FUAL

The Love of Strangers

The Love of Strangers

WHAT SIX MUSLIM STUDENTS LEARNED IN JANE AUSTEN'S LONDON

Nile Green

Princeton University Press

Princeton and Oxford

Copyright © 2016 by Princeton University Press
Published by Princeton University Press, 41 William Street,
Princeton, New Jersey 08540
In the United Kingdom: Princeton University Press, 6 Oxford Street,
Woodstock, Oxfordshire OX20 1TW

press.princeton.edu

Jacket images: Sultan Abdülmecid with Queen Victoria and Napolean III. Background:
Cheapside and Bow Church in London. Engraving by W. Albutt after T. H. Shepherd, 1837.

Library of Congress Cataloging-in-Publication Data

Green, Nile.
The love of strangers : what six Muslim students learned in Jane Austen's London /
Nile Green.
    pages cm
Includes bibliographical references and index.
ISBN 978-0-691-16832-6 (hardback : acid-free paper)   1. Iranians—Travel—England—History—
19th century.   2. Muslims—Travel—England—History—19th century.   3. Students, Foreign—
England—History—19th century.   4. Mohammed Saulih, Mirza—Diaries.   5. London
(England)—Social life and customs—19th century.   6. Friendship—England—History—19th
century.   7. England—Ethnic relations—History—19th century.   8. England—Relations—
Iran.   9. Iran—Relations—England.   10. East and West.   I. Title.
DA125.I68G74 2015
942.107′3092—dc23
[B]
             2015008234

British Library Cataloging-in-Publication Data is available

This book has been composed in Linux Libertine O with Dorchester Script MT Std

Printed on acid-free paper. ∞

Printed in the United States of America

10 9 8 7 6 5 4 3 2 1

پادشاهی پسری را به ادیبی داد و گفت این فرزند تست، تربیتش همچنان کن که یکی از فرزندان خویش

A shah entrusted his son to the care of a tutor, and said, "This is your son. Educate him as though he were one of your own children."

—Sa'di of Shiraz

For my Muslim friends

Contents

Preface

During the late 1990s, I was studying Islamic history in a London that seemed at ease with its role as the Muslim melting pot of Europe. Having spent a worrying number of gap years wandering around the Middle East, and Iran in particular, I had many Muslim friends. Outside of library reading rooms, I spent much of my time hanging about Brick Lane. Its streets appeared to me a palimpsest of London's immigrant history, from the original Huguenot *réfugiés* to persecuted Jews fleeing pogroms in Russia and the Bengali-speaking Muslims who more recently replaced them. Over time, the original Huguenot church, built in the eighteenth century, had become a synagogue and then a mosque. Looking at Europe's Muslims through the prism of Brick Lane, their presence seemed less an aberration than a continuation of British history. For the Brick Lane mosque was not the ancient mosque of Cordoba in Spain, evoking the lost Andalusian days of a distant *convivencia*. It was not a museum to a reconstructed world but part of a living and organic history with roots in the more reachable past of the eighteenth and nineteenth centuries. Since so much of London gained its present shape at that time, that more proximate past seemed more tangible and connected to the lives that Londoners were pursuing around me in those same spaces of memory. When, a few years after my Brick Lane ramblings, I came across the Persian diary that a Muslim student had kept in London two hundred years ago, it felt like I had found an ink-and-paper time machine to connect our two eras. The diary, printed but never translated, seemed like the key to an unknown Muslim psychogeography of the city, a walking tour of Islamic associations that gave entirely different meanings to Soho and Fleet Street. As I read more of the diary, I found that its author, Mirza Salih, and I had walked the same streets, visited the same museums and theaters, supped at the same taverns, and shared the same

sentiments of uncertainty, intellectual and financial, that are the pe-
rennial stuff of student life. I also learned that we were both rescued
from penury by the same sponsors, he by the fraternal orientalists Sir
William and Sir Gore Ouseley and me by the trust later established in
their name. When fortune eventually shone on me by way of a fellowship at Oxford, I found myself sitting under Sir Gore Ouseley's portrait reading the original manuscripts of two works composed by
Mirza Salih for our common patron. Again: history just out of arm's
reach.

In the meantime, between my happy afternoons in Brick Lane and
my arrival in Oxford, in September 2001 the world was turned on its
head. In the summer of 2005, the maelstrom reached London. The two
worst bomb attacks, at Tavistock Square and Russell Square, took
place a few minutes' walk from where I and many before me at the
School of Oriental and African Studies had been taught to study Muslims with postcolonial sympathy. Yet even in those more innocent
days before 9/11, I was all too aware of the horrors of Islamism. In my
college winter holiday of 1999, I was in Yemen, resuming my former
life of leading Europeans through the Middle East, when a group of
tourists was kidnapped and murdered. They were one of two tour
groups in the region that season, mine and theirs. Twenty minutes
before they were captured, I had watched their Land Cruisers drive
past as I paused at a village market to buy food for my own group. I
still cannot voice how sickened I felt when, after returning to London
on the plane with survivors who had seen their loved ones murdered,
I learned that the order for the kidnap came from London's Finsbury
Park mosque, just a couple of miles north of my college classrooms.

I am not blind, then, to the profound dangers of Islamism, nor to its
presence in the heart of Europe. But that is only, and at most, half of
the story of the Muslims in our midst, even if it is the spectacular half
that has garnered far more books than the quieter lives lived by millions of Muslim good citizens throughout Europe. In this book, I want
to tell that other side of the story—of quotidian camaraderie and personal attachments—that I found in the diary of that forgotten Muslim
student. *The Love of Strangers* is not a book about such abstractions as
"Islam and democracy" or "Sharia and civil rights." It is a book about
real people, living alongside one another, rubbing along and even get-

ting along with each another. It is a story about Europeans and Muslims as flesh and blood individuals brought together in a London on the verge of its transformation into the global city we know today.

There are many books taking rage and hatred, distrust and disappointment as defining the relationship between the Middle East and the West, a relationship that is increasingly seen through the rubric of cultural difference. What I want to achieve with this book is to write Muslims into the cultural history of Europe, as both participants and admirers of that culture. I want to do so in a way that does not treat them definitively as "Muslims" defined by the dictates of religion, but as complex creatures who are caught, like all of us, in the contest of emotion and reason. In many popular representations at least, the Regency decade of 1811 to 1820 when this book is based serves as an epitome of European civilization. So by adopting the rubric of "Jane Austen's London," that self-admiring synecdoche of European civility, I want to show Muslims as enthusiastic participants in a society that is usually seen as exclusively English. Slyly swiping at this potent model of the British past, the Anglo-Iranian comedian Omid Djalili has poked fun at it through hilarious sketches about the boisterous intrusions into that whitewashed world of a Middle Eastern "Mr. Farsy." Consciously or not, Mr. Djalili has reached toward a larger historical truth. For the young Iranian Muslims discussed in this book—my six "Mr. Farsys"—were not literary characters, not fictions from the margins of Jane Austen's oeuvre. Theirs was a genuine historical presence that points to a larger converging world—of industry and empire, of Islam and England—that Austen's novels do as much to conceal as reveal. Since Jane Austen was living in London with her brother during the autumn of 1815 when the Iranians arrived, it seems fair to describe the city they came to know as "Jane Austen's London." By bringing six foreign Muslims to the center stage of its past, I hope to take some small steps to writing a history of England for our more pluralistic present times.

In so doing, at a time when anti-Muslim rhetoric is sweeping through Europe, I want to demonstrate that Muslims are not inherently inimical to "Western" values. Instead, I want to show that Muslims were very much a part of Europe's past and that, some of them at least, were enthusiastic and even reciprocal participants in the science, reason, and tolerance that is surely the better part of Europe's modern civilization. To what extent different individual Muslims want to participate in that civilization today lies beyond the scope of the story told here. But the point is that because they did before, they can do so again.

Unlike many accounts of the relationship between "Islam and the West," this book tells a story of cooperation and friendship. By using the Persian diary of that Muslim student, and the evidence of his five companions, *The Love of Strangers* traces a series of relationships between the Iranians and their English hosts. By reconstructing those relationships, I hope to contribute to a better understanding of the history not only of the Middle East but also of England by presenting an intimate portrait of the little-known links of Regency England to the wider world of Islam. As a guidebook to the English no less than the Iranian past, Mirza Salih's diary is the lost Muslim counterpart to his contemporary William Cobbett's *Rural Rides*; it is a part of English as much as Iranian history. The presence of the Muslim students complicates our picture of Jane Austen's era by adding portraits of Iranian Muslims conversing with East India Company orientalists, Christian evangelicals, and rationalizing scientists. Despite the careful literary excavations in the gardens of Mansfield Park carried out by the critic Edward Said, such figures rarely appear in our imaginings of that age. And so, with the help of Mirza Salih, I have endeavored to place them there to show the pluralizing society behind the tired and too familiar sets of a *Downton Abbey* England.

For readers primarily interested in the Middle East, the book re-creates in detail the first sustained Muslim contact with a Western European society and its forms of knowledge. For aside from the shorter embassies of Askar Khan Afshar to Paris in 1808 and Abu'l-Hasan Khan to London in 1810, the far longer stay in London of Mirza Salih and his companions between 1815 and 1819 represented the most extensive Middle Eastern investigation to date of the cultural and intellectual life of a European nation. To re-create that encounter is to return to the point of first contact in the modern era between Muslim Iranians and Christian Britons, recovering the contexts and concerns that shaped the attitudes of each side to the other. Perhaps most importantly, the book reconstructs in detail exactly to whom and to what these pioneering Muslim explorers were exposed in *Inglistan*. For wherever possible, I have tried to detect which people, which places, which technologies, which books, which ideas, and which ideologies Mirza Salih and his fellow students discovered in England. The degree of impact that these new influences (if such they were) had on Iran after the students returned home is a separate matter, albeit one that I necessarily discuss in the "Afterlives" epilogue. But by reconstructing their explorations, I hope to advance a pluralistic globalizing approach to Middle Eastern no less than British history. And as a contribution to global history, I hope the following chapters demonstrate the intricacy and scale of Islamic interaction with Europe in a period when the colonization of Muslim lands was just beginning. What is presented here, then, is a particular kind of global history that is written on the micro-historical scale: it is a story of six men—and of one man in particular—over the course of less than four years. For this reason, I have chosen to frame the book around people and not processes, albeit with the historian's hope that the latter are revealed all the better amid their full human texture.

My final and most general hope is that, by humane illustration, this book can challenge the dangerous premise of an inevitable "clash of civilizations" by exploring cultural encounters on the manageable scale of daily life by which history is truly measured. By looking closely at the men and women whom Mirza Salih and his companions met, my aim is to challenge the no less persistent stereotype of European progress and Muslim obscurantism. For the English people whom the students encountered comprised Christian fanatics and evangelical zealots no less than the cosmopolitan and learned heirs of the Enlightenment. In Oxford and Cambridge especially, the Muslims found scholars and schools that were no less torn between religious dogma and free inquiry than those of Iran. Seeing the black-gowned students and religious rules of Oxford, it was with good reason that in his diary Mirza Salih described its colleges as *madrasas*. Overall, taking its cue from Mirza Salih, this book is a study in the neglected virtue of xenophilia. Through the affection that Mirza Salih felt for the strange *Inglis*, and the affection felt for this Muslim stranger by his English friends, I hope to bring to life a less dystopian past that may in some small measure help us find a less dystopian future.

Having previously written books about such distant cities as Hyderabad and Bombay, I have finally decided to write about London because it is the city I know better than any other in the world. The story I have tried to tell is part of the larger story of how London became the multicultural and multiracial city that captivated me as a student a hundred and eighty years after the Iranian students' time there. I hope that the tale of the true Muslim *taliban*—these "seekers of knowledge" who were some of the earliest Muslim residents in London—reveals something of the genesis of a city that since their time has been far more than a national capital. It was in that larger London, the cosmopolitan world city, that both those students and I learned much.

What readers will glimpse in the following chapters is London, and England more generally, as it was seen through Muslim eyes. This was an England at the dawn of the industrial revolution, at the onset of imperial expansion, and in the midst of the great social experiment of religious pluralization. The past, it is often said, is a foreign country. But that is only partly true, for the England seen by Mirza Salih and his fellow students is still a recognizable country today. Most of the places they visited and described—the theaters, the colleges, the pubs, even the houses they lived in—still stand. Theirs is the London in which I also once lived; it is the substantially Georgian city that millions from around the world visit each year. At the same time, behind its classical Regency facades, the country the students saw was an England that was in the process of *becoming* the country we recognize today, because it was a land just embarking on the transformations that immigration from outside Europe would bring. Because in September 1815, two centuries to the month before this book was published, the entry to London of those six Muslim students announced the birth of the nation of today that is both multicultural and a little bit Muslim.

Nile Green
Los Angeles, January 7ᵗʰ 2015

The Love of Strangers

Map 1. The Students' London.

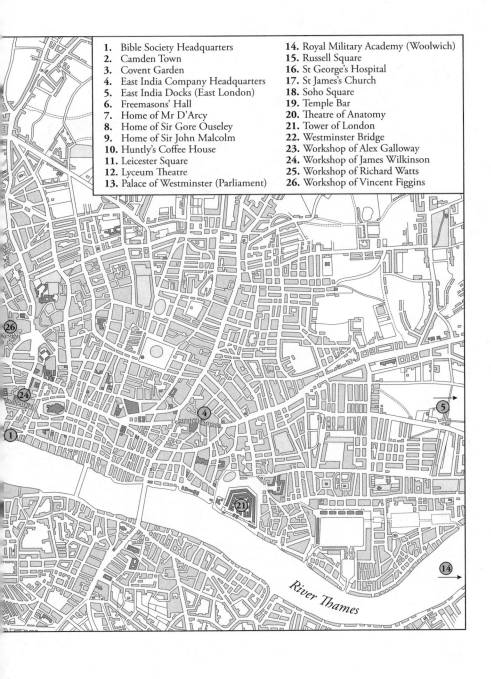

1. Bible Society Headquarters
2. Camden Town
3. Covent Garden
4. East India Company Headquarters
5. East India Docks (East London)
6. Freemasons' Hall
7. Home of Mr D'Arcy
8. Home of Sir Gore Ouseley
9. Home of Sir John Malcolm
10. Huntly's Coffee House
11. Leicester Square
12. Lyceum Theatre
13. Palace of Westminster (Parliament)
14. Royal Military Academy (Woolwich)
15. Russell Square
16. St George's Hospital
17. St James's Church
18. Soho Square
19. Temple Bar
20. Theatre of Anatomy
21. Tower of London
22. Westminster Bridge
23. Workshop of Alex Galloway
24. Workshop of James Wilkinson
25. Workshop of Richard Watts
26. Workshop of Vincent Figgins

River Thames

Map 2. The Students' England.

RUSSIAN EMPIRE

BUKHARA

KHIVA

Caspian Sea

oTabriz

OTTOMAN EMPIRE

Mashhad○

○Tehran

AFGHANISTAN

○Isfahan

I R A N

○Kerman

INDIA

○Shiraz

OTTOMAN EMPIRE

○Bushire

ARABIA

Persian Gulf

Iranian losses to
Russia (1804–13,
1826–28)

Iranian gains

Arabian Sea

RUSSIAN
EMPIRE

RUSSIAN EMPIRE

OTTOMAN
EMPIRE

CHINA

AFGHANISTAN

IRAN

ARABIA

EGYPT

INDIA

SUDAN

0   100   200   300   400   500 km

0   100   200   300 miles

Map 3. Iran.

Introducing
Mr. D'Arcy's Persians

Iranians in Jane Austen's England

*I*n late September 1815, a ship sailed into the provincial harbor of Great Yarmouth carrying what was at the time a most unusual cargo: a party of frightened Iranian students. In the hope of furthering their studies, they were traveling to the land they called *Inglistan*, seeking in particular what they called the *'ulum-i jadid*, or "new sciences," for which England was gaining fame. Four years earlier, two other Iranian youths had arrived with the same purpose, though in 1813 one of them had died; he was buried in St. Pancras churchyard in London. And so there remained six of them.

In December that year, there appeared a famous depiction of the country into which the young Muslims had wandered: Jane Austen's *Emma*. To this day, *Emma* defines our image of the time, an age of elegant ballrooms, exquisite manners, and crimson-jacketed captains. It was into the living version of that fictionalized world that the Iranians had sailed. Though Miss Austen would die two years after their arrival, her novels *Northanger Abbey* and *Persuasion* did not appear till 1818, when the six Muslims were still living in London and exploring other towns like Bath. But in September 1815, it was all just beginning, and over the following months, these Muslim gentlemen would be more fully, and politely, introduced to Miss Austen's country by their aptly named chaperone, Mr. D'Arcy.

In principle, there was nothing strange about Muslims coming to study in a distant non-Islamic land: the Prophet Muhammad had famously urged all Muslims to "seek knowledge unto China"—that is, to follow learning wherever it led, even to the ends of the earth. Nonetheless, these pioneering Muslim students—*taliban* or "seekers of knowledge," as they termed themselves—marked the beginning of a new age in the old relationship between Europe and Islam. Arriving in London over a decade before the Egyptian scholar Rifaʿa al-Tahtawi led his delegation of Arab students to Paris, the six Iranians were the first group of Muslims to ever study in western Europe. At a time when the presence of Muslims in Europe is increasingly brought into question, what they learned—and the friendships they made with non-Muslims—gives us a different way of imagining the relationship between "Islam and the West." Their human story lends an alternative etiology, a more harmonious genesis, for modern Muslim and Christian relations. For if nothing else, the following pages show that Muslims could be rationalists and progressives and Europeans religious bigots.

One of the Iranian students, Mirza Salih of Shiraz, wrote in his native Persian a diary that describes their student years in England. Never translated, at a distance of two centuries, the diary allows us to follow the fortunes of the shivering youths who arrived on the coast of East Anglia that early autumn evening in 1815. Recounting their escapades in detail, the diary tells of adventures that involved industrialists, freemasons, professors, political radicals, missionaries, and more than a few of Miss Austen's wise and beguiling women. In his *Culture and Imperialism*, the celebrated critic Edward Said tried to deconstruct Jane Austen's novels to detect in them a hidden imperial underworld, to as it were find slaves in the cellars of Mansfield Park. Mirza Salih's diary is the key to the cellar door, leading us from the novel's dark allusions to foreigners into the bright sunlight of the larger, international world that encompassed Austen's little England. For his diary metaphorically opens the cellar door onto the immigrant corridors above to show how a group of Muslim migrants found their way into the fashionable soirées of London and Bath. Since Mirza Salih had a sense for pathos and drama, his diary entries carry the wit and charm of their era. Together with a cache of the students' letters stored for two hundred years in the files of the Foreign Office, these sundry forgotten jottings drill a spyhole through the centuries into the neglected Muslim wing of Mansfield Park.

Hoping to learn English to access the knowledge held in what he called "the *madrasas* of Oxford," Mirza Salih was a man with a mission. And it was a mission of the highest importance. For he and his companions had been dispatched by the crown prince of Iran to acquire the latest scientific learning with which to protect Iran from the Russian Empire that just two years earlier had seized Iran's northwestern provinces. The son of a court official, Mirza Salih had no illusions as to the importance of his mission. Faced with a seemingly unstoppable Russia that had already defeated the far stronger Ottoman Empire, Iran lacked not only the technology to defend itself but also the diplomatic ties and knowledge of European ways to negotiate with or even understand its hostile neighbors. Fearful of Russian expansion into Asia, and suspicious of the ambitions of Napoleon, in around 1810 Britain had offered assistance to Iran, sending a handful of officers to train its military, some of whom served alongside Iranian soldiers in the latter stages of the ill-fated war against Russia from 1804–13. It sounds a familiar story, except that by a peculiar coincidence of history and fiction among the officers was a man who seemed to have stepped from the pages of *Pride and Prejudice*: a real-life Mr. D'Arcy (if not Jane Austen's Darcy). This was Captain Joseph D'Arcy (1780–1848) of the Royal Artillery, the man who in 1815 stepped ashore with the students in Great Yarmouth to introduce them to the society from which Miss Austen was then spinning her novels. For when Mr. D'Arcy completed his tour of duty training soldiers in the mountainous northwest of Iran and was about to leave for his long journey home, he had been collared by the crown prince ʿAbbas Mirza. Persuaded against his instincts, he finally agreed to escort to England the group of would-be students. As Mr. D'Arcy delicately phrased the matter at the time, writing to the Foreign Office in London from the crown prince's court at Tabriz, "His Royal Highness has required me to take charge of five individuals of his nation for the purpose of procuring them such an education in England as may make them of service to his government hereafter."

That faded letter from a mountainous city in northwestern Iran marked the students' entry into English history. In it, Mr. D'Arcy recorded their names and intended subjects of study: Mirza Riza, who sought "a knowledge of artillery"; Mirza Jaʿfar, "a young man, to learn chemistry"; Muhammad ʿAli, "a smith, to learn to make locks"; Mirza Jaʿfar Husayni, "to learn engineering"; and Mirza Salih (or Mirza Solley, as D'Arcy transcribed his name), "to acquire knowledge of the English language to become translator to the Persian government."

Reaching England's damp and pleasant land in the early autumn of 1815 after more than four months of travel, Mirza Muhammad Salih ibn Hajji Baqir Khan *marhum* Shirazi ("Mirza Muhammad Salih son of Hajji Baqir Khan, *deceased*, of Shiraz") surely wobbled and stared around him. He was no refugee stowaway, but owing his passage to the polite inability of an English officer to refuse a princely request, he was not an entirely welcome guest either. It was not the first time this had happened: in 1811, the British ambassador to Iran Sir Harford Jones had been similarly persuaded to bring two young Iranians home with him. The costs had proved considerable. Although one of them, Muhammad Kazim, died in London in 1813, the medical education being given to the survivor, Hajji Baba Afshar, was becoming expensive. Mr. D'Arcy was fretting from the moment they reached dry land at Great Yarmouth. Still, both he and the young Muslims were gentlemen—he a military officer; they court officials, or *mirzas*. And their master in Iran was none other than the crown prince 'Abbas Mirza, whose name was already known to readers of *The Times* in London. Perhaps that would help Mr. D'Arcy pass them on to more willing or wealthy patrons. Then as now, class was an international currency, and fully aware of its value, neither Mr. D'Arcy nor the *mirzas* wished to debase it. But then as now too, a good education was expensive, and it was already clear to Mr. D'Arcy that his role as chaperone could easily turn financially ruinous. Foreign "infidels" in what was still very much a Christian land, for their part the Muslim strangers were all too aware that they would need more than a little help from their friends. And as yet, their only English friend was the sulky and reluctant Mr. D'Arcy.

The year 1815 was remarkably early for Middle Eastern Muslims to come to study in Europe. Even progressive Egypt, which for centuries had kept much closer trading ties with Italy and other regions of Europe, did not send its first small party of students to London until 1818, with a larger group reaching Paris in 1826. Dispatched to Paris as a group of more than forty young men, the Egyptian student mission was better organized than its Iranian predecessor and even counted among its number a remarkably open-minded *imam* as chaperone. Arranged on a princely spur of the moment, the Iranian venture was an altogether more ad hoc affair in which its English overseer regretted his involvement from the start. And since Mr. D'Arcy's disinterest had already become apparent on the long journey to England via Russia, the young Iranians may have already suspected that, even though they had reached dry land, rougher seas lay ahead.

Fortunately, 1815 was also, as these things go, a good time to be a "Persian" in England. In 1809, the arrival of a handsome ambassador from Iran had captured the imagination of Regency gentlemen and the affection of their wives. Then, in 1813, Lord Byron had published his *Oriental Tales* to unrivaled popular acclaim. On the ambassador's departure, one debutante had taken to carrying a miniature of his portrait, his bushy black beard and flashing eyes the epitome of Byron's oriental heroes. Here, before the British Empire reduced the Muslim kingdoms of Asia to ridicule and rubble, was an enthusiastic orientalism that the students might turn to their own devices. Among persons both of learning and of fashion, it was a period of mutual attraction as Englishmen looked to Iranians with as much interest as Iranians looked back at them. Briefly united in the global front against Napoleon and (during the Anglo-Russian War of 1807–12) the czar, England and Iran were allies not enemies. But if the interest was mutual, its motivation was different, as each side had its own ideas of what should constitute the modern world. What the students came looking for and what they found were often quite different. For England was not only the land of science and reason that the Iranians hoped to find, a secularized and idealized England that more narcissistic historians like to celebrate today. It was also a deeply religious land, a country of committed Christians divided between their antagonistic visions of a zealous or a tolerant faith. Stumbling ashore and finding their land legs, the young Muslims were walking into an England in the midst of an evangelical upsurge that the moderate vicar's daughter Jane Austen chose to carefully downplay in her novels.

The Muslim Modernity of ʿAbbas Mirza

To understand what drove the students towards their English *Wanderjahren*, we need to turn first to the prehistory of their journey in the new diplomatic ties between Britain and Iran that were established a decade or so earlier. For they would never have departed Tabriz were it not for the spate of diplomatic missions sent to Iran in the early 1800s on behalf of the government of Great Britain and the governors of the East India Company. The presence in Iran of their hapless cicerone, Mr. D'Arcy, was itself the result of these new political ties. For after the embassy of Sir Gore Ouseley in 1811–12, the young Captain D'Arcy was left in Tabriz to instruct the Iranian army in the newest techniques of war, a tutelage that also strengthened British interests by checking Russia's march through the Caucasus. The window of educational opportunity that these diplomatic ties opened for the court of the crown prince ʿAbbas Mirza did not remain open for long. As the Napoleonic Wars ended at Waterloo in the months before the students left home, and as Britain's relations with Russia entered a different phase, Britain's diplomatic and military presence in Iran was scaled down. By the time ties with Iran reexpanded in the second half of the century, Britain's imperial ambitions began to acquire for her a distrust among some Iranians that has continued to the present day. But in 1815 at least, Britain and Iran were allies.

All in their early twenties, the students who arrived with Mr. D'Arcy were neither naïve nor blind to the rising power of the *Inglis*. Positioned as their homeland was between an expanding Russian Empire to the north and the insatiable growth of the British East India Company to the east, the students were certainly aware of the threat posed by Europeans. After all, it was concerns about Russian expansion that encouraged Iran's Qajar dynasts to forge the diplomatic relations with Britain that enabled the students to come to London. But when the students set off from Tabriz in the honeymoon glow of the Anglo-Iranian Treaty of 1812, England and Iran were partners. Enjoying all the enthusiasm of a newfound friendship, in the diplomatic exchanges between the Iranian ruler Fath ʿAli Shah and King George III the sovereigns addressed one another in the language of "friendship," or *dusti* in the Persian versions of the treaty. A product of its genteel and mannered age, it was a relationship between friendly sovereigns that was captured in a dazzling diplomatic gift that Fath ʿAli Shah sent to King George: a two-sided portrait with a painting of the shah's face on the one side and a mirror on the other. When George III looked into the mirror side, like lovers in Persian tradition, he saw his own image and the facing image of his Iranian friend join together in the reflection. So when mad King George gazed into the looking glass, even in his saner moments he saw Fath 'Ali Shah peeping back at him over his shoulder. Though the two kings never met, they were joined through a craftsman's conceit.

In such charming ways, from 1797 to 1834 the long reign of Fath 'Ali Shah saw Iran greatly expand its contacts with Europe. It was not the shah himself who was the main agitator for modernization, but one of his sons, the aforementioned 'Abbas Mirza (1789–1833). It was he who would dispatch the two parties of students to London, the first with two students (one of whom died) in 1811 and the second with five students in 1815. As the sincerest reformer of the Qajar dynasty, 'Abbas Mirza saw himself standing at the dawn of a new age, an 'asr-i jadid, that he sought to usher into Iran by accessing the knowledge that was driving England through its industrial revolution. He named his program of modernization the "new order," or nizam-i jadid, a term he borrowed from the neighboring Ottoman Empire, whose borders on the Mediterranean had already made them aware of the scale of change in Europe. As the second son of Fath 'Ali Shah, 'Abbas Mirza had been given the governorship of the western Iranian province of Azerbaijan at the tender age of ten, an appointment that placed him on the front line of Russian expansion. From the city of Tabriz on the edge of the Russian Empire, 'Abbas Mirza was gradually exposed to European ideas and innovations, far more than other members of his dynasty in Tehran and elsewhere in the remote interior. Facing an aggressive and expansive Russia, it was, then, for practical reasons that 'Abbas Mirza learned the importance of the "new sciences" if Iran was to maintain her territorial integrity.

Yet the prince was also a man of culture, who had been given a traditional princely education in the adab al-muluk, the Persian arts of kingship, an education that he complemented in his later youth by reading about the history of Europe. As a child he had been taught the heroic histories of the ancient rulers of Iran who were commemorated in Firdawsi's medieval epic Shahnama, and he retained an affection for Firdawsi above all poets as an adult. But despite his treaties with the British, the real hero of the adult 'Abbas Mirza was Napoleon Bonaparte, whom he admired for his great modernizing reforms. When the German diplomat Moritz von Kotzebue traveled to Tabriz as part of the Russian embassy of 1817, he recorded how on entering 'Abbas Mirza's residence he was "surprised to see in two niches, in the upper part of the room, a portrait of the [Russian] Emperor Alexander, and one of Bonaparte, the last of which was a striking likeness." Like his French hero, 'Abbas Mirza instituted a whole range of reforms, with Iran's first military academy, a new school system and a series of administrative reforms. It was in this connection that Mr. D'Arcy had arrived in Tabriz in a party of two royal artillery officers, two noncommissioned officers, and ten privates that was seconded to the embassy of the students' future friend, Sir Gore Ouseley. After the latter's departure in 1814, Mr. D'Arcy stayed on to help 'Abbas Mirza reorganize his army. Then, as we have seen, a year later on the eve of his departure from Tabriz, Mr. D'Arcy was persuaded to take home with him five young men to study in England.

From 'Abbas Mirza's interactions with the ambassadorial and military parties, he recognized the benefits his country could gain from learning from the English. An article in *The Times* of London praised "his intercourse with learned Europeans; his speaking the English and French languages very fluently." An obituary later written by the diplomatist Henry Willock, who knew him personally, described 'Abbas Mirza as "a prince who laboured to introduce such improvements in his country as might enable the people to emulate, in military prowess and in literary attainments, the present generation in Europe, and who studied, for the advancement of this object, to communicate to them the active habits and superior intelligence of those Europeans who visited the Persian court." There is certainly a tone of condescension in these lines; perhaps Mr. Willock was thinking of himself when he wrote of Europeans of "superior intelligence" at 'Abbas Mirza's court. But his basic observation still stands: 'Abbas Mirza led a pioneering attempt to transfer the scientific "new learning" to Iran.

The Alluring Ambassador

Intrepid as the students sent by 'Abbas Mirza were, they were not the first Iranians to find their way into Jane Austen's England. In 1809, the first Iranian ambassador in two centuries made his entry into London. His name was Abu'l-Hasan Khan. Sent to cement the new political ties between England and Iran as allies against Napoleon, by blazing a trail through London high society Abu'l-Hasan also prepared the way for the students who followed him six years later. The scion of a family with close connections to the shah's court, Abu'l-Hasan knew enough of high politics to have survived exile in India and to have returned in triumph to Tehran after a change of rulers. Worldly and assured, Abu'l-Hasan could hold his own with poets, politicians, or princes. The success of his mission is almost taken for granted in his own Persian diary, which does for the early Regency period what the travel letters of the no less worldly German prince Hermann von Pückler-Muskau does for its tail end. Through the diary, we are able to see a side of the Regency that is usually obscured from view, a picture of gentleman scholars and old East India men keen to share their enthusiasms for Persian paintings and the poetry of Hafiz. Emily, the precocious daughter of the co-director of the East India Company, Sir Thomas Metcalfe, even took to reciting lyrical Persian *ghazals* to Abu'l-Hasan. On other occasions, the ambassador was hosted at dinner parties serving great *pilaws* of rice cooked in the Persian style (possibly with the help of Indian servants) and taken to inspect the libraries of orientalists with collections of Persian texts. One such library was that of the erstwhile ambassador to Iran, Sir Gore Ouseley, which led Abu'l-Hasan to comment in detail on its manuscripts, all written by well-known calligraphers.

Just as during the British Embassy of 1810–12 Sir Gore's secretary William Price took an interest in the work of Iranian artists (he visited the studio of the noted painter Aqa ʿAli Naqash, whose "figures, though having Persian stiffness about them, were very nicely made out and finely coloured"), so did Abu'l-Hasan inspect the works of English painters. He even posed for several portraits, including two by the society portraitist Sir William Beechey (1753–1839). As well as recording his impressions of such experiences in his diary, he took notes on a vast miscellany of English customs and statistics, from the number of prostitutes on London's streets to the most popular stars at Covent Garden's theaters, such as the clown Joseph Grimaldi and the tenor Diomiro Tramezzani. For their part, the English were no less fascinated with Abu'l-Hasan. His daily rounds were regularly reported in newspaper gossip pages as London's great and good vied for the honor of hosting him for dinner or for what he considered the peculiar custom of the breakfast party. As anyone who has sat through long formal dinners making small-talk in a foreign language amid an unfamiliar culture will know, such occasions could be trying for Abu'l-Hasan, who never managed to learn English fluently. But with a diplomatic license that one suspects suited his personal inclinations just fine, the Muslim chose to quaff wine and brandy at dinner like the English rather than appear standoffish. His sociability impressed almost everyone who met him. Still, when an English custom struck him as too much, he was not averse to speaking his mind: he once refused to eat the expensive asparagus that one hostess served him on the grounds that in Iran, no one would eat grasses that grew wild on the plains no matter how much they cost! His private comments to Sir Gore Ouseley on the wonders he witnessed in England were no less to the point. He informed his fellow diplomatist that he had seen "hundred-year-old men trying to seduce young girls and hundred-year-old ladies flirting with young men at parties so crowded that you cannot move and so hot that you could fry a chicken!" His candor offers a refreshing contrast with the mannered conversations of Jane Austen's heroes.

Abu'l-Hasan was only slightly less candid when asked to write an account of his impressions of the English for the *Morning Post*. Arguing that since to describe only his favorable impressions of England would seem like flattery, he explained that he had better write something of the bad as well. Once again, for him the bad was the interminable parties that were the highlight of the London calendar: "I not like such crowd in evening party every night—In cold weather not very good—now, hot weather, much too bad. I very much astonish, every day now much hot than before, evening parties much crowd than before.—Pretty beautiful ladies come sweat that not very good, and spoil my happiness. I think old ladies after eighty-five years not come to evening party that much better." Though some scholars suspect the letter was the forgery of a contemporary prankster, its words have an air of truth and certainly echo some of the sentiments of his Persian diary.

Fig. 1. The Alluring Ambassador: *Portrait of Abu'l-Hasan* by Sir William Beechey, 1809–10, oil on canvas. Source: © Compton Verney.

With the indiosyncratic command of idiom shown in the newspaper letter, that the handsome Abu'l-Hasan captured the imagination of Regency London is scarcely surprising. While some, such as the young Emily Metcalfe and Sir Gore Ouseley, reciprocated his efforts by speaking to him in Persian, others attempted a halfway house of speaking English "in a Persian style." Helping to promote this short-lived fashion was one of the more unusual language books of the age, *Persian Recreations, or Oriental Stories, with Notes to which is prefixed some*

Account of the Two Ambassadors from Iran to James the First and George the Third, written by the pseudonymous Philoxenus Secundus, the "Second Lover of Strangers." Comparing the cultivation of Iranians to that of "the French in the days of Gallic civilization," Philoxenus offered Londoners an illustrative selection of the "wit and pleasantry" that comprised the Persian art of conversation. These were the *latifa* ("a joke"), the *nikila* ("a good thing, or *bon mot*"), the *pand* ("an admonition"), the *nuqta* ("a quaint conceit, or nice distinction"), and the *vaqi'a* ("an extraordinary event"). Samples of these gambits were given in English in the main body of the book, before which Philoxenus prefixed a set of what were clearly firsthand observations of Abu'l-Hasan that fill out the necessarily one-sided picture of his Persian diary. Abu'l-Hasan, wrote Philoxenus, "was a fine handsome dark man, and, whether on foot or on horseback, appeared to great advantage. He rode well, walked fast, and talked loud, and incessantly." Little surprise then that this cultivated Persian gallant (as Philoxenus pictured him) left an impression on London's novel-reading gentlewomen. This was so much so, Philoxenus added, that the ambassador "was sometimes too much annoyed by the insatiate admiration, fixed stare, and intense regard of the British ladies, who looked with their hearts in their eyes." In parody of lines from Virgil, the fake Roman Philoxenus added the following epithet in Latin:

> Nequeunt expleri corda tuendo
> Nigrantes oculos, voltum, corvinaque menta.

> None could sate their hearts gazing on those dark eyes,
> That face, and crow-black beard.

The original lines that Philoxenus was parodying came from Virgil's *Aeneid* and read:

> Nequeunt expleri corda tuendo
> Terribilis oculos, vultum villosaque saetis
> Pectora semiferi atque exstinctos faucibus ignis

> None could sate their hearts, gazing on those terrible eyes,
> On the visage of the brutish monster, on his shaggy bristled breast,
> And the flames quenched in his throat.

The original passage dealt with Cacus, a monster that feasted on human flesh and had just been killed by Hercules, so the comparison with the ambassador was hardly flattering. Still, Abu'l-Hasan seems not to have been averse to encouraging the infatuations of English-women and could, as Philoxenus knowingly put it, be "gallant."

Although the identity of Philoxenus, the writer behind these anecdotes, is uncertain, he has been identified as the orientalist and antiquarian, Stephen Weston (1747–1830). An underemployed but gifted clergyman of independent means, Weston published several pioneering works on Arabic literature while helping in his extensive spare time in the deciphering of the Rosetta Stone. Whatever the truth of Philoxenus's identity, the fascination with the Iranian ambassador that he documented promised well for the Iranian students who reached London five years later. For after the enchanting ambassador departed in 1810, there was the chance that Mirza Salih and his well-bred companions might serve as his substitutes at the dinner tables of the great and good. Yet it would be far from an easy role for the students to play. For unlike Abu'l-Hasan, they had neither a diplomat's purse nor credentials to ease their way.

Mutual Learning

Fortunately, the diplomatic exchanges that brought Abu'l-Hasan to London also provided an opportunity for the student diarist Mirza Salih to get to know the British before he and his companions left home. The earliest of the envoys sent to Iran on behalf of the Crown and the East India Company reached Tehran in 1799, though the first formal ambassador, Sir Harford Jones, was not to arrive till 1808. It was in response to Sir Harford's mission that Abu'l Hasan was dispatched to England and this led in turn to the embassy of Sir Gore Ouseley, who accompanied Abu'l-Hasan on his journey back to Iran, where they arrived together in 1811. It was through the army officers attached to these embassies that Mirza Salih had his first exposure to Europeans. For in 1810, he served as secretary to Henry Lindsay-Bethune (1787–1851), an infantry officer from the Madras Horse Artillery seconded, like Mr. D'Arcy, to the crown prince 'Abbas Mirza's army. Since

Lieutenant Lindsay-Bethune was "a giant standing six feet eight inches," his Iranian comrades jokingly compared him to their epic warrior hero, Rustam. He must have made a striking first impression on Mirza Salih, who perhaps wondered if the *Inglis* were all a race of giants. He would soon learn better. For a short while later, during the embassy of Sir Gore Ouseley from 1811 to 1812, Mirza Salih made the acquaintance of Sir Gore's elder brother, Sir William. A keen learner of Persian, Sir William Ouseley had persuaded Sir Gore to employ him as a secretary so he could travel for the first time to an Iran that was still largely *terra incognita* to Europeans. Looking back a decade later, Sir Gore's assistant secretary, William Price, described the circumstances in which Mirza Salih joined the embassy:

> The gentlemen and servants of the Embassy encamped in the plain, near the Palace Gardens [of Shiraz], and remained there till the 10th of July. While we were at Shiraz, I became acquainted with Mirza Saulih, well known for his literary acquirements: he entered our train and remained with the Embassy a considerable time, during which, I prevailed upon him to compose a set of dialogues in his native tongue, the pure dialect of Shiraz.

Less a prelude to his journey to England, Mirza Salih's tour through Iran with the Ouseleys was more of a trial run, exposing him to these worldly and Persian-speaking *Inglis*, showing him how and what to learn from them, and teaching him how to enter the pedagogical bargain of instructing them in return. Over and again, this pattern of mutuality, born of interest and sympathy for each other's culture, would recur after Mirza Salih reached England and define what was best about his time there.

We know more of the early links that Mirza Salih forged with the Ouseley circle during those months in Iran back in 1812 through the collection of Persian manuscripts that Sir William later donated to Oxford's Bodleian Library. For within the Ouseley Collection lies the original manuscript of the set of Persian "dialogues" that Mirza Salih composed for the two secretarial Williams, Price and Ouseley. Titled *Su'al u Javab*, "Questions and Answers," the dialogues were sample conversations with the people whom a traveler might meet in Iran, from servants and merchants to gardeners and scribes. Written in a large, scrawling hand on what was clearly the blue English notepaper that one of the two Williams had carried from England, this early example of a "teach yourself" language guide was signed with the name "Mirza Muhammad Salih, the son of Hajji Baqir Khan, of Shiraz," the Islamic date of 8 Jumada al-Awwal 1227 (corresponding to May 20, 1812) and a dedication to Sir William Ouseley, the latter's name also written in Arabic script.

Bound together in the same volume in the Bodleian Library is another manuscript that Mirza Salih wrote for Sir William, perhaps at the latter's request. Forty folios long, the manuscript contains a description of the villages and towns through which the Ouseley embassy traveled on its journey from Isfahan to Tehran. On the front page of the manuscript, Sir William later wrote out a descriptive title in English: "The Journal of Mīrzā Mohammed Sāleh of Shīrāz, who accompanied the English embassy under Sir Gore Ouseley from Isfahān to Teherān, describing the different towns and stages on that journey. Q. 78 pp., in his own handwriting, and probably unique." Unlike the later dairy of Mirza Salih's student years in London, the Bodleian manuscript is an impersonal text, its dry descriptions of the countryside, buildings, and markets along the route making it more a work of geography than a true journal. Since it ends with another dedication to Sir William and a date of three days later than the language guide, together with its contents this suggests that Mirza Salih traveled with the embassy as one of its Iranian assistants, perhaps working as a local secretary in the same way that he already had for the giant Lieutenant Lindsay-Bethune. That he did not hold any important office we can surmise from the absence of any mention of him in the unpublished diary that Sir Gore wrote along the way (though he did note the presence of nine unnamed "Persian servants"). Nor was Mirza Salih mentioned in the surviving accounts of the embassy written by its two official secretaries, Sir William Ouseley and William Price, though as we have seen, the latter did mention him when he came to publish Mirza Salih's language book a decade later. In any case, Mirza Salih was certainly not the embassy's official guide, or *mihmandar*, whose name was Muhammad Zaki Khan. Aged around twenty as he was at the time, it is probably safe to conclude that Mirza Salih was one of the local secretarial staff employed to smooth interactions between the British mission and the governors through whose territories they passed.

What is important about the two manuscripts Mirza Salih wrote during the Ouseley embassy, though, is that they show him becoming acquainted with the Ouseley brothers almost three years before the students reached the shores of England. For in the youthful manuscripts that Mirza Salih wrote in the roadside camps of central Iran, he had already grasped something about mutuality of interests, of learning from Britons who were likewise learning from him, that would prove useful later. Friendship, tolerance, understanding: these are mutual values built on sympathy, travel, and learning. Already nurtured on that journey through Iran in 1812, this two-sided process was to characterize the students' subsequent years in England where they and their hosts learned the merits of shared understanding.

As Mirza Salih's journey to England grew out of Sir William Ouseley's Iranian travels beforehand, the pattern of learning, and travel as part of it, was intertwined and mutual. Like Mirza Salih and his companions, who would later carry back knowledge of England to Iran, the Ouseley brothers were cultural middlemen, founder members of the Royal Asiatic Society and Britain's greatest early promoters of Persian studies. In an age that has been called "the Second Great Age of Discovery," these journeys were formative for both parties, firsthand experiences of distant and little-known cultures. In the books they later wrote about each other's countries, both Sir William and Mirza Salih were what we would today call ethnographers. Describers of the ways of strangers, explainers of foreign peoples they had come to understand and admire, they were bridge-builders between societies that often saw themselves as adverse and inimical. Yet however unfamiliar, as Mirza Salih and Sir William recognized, their worlds were interpenetrable and intelligible; because, of course, they were not two worlds but one. It was, moreover, a world that they bound together through learning, and in time, through friendship. For as we will see in later chapters, Mirza Salih would use the diary he later wrote in England to create an ethnography of amity.

All this suggests that we should not to confine the students' relationship with their English hosts within the conceptual bonds of colo-

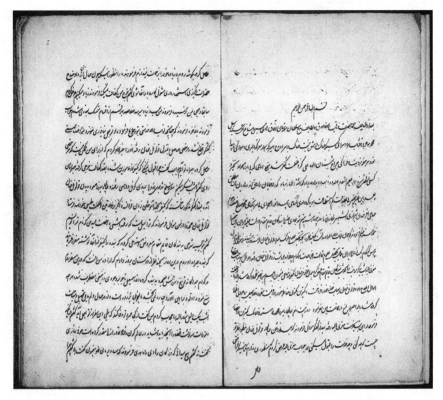

Fig. 2. A Lost Window on the Regency: The Manuscript of Mirza Salih's Diary. Source: © The British Library Board. Add.24034 f255.

nialism. When they reached London in 1815, Britain's power in Asia was still only nascent and Victoria, the future "Empress of India," was not even born till the year of their departure. If much of the wealth behind the gilded world of Jane Austen's novels was indeed built on the sweat of Caribbean slaves, it is no less true that the East India Company had far from finished building its Asian empire. Much of India still remained to be conquered, while the Company's expansion into Southeast Asia was still over the horizon, with Singapore and Malacca not acquired till 1819 and 1824 and Burma not defeated till 1826 and 1853 (itself a task in which Jane Austen's brother, Charles, played a leading if fatal role). In Africa, British rule was just beginning in 1815 with a small settlement at the Cape of Good Hope allowed by the Congress of Vienna only that year. As for expansion into the Middle East, it was Russia and France that had by this time battled the still-mighty Ottoman Empire, and it would not be till the 1830s that the first European colony in the Arab world was initiated with the French conquest of Algeria. To point this out is not to pretend that colonialism did not happen; it is merely to point out that by 1815 much of it had not happened yet. Thus it was that when the Muslim students landed in Great Yarmouth, they entered a land they saw as an ally against their old enemy, Russia. If many future Iranians would come to see a hidden English hand behind every blow to their nation, then the students had not yet learned this reflex. England was a friendly but still unknown entity; like other Muslims, the students did not yet know what to make of the English; nor did they know how to relate their ideas to their own, which to accept and which, if any, to reject. Through their learning and affections, when they landed in Great Yarmouth Mirza Salih and his companions were set to become Muslim cosmopolitans, eastern counterparts to the Hafiz-quoting Ouseley brothers who were already Mirza Salih's friends. Through mutual interest that fostered mutual respect, both parties learned to trust one another. And this will only become clear by telling a story not of "civilizations" and "cultures" in the abstract, but of individual people in all their complex humanity.

Great Stakes, Small Steps

It is hard to overestimate the mutual novelty of England and Iran to one another in the early 1800s, a time when both countries relied on the patchy, dated, and indirect knowledge passed down from a brief but intense exchange of ambassadors and traders in Shakespeare's time. It is true that by the early 1800s, the East India Company was employing local agents in the Iranian port of Bushire and inland cities such as Shiraz, but they were usually Indians or Armenians and the messages they sent by mule and ship had to be interpreted in distant London or Calcutta through a fog of misunderstanding. It was not until the year of the students' arrival in London that the East India Company's former emissary to Tehran, Sir John Malcolm, published his pioneering *History of Persia* (the students were already on their way home by the time Sir William Ouseley and William Price published their accounts of Iran). Against this background, travel diaries served as a crucial medium of knowledge for both sides. The travelogue was not yet the armchair traveler's celebration of the picturesque. It was a serious, multipurpose genre for collating information on transport, languages, commodities, institutions, customs, and of course culture. Using the same methods of learning, Mirza Salih and the two Williams, Price and Ouseley, traveled, observed, and wrote about what were to their readers back home scarcely known regions still wrapped in legend. For most people in England, Iran was still Shakespeare's mysterious "land of the Sophy," while for Iranians England was vaguely recalled as the land of Shah 'Abbas's exotic servant, the Elizabethan freelance Sir Robert Shirley. For both the English and the Iranians, travel was the primary means of learning about a wider world that, even as late as 1800, was still unfamiliar in detail.

The traffic in knowledge was two-way. The same period that witnessed the explosion of the English travelogue in the eighteenth and nineteenth centuries saw Iranian (and Indian) Muslims write accounts of their own experiences in distant *Firangistan* or Europe. Mirza Salih would draw on this genre of the Persian *safarnama* or "travelogue" in the writing of his diary which he had begun as soon as he left Iran with his compatriots and Mr. D'Arcy, recording in detail their passage through Russia and thence towards England. Though it would not be published till the 1960s, he wrote it with the intention that on his return home manuscript copies would be made for his royal master and his peers in Tabriz. It was, then, a part-public, part-private text, both diary and travelogue.

If student diaries are not often seen as the transformative stuff of history, then they should be. For over the course of more than a century and a half, the transfers of knowledge made by Mirza Salih and his companions would utterly transform Iran. When they set off from Tabriz, their homeland possessed almost nothing of the technology that was busily transforming Jane Austen's country estate England into the land of dark satanic mills bemoaned by William Blake. In 1815, Iran did not have a single printing press or newspaper; it had little scientific equipment beyond antiquated astrolabes; its doctors knew nothing of the changing methods of medicine or the geological, chemical, and other applied sciences that were driving England's industrial revolution. Yet through its contacts with Britain and Russia, the court of ʿAbbas Mirza in Tabriz was aware that Europeans had come to possess powerful new forms of knowledge, the *ʿulum-i jadid*, or new sciences, that were transforming Europe's place in the world. As the sons of court bureaucrats, the six students sent to England already recognized the value of these new sciences and hoped to spend enough time in London to master their various components. Their mission was no exercise in education as self-promotion. As their princely patron admonished them, their responsibility was to Iran as a whole, whose destiny they held in their skilled hands and sharp minds.

What they and other Muslim students sent to Europe after them achieved would transform their homelands into recognizably modern nations, albeit never into economic powerhouses. There are complex reasons for this, but one of them is the uneven flow of knowledge caused by barriers to education both around and inside Muslim nations. It is here that the students' story helps us grasp the human complications behind such abstract ideas as "divergence," "development" and "progress." For what Mirza Salih's diary recounts is less a tale of unmitigated success than a parable of the false starts and repeated efforts required to even access let alone acquire an education two hundred years ago when Europe began its "great divergence" from the Middle East and Asia at large. The saga of Mirza Salih and his companions is one of the struggles of foreign Muslims to break into the social circles of English learning, before even attempting which they first had to master the unknown language of the *Inglis*. The challenges ahead as they walked down the gangplank at Great Yarmouth were manifold. Faced with the great stakes of the future of their homeland, they took their first small steps onto English soil.

Now we must pursue them. If what follows is a tour of Jane Austen's world led by six meandering Muslims, then it has the virtue of revealing an alternative history of England, a history in which Muslims were present at the birth of modern Europe. What is more, it is an amicable tale, a story of xenophilia. For theirs was a journey through knowledge and faith unto friendship. Let us join them at the start of their adventures.

Knowledge

1

In Search of a Teacher

An Entry to Inglistan

Mirza Salih began the diary of his English journey by recounting the circumstances of his companions' departure from Iran in the company of Mr. D'Arcy. Since the crown prince 'Abbas Mirza wished to send several persons to study the *'ulum-i farang* or "European sciences," Mirza Salih wrote, using another term for the "new sciences," he was chosen for the task along with Mirza Riza, two youths named Mirza Ja'far, and a craftsman called Muhammad 'Ali. Once they reached England, they would join their compatriot Hajji Baba, who had been studying in London since 1811. After several months traveling overland through Russia and then across the Baltic Sea from Saint Petersburg, we have seen their ship arriving at Great Yarmouth on England's eastern seaboard. As a seaside resort since the 1760s, the town was lit that late September evening with bright and colorful lights; perhaps the wind even carried the tune of a flute or fiddle to where they stood gazing at the shore from the deck. While Mr. D'Arcy and the ship's captain went ashore to visit relatives who lived in the neighborhood, to their disappointment the students were told to remain aboard ship and delay their first taste of England till their chaperone returned. Fortunately, the captain's deputy took a less schoolmasterly approach, and when D'Arcy and the captain were rowed to land he sneaked the young foreigners ashore on a cutter. Smuggled into England by a cunning old seadog, it must have been an exciting start to their great venture.

Even by the standards of a coastal port, the students must have proved a strange sight as they wandered wide-eyed in their robes and turbans through the streets of Great Yarmouth, a port more used to local fishermen and the occasional Dutchman than visitors from the distant East. To the students, the small town of Great Yarmouth appeared as one of the gathering places of a new world: it provided many a "spectacle," many a *tamasha*, to use a word of which Mirza Salih would grow fond. The Iranians and the English looked at each other with matched curiosity, for this was still a time when these different peoples had not yet classified one another as friends or foes, moderates or fanatics. Not least among the "spectacles" that struck the students was a hall in which they saw men, women, and girls mixing gaily and freely, enjoying each another's company unashamedly in public. It was something that the students had never seen in Iran, at least among the respectable classes; the different morality of public space would be one of their earliest and least expected lessons. By the time they crept back aboard ship that night, they had already seen much; some of it was comparable to home; much of it was beyond their ken. Mirza Salih recorded the date in his diary as the 23rd of Shawwal; it was the 28th of September, 1815, and three months earlier the duke of Wellington had defeated ʿAbbas Mirza's hero Napoleon at Waterloo.

The students passed three dizzying days in Great Yarmouth, days in whose new experiences Mirza Salih was too absorbed to record much of detail in his diary. And then, still aboard ship, they sailed down the coast and, entering the Thames estuary, reached the port of Gravesend in the garden county of Kent. As the first major port in from the coast up the Thames, Gravesend lay about twenty miles east of London's new East India Docks and had for centuries connected the capital with the continent. By the year the students arrived, Gravesend was already seeing steamboats plying the river route up to London. In January that year, the steamship *Margery* had begun a regular service from Gravesend for the London firm of Cortis & Co. It must have been a startling sight after sailing so far powered only by the wind and such sights as the *Margery* would have been of special interest to Mirza Jaʿfar, who planned to study engineering. It was a timely ambition. Steam power was being deployed for many new purposes, and James Watt (1736–1819), the greatest of all steam engine inventors, was then still alive in Birmingham (he would die just a month before they returned home). Many such possibilities lay ahead of them, and many challenges as well. As yet, they did not even speak English and, as

Mirza Salih's diary shows, even in their own language they struggled to find words for the new things they saw.

Despite sneaking ashore at Great Yarmouth, it was at Gravesend that the students officially disembarked and passed through customs into the realm of the *Inglis*. Absorbing everything around him, Mirza Salih described the customs house itself. Though a few Iranian ports had some form of customs houses (or *gumruk*), as an early sign of the orderly governance with which he would come to associate England's island realm, the Gravesend *gumruk* were novel enough to to be worth recording. From Gravesend, the party traveled by coach to visit Mr. D'Arcy's family at the great naval port of Chatham, where his father was commandant of the garrison. The father, Major General Robert D'Arcy, cut a striking figure. Since being wounded in the Napoleonic Wars, he had taken to wearing a stark black eye patch that made a bold contrast with his white powdered wig. Here was a gentleman warrior, at once frightening and a little bit effeminate.

After the students ate supper—their first proper English meal—in the company of the D'Arcy family, they listened to the ladies of the household play instruments. Mirza Salih described these as *chang u saz*, which given the setting seem to have been the harp and guitar. Here perhaps was a sight such as that found in Miss Austen's Mansfield Park, where "a young woman, pretty, lively, with a harp as elegant as herself . . . was enough to catch any man's heart." The students were gaining their first taste of the domestic culture of the Regency's happy middle classes. It was one of the first images of a contented society that Mirza Salih would redact into his diary and later carry back to Iran. It was in many ways a false image, for this was also the age of the struggles of the laboring classes that would erupt in the Peterloo Massacre of August 1819 a few months before the Iranians departed. But proud bourgeois patriot as Mr. D'Arcy was, this proletarian world was not one he wished to show his foreign guests. Nonetheless, some of them at least would find themselves forced to enter it. As they would learn, English life was not all harps and guitar lessons.

The next days were filled with the sights and sounds of other new spectacles. Both Mr. D'Arcy and his young charges were keen to start their mission on the right foot, and for D'Arcy at least that meant a military footing: bright and early, he took them to inspect one of Chatham's cannon and gun foundries. Having equipped England's burgeoning navy in its wars against Napoleon, Chatham's naval foundries also supplied the ships that just a few years earlier Jane Austen's two sailor brothers had commanded in the sea war against France. All told, it was the type of visit of which Crown Prince 'Abbas Mirza would have approved; it was also the kind of tourism to which his former military advisor Mr. D'Arcy was best suited. Whether the students were quite so keen we can only guess, though Mirza Salih's diary suggests the sight of people making music and dancing was more immediately appealing.

Even so, the Christian culture that underlay Miss Austen's lighthearted depictions of gentle country parsons meant that the next items on Mr. D'Arcy's itinerary were visits to the churches of nearby Rochester. And so the next day, they made their next steps toward exploring the strange new society around them by entering their first English city. Miss Austen had visited Rochester when she was around the same age as the students. Though small, it also made a good impression on Mirza Salih. As he wrote in his diary,

> There is a huge bridge there made of stone; it has twenty-one arches. It was built in the time of Edward III and completed in the Christian year 1256. We crossed over that bridge and entered the city. It has fine buildings and three well-built churches. And there was one other church that they call a "kathral." It belongs to a "beshap," who is one of the great priests.

If, after his years among the mosques of Tabriz, Mr. D'Arcy was seeking to correspondingly impress the Muslims with the architectural splendor of Christendom, then Rochester was not an altogether bad choice. Founded in the year 604, the cathedral was the seat of England's second oldest bishopric, after Canterbury, and though small, the cathedral is an early Norman gem of a building. But young men that they were, the students had other curiosities and thankfully their early days were not all filled with stained glass and cannons. Wandering around town in the evening, Mirza Salih described him and his companions looking into a dance hall, where they gazed at the happy sight of young couples dancing, playing cards, and flirting till the early hours of the morning. They had already stood and stared at such a gathering in Great Yarmouth, and here they were again a few days later, young men who were clearly drawn to such sights. It is tempting to call them "innocent sights," but perhaps at first, and by comparison with their homeland, they seemed far from innocent. They were fascinating nonetheless.

The following day, they rode horses across Kent and finally entered London, crossing the Thames from the south via Westminster Bridge. With the eye he was acquiring for detail, Mirza Salih described it as four hundred paces across. From there, on another September morning thirteen years earlier, the young William Wordsworth had gazed out to see where

> Ships, towers, domes, theatres, and temples lie
> Open unto the fields, and to the sky, —
> All bright and glittering in the smokeless air.

Mirza Salih's first impressions of the view along the Thames were more reserved; "there are some good houses, buildings and other places along the way," he noted simply. They would have to wait for the glitter of the big city.

To recover from their ride and make them feel more at home, the students were taken to one of the Turkish-style *hammams*, or bath-houses, that were currently fashionable in the capital. London guide-books from the period list many such bathhouses, many of them attached to hotels and coffeehouses. Others were located all over central London, whether at the "Old Hummums" on Covent Garden; on Great Windmill Street and Long Acre in Soho; on Great Coram Street just off Russell Square; and on Leicester Square, where Mr. D'Arcy lived and the students were heading. These were all in any case addresses with which the students would become closely associated over the following years: far away from Iran as they were, they were never to be far from a *hammam*. However, Mirza Salih soon learned that the etiquette of these bathhouses was embarrassingly different from that of their Iranian equivalents. When he first went to one (presumably Bartholomew's Leicester Square Turkish Baths), he decided to spruce up his appearance for the new city by dyeing his beard. But as soon as he started applying the bold henna dye, the Englishman sitting beside him in the tepidarium was alarmed and began to speak to him, in English, and then, seeing that Mirza Salih didn't understand, trying again in French. When he realized that the stranger with the dye running down his body didn't understand French either, the Englishman became frantic. But it was to no communicational avail. Mirza Salih carried on with his plan of staining his beard with what he jokingly referred to as *haft-rang* or "seven colors." Later in the evening when he was back at his lodgings, a message was sent to Mr. D'Arcy explaining what had happened. Apparently, Mirza Salih had broken the rules of the bathhouse on two counts: first, by not going directly to the pool and instead sitting around on the benches; and second, by letting his dye run all over the place, leaving stains on the expensive marble. It was one of Mirza Salih's earliest lessons: even in the *hammam*, they did things differently in England.

Nevertheless, after the students' long journey it was a relief to have finally reached their destination. Their first weeks in London seem to have been enjoyable ones. If one had money in one's pocket, London was a wonderful place to be in that post-Waterloo autumn of 1815. Even Jane Austen, having her own income for the first time now that her books were selling well, chose to spend the months between October and December 1815 living in London. As for the students, their days were filled with some of the same pleasures of tourists to the city two centuries later; perhaps Miss Austen even encountered them in the street as they went to watch the changing of the guards, for example. Even if this was a touristic "spectacle" (to use Mirza Salih's term), it was also a demonstration of England's fighting power. Against the background of the crown prince 'Abbas Mirza's *nizam-i jadid*, the Russian wars with Iran and the many military men (sailors especially) who feature in Miss Austen's novels, the changing of the guards served as a vivid reminder of the highly militarized societies of the Russians and English who were encircling Iran.

In fitting with their status as protégés of 'Abbas Mirza, during their first week in London the students were introduced to several important people, particularly those associated with the embassies to Iran of the previous decade or so. They met James Morier, who may have drawn from the students some inspiration for his later best-selling novels depicting the misadventures of the semifictional Iranian Hajji

Baba in England. They also met the former ambassador to Iran, Sir Gore Ouseley, in whose company we have seen Mirza Salih traveling across Iran in 1812. By chance (for London society was small enough in those days), they also ran into Sir Gore's predecessor as the East India Company's emissary to Iran, Captain (and by now Sir) John Malcolm. It would have been a comfort to the students that he not only spoke Persian but also understood its idioms and social etiquette. As Mirza Salih recorded the meeting in his diary, Sir John "treated us in a kind, gentle, and loving manner and even presented his wife to us. Afterward, when we left, he escorted us out into the street and said, 'Consider my house to be your house. I am a servant of the great government of Iran, for I have eaten the salt of the shah. If there is any help you require, then I am at your service.' " Since Sir John knew their princely patron ʿAbbas Mirza, the students must have been excited to meet him, not least since earlier that year he had published his groundbreaking *History of Persia*, a work that had already established him as England's leading authority on Iran. He might prove to be both a gracious and useful contact.

As it turned out, the students soon needed all the help they could get. As Mr. D'Arcy began to make inquiries about the cost of their education, it quickly became clear that the funds given to him by ʿAbbas Mirza on the eve of their departure from Tabriz would prove manifestly inadequate. In a letter dated after the students' arrival in London, he gave a breakdown of the funds provided to him by the crown prince as follows: for Mirza Salih, "the secretary," £250; for Mirza Jaʿfar, "the engineer," £250; for Mirza Riza, "the artillerist," £300; for Mirza Jaʿfar, "the medical student," £300; and to Muhammad ʿAli, "the locksmith," £100. In addition to this total sum of £1,200 (around £100,000, or $160,000, in today's terms), he explained, the crown prince had promised to send the same amount again for the following year, but so far there was no sign that this money would be forthcoming. Financial trouble was already on the horizon, then, not least in view of the expenses that Mr. D'Arcy had already incurred on the long journey from Iran, with the well-born *mirzas* having required suitable accommodation all the way across Russia.

So it was that, desperate both to honor his promise and defy bankruptcy, shortly after they reached London Mr. D'Arcy began a long and protracted series of negotiations with both the Iranian and the British governments, as well as the directors of the [...] ndia Company on Leadenhall Street. In letter after letter, he asked for supplements and increases to the students' allowance, so as to save himself from the ruin he faced were he forced to fund their education on his junior officer's salary. The correspondence generated by his increasingly frantic efforts survives today in the National Archives in London's Kew Gardens as testimony to his dilemmas and frustrations. It was an unfortunate and unenviable position: by March 1816, five months after the students' arrival and after months of their perpetual complaints, D'Arcy would be writing of "the very distressing and remarkably unpleasant situation in which I find myself." But from the moment the students arrived, the situation was one that His Britannic Majesty's Government considered to be of D'Arcy's own making and the government refused to take responsibility for a situation they saw the foolish young officer as having brought upon himself.

The other side of the story appears in Mirza Salih's diary. There, his early jokes about bathhouse misunderstandings were rapidly replaced by financial fears and complaints about his chaperone. He repeatedly voiced his and his companions' frustrations at what, as the weeks turned into months of apparent inactivity, began to appear like Mr. D'Arcy's prevarication, stonewalling, and plain avoidance of responsibilities. While Mirza Salih poured his frustrations into his diary, the other students vented their anger more directly. As Mr. D'Arcy wrote in one of his increasingly desperate letters from this period, "they place no bounds to their reproaches, load me with insults and have even gone so far as to threaten my person unless I will deliver up the remainder of their funds (about £310) to gratify their extravagances." For Iranians no less than Englishmen, this was an age in which the honor of one's word carried great weight. And as the students constantly reminded him, as an officer and a gentleman, Mr. D'Arcy had given his word to no less a man than the princely heir to the Peacock Throne.

Matters were hardly helped by D'Arcy's insistence that the students do nothing in the meantime but wait at his London home till these financial matters were resolved. And so their first weeks and then months were spent ambling and idling in the neighborhood of his Lon-

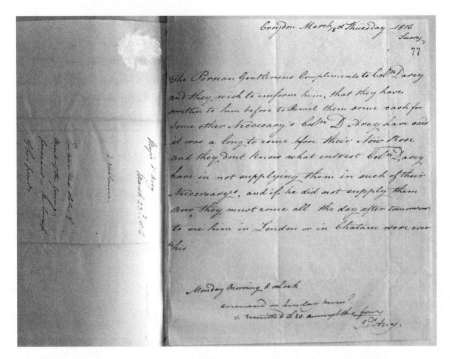

Fig. 3. "The Persian Gentlemen's Compliments": The Students Write to Mr. D'Arcy. Source: Courtesy The National Archives. F.O. 60/11 (77)

don home. The house where they lodged with Mr. D'Arcy stood at 27 Leicester Square. It was demolished in the 1850s, but its surviving neighbor at number 28 shows it to have been a grand Georgian terrace building. Less than two miles away, Jane Austen was then staying with her brother Henry in a similar house at 64 Sloane Street. But she by now had an independent income and that made all the difference to her in that happy season of success. For the Iranians, their early fascination was turning into frustration, especially as regarded their quest for the new sciences.

Still, even if it was hardly the educational core of the capital, Leicester Square held many diversions for the young men from Iran. A London guidebook from a few years after their arrival lists 27 Leicester Square—the same building in which they lodged on one of the upper stories—as the location of one of the public bathhouses of which they were so fond. Given Mirza Salih's mention of visiting such *hammams* during the period of their residence there, they must have frequently (and forcibly) idled in that bathhouse that occupied the ground floor of number 27. Not only the location of London's *bagnios*, Leicester Square was also the site of Huntly's Coffee House, where during those first redundant months they ran up a bill of over £35. In today's terms, this was around £3,000 (or $5,000): even in 1816, it was a sum for which one could rent a large London house. Needless to say, Mr. D'Arcy was furious and used the bill as proof of their profligacy. Nor was Huntly's their only leisure-time option. Just around the corner at the back of 27 Leicester Square, on Bear Street there stood the Bear & Staff tavern, run by the landlord John Philips. Perhaps these were the kind of "extravagances" about which Mr. D'Arcy was writing letters at the time.

If education was in short supply during those early months, then there was at least entertainment available in plenty. But as autumn passed into winter, and the daylight in Mr. D'Arcy's dimming apartment grew shorter, so did the students' patience. Finally, they took the decision to take matters into their own hands. And so, with the impatience of youth and spirit of enterprise that would carry them through their English adventures, Mirza Salih set about organizing his companions' education himself. This was far from easy, since by now they had next to no money and in Regency London an education was the prerogative of gentlemen of means. And in any case, before they could embark on their intended studies in engineering, medicine, and other branches of useful knowledge, they would have to master the English language. With this in mind, and recognizing the reciprocal demand for learning Persian in England, Mirza Salih tried to find someone who would teach him English in return for lessons in Persian. As a pioneering experiment in the language exchange principle that has since carried many a foreign student through their gap years in England, it was an early sign of Mirza Salih's practically minded ingenuity. At a time when Persian has fallen far behind English and Chinese as a useful language for ambitious students, it is difficult now to recognize the value of Persian in the England of 1815, which aside from the exchange of a few strategic embassies had hardly any commercial interests in Iran. But Persian was not only the language of Iran: in the early nineteenth century, it was still the most prestigious *lingua franca* of India and other regions around the Indian Ocean. At a time when vast chunks of India were tumbling into British hands, Persian was the East India Company's language of bureaucracy.

It would not be till 1847 that the prime minister Benjamin Disraeli would declare "The East is a career!" But ever since the formation of the East India Company in 1600, hundreds of other Britons had already recognized this. And in doing so, they saw that mastery of Persian was the key to such a career. Since the East India Company would continue to use Persian until 1837 as its language of administration, 1815 was a time when knowledge of Persian was a prerequisite for many a profitable position in India. Given that there were few useful learning aids to speak of, the ways in which such Britons chose to study Persian were at first ad hoc, by employing Indians (and typically Muslims) when they reached India as their *munshis* ("teachers," in this usage). Clearly, this was the role that Sir William Ouseley had envisaged for Mirza Salih three years earlier when he had asked him to write his Persian phrasebook during their journey through Iran. It seems similarly likely that the phrasebook was the written legacy of verbal lessons that Sir William received from Mirza Salih. Given that language is at heart nothing more than the process of two people talking to one another, such conversational learning formed an effective method. But communication facilitates much more than learning: it also facilitates friendship and the bonds and responsibilities that friendship requires. It was this radically humane potential of one-to-one communication that eventually rang the death knell of the *munshi* system in India. In 1806 and 1809, the East India Company established two new colleges, one at Haileybury in Hertfordshire for the education of its civil servants and another at Addiscombe in Surrey for the education of its military officers. So it was that less than a decade before the students arrived in England, Persian had become part of a respectable English education.

Yet the interest in Persian spread well beyond the Company's employees. The students had reached London at the height of the Romantic era, when it had also become fashionable for literary-minded young men and women to learn (or at least pose as learning) the sweet language of Hafiz. Since Mirza Salih hoped to find conversational partners to learn English, he had reached London at a fortunate time indeed, since there was a good chance that he could find partners in his plan to exchange English conversation for Persian. We do not know whether his former student Sir William Ouseley wrote him a testimonial, but the fact that he had taught Persian to England's leading gentleman orientalist would surely have been helpful.

Before long, Mirza Salih did find a young man who was eager to improve his Persian and an arrangement was agreed upon. In his diary, he recorded his conversation partner's name as Mr. Balfour (or Belfour; spelling in Arabic letters always scrambles English names). Judging from the circles in which the Iranians were moving by this time, the man in question could have been one of several Balfours linked to the East India Company. One possibility is Francis Balfour, who had earlier translated the well-known Mughal bureaucratic manual *Insha'-yi Har Karan* (which he rendered as *The Forms of Herkern*); it had been the first book using Persian type ever printed in India. In 1807, he had retired back to Britain and was still alive in 1816, when Mirza Salih and his companions encountered their "Mistar Balfur," as Mirza Salih wrote his name in Persian's Arabic script. Since Francis Balfour's *Forms of Herkern* provided templates for composing diplomatic correspondence with Persian-speaking princes, he would certainly have been interested to meet a group of young representatives from the court of 'Abbas Mirza. But given the spelling of the name as "Belfour" in one of Mr. D'Arcy's letters from the period, a more likely candidate is Francis Belfour. A recent graduate of Magdalen Hall, Oxford, Francis Belfour was deeply invested in learning Persian at this time and by the early 1820s he would go on to make his name as a reputable scholar of the language. Moreover, as we will see in later chapters, Magdalen Hall was the Oxford college with which Mirza Salih and Mirza Ja'far would become associated. Since the period of Mirza Salih's language exchange with Mr. Belfour coincided with his first ambitions to study at Oxford, this early connection with Magdalen Hall via Francis Belfour helps confirm the identity of Belfour himself. But whether the teacher was ultimately this Belfour or another, Mirza Salih and his companions at last felt able to settle down to the lessons in the language they would need to master before moving on to their chosen scientific subjects.

Finally they had made a step forward. But this initial streak of luck in finding someone who would teach them English for a verbal swap instead of a fee did not last long. For shortly after their English lessons began, Mirza Salih haplessly recorded, Mr. Belfour departed for Paris. It was only fair; he was pursuing his own education; Paris was the center for the study of Islamic languages: twenty years earlier it was there that Sir William Ouseley had similarly spent time furthering his language studies. So the students were back to square one. This time, like many another immigrant before and since, Mirza Salih hit upon the idea of turning toward the help of one of his fellow countrymen. As we have already seen, a few years earlier in 1811 'Abbas Mirza had sent two other students to London. One of them, Muhammad Kazim, had died in 1813—"the funeral . . . performed . . . in St Pancras Church-yard with all the Respect and Ceremony due to the Mussulman Reli-gion"—leaving his companion in London alive and, Mirza Salih hoped, financially well. Unlike Indians, who were far more numerous in Lon-don at this time, Iranians were a tremendous rarity in Regency En-gland: the only Iranians known to be in England at this time were the six students. So with their common purpose and shared friends back home, it is scarcely surprising that they felt able to rely on one another. The fellow Iranian to whom Mirza Salih turned was by now a student of medicine; his name was Hajji Baba Afshar and he was the sixth of our student gang.

Hajji Baba may have been the inspiration for the best-selling novels, *The Adventures of Hajji Baba of Ispahan* (1824) and *The Adventures of Hajji Baba of Ispahan in England* (1828), written by James Morier, whom we have already seen the students meeting in London. In Per-sian translation, the books later became bestsellers in Iran, but though they have usually been seen as caricatures of Ambassador Abu'l-Hasan (who was certainly upset when he heard of their contents), given the fact that James Morier knew the student Hajji Baba, it seems likely that he was at least partly the inspiration for Morier's comic hero. Yet all that was still in the future when Mirza Salih tracked down Hajji Baba at his London address. With what questions he must have plied Hajji Baba when they met! We will never know, for the entry in Mirza Sa-lih's diary that day was a brief one: "I met Hajji Baba Afshar, who has been in this land for five years already . . . he was dressed in English clothes. We had a conversation."

Unfortunately, Hajji Baba left no diary of his own, but surviving records allow us to reconstruct something of his circumstances. By the time Mirza Salih and his companions turned to Hajji Baba for help in early 1816, he was lodging in north London's Camden Town. Camden Town had not even existed a little over twenty years earlier and had been farmland belonging to Charles Pratt, the 1st Earl of Camden. Like other aristocrats at the time, the Earl of Camden decided his farmland would make more profit if developed into rentable residences and so in the 1790s he began to transform it into housing. Within a few years, almost 1,500 homes were built, many of them small terrace houses for lower middle class tradesmen and skilled members of the working class. Although Camden Town was therefore anything but a fashionable neighborhood, in Mirza Salih's frustration at the lack of progress with his studies he decided to leave Mr. D'Arcy's more spacious residence on the West End's exclusive Leicester Square and instead to move in with Hajji Baba. The address of their house was number 2, Camden Street, Camden Town. The building no longer exists, but surviving houses nearby suggest that it was one of the respectable if small two-story townhouses constructed as part of the Earl of Camden's development. Having left his companions in Mr. D'Arcy's more spacious residence at Leicester Square, Mirza Salih recommenced his English education in vicarious mode by making use of his Anglicized compatriot. He was to spend the next four months living in Camden Town.

For the son of a court notable who until this point had only visited the capacious residences of England's military and diplomatic establishment, his small new lodgings must have come as a shock to Mirza Salih. But the deliberateness of his change of circumstances points to his determination to succeed with his education. As well as an escape, the move was also something of a calculated insult, an indirect but unambiguous way of telling Mr. D'Arcy that he preferred the humbler circumstances and vicarious lessons of his fellow countryman than the gilded prison on Leicester Square. But Mirza Salih was no fool and knew all too well the importance of influential social connections. So during his four months in Camden Town, he was careful to take Sir John Malcolm up on the offer of assistance he had made when the students met him during their first months in London. He visited Sir John's house one evening each week for dinner and conversation, taking his companions along with him at least sometimes. It was a good time to encounter Sir John. Not only had his Indian-learned Persian been "Iranianized" by his stay as ambassador to Tehran. By the time Mirza Salih began visiting him at his house on Manchester Street toward the end of 1815, Sir John had just been blessed with a daughter, a gift indeed for a soldier on home leave. Taking advantage of the post-Waterloo peace, Sir John had recently returned from an extensive tour of France and Germany—given its timing, we would now call it a book tour for his *History of Persia*—during which he had met many of the continent's leading orientalists. While the tour had also seen him pay a visit to Waterloo to inspect the battlefield and dine with the victorious duke of Wellington, Sir John was far more than a man of war. By 1816 when Mirza Salih was regularly visiting him, he was becoming equally celebrated as a scholar, precisely the kind of company that the students sought, then. Mirza Salih's decision to trade up his relationship with Mr. D'Arcy for the acquaintance of Sir John may also have reflected his increasing awareness of his chaperone's true status in England: the "Colonel Khan" who had appeared so important to Mirza Salih as the trusted advisor of the crown prince 'Abbas Mirza back in Tabriz was slowly being revealed as an ineffectual junior officer with little clout among the ruling powers of his own country. Besides, with Sir John at the height of his success (his recently published *History of Persia* was a best seller; even Byron praised it), his dinner table must have been a busy one at which Mirza Salih made many new acquaintances.

While some of these new acquaintances were stolid and sensible men like Sir John, this was also an opportunity for Mirza Salih to make his first English friends of his own age. It was at one of the dinner parties during these months that Mirza Salih made friends with Sir John's younger relative, Major Beazley. From around March 1816, the gallant young major (retired early after Waterloo) took Mirza Salih on regular visits to the opera houses and theaters that Ambassador Abu'l-Hasan had enjoyed five years earlier. Mirza Salih took great pleasure in these outings, despite in his diary ruing the fact that his command of English was such that he still missed much of the word play that was so central a feature of Regency comedy. Even so, he was in good company, for what he wrote of his new friend suggests that he was Samuel Beazley (1786–1851), who had earlier served as an officer in the Peninsular War before returning to London in 1815 and setting himself up as a theatrical architect and impressario. In early 1816, when Mirza Salih met him, Beazley had just redesigned the Lyceum Theatre off the Strand, which was also one of Jane Austen's favorites when she was "in town." Beazley reopened the Lyceum as the English Opera House; in 1831, he would add a graceful portico, rotunda, and colonnade to the Theatre Royal just up the road where he also surely took Mirza Salih. In the 1810s, only the two Theatres Royal at Covent Garden and Drury Lane were allowed to stage serious drama, so most of the plays Mirza Salih (and perhaps the other students) saw with Beazley would have been comic pieces that, to get around the legal definition of serious drama, contained a good deal of singing, clowning, and pantomiming. While we may look back on the era as that of Austen, Scott, and Byron, the kind of "English literature" to which the Muslim students were exposed hardly stood at the artistic zenith of Western civilization.

So it was that in 1816 when Mirza Salih first met Mr. Beazley, his own comic operetta, *Is He Jealous?*, was being staged at the Lyceum. That theater, to which he surely took his Iranian friend, would maintain its importance in England's artistic life through the coming decades: it was here that the great actor Sir Henry Irving later gave his most famous performances and where Bram Stoker wrote the novel *Dracula* while working as its manager. With such visits to the Lyceum, Mirza Salih—and perhaps some of his student companions—was beginning to enter a wider social world than that to which Mr. D'Arcy had access. Through these theater visits and the regular dinners as guests of Sir John Malcolm, the young Muslims and Mirza Salih especially were beginning to meet people who would open up to them a side of English life that lay beyond the martial tours of cannon foundries that had announced their entry to *Inglistan*.

Yet it was still a frustrating time. They had now been in London for over six months and though their English had improved, they had made no progress at all toward accessing the new sciences. And the longer they stayed in London, the more they were learning of the opportunities for education that the capital offered. They were not so much in a slough as a cycle of despond. As Mirza Salih's diary makes clear, by now he had become aware of London's distinguished ancient schools, such as Westminster, Charterhouse, and Merchant Taylors' (from where the youthful Clive of India had earlier been expelled), all of whose names he carefully spelled out in Arabic letters. He had also learned of the city's charitable schools that offered free education to uneducated rural children and realized that there were even reform schools for young thieves and prostitutes in London. He also heard that outside of the capital, there existed charity schools in almost every town and village of the land, where the children of the poor could receive an education. Perhaps for a moment he was tempted by this chance of a free education, but he and his companions were *mirzas*, gentlemen, and not the offspring of *dihati*, or "country bumpkins." For persons of social standing in their own land who had traveled so far on the promise of an education, it must have been galling for the young Muslims to sit waiting in London for the time when their education would properly begin. Even though Mr. D'Arcy constantly complained about the lack of money, the many charity schools seemed to suggest that there were other options available. It must have seemed to Mirza Salih that from prostitutes to lords, everyone in England was being educated except him and his friends.

Although Mirza Salih was admittedly making some kind of progress toward his educational goals between his language lessons with Hajji Baba and his theater visits with Major Beazley, distinctly less progress was being made with Mr. D'Arcy's attempts to make the British or Iranian government provide money to pay for proper instructors. If funds were short, then as seen through the services offered by Indian teachers of Persian in London, there were certainly opportunities for Mirza Salih to pay something of his own way, to get a job. In fact, the daughter of one of Mr. D'Arcy's friends actually asked Mirza Salih for Persian lessons, perhaps from a desire to match what we have already seen were the fashionable accomplishments of Miss Emily Metcalfe in writing Persian verse. But since the suggestion emerged from the young lady's having learned of Mirza Salih's precarious finances, the young Iranian gentleman took umbrage. According to his diary at least, he proudly replied that even if the king of England's own daughter asked for lessons, and offered the princely sum of a hundred Iranian *tumans* per lesson, he would still say no! As he increasingly found his way around London, one senses that Mirza Salih was anxious to set himself apart from the Indian teachers of the Persian language who were setting themselves up in the capital at the time by advertising their services in newspapers. The Iranian students were after all the courtly representatives of an independent prince and not the paid servants of an overblown trading house such as the East India Company. Whether it was with the Indians or the Company that Mirza Salih wished to avoid being associated, he was clearly aware of the importance for his own and his country's independent status of distinguishing himself from the Indian subjects of the Company Empire. But with no financial backing, and English patrons who even after a year of careful cultivation seemed only willing to provide dinner parties and theater trips, Mirza Salih and company were going to have to come up with a masterplan if they wished to both keep their independence *and* gain an education. It was time for a radical rethink.

A Retreat to the Provinces

Mirza Salih's linguistic and cultural lessons with his compatriot Hajji Baba had now taken their course and he felt ready to gain an English education firsthand. Despite Mr. D'Arcy's protests that Mirza Salih should come back to his house and wait patiently for the two governments' response, on March 13, 1816, Mirza Salih made the bold decision to leave London and take his companions with him. While Hajji Baba would stay in Camden Town, instead of staying in the capital, Mirza Salih and the other four students would move to the small town of Croydon, some ten miles to the south. Given the fact that everyone they knew with an interest in their well-being resided in London, the decision may seem a strange one. It was certainly a bold move. If they were seeking to further their education, they might at least have been expected to move to Oxford or Cambridge, both less than sixty miles from London and accessible by regular stagecoach. Yet unlikely as it may now seem, what is today the grimy commuter town of Croydon was for over half a century more important for the study of Persian than either Oxford or Cambridge.

As we have seen, a few years earlier the East India Company had founded one of its new colleges for the education of its military officers at Addiscombe; it lay just on the outskirts of Croydon. With the East

India Company's desire to reduce the influence of the Indian *munshi* teachers over their British employees, the teaching of Persian—along with Sanskrit and other useful languages like Hindustani—had finally found a home on English soil. Founded in 1809, Addiscombe's East India College was intended for the Company's officers. In addition to their training in the arts and logistics of war, trainee officers received instruction in the languages necessary for commanding their regiments of Indian soldiers, chiefly the "Hindustani" (we would today call it Urdu) that was becoming the *lingua franca* of the Company's armies. Since it was originally envisioned that at least two of Mirza Salih's fellow students would acquire an education in the engineering techniques associated with modern warfare (a necessary preoccupation of their princely sponsor 'Abbas Mirza, whom we have earlier seen employing D'Arcy to modernize his armies in Iran), Mirza Salih's decision to lead his companions to Croydon was therefore a sensible one. For the Company colleges operated on a model of British professors and "native" language teaching assistants; here lay the chance of gainful employment.

By the standards of the day, these Indian and Iranian language teachers were well paid. For all their contribution to England's relationship with the wider world and their foundational work in the teaching of Asian languages, the East India Colleges (both of which were disbanded in the 1850s) are scarcely remembered today. Yet the faculty of the two colleges—and the Indian teachers in particular—were the pioneers of a multicultural Britain, spreading appreciation of Islamic learning, taking English wives and bringing Persianate culture to the small town Home Counties.

If most of the language teachers at the East India Company colleges originated in India, then the college at Haileybury, to the north of London, did later employ one Iranian scholar. This was Mirza Muhammad Ibrahim, who joined the college in 1826 and earned a good salary there until his retirement (with a pension) in 1844. Though he joined the college a decade after the Iranian students moved to Croydon, his success shows that Mirza Salih's plan was far from outlandish. Since the college outside Croydon at Addiscombe was intended for training soldiers rather than administrators, it employed fewer language and literature teachers, though there was one Indian teacher of Persian

Fig. 4. Teaching Persian in the Provinces: The East India College at Addiscombe, Croydon. Source: *Addiscombe, its heroes and men of note*; by Colonel H. M. Vibart (Westminster, London, 1894).

employed there. This was Mir Hasan ʿAli, who came from the north Indian city of Lucknow and taught at Addiscombe for six years before resigning his post in 1816 and returning to India with his English wife early in 1817. Since the date of Mirza Salih's move to Croydon coincided exactly with Mir Hasan ʿAli's resignation, his decision to relocate to Croydon seems to have been inspired by the hope of taking up the Indian's position as Persian teacher. We certainly know that he had a low opinion of the Indian *munshis* and their standard of Persian, for his associate William Price recorded Mirza Salih's assessments in the preface to the Persian conversation guide they had written together during the months traveling across Iran four years earlier. Looking at a Persian language guide written by the Englishman Francis Gladwin and his "Indian Moonshees, unaccustomed to modern Persian," Price explained in his preface that it was "so full of pedantic phrases and obsolete words, that whenever Mirza Saulih took up the book to read them, he appeared disgusted with the style." With his links to the Ouseley brothers in London, Mirza Salih would have easily learned of Mir Hasan ʿAli's departure from the college; after all, Sir Gore Ouseley (who was cropping up regularly in Mirza Salih's diary by this time) had lived in Mir Hasan's hometown of Lucknow for many years. Moreover, a few years later Sir Gore would be instrumental in convincing the other college at Haileybury to hire an Iranian rather than an Indian teacher, persuasion that led to the employment of the aforementioned Mirza Ibrahim.

Yet whatever Mirza Salih's precise intentions in moving to Croydon, despite his pressing financial needs, he was never to enter the formal employment of the East India College. Even so, it is hard to imagine that his decision to move and then remain there was unconnected to the presence of the college and its many cadets anxious to pass their Persian exams. While Mirza Salih was always discreet in the details of his life he committed to paper, knowing that his diary would later be read by others on his return home, given his straitened circumstances in Croydon it seems likely that he and his companions supported themselves by quietly giving private Persian lessons to officer cadets from the neighboring college. Even though they did not work directly for the college, then, they were nonetheless associated with it. Away from the direct circle of his London associates, where Mirza Salih had publicly turned down the offer to teach Mr. D'Arcy's lady friends, Croydon was a venue of discreet retreat where, beyond the probing eyes of Sir John and Sir William who knew him as a man of status and not a mere *munshi*, he could hope to buy an education by, in reciprocal manner, selling one.

Even so, we know that the students' situation in Croydon remained difficult through several letters that they wrote from there that described their straitened circumstances. On March 18, 1816, just after settling in Croydon, they wrote a collective letter to Mr. D'Arcy demanding more money.

> The Persian Gentlemens compliments to Col. Darcy and they wish to inform him, that they have written to him before to Remit them some cash for some other Necessary's. Col. D Arcy have said it was a long to

come before their Now Rose and they don't know what intrest Col. D,arcy have in not supplying them in such of their Necessary's, and if he did not supply them now they must come all the day after tomorrow to see him in London or in Chatham where ever he is.

Despite its occasional mistakes and its borrowing of certain idioms from the Persian (such as the politely indirect addressing of Mr. D'Arcy in the third person), the letter is a valuable informant on their progress with their English. Their attendance at dinner parties and theaters had clearly proved worthwhile. But the letter also documents the precariousness of their financial situation when they reached Croydon, suggesting again that they may have finally resorted to language teaching.

The letter also marked the worsening situation with Mr. D'Arcy: they were after all threatening to come and see him as a group to demand their money. Whatever their motivations, educational or festive, the second letter that soon followed it was even more pressing than the first:

> We received your letter, and we are very much obliged to you, for all the compliments you have paid us in it, you have wrote sens [since] we are Instrument of the other we do not deserve to be calls Gentlemen, but on the contrary you act by your self very unhandsomely and very ungentlemanly. You inform us that you have left orders with your Servants in London and in Chatham not to admit us in your company, but do you know that we should not wish to see you or speak to you if you did not possess our money. You talk a good deal about your Protection and Assistance but we have not seen any of it sens [since] we have been in England, but only your promises going on, these 6 months past, and we are left unprovided for and unsettled, in every respect, but now only we have to give you a wright understanding sens [since] you have declared not to give us any more of your assistance (which was but very *trifling*) so therefore you must settle our accounts with us, becaus we have been 6 months heer using the Money of our Benefactor [that is, Prince 'Abbas Mirza], not doing any service to him, and now we will Endeavour to be *Sedulous* in our undertaking without your Assistance and Protection, we therefore beg you to return us an amid'et ancer [immediate answer] and inform us what property of ours you possess now.

While the students' situation was undoubtedly incredibly frustrat-ing, it was little less so for Mr. D'Arcy. As testified by the long se-quence of surviving letters he wrote to the foreign secretary and other influential persons, he was actually working hard to resolve their situ-ation. Indeed, he felt no less trapped by the relationship with the stu-dents than they did with him. In response to the demands to hand over all of the funds that the two letters voiced, Mr. D'Arcy wrote to Edward Cooke at the Foreign Office to ask if he could indeed hand over all of the money and so be done with the whole affair. That he was not em-bezzling the students seems clear from the scrupulous accounts he repeatedly presented to the Foreign Office and that survive in its re-cords today (assuming, that is, that he didn't cook the books). Hoping to disprove any imputations of impropriety, in June 1816 he asked Sir William Ouseley and the accountant R. P. Percy to independently check the expense claims and accounts he had made on the students' behalf. It was, then, an impossible situation for both D'Arcy and the students, and one which neither party had the means to resolve them-selves. After all, the heart of the problem lay in the fact that the stu-dents' princely "Benefactor" 'Abbas Mirza had neither provided them with sufficient funds in the first place nor followed through with his promise to provide regular additional stipends (a matter about which he had since been reminded, to no avail, by the British *chargé d'affaires* in Tabriz). As a result, the students were left demanding money from Mr. D'Arcy, and he was in turn left begging money from the Foreign Office, who in turn tried to stonewall him by insisting that this was his own private matter and responsibility.

While the two letters from Croydon quoted earlier conjure an air of desperation, the students were in fact far from indigent. As D'Arcy wrote to Mr. Cooke at the Foreign Office in connection with their de-mands, they already had "their board & lodging, washing & pocket money regularly paid by me & therefore cannot be in want." His state-ment is confirmed by the accounts he presented during the students' months in Croydon, which clearly document the sums he paid out to their Croydon landlady for bed and board. Moreover, the accounts also document certain other expenses that cast a rather different light on the epistolary pleas of desperation. For among the expenses listed was the sum of £12 and 6 shillings for "theatre and other amusements" and

£10 and 10 shillings "for a watch" that Muhammad ʿAli had bought from a French or Swiss watchmaker called Mr. Bazzand. Given that the cost of the watch alone would be equivalent to at least £875 (or around $1,500) today, the "Persian Gentlemens" clearly had elevated expectations of a student lifestyle.

Considering that the earlier coffeehouse bill added up to more than a month's rent and food for all of the students combined (as paid by Mr. D'Arcy to Mrs. Starcy in Croydon), the accounts' cold mathematics present a somewhat different picture of the students' circumstances. Without lessening their genuine frustrations and sense of urgency about the need to move forward with their intended studies, when we scrutinize the two letters more closely, another factor appears that may help explain the particular urgency of the two letters they sent to Mr. D'Arcy in so short a time. For their writing of two insistent letters within forty-eight hours on March 18 and March 20 suggests that their urgency had more than a little to do with their wish to be able to celebrate the Persian New Year in a degree of comfort that fitted their background as well-born associates of the Qajar court. They had, after all, mentioned the "Now Rose" holiday in the first letter, and the spring of 1816 was to be the first time that they celebrated this most important of Iranian celebrations in England. In falling on the vernal equinox, it would have occurred on March 21, 1816, the day after the second urgent letter.

Whether or not their situation genuinely consisted of desperation may be doubted, then. As the various English records surrounding them insisted, they were "Gentlemen," with all that this implied in Jane Austen's era, including certain expectations as to an appropriate standard of living. Even so, while their depravation was more relative than absolute, they clearly felt themselves short of sufficient funds for their preferred endeavors and lifestyles. And this may have led them to teach Persian to some of the hundreds of trainee East India Company officers who were stationed at Croydon. Even though their aim in coming to England was of course to learn and not to teach, Croydon's proximity to the East India College still rendered it a sensible place of retreat. It was less expensive than London and was also a town with a relative abundance of professors and tutors, many of whom had experience of India and even Persian and so would not have been mystified at the prospect of taking on an Iranian student or two. This is confirmed by an official statement of the students' activities written during their months in Croydon, which declared that they were "availing themselves of the instruction of the several masters that the vicinity to the college at Addiscombe afforded."

Mirza Salih's diary again helps us here, for he recorded meeting in Croydon a Mr. Shakespear, whom he described as a professor who also knew Persian. Once again taking his and his companions' education into his own hands, Mirza Salih made arrangements for this aptly named fellow to improve their English. This new association enables us to work out with more precision Mirza Salih's contact with the East India College. Although he did not commit to his diary any demeaning contacts with its humble cadets, he was willing to record his meetings with one of its professors. For the Mr. Shakespear in question was John Shakespear (1774–1858), professor of oriental literature at Addiscombe's East India College since 1809 and compiler of what still serves as one of the two standard dictionaries of "Hindustani" Urdu. Mirza Salih's sudden appearance in John Shakespear's company is further evidence of his intention of replacing Mir Hasan 'Ali as the Persian language instructor at Addiscombe, for Mir Hasan's official position was as assistant to the same Professor Shakespear with whom Mirza Salih was now keeping company within weeks of the Indian's departure.

The son of a laborer on a small farm in the Midlands, the young John Shakespear had the most modest of upbringings. But after being taken under the wing of the local lord of the manor, he was sponsored in pursuing language studies toward a military career, working his way up to the Royal Military College in Marlow before moving on to teach at the college founded at Addiscombe in 1806. A portrait drawing of Shakespear by the Maltese lithographer Maxim Gauci (1776–1854) from around the time he met the Iranians depicts him as a thin-lipped and self-satisfied fellow; an oil painting preserved in the country manor to which he later retired shows him having become a brooding headmasterly figure. Such was the man who, for a while at least, was the students' first formal teacher in England. While we know nothing in detail of the contents of those lessons, there is something fitting in their studying English with a man who, after his rise up in the world, liked to claim he was a descendent of William Shakespeare, that other son of the Midlands who made his fortune in London.

However promising it first looked, the teaching arrangement didn't last very long. Conscious as ever of his limited funds, Mirza Salih tried to bargain with Professor Shakespear about the rate of his remuneration. When Mr. D'Arcy was asked to intervene in the matter, the unseemly question of cash became a matter of embarrassment for the two English gentlemen. In the early decades of the nineteenth century, when East India Company officers were well used to paying Indian *munshis* to instruct them in oriental languages, Mirza Salih's request was an unusual turning of the table: he was making a *munshi* of Mr. Shakespear. And then telling him he was worth less than he demanded. Like Britons in India by this time, Mirza Salih probably considered it his right to set the rate of payment of a teacher who would, after all, be in his employment. But due to the prestige that surrounded the small number of Englishmen who had mastered Asian languages, and the fact that John Shakespeare was Addiscombe's professor of oriental literature, Mirza Salih's attempt to barter for a better bargain no doubt struck the professor as *infra dignitatem*. And all this added more to the embarrassment of Mr. D'Arcy. Born into poverty, Professor Shakespear was notoriously punctilious in matters of finance. By making more lucrative arrangements with other students, he built a considerable fortune over the years. Pledging to posterity his claim to be a descendant of The Bard (a claim he must have made unmistakably clear to the Iranians), on his death John Shakespear bequeathed £2,500 for the endowment of a museum in William Shakespeare's birthplace. The same museum in Stratford still attracts thousands of visitors today.

Back in Croydon in the spring of 1816, Professor Shakespear continued to drive a hard bargain with Mirza Salih. Since payment in money was clearly a problem for the students, it seems feasible that they may have tried to arrange with the professor the kind of language exchange that they had earlier agreed with Mr. Belfour in London. After all, Shakespear was at this time preparing for the press his *Dictionary, Hindustani and English* that, as one of the earliest and most enduring dictionaries of the language we now call Urdu, would be published the following year in 1817. Since a large proportion of the words in Shakespear's dictionary were effectively Persian, it would have been very much in his interest to accept the advice of educated native speakers. Perhaps he did draw on their advice; and perhaps, in the midst of their disputes, they were heavy-handed in their critiques of his lexicography. In view of Mirza Salih's dispute with him over the rate that the nobly born Iranians would pay for the lessons of the English farm laborer's son, it is tempting to trace an echo of their encounter in the dictionary Shakespear was finalizing at the time. For in his definition of the adjectival form of Mirza Salih's name in the dictionary, the insulted professor wrote: "Mirza'i: The behavior or manners of a *mirzā*; gentility, arrogance."

If Mirza Salih's pride prevented him from recording in his diary any of his own teaching activities, then he was not averse to describing how he had to sell certain possessions to pay for his lessons. After all, selling precious belongings was considered far less demeaning than manual work or lowly service positions such as the *munshi* teaching he publically scorned. He harbored high ambitions for his future and had no desire to spread the word that he held humble occupations in his student years. Having already sold two embroidered *tirmah* shawls that he had brought with him from Iran, he returned to London to collect his remaining funds from the sale before setting off again for Croydon to pay Professor Shakespear his wages. Quite what became of the final arrangement is unclear, but it seems that the professor eventually priced himself out of Mirza Salih's budget (unless he resigned, offended by the arguments over his remuneration). But we do know how much Professor Shakespear was paid, because it was recorded in one of the accounts statements written up by Mr. D'Arcy, anxious as ever to document the honesty of his dealings with the students. From the statement in question, we know that Shakespear was paid the sum of £31, 16 shillings, and 6 pence "for five weeks of instruction." No wonder Mirza Salih had tried to bargain: the sum is equivalent to over £2,500 (or around $4,300) today. Since we can calculate from the same accounts statement that the collective costs for the students' food and rent in Croydon came to the similar sum of £33 per month, we can understand Mirza Salih's anxiety that a few hours of lessons per day were costing around the same as his and his fellow students' living expenses.

Yet even without Professor Shakespear's lessons, it is clear from Mirza Salih's diary that he decided that Croydon remained the students' best option. And so with the exception of the their craftsman and medical companions Muhammad ʿAli and Hajji Baba, who both stayed behind in London, Mirza Salih and the others students decided to remain in Croydon, where comfortable lodging was at least less expensive than in London and where they were less than a mile away from the college at Addiscombe and its lucrative learners of Persian.

If it was not Mr. D'Arcy's Leicester Square, then Croydon was still not a bad place to be during the Regency. A few years before the Iranians arrived there, the town entered something of a golden age. During the early nineteenth century, it stood at the center of a flourishing local economy that relied partly on the stationing of so many troops there, at the Croydon Barracks (opened in 1794) as well as the East India College. The town was also home to Messrs. Gillett, Bland & Co., one of the most important bell and clockmakers of the period, who were one of its largest employers. But it was as a transport hub that the town gained much of its wealth, not only from the Croydon Canal that opened in 1800 and connected the town with the dockyards in London's Rotherhithe but more prestigiously from the coaching road that passed directly through the town to connect London with Brighton. As the Regency's coastal pleasure resort, Brighton saw the prince regent remodel his Royal Pavilion there between 1815 and 1822 in fashionably Islamic style after the designs of the period's most celebrated architect, John Nash (1752–1835). With so much of London's high society passing through Croydon, the downs outside the town became a favored spot for coursing with greyhounds. An entire industry of coaching inns developed to attend to the visitors, such that by 1820, upward of forty coaches a day were stopping in Croydon to refresh their passengers and change their horses. It may have been from witnessing this constant traffic that Mirza Salih wrote the account of England's efficient stagecoach system that appears undated in his diary. Even the prince regent changed his horses in Croydon, always

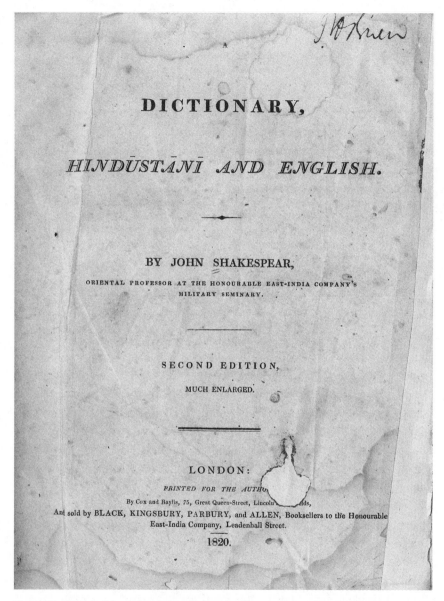

Fig. 5. The Swan of Croydon: John Shakespear's *Dictionary of Hindustani.* Source: "Dictionary: Hindustani & English" (London, 1820)

at the Greyhound Inn (though there were other coaching inns vying for his custom, such as the appropriately royalist rivals, The King's Arms, and The Crown). Given the students' finances, it seems unlikely that they lodged at these finer establishments. But the passing trade ensured that Croydon had a surfeit of accommodation, and they may have resided at the more economical Dartmouth Arms that overlooked the canal and its less distinguished local pleasure boaters. While one of Mr. D'Arcy's statements of account names their landlady in Croydon as a Mrs. E. Starcy, a lack of further records means it remains unclear whether she was the landlady of a coaching inn or an ordinary lodging house. In either case, the rent they paid suggests that it was comfortable accommodation, if not quite of the standard of the prince regent.

In the end, they remained in Croydon for eleven months, and wherever they lodged, Mirza Salih, Mirza Riza, and the two Mirza Ja'fars would certainly have gotten to know the town's prominent public buildings, such as its parish church of St. John the Baptist. In 1818, it was described as "a very beautiful and stately Gothic structure, far surpassing every other church in the whole county of Surrey." Every Sunday morning, they could have watched the spectacle of cadets from the East India College marching in uniform to the church to the accompaniment of a military band. When Mirza Salih later wrote in his diary an account of the rise of British power in India, he may well have thought back to these soldierly displays of strapping lads who would shortly be dispatched to Bengal. Given that Mirza Salih was also developing a special interest in English Christianity, the grand old church of St. John near which he lived for almost a year may have shaped his appreciation for Anglican worship. But the church was by no means Croydon's only public building: in 1809 an imposing town hall was completed on the High Street. Built of stone in classical Regency style with columns in both the Doric and Ionic orders and a cupola at its summit, it was designed by the fashionable architect Samuel Pepys Cockerell (1754–1827). A surveyor to the East India Company and a descendant of the diarist Samuel Pepys, Cockerell was a leading player in the orientalizing fashions of the period. Though the good burghers of Croydon opted for a more classical style, Cockerell was better known as the architect of Sezincote House. Begun in 1805, its Mughal-derived dome and arches made it look more like an Indian mosque than the seat of a country squire. Croydon certainly had none of that—even the East India College was in colonnaded neoclassical form—but walking past the town hall as they regularly did along the High Street, the Iranians would have been well placed to detect an Islamic influence in Cockerell's signature cupola that surmounted the building. They would have seen other such buildings during their time in England. For their student years coincided with the craze for Indo-Islamic designs triggered by the superb architectural drawings published by Thomas and William Daniell in their *Oriental Scenery* (1808) and *Picturesque Voyage to India by Way of China* (1810). These costly volumes each contained dozens of aquatints depicting the crumbling grandeur of the Mughal Empire with the fine detail afforded by camera obscura. An immediate success, the volumes were bought by aristocrats who then employed architects such as Cockerell, Nash, William Porden, and Humphrey Repton to return the Daniells' drawings to three dimensions on English soil. And so it was that, above the neoclassical façade of the town hall, Mirza Salih and his pals came to walk beneath a Mughal dome every morning in Croydon.

Living there for almost a year, they would have become familiar with some of Croydon's shops: Barnes the baker, Broad the butcher, Page the fishmonger, Walker the greengrocer, and Roy the pie-maker. Mirza Salih did not waste the opportunity for learning and among the various entries he was making on English lifestyles in his diary, he included a section on eating habits and the foods enjoyed by ordinary people. Though the better-off ate beef, mutton, and venison, the only wild animal left for poorer people to hunt was rabbit, he explained. Still, most people of the middling sort could afford to finish their evening meal with some cheese or a pudding. Though he used ordinary Persian words in his diary, he must have been eating in the inns and taverns of Croydon during this time, and so with his gastronomic interests he must have heard some of the colloquial terms for the foods that were served in those taverns. Even after Professor Shakespear's English lessons, what must he have made of a chalkboard covered with the names of such dishes as "German duck" (half a boiled sheep's head), "scratch platter" (bread sopped in oil and vinegar), and "old crowdy" (plain porridge)?

Having left Mr. D'Arcy's fashionable lodgings on Leicester Square, during these months in Croydon Mirza Salih, Mirza Riza, and the two Mirza Ja'fars would in such ways have learned more about the lifestyles of ordinary English people. Having been introduced to the pleasures of the theater by Major Beazley, Mirza Salih wrote various descriptions of English entertainments, and in particular of the theater. Though the specific theater visits he recorded were mainly to the more prestigious venues around London's Covent Garden, there was also a flourishing theater in Croydon during the year the Iranians lived there. On various occasions at this time, it hosted the great Regency actor Edmund Kean (1787–1833), including in his signature role as Sir Giles Overreach. The great thespian Kean often featured in the letters of Jane Austen, who much admired his performances and always enjoyed her own visits to the theater. The students were entering her cultural world.

Although Mirza Salih did not mention the fancy dress parties described a few years earlier in the diary of Ambassador Abu'l-Hasan, these were also a part of Croydon's regular entertainments. In response to the fashions of the day, Croydonian pastimes of the period included oriental fantasies, such as the performing troupe associated with the Croydon Barracks that often marched through the town. As recollected by the Croydonian William Page around 1820, the troupe included "some fine black men who played accessory instruments, viz. drums, cymbals, tambourine, triangle and bells. . . . Their fine stature and the picturesque dresses of the blackmen . . . corresponding between that of a Turk and a [North African] Zouave; being short red jackets embroidered in gold, very loose trousers, and high Turkish turbans." We cannot know whether the Muslim students witnessed this particular spectacle, but the "exotic" nature of their dress, comparable by locals to that of the marching troupe and other performers, may have contributed to a significant decision that Mirza Salih made during his time in Croydon. On several occasions during these months, Mr. D'Arcy had suggested that the students start to wear English clothes. Although this was a proposition that Mirza Salih at first adamantly refused, seeing the abandonment of his Muslim dress as a matter with no relation to the pursuit of an education, he gradually acquiesced. "If Colonel Khan strives to make me wear English clothes because he thinks that way I will learn something and that it is the appropriate thing to do at this time, then that is easy enough for me," he wrote in his diary. "And as a matter of fact, being in conflict with this or that minor matter, whether to prefer a fur hat to a foreign beret, is actually quite fun." For Mirza Salih it was a trivial matter; he had larger concerns than clothing. Understanding that knowledge was more than a matter of outward dress, he quoted the poet Sa'di in his diary:

> It makes no difference to the water
> If the jug is made of gold or clay.

After all, the students' mission was to acquire English scientific knowledge—the *'ulum-i jadid*—and not English manners. Even so, as a contemplative young man Mirza Salih pondered carefully the dilemmas that acculturation posed to self-identity. In the end, he jotted in his diary his conclusion that the obstinacy of his earlier refusal to adopt English dress was unreasonable—in his own words, it was *az 'aql dur*: "far from reason." What he wore on his head was no matter of deep significance, he concluded; and like wool, his beard would also grow back soon enough.

Living in Croydon as he was at the time of this decision, he may have acquired his new English outfit from the ready-made (and so less expensive) gentlemen's clothes shop run by Mrs. Rochfort, the genteel widow of a former officer aboard *HMS Royal George*; his shoes may have come from Mr. Fisher, the town's fashionable boot-maker. In this act of open-mindedness, Mirza Salih again sought solace in Sa'di, the medieval Persian poet whose own lifetime of travel lent him a wry worldliness that has cheered Iranians for centuries:

> Don't be so proud of your turban and beard:
> They're just the same as cotton bolls and weed.

Changing clothes and quoting Sa'di was all very well, but the matter of the students' education remained a pressing one. After all, they had moved out of London in search of a more affordable education in Croydon and as the months had gone by, the costly arrangement with Professor Shakespear had been abandoned. Finding their own way as they were, the students tried out a number of other tutors, and Mirza Salih's

diary records them being taught a range of subjects by several unnamed teachers as well as by someone whose name, as recorded in
Mirza Salih's Arabic script, might be read as "Baldwin" or "Bordwine."
Given their prior association with Professor Shakespear from the East
India College, the person in question appears to have been Joseph Bordwine (d. 1835), the college's professor of fortification and artillery.
Since Mirza Riza had traveled from Iran to learn modern artillery
methods, and Mirza Ja'far to learn military engineering and fort-
building, Mr. Bordwine would have been an appropriate choice. We
know that he was already working at the East India College when the
students arrived in Croydon in the early spring of 1816, having been a
regular professor there since 1811. But if such a teacher would have
well suited Mirza Ja'far and Mirza Riza, then Mr. Bordwine had little
attraction for Mirza Salih. And so he continued his search for an instructor more suited to his own interests in language and culture.

Since there was still no sign of support from the Iranian or British
governments, at some point during their eleven months in Croydon,
they were eventually forced to move downmarket and abandon their
studies with the distinguished and costly professors of the East India
College. Less than a mile away from the college, the town of Croydon
itself offered alternative sources of teachers, including Archbishop
Tenison's School; the Whitgift School; and a newer "Academy for Gentlemen" set up in response to the town's recent gentrification. In the
first of what would become a series of associations with English clergymen, from among these schools Mirza Salih found the students'
most permanent teacher in Croydon. Noting his disbelief at being by
this point effectively abandoned by Mr. D'Arcy, the English government, and the Iranian court, he recorded his circumstances at this time
in his diary:

> This humble slave was in a state of bewilderment. It was in this condi-
> tion that I found Mr Bissit, a priest in one of the churches of Croydon.
> I arranged for him to give me two hours of teaching for three days
> each week. The fee was one guinea, which is more than two Iranian
> gold coins [*ashrafi*].

The "Mister Bissit" whom Mirza Salih implicitly described over-
charging him was Reverend John Bisset (1785–1852). Despite the high

fees, through his limited options Mirza Salih stuck by him, bringing his companions along to lessons, where they immersed themselves in a course of private tuition for their remaining months in Croydon. The son of a local schoolmaster, Bisset had graduated from St. Edmund Hall, Oxford in 1808. He then inherited from his father Alexander the "Academy for Gentlemen," a small family affair that did not have a schoolhouse of its own and had its lessons conducted at the George Inn, one of the town's many coaching inns. It was not an unusual occupation for a fresh Oxford graduate. A generation earlier Jane Austen's father, George, himself a young reverend Oxonian, set up a similar one-man-school for the sons of local gentlemen which he ran for many years to supplement his clerical stipend. In Mr. Bisset's case, by 1812 he had also assumed the positions of chaplain and headmaster at Croydon's distinguished Whitgift School (founded in 1596), offices to which he was appointed by no lesser a patron than the Archbishop of Canterbury, Charles Manners-Sutton (1755–1828). Even so, his lucrative Academy for Gentlemen still left him open to requests for private tuition and so it was that he took on the young Muslims.

Mr. Bisset was still a young man aged less than thirty during the time they were studying with him. He was also teaching some fifteen boarders and thirty day students at the Whitgift School, for which he was paid a mere £20 per annum, so the extra guinea (that is, a pound and a shilling) he made from the Iranians for each three days of lessons would have been a considerable supplement to his salary. Here was an early English exercise in seeing "overseas students" as a revenue booster. According to the arrangement recorded in Mirza Salih's diary, Mr. Bisset's lessons were given every day between seven and nine o'clock at the students' lodgings, though it seems inevitable that they would at least sometimes have encountered him where he ordinarily held his Gentlemen's Academy in the somewhat surprising setting of the George Inn. The motivations for this location were perhaps more bibulous than pedagogical: that Bisset was fond of such establishments we know from a description of him from as "a stout, jolly fellow who after his tuition labours were over used to saunter down to the old 'Ship' and have his glass." Another account from the period describes his lively presence at The Ship Inn, where "after the fashion of Dr. Johnson, [he] held forth to admiring company." Presumably this blend of jollity and learning helped the students warm to him, because this provincial scholar became one of their most important teachers. For under his tutelage, they began to learn more not only of English knowledge in the abstract but also about the English themselves in flesh and blood.

Having earlier begun studying British history with Professor Shakespear and developed a taste for the subject, Mirza Salih asked Mr. Bisset to continue their lessons in this subject as well as to teach them Latin. As a churchman—Bisset was curate of the parish of Addington in Surrey as well as the chaplain and schoolmaster at the Whitgift School and master of his Gentlemen's Academy—he would certainly have known his Latin, which had been a central part of his education at Oxford. Even so, he was not Croydon's only classical scholar and a stone's throw from his two teaching posts at the Whitgift School and the George Inn, there lived on George Street the Reverend Jonathan Cape (1793–1868), professor of mathematics and classics at the East India College. But Cape arrived in Croydon a couple of years too late to help the students with their Latin, and they had anyway now decided to opt for less costly teachers than college professors. Even so, the presence in Croydon of such men of learning shows that Mirza Salih's choice of the town as an alternative to London was more sensible than it first seemed.

It is less clear what their actual intentions were in studying Latin, since by this period Latin held far less importance as a language of scholarship and diplomacy. Although over the past century Latin had been replaced as the language of science by English and French, the students may at this point have thought it was still an essential key to their education. Though it was certainly not the language being used by specialists in the mechanical sciences, as yet they probably did not realize this. Given the importance in a traditional Iranian education of learning Arabic, as they all had, they may have considered Latin to be Arabic's natural counterpart. However, given the deliberation that Mirza Salih was by now showing in the art of self-advancement, he may have recognized the importance of a Latin-based education for gaining entry to Oxford or Cambridge. He and Mirza Ja'far at least now had aspirations in this direction and may already have been working toward this goal. If so, they had chosen an appropriate prep teacher in the Reverend John Bisset, for both the Whitgift School and his Gentlemen's Academy regularly dispatched boys to the two varsities. But whether Mr. Bisset could achieve the same success with two foreign Muslim students remained to be seen.

Whatever the future held, the lengthy summaries of English history that Mirza Salih wrote in his diary show that they learned much from the Croydonian reverend. As a result of their more permanent and affordable arrangement with that "stout, jolly fellow," the students were to spend nine of their eleven months in Croydon studying at least the basics of an English education, comprising English grammar, history, and Latin. It was not the "new learning" they had come in search of, but it was at least more solid progress than any they had made so far. As 1817 began, their time in Croydon had been a year in which they had begun to adapt to English life more comfortably as well as consciously. We have seen Mirza Salih decide to start wearing English clothes, a decision his Iranian housemates may have shared. We know that Hajji Baba, whom they sometimes visited in Camden Town, also dressed the English way. More importantly, there were finally studying and finding their way. In educational terms at least, things were looking up.

Managing their education as best they could on their own, by now they were keeping only minimal contact with their supposed chaperone. In desperation at his financial responsibilities, in July 1816 Mr. D'Arcy had in any case fled to Paris to stay with his brother; short of running back to Iran it was as far away from the students as he could reasonably get. As he wrote in a letter to Mr. Cooke of the Foreign Office just before his departure, the £1,200 given to him by the crown prince 'Abbas Mirza was now entirely spent (a situation that helps explain the students' switch from Professor Shakespear to Mr. Bisset early that summer). Worse still, despite the students' perpetual complaints and requests for more money, by the time he fled to Paris Mr. D'Arcy had spent 144 pounds, 17 shillings, and 6 pence of his own money on them. In fairness, for a junior officer on extended leave it was a very considerable sum, being around £12,500 (or $20,000) today. Moreover, since the Napoleonic Wars were now over, D'Arcy was part of a huge glut of recently decommissioned officers who had flooded back into England. The dashing officers who heroically populate Jane

Austen's novels were dreamed up when the wars were at their height, and such men were a viable financial catch. By 1817, when Jane Austen died and Mr. D'Arcy was living at his brother's expense in Paris, the situation had changed drastically. The real Mr. D'Arcy's prospects were little better than those of the immigrant students.

As for the students themselves, despite their progress with Reverend John Bisset, the letters shared between Mr. D'Arcy and the Foreign Office show that the problem of finances reached crisis point after their money was all spent. Losing patience, during their last months in Croydon they finally gave up on their technique of writing threatening letters to Mr. D'Arcy, who was in any case now abroad and not answering them. Instead, they decided to write directly to the foreign secretary, Lord Castlereagh. "At present, we are in extreme anxiety of mind," they entreatied, "and our debts are become so great that we know not what to do." But in shifting the direction of their pleas from Mr. D'Arcy to Lord Castlereagh, they were hardly addressing the most sympathetic man in England. For the foreign secretary was the very person of whom the poet Shelley was to write two years later,

> I met Murder on the way —
> He had a mask like Castlereagh —
> Very smooth he looked, yet grim;
> Seven blood-hounds followed him.
> . . . one by one, and two by two,
> He tossed them human hearts to chew.

A Benefactor, at Last?

The desperate appeals that were voiced in the letter to Lord Castlereagh could not have been sent to a less likely source of charity. After the persistent crowing of critics like Shelley pressured Castlereagh into suicide in 1822, Lord Byron penned a savage epitaph in which he urged anyone passing by his grave to "stop, traveller, and piss." Yet for all his many enemies, Castlereagh was a masterly politician and a brilliant tactician of the complexities of foreign affairs. Even though the threat of Napoleon that had originally made England an ally of Iran had disappeared, in early 1817 Castlereagh still recognized that the good favor of Iran's rulers could be lost or won for the cost of maintaining a handful of students. And so, reversing the foreign office's earlier opinion that the students' well-being was the private responsibility of Mr. D'Arcy, Lord Castlereagh decided to turn the students' education into a matter of state. And so, by the beginning of 1817, there appeared a break in the deadlock between the by now indebted Mr. D'Arcy and the stonewalling British government. Writing to the distraught D'Arcy with the good news, Castlereagh acknowledged the "considerable difficulties" that had arisen "from the want of a proper authority and control" over the students. More importantly, he accepted that the funds originally provided to Mr. D'Arcy by the crown prince 'Abbas Mirza were indeed far too little. And then came the really good news, for D'Arcy not least: since the original funds "have been found so inadequate," Castlereagh informed him, "The Prince Regent, as a mark of his esteem and friendship for the Prince of Persia, has not hesitated to advance the further sum necessary for their maintenance hitherto." If Mr. D'Arcy would be recompensed and, financially at least, the students were finally being put in a position to pay for a more adequate education, their problems were far from completely resolved by the prince regent's largesse. Who after all would they now study with? And where? And precisely how?

Still, there was no doubt that matters had suddenly taken a turn for the better for the students. With more clout than the junior officer Mr. D'Arcy, it was Mirza Salih's former traveling companion the baronet and former ambassador Sir Gore Ouseley who had been working behind the scenes to make the Foreign Office realize that the students' education was a matter of policy and not the private muddle of a foolish subaltern. As a result, Lord Castlereagh agreed to assign £300 (today around £26,000, or $42,000) to each of the students to pay for their instruction and lodging. Their exile in the provinces was over: they were able to return to London from Croydon. Mirza Salih recorded happily his arrival back in London on January 25, 1817, after almost a year in Croydon. There was still no word about financial support from the distant government of Iran, but at least Lord Castlereagh and the prince regent had decided to supply the funds for their education. Perhaps now, crossing Westminster Bridge from the south as he reentered the capital that January morning, he did finally feel as Wordsworth had traversing the same bridge fifteen years earlier:

> Never did sun more beautifully steep
> In his first splendour, valley, rock, or hill;
> Ne'er saw I, never felt, a calm so deep!

His struggles, and those of his companions, it seemed, were over. Through efforts that had been made by Sir Gore Ouseley during their months in Croydon, places were soon found for their education in different parts of London. Trained as a blacksmith in his home country, the craftsman Muhammad ʿAli was the easiest to place. Since he desired to learn "fabricating guns, sabres, etc" he had been found a tradesman's apprenticeship before the other students even returned from Croydon. After all, such an apprenticeship was both far less expensive and far easier to organize than the courses of military and medical instruction sought by most of the other students. As a result, by 1817 Muhammad ʿAli was reportedly "perfecting himself in his trade by working in some of the best shops." The shops in question included that of "the Gun Maker to His Majesty," James Wilkinson and Son, who traded from 12 Ludgate Hill in the old medieval City of London. The military preoccupations of an Iran facing Russian invasions were all too clear in Muhammad ʿAli's apprenticeship to a gunsmith capable of teaching him to make weapons at least as efficient as those of the czar's Cossacks.

The next students to be placed were Mirza Jaʿfar and Mirza Riza, who left their studies with Mr. Bisset in Croydon to attend the Royal Military Academy at Woolwich. It was a vast step up in prestige, moving from Bisset's shoestring Gentlemen's Academy in a Croydon inn to the prestigious Royal Military Academy on the south bank of the Thames in the leafy outskirts of London. Originally established in 1741 to produce "good officers of Artillery and perfect Engineers," the Academy provided an excellent venue for Mirza Jaʿfar and Mirza Riza to be trained to the same scientific standards as British military engineers and artillerymen. Its atmosphere gave them the sense of receiving an education fit for protégés of the shah, for they arrived at the Academy just a decade after the architect James Wyatt (1746–1813)—the rival of the more famous Robert Adam (1728–92)—had finished rebuilding it. In a bid at innovative one-upmanship, instead of Adam's neoclassicism Wyatt opted for a grandly castellated style that responded to the Tower of London in its parallel setting along the Thames to the east. Wyatt may have been amused had he learned of the Muslims' presence at the Academy, for his previous commission was the fantastical Fonthill Abbey that he designed for William Beckford, the author of England's most celebrated orientalist novel, *Vathek, an Arabian Tale*. Between Fonthill Abbey and the Royal Military Academy, Wyatt effectively launched the gothic revival that would eventually overtake the classical fashions of the Regency. Though Mirza Ja'far and Mirza Riza had come to study artillery, they were caught up in the beginnings of an architectural revolution. Perhaps it was no coincidence that, after their return home to Iran, both of them took up a professional interest in public architecture.

As soon as the two young Muslims reached Woolwich, a plan was drawn up for what precisely they would study there. As the governor of the Academy, Colonel William Mudge, wrote in a letter regarding Mirza Ja'far and Mirza Riza, they would be allowed "access to the several establishments of the Royal Arsenal and daily attendance on gun and mortar practice with the cadets, [which would] afford the best possible means of conferring on the persons a complete knowledge of all that is necessary for a military profession." There were also, he added, "certain public lectures delivered at the Academy which these students might attend . . . and access to the models of fortifications and artillery might be freely afforded to them." Recommending that they be placed under the special supervision of a single instructor, Colonel Mudge suggested "Dr. Gregory of this Academy to be selected as the person under whose immediate care these Persian gentlemen should be placed."

The man in question was Dr. Olinthus Gregory (1774–1841), a mathematician by profession (and also a noted astronomer) who wrote many works on the topics of his expertise that were well-regarded by his contemporaries. Among these writings were *Lessons Astronomical and Philosophical* and *Mathematics for Practical Men*, the practical men in question being engineers (and specifically military engineers) such as Mirza Ja'far hoped to become. More importantly, a year earlier, Dr.

Fig. 6. Engineer, Mathematician, Moralist: Olinthus Gregory. Source: Courtesy Museum of the History of Science, University of Oxford.

Gregory had published the third edition of his highly successful *Treatise of Mechanics: Theoretical, Practical and Descriptive*. In modern terms, this was a course in engineering written during the age of England's first great civil engineers, such as Thomas Telford (1757–1834). More or less containing a degree course in its two volumes, Gregory's *Treatise of Mechanics* was a highly complex book, explaining in a mixture of algebra and prose the theories of statics, dynamics, hydrostatics, and pneumatics, before moving in its second volume to the practical application of these physical laws and then concluding with "Descriptions of Many Curious and Useful Machines." Challenging as it was, this was exactly the kind of education that Mirza Ja'far and Mirza Riza had been seeking.

Not only were they now in good hands with Dr. Gregory, they were also fortunate in making their association with Colonel Mudge, who oversaw their education as a whole as the governor of the Royal Military Academy. For Colonel William Mudge (1762–1820) was one of the most important surveyors of the age, whose pioneering surveys of the geography of the British Isles laid the basis for the Ordnance Survey maps that took their name from Mudge and his assistants' affiliation to the Royal Artillery. A pioneer in the trigonometric observations that were revolutionizing the making of maps for military and civilian purposes, by the time Mirza Ja'far and Mirza Riza came under his charge Colonel Mudge was a long-standing fellow of the Royal Society, England's most prestigious scientific association. Since one of his policies at the Royal Military Academy was that all the cadets there should study his new techniques of surveying and topographical drawing, the two Iranians also learned these skills there. This would prove to be important, because in the years after their return to Iran, their government became obsessed with the drawing of maps and the charting of borders. This was not least the case in the northwestern provinces governed by their princely patron 'Abbas Mirza, provinces that bordered both the unfriendly Russian and Ottoman Empires. Mirza Ja'far and Mirza Riza would be the first to transfer these new surveying skills to Iran.

Another new invention that Mirza Ja'far and Mirza Riza would have witnessed at Woolwich was the Congreve rocket, the first modern battlefield missile. The rockets were named after Sir William Congreve (1772–1828), who after a solid education at Wolverhampton Grammar School entered the Royal Laboratory, which was part of the Military Academy at Woolwich. It was there that he learned of rockets being used by the Indian soldiers of Tipu Sultan at the Battle of Seringapatam in 1799, when they were defeated by the East India Company. After the battle, Company soldiers not only recovered a cache of seven hundred unused rockets, but also looted a Persian military manual from Tipu Sultan's library that described the rockets' strategic value. Titled *Fath al-Mujahidin* ("Victory of the Holy Warriors"), the manual had been written by Zayn al-'Abidin Shushtari; Congreve and others saw that it was quickly translated into English. Strictly speaking, then, the rockets were not Congreve's invention, but through his series of experiments at Woolwich, he created the sequence of stablilized and improved versions of the missile that came to bear his name. The most indirectly celebrated use of Congreve rockets came during the Anglo-

American War of 1812 when the British fired Congreve rockets at Fort McHenry, Baltimore, inspiring the famous line in the first verse of the *Star-Spangled Banner*: "and the rockets' red glare, the bombs bursting in air." Three years later, some eight hundred Congreve rockets were used to defeat Napoleon at Waterloo. Then, during Mirza Ja'far and Mirza Riza's first weeks at Woolwich, an even larger number were launched from specially equipped rocket ships to bombard the Mediterranean's last Muslim pirate enclave at Algiers. Since Sir William had only created his final version of the rockets in December 1815, and was testing them at Woolwich during the following eighteen months, his noisy and spectacular demonstrations would made a dramatic welcome for Mirza Ja'far and Mirza Riza and at the very least have attracted their attention. Since he both lived and worked at the Academy, they may well have met Sir William or read some of his published works in the library at Woolwich (perhaps the simplified 40-page booklet titled "Details of the Rocket System"). For if such rockets had helped defeat the mighty Napoleon, then they might also be used to keep the Russians at bay from Iran. And Mirza Riza had after all come to study the latest methods of artillery. Whatever one makes of the reasons, there is clearly nothing new in Iranian interest in acquiring the latest weapon technology.

With Mirza Ja'far and Mirza Riza thus settled at the Royal Military Academy, aside from Mirza Salih this meant that Sir Gore Ouseley also had to arrange the studies of the other Mirza Ja'far and Hajji Baba, the surviving member of the party of two students sent to London in 1811 who never went to Croydon. Both were interested in the study of medicine; indeed, through an earlier source of funding, Hajji Baba had been making progress in his medical studies for several years. Nonetheless, the newly released funds from Lord Castlereagh bettered his prospects as well as Mirza Ja'far's. They were soon assigned to a London surgeon called Dr. Babington. The man in question was Dr. George Babington (1794–1856), a junior surgeon at London's St. George's Hospital who when the students took up with him had just been appointed as a member of the newly founded Royal College of Surgeons. He was also a fellow of the Royal Society, like Mirza Ja'far and Mirza Riza's overseer at the Royal Military Academy, Colonel Mudge. The medical students were certainly being placed in good hands, for a few years later, Dr. Babington would take up the official position of lecturer in surgery at St. George's Hospital, one of the highest surgical posts in the country. Founded in 1733, by the time Mirza Jaʿfar and Hajji Baba began taking lessons there, St. George's occupied a grand Georgian building called Lanesborough House on Hyde Park Corner, divided into multiple wards kept separate for men and women. If this incarnation of St. George's was not yet the celebrated edifice it was transformed into after its reconstruction in 1827 (and that survives today as London's most exclusive hotel, The Lanesborough), it was still a privileged part of London in which to study. For a few months after Mirza Jaʿfar and Hajji Baba began studying at St. George's, no lesser a figure than England's national hero, the duke of Wellington, moved into the opposite building, Apsley House, which possessed the superb address of No. 1, London.

Nonetheless, St. George's promised Mirza Jaʿfar and Hajji Baba more than prestigious neighbors. In the period when they studied there, it was training some of the most famous physicians of the age, including the "father of immunology," Edward Jenner (1749–1823), and the surgeon and celebrated author of *Gray's Anatomy*, Henry Gray (1827–61). Mirza Jaʿfar and Hajji Baba did not study only with Dr. Babington, for Mirza Jaʿfar was also sent to study with Dr. John Shaw (1792–1827). Along with his own teacher Sir Charles Bell (1774–1842), Dr. Shaw was the era's pioneer in understanding the workings of the nervous system. During the period when he was associated with Mirza Jaʿfar, he was teaching at the Theatre of Anatomy at 16 Great Windmill Street in Soho established by William Hunter (1718–83), the celebrated Scottish anatomist who was also an alumnus of St. George's. As England's most famous "theater" of surgery, the Theatre of Anatomy trained the most distinguished surgeons and anatomists of the age. A monument to the many medical advances made there, the Theatre of Anatomy still stands on Great Windmill Street today.

It is important to recognize how new the methods of surgery being promoted there were. For surgeons had only recently formally separated themselves from the barbers with whom they had been associated for centuries, with the year 1813 formalizing the separation through the opening of the grandly neoclassical Royal College of Surgeons on London's Lincoln's Inn Fields. Learning about it through his medical student companions, Mirza Salih described the Royal College of Surgeons in his diary, suggesting that the students shared a good deal with another about the different educations they were now receiving. Mirza Ja'far and Hajji Baba's medical teacher, Dr. Shaw, was central to this revolution in surgical techniques. Just a couple of years before taking on his Muslim understudies, he made his breakthroughs in understanding the nervous system through studying the effects of gunshot wounds at the Battle of Waterloo in 1815. The improved amputation techniques that he and his own teacher Sir Charles Bell brought to the battlefield raised the survival rate for Waterloo's amputees to an astonishing 90 percent. There could scarcely have been a more appropriate teacher for the young Iranians. For Dr. Shaw's expertise was perfectly matched to the military concerns of their princely patron, 'Abbas Mirza, whose troops were repeatedly mown down in battle with the Russians during the 1810s (and then 1820s).

We cannot be certain precisely what Dr. Babington and Dr. Shaw taught their Iranian charges, for unlike Dr. Gregory and Colonel Mudge, Babington wrote no teaching manual on his field of expertise and Shaw's celebrated *Manual of Anatomy* did not appear till 1821. But we can be reasonably sure that their lessons would have included the surgical techniques in which they specialized, for it is hard to see why else the students would have been assigned to these celebrated surgeons. We are able to reconstruct their more basic medical studies (which Hajji Baba at least had already completed by this time) from the detailed "Plan of Education for the Persian Youth," written earlier in 1813 by Hajji Baba's first medical teacher, Dr. Fromager, who specially designed for Hajji Baba "an elementary course of Natural Philosophy and Chemistry illustrated by a suitable number of experiments, which he will be required to perform himself." After he had acquired "a knowledge of decimal arithmetic," the Iranian was expected to master practical astronomy by "computing . . . the latitude and longitude of places," then to learn how to use a theodolite and enough mathematics "so as to be able to comprehend the principles upon which machines are constructed and perform their various operations." In addition, Hajji Baba was taught enough Latin to understand the technical terminology of surgery and anatomy, after which it would "be necessary for him to attend dissections, to perform the necessary operations on the dead subject, and to see them performed on the living." (This is presumably where the surgical masters came in.) As though this were not enough, his daily routine of studies was expected to continue through the evening, when he would "drink tea at six and in the evening study anatomy and occasionally make astronomical observations."

What is immediately striking about Dr. Fromager's syllabus is its comprehensiveness, taking in arithmetic, astronomy, and trigonometry, as well as more clearly medical skills such as dissection. Having arrived in London in 1811, Hajji Baba was to stay in London longer than any of the students, exposing him to a tremendous amount of the new scientific learning. One way or another, it was medical knowledge that he and Mirza Ja'far hoped to transfer back to their homeland, which still relied on an Islamicized version of Galenic Greek medicine. The medical associations that the two Iranians forged with England were to endure long after they left for home, for in 1845 another Iranian student, Mirza Sadiq, arrived in England to study in Manchester with Dr. Shaw's medical companion at Waterloo, Dr. Charles Bell.

In such ways, whether through learning gun-making, military surveying, or medicine, the students were now able to busy themselves with acquiring the key skills that would help the "new order" that the crown prince 'Abbas Mirza had initiated in Tabriz with the imported assistance of the likes of Mr. D'Arcy. The six young Muslims represented nothing less than a national development policy. All too aware of the responsibility, the students were hugely relieved that their teaching arrangements now seemed to be settled. But their road to knowledge never ran smoothly and the matter of their finances still hung heavily over them. The fees for Mirza Ja'far and Mirza Riza at the Royal Military Academy were £300 (today around £26,000 or $42,000) each per year. Since this sum was the precise figure that Lord Castlereagh had assigned each of them, it left little margin for necessities, let alone luxury. But if there was little money left over for entertainment, then Mirza Ja'far and Mirza Riza were at least having the best military education that money could buy.

Although the education of his companions now seemed settled, Mirza Salih's own program of learning was still hanging in the balance. Since his aim was not to acquire either a military or a medical education, and was instead to study languages, the obvious place to send him seemed to be one of the universities, Oxford or Cambridge.

Unfortunately, both universities required an oath of allegiance to the Church of England and its Christian tenets. Determined not to let the uncertainty about his future interfere with his self-managed education, Mirza Salih once again set about arranging his own studies as best as he could. Recalling that an acquaintance of one of his recently made English friends from Croydon had also moved to London, he went to meet this man to discuss with him the possibility of arranging further lessons in the capital. It is unclear who exactly this figure was, though between Foreign Office documentation and the Arabic spelling of his name in Mirza Salih's diary, we can determine that his name was John Garrett. Whoever this Mr. Garrett was, we know that he lived on Queen Square in the Bloomsbury quarter of London. It was soon arranged that Mirza Salih would join him there as a lodger to better enable Mr. Garrett to improve both his English and his Latin, as well as introduce him to the natural sciences that he had himself apparently studied. Mirza Salih described the conditions at Mr. Garrett's house as being rather frugal, and it is certainly true that Queen Square was not one of the capital's grander districts. To supplement his income—as we have seen, Castlereagh and the prince regent were more concerned with funding the students' educations than lifestyles— Mirza Salih sold another of the fine shawls that he had brought with him from Iran. They had made shrewd imports, for such shawls (the word is originally Persian) were extremely valuable commodities in Regency London. Jane Austen, her sister, and her aunt all counted such imported shawls from India or Iran among their most treasured possessions. Such was their rarity that in *Mansfield Park*, Lady Bertram declared, "William must not forget my shawl, if he goes to the East Indies," adding in a rush of sartorial self-interest that "I wish he may go to the East Indies, that I may have my shawl." Once again, Mirza Salih's timing was fortunate, for these were the last years before the price of such hand-embroidered shawls collapsed with the introduction of the mechanical Jacquard loom to the textile mills of Scotland's Paisley in the 1820s. From then on, industrializing factories were able to mass-produce cheap but high-quality copies of the *tirmah* shawls of Iran and Kashmir.

Harboring hopes of entering one of the universities, throughout 1817 and into 1818 Mirza Salih kept busy with his lessons with Mr.

Garrett, in his spare time keenly discussing his options with all of the influential men he now knew in London. At the center of his circle of supporters during this time were Sir Gore Ouseley and Colonel D'Arcy senior, who became two of his closest confidants. When Colonel D'Arcy (the father of the students' lapsed chaperone) agreed that Mirza Salih might try to study at Oxford University, someone was dispatched to Oxford to try to find him a place in one of its colleges. Mirza Salih's diary is silent on the question of allegiance to the Church of England that entering an Oxford college would have involved. There was also the possibility of studying privately at Oxford without actual admission to a college; after all, this was sometimes arranged for women (including the young Jane Austen in 1783), who were excluded from formally matriculating at any of Oxford's colleges. While the diary is ambiguous about the results of Colonel D'Arcy's messenger, for the time being at least Mirza Salih felt buoyed by the prospect that a new stage in his education was being planned. Over dinner one evening, he announced his intentions to a new friend, Colonel Holden, an architect who spoke Arabic and Persian (perhaps through service in India). But on hearing Mirza Salih's Oxford plans, Colonel Holden explained that since it was by now late spring (of 1818), there would be no more classes in Oxford until the start of Michaelmas term in the autumn. Mirza Salih was disappointed and annoyed that Colonel D'Arcy had not told him this earlier. But then he realized that Colonel D'Arcy was after all an army man who had no idea of arcane academic timetables. And so, forced to stay put in London, the studious young Muslim resorted to his diary, recording in high-minded mood the thought that spending the summer months in Oxford in mere pleasure and relaxation seemed a poor use of his time. It would be better, he wrote, to stay in London with his teacher till the autumn, and continue his studies in Latin and English under the guidance of Mr. Garrett.

Coaching Ways and Coaching Days

Even though Mirza Salih would not allow himself to be distracted by the summertime frivolities of student life in Oxford, when he was presented with the offer of a tour around Devonshire he persuaded himself that it would not be a mere tourist's excursion but an opportunity to learn more about England as a whole. And so on May 21, 1818, he set off from London by stagecoach in the company of one of the acquaintances of his London friends, whom he named in his diary as Mr. Robert Abraham. Based on the fact that he described Mr. Abraham as having Devonshire connections, as having a sister called Sarah, as having introduced Mirza Salih to the topic of the Catholic population of Devonshire, and discussed him in connection with the new buildings of Regent Street, the man in question seems to have been the architect Robert Abraham (1775–1850), who worked together with the more famous John Nash, the guiding architectural spirit of the Regency. Born in London to a Devonshire father, Abraham would keep up his Devonshire connections even late in life by marrying his second wife there in 1837. He had a London-based sister, Sarah Abraham (1771–1852), whom Mirza Salih described meeting ("Miss Sarah"), and he did much of his business with England's leading Catholic families. Helping confirm the identification, Mirza Salih recounted how on their tour together Mr. Abraham took him to the stately home of a Catholic nobleman. When Mirza Salih first met him in London, Mr. Abraham was busy designing the County Fire Office and the Quadrant on Regent Street (completed 1819) and the elegant Regency terrace of 177–186 Regent Street (completed 1820). Given that much of their tour of Devonshire and their route thither would be dedicated to looking at fine buildings, such as the cathedral at Salisbury in the unique uniformity of its early English style, Mirza Salih surely learned to see through the trained eye of his companion.

The coach trip was in itself a new experience, for this was the heyday of the horse-drawn coach and the turnpike road, though highwaymen like Dick Turpin had fortunately been vanquished a generation earlier. Mirza Salih keenly described such coach travel, which in its new organization offered a considerable contrast to the rudimentary and ad hoc affair of traveling across an Iran whose roads (such as they were) were still the prey of not merely highwaymen but whole tribes who owed their livelihoods to extorting tribute from travelers. In several places in his diary Mirza Salih commented on the state of England's roads, including its system of toll roads. It was with good reason, for through the work of such engineers as Thomas Telford, over the past few decades the British Isles had gained the finest road system in Europe, both in terms of the quality of the roads themselves (as funded by turnpike fees) and the regular coach services (and coaching inns) that served them. It was only half in jest that around this time the poet laureate Robert Southey dubbed Thomas Telford the "Colossus of Roads."

As Mirza Salih's first extensive visit beyond London, Croydon, and the East Anglia he had glimpsed during his first week in England, the road trip was a genuine adventure in a period when Muslims were a great rarity outside the capital and a few ports. Even so, he was far from the only foreigner on the open road. About the journey from London to Salisbury, he wrote,

> Your humble servant was one of several passengers seated inside the coach, who looked at me as I sat down. One of the people in the coach was a young Spaniard and another was one of the people of Devonshire. The Spanish youth had lived in England for some time, but his accent was so strong that I couldn't understand a single word! And it was likewise with the Devonshire man. He belonged to a community of farmers who have a special accent of their own, so I couldn't make out much of his conversation either.

He went on to explain that, since he had learned English in London, the experience with the farmer made him realize that he only really understood the accent of Londoners. But there was more to it than this. The farmer's incomprehensible accent was testimony to the fact that Devonshire was far distant from England's political and cultural centers. Jane Austen used the county as a symbol of remoteness and social exile, as in *Sense and Sensibility* when Mrs. Dashwood moved with her daughters to live in Barton Cottage in Devonshire. After all, for the remainder of the nineteenth century, there were still many people there who spoke the Celtic language of Cornish. Just as his friends the Ouseley brothers had in Iran, Mirza Salih was now exploring the remotest regions of England.

Stopping in Salisbury, where the stagecoach made one of its scheduled halts, he and Mr. Abraham made a tour of the city. As he had of the Iranian cities in the travel diary he had written for the Ouseleys in

Iran, Mirza Salih recorded Salisbury's civic assets in detail: its cathedral was founded in the year 1219 and at 409 feet high its "minaret" was the highest in all England; its wealth derived from wool-spinning and the manufacture of knives; and there were good schools for boys and girls, including a charity school for the children of the poor. Moving on with his Devonshire tour, he next described Exeter in similar detail, as well as the pleasure he derived from being squeezed in a post-chaise carriage between Mr. Abraham's female relatives, Miss Sarah and Miss Goodwyn. In Plymouth, he made a tour of the lighthouse, docks, and barracks and spent an entertaining day attending the birthday celebrations of King George III. Prefiguring his later interest in England's religious minorities, it was here that he was introduced to a local churchman, Mr. Keaton, who spoke to him of the Catholics of nearby Ashburton. It was through Mirza Salih's ventures into rural and small-town England that he was able to hear of and eventually meet such religious minorities, opening up to him the complexities of a Christian society that few if any Muslim travelers had ever seen in its plurality. It was a tour through another England from that he had come to know in London and Croydon.

Education in the Age of Reason

After almost four weeks away, on June 16, 1818, Mirza Salih returned to London from his tour of the rural southwest, only to have a heated argument with Mr. D'Arcy over the ongoing delays in organizing his education. It had, after all, been almost three years now since he arrived. Matters had now reached a peak, and Mr. D'Arcy twice swore that he would have no more to do with his Muslim protégées. Mirza Salih retreated to his books. Perhaps to distract himself from his worries no less than to make best use of the summer months before taking up his hoped-for place at Oxford in the autumn, he set himself the task of recording a lengthy account of British history in his diary. He began with the Roman conquest under Julius Caesar in 55 BC, at which time, he wrote, the English lived in forests in houses made of straw and wood and had neither towns, manners, nor learning. Reflecting the Whig vision of English history that was taking shape at this time (and that we may assume he had been taught by Professor Shakespear and Reverend Bisset in Croydon), he went on to recount the days of King Arthur, of the Danelaw, of Alfred the Great, and Magna Carta, before moving on to the ancient development of English common law and the evolution of the institution the English called the "jury." When he came to write down the history of the universities, he unwittingly drew on invented traditions that flourished in an era of growing English self-confidence. The foundation of Cambridge was thus projected back to the year 955, when the patron of Olde England's scholars Alfred the Great was succeeded by his son Edward.

The question of the source of this history beyond Mirza Salih's Croydon teachers is one that is worth asking. Given the huge popularity at this time of the historical writings of David Hume (1711–76), there is good reason to think Mirza Salih was drawing his vision of British history—and of its tortured progress toward liberty—from that paragon of the Scottish Enlightenment. Although Hume is primarily thought of today as a philosopher, both during his lifetime and during the Regency period, he was more widely celebrated as a historian. Published in six volumes between 1754 and 1761, his *History of England* was the standard history till its place was usurped by the work of Thomas Babington Macaulay in the 1840s; Jane Austen owned a complete edition. Hume's history not only foreshadowed the narrative laid out by Mirza Salih (beginning, for example, with Julius Caesar's invasion, and moving on through King Alfred, the Magna Carta, and so on). It also laid out the basic lessons about the struggle for constitutionalism and liberty that Mirza Salih took as the core meaning of England's past. With his growing interest in political institutions, he devoted extra detail to the circumstances surrounding the signing of Magna Carta and the reasons for the English Civil War, again, likely drawing on Hume's great vision in which Magna Carta and the Civil War served as synecdoches for the whole of English history. And so, as Mirza Salih continued his historical résumé by summarizing the notable events of each king's reign, like Hume before him, he pointed to larger constitutional developments. Then, like Hume again, he moved beyond dynastic matters by bringing in cultural and intellectual figures to his narrative, echoing both his friends' and the wise Scotsman's interests by discussing the development of science as a central part of history. At the time, this was a novel way of writing history, and yet both Hume and Mirza Salih singled out for special attention William Harvey (1578–1657), the Jacobean physician who first discovered and fully described the circulation of blood throughout the human body. Through reading Hume and translating his views into Persian, Mirza Salih became a Muslim champion of liberty, constitutionalism, and scientific free inquiry.

Since Hume's history terminated in 1688, that great year for English liberty, Mirza Salih clearly drew on other sources for the later sections of his summary. His account of the century or so between 1688 and his own time moved in broader directions than Hume's by looking out onto the wider world. He gave a summary of North America's history, which was one of the earliest (and certainly the most up-to-date) Muslim accounts of its kind. Beginning with the discoveries of Vasco da Gama and Christopher Columbus, he next outlined the struggle between the Spanish, French and British for control of America, which he noted as due particularly to the trade wealth that America generated. There were vast gold and silver mines in the continent, for example. Moving forward in time, he singled out for attention Benjamin Franklin, "one of the philosophers and learned ones," and described with sympathy Franklin's unsuccessful mission of conciliation to the English Parliament. He respectfully described "General George Washington" and his war for independence, or *istiqlal* (ironically using a term that Iranian revolutionaries in the twentieth century would use to declare their own "independence" from the United States). He then turned back to Europe and to the beloved Napoleon of his royal master, ʿAbbas Mirza, before moving from Europe to Asia to chart the rise of the British in India via the East India Company, Clive of India, Warren Hastings and the Battle of Seringapatam, which saw India's last great Muslim power defeated in 1799. Finally, he brought his English history up to date via William Pitt, and the prince regent, whom he described as a lighthearted and fun-loving character who always spent in excess of his income. (Perhaps the prince reminded him of one or two of his friends and their watch-buying extravagances.) There was more to come, for he next devoted a lengthy number of pages in his notebooks to depicting the present state of England, with a particular emphasis on its constitution, laws, and institutions. He spent pages praising the flourishing state of its centers of learning, from the Royal Society and the Royal College of Physicians to the universities at Oxford, Cambridge, Edinburgh, and Dublin. In the course of the next chapters, we will return to many of his comments and the insight they provide on his engagement with the intellectual and religious life of Regency England.

It was during this London summer of reading and note-taking that Mirza Salih and his companions came into closer contact with another now obscure figure from the days of Jane Austen. This was Dr. Olinthus Gregory, who as "Daktar Grigri" appears repeatedly in Mirza Salih's diary. As we have seen, since 1817 Dr. Gregory had been appointed as the tutor of Mirza Ja'far and Mirza Riza at the Royal Military Academy. But over the course of the next year he informally expanded his role to become an educational advisor to the other students as well. Since Mirza Salih was still not enrolled in any formal course of study at an institution comparable to the Academy, Dr. Gregory seems to have singled him out in particular for help with his education. Despite his mathematical specializations that we have already seen in his several book publications, Dr. Gregory was something of a polymath. Before being appointed to the Royal Military Academy, he had an earlier career as a bookseller in Cambridge and was one of a handful of contributors who compiled an encyclopedia titled *Pantologia*, which was published in 1813, two years before the students reached England. With such a broad knowledge base, he was clearly a fine figure to serve as an informal all-round tutor to Mirza Salih as well as instructing Mirza Ja'far and Mirza Riza in matters mathematical.

Yet if Mirza Salih's readings of Hume were inculcating in him a love of reason and the liberty of free thought, and the other students were now venturing deeply into the new sciences, through their many encounters with Dr. Gregory they were reminded that even in England the dawning of the age of reason did not go unquestioned. For even mathematical men such as Dr. Gregory were dedicated to restraining the reach of reason into what they saw as the higher realms of Christian faith. Here, we begin to see a pattern emerging which saw the students' attempts to study science become enmeshed with attempts to teach them the merits of Christianity.

Since 1815, Dr. Gregory had begun to turn toward theology, responding to the rationalizing trend set by William Paley's *Natural Theology* of 1802 by writing his *Letters to a Friend, on the Evidences, Doc-*

Fig. 7. Training Officers, Gentlemen, and Mirzas: The Royal Military Academy, Woolwich.

trines, and Duties of the Christian Religion in which he drew on his knowledge of mathematics and astronomy to formulate a substantial rejection of the Deistic premise of "natural religion" and by extension of the arguments that Paley had presented in his *Natural Theology*. Defending the truth claims of scripture and the need for divine revelation to transmit knowledge that was inaccessible to reason alone, Dr. Gregory was trying to undermine the rationalistic presumption of what he termed as "the absurdity of Deism." Defending the existence of divine "mysteries" that cannot be understood by reason, he drew on his expertise to provide mathematical equations that served his argument about the limits of mathematical or other forms of rational knowledge. He even went as far in his defense of these mysteries as to state that even math has its fundamentally "incomprehensible elements." Even more surprisingly for a man of science, he also wrote a spirited vindication of miracles. In a familiar circular argument, he claimed that Christians can believe in miracles because the Bible states that they happened; and they can in turn believe the truth claims of the Bible because of the evidence of miracles. For a leading mathematician employed to train the nation's military engineers in the subtle trigonometry of cannons and the quick geometry of the campaign bridge, Dr. Gregory shows the strange ways in which some Regency scientists were still committed to positions of extreme scriptural literalism. Today we would call him a fundamentalist.

That the Muslim students had a close familiarity with Dr. Gregory's work may be surmised through his role as the personal tutor of Mirza Riza and Mirza Ja'far since early 1817 and his increasing influence on the other students by the following year. Given what we will see in later chapters of the students' increasing interest in theological matters, it seems probable that Mirza Salih, Mirza Riza, and Mirza Ja'far all discussed with Dr. Gregory his ideas on theology and the epistemological limits of the math and science that he was nonetheless employed to teach them.

A few years later, Dr. Gregory busied himself with editing the sermons of his role model, the Baptist preacher Robert Hall (1764–1831). In this book, he included a sermon that Hall had delivered in London in the year before the students' arrival there in which Hall expatiated on the necessity of converting all the heathen of Asia. "In India," Hall had declared, "Satan maintains an almost undisputed empire, and the powers of darkness, secure of their dominion, riot and revel at their pleasure." One suspects he had no better opinion of Iran than India. We do not know whether Dr. Gregory himself considered his Muslim students as members of Satan's "undisputed empire," though it is hard to imagine that his zeal did not lead him to attempt to convert them. Knowing that his diary would be read by his superiors when he returned home, Mirza Salih was careful not to mention any such Christian influences on his education. But in the following chapters, we will see that Dr. Gregory was far from the last evangelical the students would encounter in their quest for the new learning.

In an age in which science had not separated itself from religion, Dr. Gregory was Mirza Salih's main social link to the scientific institutions that he described himself visiting in London around this time. These included the Royal Society and the British Museum (though it was probably through the connections of his medical student companions that he visited the Royal Colleges of Physicians and Surgeons, the Chelsea Royal Hospital and the Magdalene Hospital). At the Royal Society, he was able to see (if, it seems, not actually meet) its celebrated president, the great naturalist and explorer Sir Joseph Banks (1743–

1820), whom he estimated as being around eighty years of age (he was in fact not yet seventy-five). By the time Mirza Salih saw him grandly receiving visitors who presented him with new books or inventions, Sir Joseph had been president of the Royal Society for forty years. Seeing the famous scientist greatly pleased Mirza Salih (remember that he was also studying "natural philosophy" with Mr. Garrett at this time), and he described with admiration the Royal Society's headquarters at Somerset House on the Strand as the place where all of London's philosophers came to meet. Moreover, he noted, this palace of high learning was not reserved for social elites, since for four months each year lectures were freely given there on philosophy, chemistry, and other subjects, allowing ordinary people to attend for an hour or two before returning to their places of work. Mirza Salih also admired the British Museum, albeit in its original quarters at Montagu House, a seventeenth-century mansion in Bloomsbury, rather than its current neoclassical home, whose construction did not begin till 1825. Yet what excited Mirza Salih was not the building but the fact that it too was open for all people to visit and, as a result, attracted around fifty thousand visitors every year.

Not only did the British Museum possess a library with books in every language, he wrote, it also displayed sculptures from Rome, Constantinople, Egypt, Syria, even from the ancient Iranian ruins that the English called Persepolis and the Iranians called Takht-i Jamshid. Persepolis had in fact been discussed, measured, and sketched by Mirza Salih's friends, the two Williams Price and Ouseley, who described the ruins in great detail in their own travel diaries. Since Persepolis lay a short distance from Mirza Salih's home city of Shiraz, where in 1813 he had joined Price and Ouseley's diplomatic caravan, there is a good chance that he had visited the ruins in their company, bringing a different dimension to his appreciation of the sculptures in London. Even if he hadn't made it to Persopolis, the museum's display of statues from the seat of Iran's ancient rulers near his home city must have been a moving sight after three years away. But for the increasingly intellectual Mirza Salih it was also surely a thought-provoking sight. For here he could see the statues of Persepolis not through the mythical tales preserved in Firdawsi's medieval epic *Shahnama*, which had lent the ruins their Persian name of Takht-i Jamshid or the "Throne of

Jamshid" after the pre-Islamic king of that name. At the British Museum, he could instead see Iranian history in a comparative setting, its artistic achievements displayed side by side with those of ancient Egypt, Rome, and especially Greece. For his visits to the British Museum happily coincided with the opening of its first galleries for the Elgin Marbles, the Greek sculptures rescued or plundered by Lord Elgin from the Parthenon in Athens and placed on display at the British Museum in the summer of 1816. It was an exciting time to be a student in London, and Mirza Salih made his educational best of the days when he wasn't studying with Messrs. Gregory and Garrett.

To someone who had by now had many history lessons that began with ancient Greece and Rome, seeing objects from Persepolis under the same roof as the Elgin Marbles helped him see history in a new way. We can detect the influence of this side-by-side approach in his diary's lengthy summary of world history, where he applied this comparative method to the history of France, America, and India by making sense of historical developments through connection and comparison. Yet the British Museum provided Mirza Salih with more than lessons in the comparative history of civilizations. It also provided him with a dazzlingly new and truly global sense of the artistic achievements of humankind, in Persian *insan*, as a whole. For on display, he wrote, were not only statues from the old world's ancient kingdoms in the Middle East and Europe but also countless items carried back from Captain Cook's circumnavigation of the planet.

> On the travels of Captain Cook, he made a circuit of the entire world, visiting every island and every country, from where he sent all sorts of curiosities as gifts to the museum, such as clothing, weapons and pottery.

The museum housed nothing less, he declared, than the "wonders of the whole world."

Despite these fascinating distractions, Mirza Salih was focusing his mind on his goals. Having left Croydon at the same time as his companions, and then moved in with Mr. Garrett in Bloomsbury, by that summer of 1818 he was living in Woolwich. Sharing the same house as Mirza Ja'far and Mirza Riza, who were training at the nearby Royal Military Academy, by living in Woolwich he became closer to the evangelical mathematician, Dr. Gregory. Despite the latter's work at the Academy, he did not allow Mirza Salih to be distracted by the marching soldiers outside. He insisted that he study through what remained of the summer and at the beginning of autumn prepare himself for what Mirza Salih hoped would be the beginning of his long-awaited studies at Oxford. With characteristic practicality, Mirza Salih worked on French, as well as continuing with the Latin lessons he had begun with Reverend Bisset back in Croydon. Since Mr. Garrett did not know French (we do not know about Dr. Gregory), Mirza Salih also took lessons from another teacher. This was the same Mr. Belfour with whom he had briefly studied before Croydon and who had now returned from Paris, allowing French subjuntives to roll effortlessly from his tongue. Inspired by the scientists he had seen at the Royal Academy, Mirza Salih also decided to learn something of astronomy. Though this was a subject in which his princely patron 'Abbas Mirza had a keen interest, he was probably drawn into it at this time by Mirza Ja'far, whose mapmaking lessons at the Military Academy involved the use of telescopes and other new viewing devices.

Hearing in early autumn that the new term in Oxford was about to begin, and that this would be accompanied by the sight of different students arriving, sitting examinations, and being given degrees, Mirza Salih and Mirza Ja'far asked permission from Dr. Gregory to visit the university. Dr. Gregory had connections in Oxford, and together with Sir Gore Ouseley, he promised to try to make arrangements for Mirza Salih and Mirza Ja'far to study there for at least a year. For the moment at least, he heartily gave his permission to pay the city a preliminary visit. So it was that the two students headed out from the suburb of Woolwich into the center of London, where they could buy a coach ticket for their journey to Oxford.

2

The Madrasas of Oxford

To the Varsity at Last!

*T*he Oxford that Mirza Salih and Mirza Ja'far visited was a very different institution to what it became in the reign of Victoria, when reformers took the upper hand of the administration to promote the virtues of a "liberal education" based on free inquiry. Although Oxford was already on the road to reform—not least through the University Statutes of 1800 and 1807 that provided the basis for the formal examinations system that Mirza Salih would witness—the varsity was still dominated by churchmen and their Christian concerns. In the early nineteenth century, around two-thirds of Oxford graduates went on to careers in the church and the study of divinity remained central to its tripos degree system. Jane Austen's Oxonian father and two of her brothers were clergymen; so were Edward Ferrars, Henry Tilney, and Edmund Bertram, the heroes of *Sense and Sensibility*, *Northanger Abbey*, and *Mansfield Park*. Until the impact of the great social reforms of the 1830s, to matriculate (that is, formally register) as a student at any of Oxford's colleges it was obligatory to swear allegiance to the Thirty-Nine Articles of the Church of England; to the King; and, depending on the college, to other pillars of the Anglican establishment. It was certainly a challenge for the two Muslim subjects of the shah of Iran.

Of course, not everyone in England took those oaths seriously. In his 1823 Oxford comic novel *Reginald Dalton: A Study of English University Life*, J. G. Lockhart recounted the series of oaths the eponymous hero of his novel was obliged to swear on being admitted to his college:

> The passive youth, of course, took all the oaths they proposed to him.
> He renounced in due form the Devil, the Pope, the Pretender, and the

authority of the Mayor of Oxford. He swore that he would never believe anything but what is written in the XXXIX Articles of the Church of England—he swore that he would never miss the prayers, the lectures, or the dinners of his College—he swore that he would wear clothes "coloris nigri aut subfusci," and cut according to the University pattern (which, by the way, has undergone no alteration since the time of Charles II.)—he swore that he would never "nourish whiskers or curls," nor indulge in "absurdo illo et fastuoso publicè in ocreis ambulandi more," which means, being interpreted, "that absurd and arrogant fashion of walking publicly in boots or gaiters,"—he swore that he would never drive a tandem, nor neglect to cap a Master of Arts.

But the fact of the matter was that the oaths were no joke. The struggle to repeal them—and in so doing finally free England's intellectual life from the Church—was a long and bitter one. And in 1818 quite where these oaths of Christian loyalty left two Muslim would-be students remained to be seen. The oaths even presented a challenge to their greatest supporter at this time, Sir Gore Ouseley, who for all his knightly connections was not an Oxford man with the local clout to negotiate a way round the varsity's regulations.

The Christian basis of the university did not mean that there was nothing taught there except theology; the study of the Latin and particularly the Greek classics was of no less importance. But given the fact that all of its teaching fellows were unmarried and theoretically celibate men who had taken holy orders, even the study of pagan literature was often undertaken through a moralizing Christian lens. At times, there was something of a culture clash between the undergraduates and the dons responsible for teaching. In a period in which 70 percent of Oxford undergraduates were gentlemen, esquires, or peers, the aristocratic celebration of classical culture that was one of the defining characteristics of the early nineteenth century offered a considerable contrast to the pious Christian inclinations of the teaching fellows. In 1807, the future Anglican bishop of Calcutta, Daniel Wilson, wrote to a friend about the dilemma faced by a young tutor he knew at Oxford's St. Edmund Hall, the former college of Mirza Salih's teacher, Reverend John Bisset. The tutor's dilemma was that he was required to teach Aristotle, Aeschylus, and logic as well as the New

Fig. 8. Friend, Patron, and Persianist: Sir Gore Ouseley.

Testament, when his only real goal in teaching undergraduates was "to instruct them in the saving knowledge of God, and so imbue their minds with true piety, that, however little they may profit by me in secular matters, they may nevertheless learn to love God, to believe in Christ, to despise and reject the vain traditions and fancies of men." As we will see in more detail later, this spirit of Anglican zeal was laying the foundations for a new evangelical movement that would sweep through both Oxford and Cambridge. This too did not bode well for the Muslim students.

With Oxford's historic emphasis on the study of divinity and classics, for all its association with such pioneering scientists as Edmund Halley and Robert Boyle, by the early nineteenth century the univer-

sity was failing to keep apace with the "new sciences" that so interested Mirza Salih and especially Mirza Ja'far. Such was the scale of the
neglect that politicians began to worry about the implications of rear-
ing a generation of gentlemen whose technical and scientific knowledge could not compete with that of the rising class of tradesmen and
industrialists from new cities such as Birmingham. The consequences,
it was feared, would be a social revolution in which, equipped with
their mastery of science and engineering, a rising class of upstarts
would seize the reins of power from the ruling tribe of intellectually
outmoded gentlemen. The kind of knowledge the Iranians were seeking was therefore a much debated and socially disruptive force in its
own country of origin.

Even so, the Oxford that the two Iranians were visiting was not only
a place of learned controversy. It was also a place of entertainment and
pleasure, even a place for avoiding study. As John Campbell, a BA of
Balliol College, admonished freshmen in his 1823 *Hints for Oxford*,
students should take reading "like everything in life, coolly and mod-
erately," for "a course of excessive study is the most ruinous of all
attacks that can be made upon the constitution." For all the worldly
cynicism of the recently graduated Mr. Campbell, his *Hints for Oxford*
provides a perspective on Regency Oxford that the Iranians soon found
themselves sharing. For Campbell claimed that anyone "acquainted
with the civilized world at large" would find Oxford formal, stuffy, and
pretentious, its spirits reined in by what he termed as its "monkish
constitution." And as for the "new learning" that the Muslims were
seeking there, Campbell claimed "there is no free discussion and no
zeal of enquiry" to be had in Oxford. But if the university was not the
great fountain of England's new sciences that the Iranians hoped to
find, neither (to them at least) was it the closed-by-class institution
encountered by Thomas Hardy's Jude Fawley later in the century. For
if the self-educated English stonemason found the gates of Oxford's
colleges closed to him as a lower class laborer, then the status of Mirza
Salih and Mirza Ja'far as the courtly Muslim protégées of a foreign
prince lent them advantages lacked by the Christian Jude the Obscure.
Remembering the importance of their mission, these were social advantages that Mirza Salih and Mirza Ja'far were more than willing to
deploy.

Yet there still remained the matter of Christianity. For in the Iranian students' time no less than Jude Fawley's time at the opposite end of the century, Oxford was a city in which religious preoccupations were central to the organization of knowledge. For the Iranians, there was nothing unfamiliar about this: in their home society the great colleges were similarly dominated by religious concerns. Like their counterparts in Oxford, whose sworn allegiance to the Thirty-Nine Articles offered theological constraints on their teaching, the clerical seminaries of Isfahan and Qum also taught mathematics, grammar, law, astronomy, and the writings of the Greek philosophers. In a very real sense, the colleges of Oxford in 1818 were counterparts to the Muslim colleges of Iran. Little wonder that Mirza Salih referred to them in his diary as the "*madrasas* of Oxford."

A Persianate Oxford

Mirza Salih and Mirza Ja'far were not the first Muslim visitors to Oxford, and Persian travelogues from the period record other scholarly engagements between visiting Muslims and their Christian counterparts there. One of the earliest such travelogues to describe a visit to Oxford was the *Shigarfnama-yi Vilayat*, or "Book of Blighty's Wonders," itself one of the earliest firsthand Persian accounts of England. Written by an Indian Muslim called I'tisam al-Din (1730–1800), the *Shigarfnama* describes a diplomatic mission from Delhi to London that commenced in January 1766 and that I'tisam al-Din made on behalf of the Mughal Emperor Shah 'Alam II, whose authority was being diminished through the rise of the East India Company. I'tisam al-Din made his journey in the company of an Englishman called Captain Archibald Swinton (1731–1804), who quit his position in the East India Company to take on the role of ambassador of the Mughal Emperor. In diplomatic terms, the mission was far from a success. But it did give I'tisam al-Din the opportunity to record his impressions of the new *vilayat*, the "Blighty" or "mother country," that via the East India Company was slowly displacing the Mughal Empire.

Like Mirza Salih and Mirza Ja'far, I'tisam al-Din had keen scholarly interests and so eagerly availed himself of the opportunity to visit

Oxford. The university served by way of a respite to the misfortunes of his mission. "At seeing this city," he wrote in his *Shigarfnama*, "my dejected heart was gladdened, and from the beauty and clean appearance of it, the bird of joy constructed a nest on the branches of my heart." He took special pleasure in the college gardens and the statues and paintings he saw on display in the college libraries. Like Mirza Salih and Mirza Ja'far, he was fascinated by the novel studies in astronomy going on at the university and swapped expertise with Thomas Hunt (1696–1774), the Laudian Professor of Arabic, who showed him many of the Persian manuscripts held in the Bodleian Library. As we see more fully later, I'tisam al-Din also met with the most famous scholar of Persian that Oxford ever produced, Sir William Jones, to whom I'tisam al-Din claimed he gave substantial but unacknowledged help on his famous *Grammar of the Persian Language*, which was printed in 1771 a few years after I'tisam al-Din's visit.

As we have already seen, demand for instruction in Persian was high in England in the decades on either side of 1800. Despite this, Oxford refused to countenance the idea of a professorship in the language, leading "Oriental Jones" to pursue his career in Calcutta and found the Asiatic Society of Bengal to promote the learning that his alma mater would not. Even so, Oxford still attracted other Persian-speakers in the years prior to the arrival of Mirza Salih and Mirza Ja'far. One of them was another Persian-speaking Indian scholar, Abu Talib Khan Isfahani (1752–1806), who traveled to London in 1799 and spent three years there, during which time he too visited Oxford. As his name suggests, Abu Talib Isfahani belonged to an Iranian family from the city of Isfahan; it was his father who had migrated to India. Like I'tisam al-Din beforehand and Mirza Salih afterward, Abu Talib described his visit to Oxford in his Persian travel diary. The similarity of his itinerary around the city to that we will see of the Iranian visitors points to a similar set of concerns between Persian-speaking Muslims from India and Iran.

Abu Talib is of special interest because he penned a unique poetic celebration of the university (as well as of its rival on the river Cam). Today the sole surviving manuscript of Abu Talib's *masnavi* poem is a small leather-bound volume in Oxford's Bodleian Library, in whose stacks it has sat scarcely noticed for the past two hundred years. It was perhaps already there when Mirza Salih and Mirza Jaʿfar visited in the autumn of 1818. Abu Talib also wrote a Persian panegyric about England, in which, stanza by stanza, he eulogized each of London's "wonders," hitting on many of the same places that impressed Mirza Salih. The Iranians were therefore not unique in their interests, whether in visiting London or Oxford. But they were unique in trying to formally study at the university. So, having left their friends to continue their medical and military studies in London, let us return to Mirza Salih and Mirza Jaʿfar on their journey.

From a comparison of the details in Mirza Salih's diary with a memoir of coaching in and out of Oxford written by an English contemporary, William Bayzand, we can establish that he and Mirza Jaʿfar probably traveled to Oxford on the London, Blenheim, and Star coach service, perhaps even the coach driven by Charles Holmes or James Castle. As a contemporary advertisement described it, "This coach is the only one running from Oxford to which Patent Detainers have been applied, and will be found to merit the patronage of the Members of the University and of the public in general." Having departed from Charing Cross in London, Mirza Salih recorded that on arriving in Oxford they stayed at the Star Inn (where the London, Blenheim, and Star coach arrived every day at five in the afternoon). The Star Inn was run at the time by a Madam Dupré, who an English source described as "a fine old lady, always dressed in black silk, with old fashion[ed] mob-cap." Such was the hostess who on October 11, 1818 welcomed the two Iranian *taliban*, or "knowledge seekers," when they finally reached Oxford.

The account that Mirza Salih wrote of their visit to the university was in some ways cursory. But it forms a central part of the students' story and so is worth quoting at some length to gain a fuller impression of how Oxford appeared to Mirza Jaʿfar and Mirza Salih.

Sihshamba Dhu'l-Hijja 24 1234 / Tuesday October 11 1818

Today we went to see Mr Hill and together with him went to see Dr Macbride, who is a calm and humane person. As well as the languages of Europe, Macbride is a master of Arabic, such that is he is the Arabic teacher of Oxford. We ate breakfast together and then went along with him to visit the colleges. We saw the chapel of New College, which is a church of splendid appearance. After looking round there, Mr Dunmill (who is the master of New College) invited us for supper.

Nearby is a mansion that is called the "Observatory." which is a place where astronomy is taught. Huge telescopes and astrolabes are kept there, and the people who are studying astronomy go there and with these telescopes trace the orbits and trajectories of the planets. The setting of the mansion is a place like paradise; the building itself large and splendid. After our visit, we went to see the Queen's College, which is also a fine place. From there we went back to our lodgings and then ate supper at a colonel's house, along with fifteen other guests drawn from among the great ones of the different colleges. We were seated there for two hours. Afterward we returned to Mr Hill's house, where we were served tea. Then, toward the middle of the night, we went to bed.

Chaharshamba Dhu'l-Hijja 25 1234 / Wednesday October 12 1818

We ate lunch at the house of Mr Pitt, the nephew of the former prime minister. Because it was raining so much, we were unable to visit the colleges and went instead to the Oxford library. It is a magnificent library! There are 300,000 volumes there in the Greek language, Latin, and the languages of Europe; there are books also in Persian, Arabic and Turkish, written in fine calligraphy and with countless illustrations. The ways of the library are such that all of the benevolent lords have made bequests to the colleges so that any student who cannot afford a particular book can go to the library between ten in the morning and four in the afternoon and ask to see any book in any language. When the Master closes the library for the day, everyone leaves, and the next day the student returns to the library at the aforementioned time. Any member of the one of the colleges may go there and make out a request slip for a book to the library master and then keep the book to read in his compartment. There are also several servants in the library who look after the books so as to prevent dust and worms from destroying them. We spent around four hours there, reading Arabic, Persian and Kufic books.

We came out of the library and went to a building that houses a school where the young students go to sit exams. The method of examination is such that those youths who come to Oxford to seek learning spend three or four years in study and then each year are gathered together in a certain place. If someone has been studying Latin and Greek, a Latin and Greek master comes along and sits at the head of the gathering and asks questions over the length and breadth of the subjects he has been studying. Both examiner and examinee propose their questions and give their answers from memory. Whatever answer is given must be from memory! If in the event the student is able to give answers on the history of Greece and Rome and the details of its events, and on the principles of knowledge and the rules and regulations of how they are employed, then he writes the answers and gives them to the examiner and is awarded a degree that makes him proud among his peers and so encourages others towards study. Whether someone studies the natural sciences, theology, logic, rhetoric, or astronomy (all of which are considered part of philosophy), he will be tested by an examiner specific to that subject. It is said that whatever book any of the youths has read, he has made a record of it in his heart. After our visit to the School, we went back to the house, ate our supper and slept.

Panjshamba Dhu'l-Hijja 26 1234 / Thursday October 13 1818

We ate lunch and then went out to the palace in which the Vice Chancellor (who is the master of Oxford) examines people for the degree of doctor. Inside, the palace contains a square room, lengthy and wide, with a great throne at the head of the assembly. Two chairs are placed to the right and left of the throne, and on both sides of the hall there are places for people to sit. When we entered there was a gathering of both men and women already seated there. When the Vice Chancellor came in all the people rose from their seats. Several persons walked in before him bearing long maces of gold and silver, and after them came the Vice Chancellor himself, dressed all in scarlet and wearing a garment like a *bashliq* thrown over one shoulder. He entered with extreme pomp and then sat down at the head of the assembly. On two chairs to either side of him were sat two other people known as proctors. Two other men, previously among the lords of learning, had examined the scholars of the colleges, written something and passed it to their hands; this was composed in the Latin tongue. So the Vice Chancellor stood up from his place and read out this announcement as the whole assembly listened. Then the two proctors rose from their seats. First stood the person seated to the right of the Vice Chancellor, and in a loud voice he read out in Latin from the aforementioned paper that was written for the scholar being presented with the degree. After that, the proctor went into the middle of the hall and then returned to his own place and sat down. Then the person who was seated to the left of the Vice Chancellor stood up, read out from the piece of paper in the same way, went out into the middle of the hall and came back and sat down again. There were three such to-ings and fro-ings in this way before the gaze of the whole assembly. In our eyes especially it seemed nothing but tomfoolery and excess.

It appears that in the past the rules were such that whoever was given a degree by one of the colleges had his achievements and behavior examined in front of the entire audience and this was done three times by each side of the assembly before the proctors went back to their seats. If someone among those present had any doubt about the candidate's achievements or worth, he grabbed the hem of one of the proctors as he passed and so forbade the reading out of the candidate's diploma. Whoever was honored with a degree had to be completely without fault in both his actions and bearing. That rule is still in force.

In the end, two people were given scarlet gowns and awarded the title of doctor. Several people from among the examiners testified in Latin that they were proficient in such and such a subject, the vice chancellor awarded the two candidates their degrees, and then the audience disbanded. Their names, degrees, and branches of learning were recorded in ledgers. Although the vice chancellor is no greater a doctor than anyone else, as the master of Oxford he is one of the notables and great ones of England, such that the aforementioned doctors become his deputies. For this reason, he was arrogant toward us in a way that none of the other *khans* of Oxford were. Indeed, from when we entered the hall until the time we left, he did not so much as utter a word to us, nor even offer a glance in our direction. And so neither did we utter a word to anyone as we exited and walked toward the festivities in the "botanic" garden. . . . Afterwards, we returned to Mr. Hill's house, ate supper, and were again served tea.

Weighty Rites and High Pomposity

Given the fact that the Iranians had been sent to England on account of its reputation for scientific "progress"—the *taraqqi* that in subsequent decades would be the leitmotif of almost every Persian travel account of Europe—the importance that the English lent to ritual in their greatest seat of learning must have come as some surprise to them. At least, so it seemed during their visit to Oxford in the damp autumn of 1818. Their reaction to the degree ceremony they witnessed was not that of modern international tourists brought up to expect and respect the pomp and circumstance of English life. On the whole, they seem to have been underwhelmed by the spectacle: as Mirza Salih laconically assessed the ceremony, "In our eyes especially it seemed nothing but tomfoolery and excess." While such arcane ritualism was not what the students had come to England in search of, Mirza Salih still regarded its existence as significant enough to record in his diary, perhaps due to its very unexpectedness. Yet even if they were no admirers of such weighty rites—after all, their princely patron 'Abbas Mirza was famously "averse to pomp"—what they observed was still broadly intelligible to them and not the hocus-pocus of an unintelligible cultural universe. They had by now much experience of English ways, of the peculiar rituals of Miss Austen's polite society. Carefully describing what he saw in his "field diary," after three years in England Mirza Salih was becoming a skilled ethnographer.

In the shrinking world—and expanding England—of the early 1800s, the ethnographic diary was a popular genre. Even Jane Austen's sailor brother Charles kept a detailed diary of the customs he observed in the East India Company's ports in Malaya. Reciprocating Mirza Salih's depictions of English ways, in his account of Iran Sir William Ouseley was similarly able to grasp the import of the rituals he observed over there. This is by no means to say that misunderstandings did not arise. But it is to point to the mutual intelligibility of these two intersecting societies, an intelligibility that allowed people to move between them. The degree ceremony the students carefully observed in Oxford is an example of this.

Fig. 9. The *Madrasas* of Oxford: Street View Showing Dr. Macbride's Magdalen Hall.

As we have seen from Mirza Salih's description, the ceremony involved the recipients of degrees being escorted before the vice chancellor on his throne before a crowd of men clad in black gowns; the uttering of Latin formulae; and the final presentation of degrees through the issuing of a paper certificate. Mirza Salih may already have had some inkling of what to expect from conversations with his friends in London. He recorded in his diary how Dr. Gregory had earlier spoken to him about the spectacle of an Oxford degree day. Moreover, on account of his recently published *History of Persia*, the students' friend Sir John Malcolm had himself been the recipient of an honorary degree from Oxford on June 26, 1816, a "commemoration [that] was very grand," he wrote in a letter to his wife. Since this event fell during the period of the students' regular visits to Sir John's house, there is good reason to suspect that he had described the scene to his Muslim guests.

The specific degree ceremony that Mirza Salih and Mirza Jaʿfar witnessed took place two years after Sir John would have described to them its symbolism and meanings. But we are able to fill in the details of what, and who, they saw in October 1818 from the university's records. The occasion was presided over by Frodsham Hodson, who had, incidentally, also been responsible for recommending Sir John for his honorary LLD and who had become vice chancellor only a week or two before Mirza Salih saw him sitting pompously on his throne. As for who was being granted a degree at the ceremony that Mirza Salih and Mirza Jaʿfar observed, records suggest that this was probably the full Convocation that gathered to confer a doctorate of civil law on the grand duke Michael, brother of the czar of Russia. Also attending the ceremony was His Imperial Highness the Archduke Maximillian of Austria, who arrived in Oxford on the Wednesday, disembarking at the same Star Inn where the students had themselves arrived a few days earlier. It is possible that it was the presence of these dynasts at the degree ceremony that led to Mirza Salih being (in his own eyes at least) ignored by the university's grandees. However, given the ambiguity of the dates given in this section of his diary, it is also possible that they attended the ordinary undergraduate degree ceremony that was held on Saturday, October 10, though since this would have fallen at the beginning of his visit, it fits more awkwardly with the sequence of events he described. Besides, Mirza Salih specifically mentioned that it was a ceremony of doctoral degrees that they witnessed. But for the record, on that alternative occasion bachelor's degrees were conferred on Josiah Forshall and Thomas Snow of Exeter College, and master's degrees on Reverend Andrew Edwards of Magdalen College and Reverend William Gurney of St. Edmund Hall, the latter the *alma mater* of their Croydon teacher, Reverend John Bisset. And so if they were present, they may have recognized the name of St. Edmund Hall and taken pride in their vicarious affiliation. In any case, the ecclesiastical presence of the two reverends would have further contributed to Mirza Salih's picture of the university as a compendium of theological colleges, a city of *madrasas*.

Having laid out the scene of the students' visit, let us now turn to the way in which Mirza Salih communicated what he saw for his readers back home. What is most striking about his description is the apparent intelligibility of what he saw going on and the ease with which he was able to find an equivalent ritual vocabulary in Persian. The first matter to note here is his repeated use of the term *martaba* for "degree." He was quite correct to do so. For *martaba* is in fact a calque, or substitute-translation, of the English word "degree," albeit a term that already had a long history in Persian ritual culture. When Iranian courtiers were awarded a new rank—say, as the commander of two thousand men—the expression in Persian was that they had been "raised to the degree [*martaba*] of so many horses or men." In signifying a series of possible different ranks (bachelor, master, doctor), the English term "degree" functioned in precisely the same way, albeit here in an academic rather than a courtly setting. What this tells us is that Mirza Salih gained a fairly accurate picture of the ranking procedure that was at the heart of the ceremony.

The ceremonial adoption of the Latin language that he described would have been similarly intelligible to the two Iranians, who after all had studied Latin for several years by this time. Mirza Salih had already designated Oxford as a city of *madrasas* and, in the *madrasas* of Iran, corresponding use was made of the Arabic language as a weightier language of learning to the vernacular Persian of the student body. By the same token, the use of paper certificates at the ceremony to testify the recipient's level of learning closely reflected the Iranian practice of issuing paper *ijazat* certificates. The final element of the ceremony's symbolic vocabulary that Mirza Salih described was the ceremonial gowns. These had been used as a sign of learning at England's universities since medieval times. While the spectacle of black-gowned students and dons strikes many modern visitors to Oxford as a peculiar sight, there is no reason to think that this was the case for the Iranians, since the wearing of a dark gown or *'aba* was similarly normal for teachers at the *madrasas* of Iran. As we have seen from Mirza Salih's description, he carefully noted the differently colored robes worn by those present at the ceremony. For example, he wrote that the vice chancellor was "dressed all in scarlet and wearing a garment like a *bashliq* thrown over one shoulder," a *bashliq* being a hood, bright in color, that was worn in the Caucasus Mountains just north of 'Abbas Mirza's court at Tabriz. It would have been clear enough to the

Iranians that the vice chancellor's distinctive outfit represented his elevated status, for the custom of bestowing gowns of different colors as a signifier of varying rank was common to Persianate tradition in India as well as Iran.

It was with such ceremonial robes—and the pomp and solemnity that surrounded them—that Mirza Salih and Mirza Ja'far came to associate Oxford. Even as they dined at New College, they may have been reminded of this by their likely host, the warden of the college Dr. Samuel Gauntlett. For he was described by a contemporary as someone who "with his quiet and rather solemn deportment looked, as he stood statue-like in the Chapel, the beau-ideal of a Warden." In dining at New College, the two *mirzas* were entering the oldest and one of the richest of Oxford's colleges at the height of its Regency excess. Unlike the latter-day Spanish visitor to Oxford described in Javier Marias's novel *All Souls*, one suspects they were far from confounded by the gongs and whispers of the high table; we have already read Mirza Salih's dismissive account of the degree ceremony. Nor with their much improved English by this time did the Muslim students need Marias's advice for academic diners abroad: "in a language not one's own, it's easy to make a pretence at listening and, by pure intuition, to agree or enthuse or now and again make some (obsequious) comment."

While Mirza Salih left no details of the food they ate on this occasion, other evidence from the time allows us to reconstruct the gastronomic scene that confronted them. One vivid description appears in the diary of Reverend James Woodforde, who transcribed several menus from New College in the years before Mirza Salih and Mirza Ja'far ate there. At the time, Woodforde was vice warden of New College and so in a comparable position to the *buzurg*, or "grandee" of the same college whom Mirza Salih recorded as inviting him and Mirza Ja'far to dine there. Mirza Salih remembered his host at New College as being named Mr. Dunmill, though the actual warden at the time of their visit was Samuel Gauntlett, a doctor of divinity who was mentioned in one of Jane Austen's letters. With a nod toward the cods and roasted meats that Mirza Salih wrote were common on English tables, Reverend James Woodforde described one New College dinner as comprising nothing less than "two fine Codds boiled with fryed Souls round them and oyster sauce, a fine sirloin of Beef roasted, some peas soup and an orange Pudding for the first course, for the second, we had a lease of Wild Ducks roasted, a fore Qu of Lamb and sallad and mince Pies." Whatever a "fore Qu" exactly was, Woodforde evokes the kind of feast faced by Mirza Ja'far and Mirza Salih that evening in Oxford. It certainly wasn't only foreign Muslims who ate strange things! Although Woodforde's grand repast was admittedly a Christmas dinner, his depiction of more regular dinners for college guests shows them as little less substantial. A more quotidian entry in his diary records that, "I gave my company for dinner some green Pea Soup, a chine of Mutton, some New College Puddings, a goose, some Peas, and a Codlin Tart with Cream. Madeira and Port Wine to drink after and at dinner some strong Beer, Cider, Ale and small Beer." While it would be tedious to list sample menus for every college at which the students ate during their visits to the varsity, suffice it to say that New College was by no means exceptional in the munificence of its table.

Yet even if Mirza Salih and Mirza Ja'far ate well, the impression they gained from the ceremonial degree day remained the same: the university was an underwhelming place of high ritual and self-importance. To see whether they fared any better away from high tables and rituals, we must turn to the scholars they met in Oxford.

Betwixt Latin and Persic

Despite Oxford's later role as the intellectual hub of the British Empire, when the Victorian Benjamin Jowett turned Balliol College into a finishing school for the likes of Lord Curzon and when Cecil Rhodes established his famous scholarships for the brightest boys from every corner of the empire, for the first three centuries of British expansion overseas Oxford remained startlingly insular in its concerns. Ironically, by 1818, it was a lesser site of oriental learning than Croydon was with the East India Company's college. The situation did not look promising for Mirza Ja'far and Mirza Salih's hopes of gaining traction there through their language skills.

According to the diary, the men with whom Mirza Salih and Mirza Ja'far were most closely associated in Oxford were Mr. Hill and Dr.

Macbride. To understand who they were, and what the significance was of their hosting the two Muslims, we must first look more closely at the confluences of learning at the university around 1818. For the meetings of Messrs. Salih, Ja'far, Hill, and Macbride were not only meetings between four men but also encounters between two systems of learning and the languages on which they were based. As we have seen, up until this point much of Mirza Salih's efforts in England had been devoted to the study of language—of English, Latin, and French—with Mirza Ja'far's education based on the engineering and surveying curriculum of the Royal Military Academy. In response to the East India Company colleges, Oxford was now slowly recognizing the wider world beyond Europe as its faculty developed interests in Islamic Asia. Since it was far from an easy proposition to admit Iranian Muslims to a university whose students and fellows were sworn to honor the Church of England, Mirza Salih and Mirza Ja'far recognized that their best chances of gaining support came through cooperating with faculty members who had an interest in Muslim affairs. Given what Mirza Salih had learned since his travelling days with Sir William and Sir Gore Ouseley in Iran, as well as during his time near the East India College in Croydon, he realized that his linguistic expertise in Arabic as well as Persian was his chief intellectual asset in England. As a *mirza*, or "secretary," Mirza Ja'far had identical skills. Language, then, would be the crux of the students' engagements with Oxford.

The study of languages is after all crucial: language learning forms the foundation of all learning. Having previously studied the scholarly language of Arabic in addition to their native Persian, the two Muslims knew this well. They had carried this model of the importance of knowing both a vernacular and a classical language with them from Iran, which had led them to study both English and Latin during their eleven months in Croydon. The corresponding attempts made by Oxford and, as we shall see later, Cambridge scholars to study Arabic and to a lesser extent Persian show the reciprocity of the learning process that they were to enter into at the universities. Although the universities had long moved on from the days when all lectures were expected to be delivered in Latin, the Oxford at which Mirza Salih and Mirza Ja'far sought to enroll was still an institution that placed great emphasis on foreign languages, albeit mostly dead "classical" ones. We have seen from Mirza Salih's diary the efforts to which he put himself to master Latin as well as English and French; as an educational prerequisite, such multilingualism would have struck someone of his background as nothing unusual. For young men destined for the court bureaucracy like himself would have been expected to know high literary Persian, Arabic, and, given his employment in the western city of Tabriz, probably Turkish as well. We also know that he understood "Hindustani" Urdu, perhaps through the presence of Indian merchants in his home city of Shiraz. These languages were his and Mirza Jaʿfar's greatest assets, and potential bargaining chips.

For centuries of English history, it had been Latin, Greek, and to a lesser extent Hebrew whose mastery had served as the linguistic markers of academic knowledge. With their long-established claim to these languages, the ancient universities had held a virtual monopoly on these linguistic commodities. But as we have seen, as England's commercial and then political connections with India became of growing importance, a new linguistic commodity began to enter the scene. This new linguistic commodity was Persian, the most reliable ticket to a sinecure in the East until the East India Company's decision to replace Persian as its language of administration in 1837. India's importance was capable of pushing to the forefront of English politics the sons of such low-born East India men as Thomas Pitt (1653–1726), with one of whose relatives Mirza Salih and Mirza Jaʿfar dined in Oxford. Yet Oxford was no more willing to make concessions to this new Indian and Persian road to self-advancement than it was to offer instruction in the building of colliery-pumps and steam-engines. Instead, it fell mainly to the East India Company's colleges at Haileybury (to the north of London) and Addiscombe (on the edge of Croydon) to teach languages more fit for an Indian than a church career. This did not bode altogether well for the two Iranians.

Arabic, however, was a somewhat different matter. Unsurprisingly, the birth of Arabic studies in Oxford emerged more from the dons' desire to better understand their own faith than immerse themselves in another. The incentives were theological, inspired by the Protestant emphasis on the proper understanding of scripture, rendering Arabic a theological fillip to the interpretation of difficult passages of biblical Hebrew. Although a small number of scholars at the medieval university were interested in Arabic (most famously the Franciscan friar and philosopher Roger Bacon), it was chiefly with Archbishop William Laud's endowment of the Laudian chair in Arabic in 1636, followed by the Lord Almoner's chair in Arabic in 1699, that the language found a permanent home among the spires. Most of the early holders of the Laudian professorship were primarily Hebraists, and years passed by during which they gave no instruction in Arabic at all. Even the great early hero of Oxford Arabism, Edward Pococke (1604–90), whose Arabic interests were more diverse than many of his successors to the Laudian chair, spent most of his time in theological pursuits. Though Arabic was endowed with two professorships, Oxford's "monkish constitution" saw the Reverend Benjamin Holloway publicly denounce the second Laudian professor of Arabic, Thomas Hunt (1696–1774), on the charge that "he set himself with all his Might, to exalt the *Arabic* Tongue, and no less to depress and degrade the Hebrew." The battle was still not over in 1818, when Mirza Salih and Mirza Ja'far arrived there.

If Arabic was at least on the syllabus, in the early nineteenth century Oxford was still spurring the worldly concerns of the East India Company by neglecting Persian. A few decades earlier, the university brushed aside a great opportunity to print its stamp on the imperial encounter with India. For in around 1768, an anonymous proposal was sent from Calcutta to establish a professorship of Persian at Oxford. It appears to have come from the governor-general of India, Warren Hastings, who was determined to bring Persian to the varsity syllabus. In spite of the rhetoric of cultural superiority that was later to shape English attitudes to "oriental" learning (most famously in Thomas Babington Macaulay's "Minute on Education" of 1835), Governor Hastings couched his proposal in the rational universalism of the Enlightenment (though in view of Oxford's clerical dons, he gave the occasional nod toward the preeminence of Christian scripture). The study of Persian was thus possessed of a double value, to "open new insights into the general history of mankind, *and* serve to corroborate the testimonies of Scripture." He went on, "there is a large collection of manuscripts in the Persic language [already] in the University of Oxford," he wrote, "where (except for a few individuals) they must be considered even in a place of Learning merely as useless curiosities . . . the whole collection might be made subservient to the most useful purposes, by being placed under the charge of some person skilled in that Language." With a further pragmatic gesture outlining the demand for students versed in Persian in the employ of the East India Company, which now "exercise[d] the rights of sovereignty over a rich and extensive country," Hastings proposed that a fund be raised to elect a "Professor of the Persian Tongue." While it went without saying that the professor himself must be British (and a sworn member of the Church of England at that), Hastings recommended that an assistant— "a native of Persia or Indostan"— be employed so that undergraduates might actually learn to speak the language before they were sent to serve in India. This might well have been an opening for one of the Iranian students had Governor Hastings's proposal been accepted.

But it was not. Despite the eloquent and pragmatic arguments that Hastings made in favor of his proposal, Oxford's infamous apathy prevailed. Persian found no official home there and Hastings instead bequeathed his wealth to private causes. In a curious example of the presence of Persianiate Asia in the smaller domestic world of Jane Austen, during the same year that the Iranian students were in Oxford, Governor Hastings left the grand sum of £5,000 (around £375,000 or $600,000 today) to Austen's cousin, Betsy. Governor Hastings's wife, Mary, was also the best friend of Austen's aunt Phila, who lived in Calcutta. So close was the link between the Hastings and Austen families that Hastings sent his young son to live in England under the care of Miss Austen's father, George. After the boy died in the latter's care, Governor Hastings came to meet George Austen in London and, seeing in him a sound and sincere churchman, made him a trustee of a fund for his god-daughter. George Austen was so impressed with the largely self-educated governor of the East India Company that he encouraged the Austen children, Jane included, to imitate Hastings's lust for learning. And so though Jane Austen never learned Persian, there is every chance that it crossed her mind as the implication of her father's advice. Her sailor brothers took more notice, though, with Charles Austen eventually dying in the cause of expanding East India Company rule into Burma.

Back in Oxford, however loud the occasional enthusiast such as Warren Hastings and William "Oriental" Jones tried to compare the

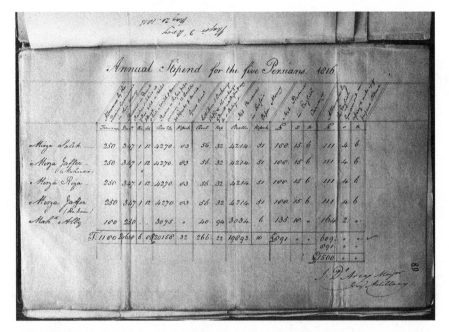

Fig. 10. Exasperating Accounts: Statement of the Students' Finances. Source: Courtesy
The National Archives. FO 60/11 (102).

merits of Persian literature to those of Greek and Latin, the varsity
remained impermeable to the entry of Persian to the syllabus. And this
implied that it was similarly indisposed to allowing entry to Persians,
including the two hopefuls who arrived on the stagecoach from London that October of 1818. Still, Mirza Salih and Mirza Ja'far had few
options but to try their luck. Only a couple of people from the otherwise influential circle of diplomats and scholars in which they now
moved in London had studied at Oxford. And the one Oxonian they
were close to, Reverend John Bisset, their schoolmaster from Croydon,
hardly held much sway.

When the two Iranians stepped down from their stagecoach, the
university's teaching fellows were all ordained churchmen and the
main profession of those graduates who had to seek work remained
that of clergyman. One of them was Jane Austen's father, the Reverend
George Austen, who had taken his Bachelor of Divinity from Oxford's
St. John's College, where he later worked as assistant chaplain. Just
seven years before the Iranians' arrived, Oxford had expelled the

young poet Percy Shelley for writing a student essay on "The Necessity of Atheism." Given that Mirza Salih had just spent the summer filling his diary with notes taken from the writing of the great Scottish rationalist David Hume, the Oxford that he and Mirza Ja'far had entered was no city of free (still less of radical) thinkers. What radicalism there was came less from rationalists and skeptics than from religious "enthusiasts," the fanatics of their day whom Miss Austen despised: the evangelicals. Moreover, one of them was the Iranians' host in Oxford.

Mirza Salih described this "Mister Hill" as a *kashish*, or church priest, and an occasional college teacher: he was the Reverend John Hill (1786–1855), an evangelical associate of Isaac Crouch, the father of Oxford evangelicalism, and of his St. Edmund Hall, the hotbed of godly "enthusiasts." By the time of their arrival in 1818, Mr. Hill had risen to the position of vice principal of St. Edmund Hall, making him in institutional terms at least one of Oxford's leading evangelicals. Since at this time he lived at number 65 on the High Street, his house would have been in close walking distance of the New and Queen's colleges and (at the far end of the High) the botanic garden to which, from Mirza Salih's diary, we have seen him escorting the Iranian students before taking them to his home for tea. Not only was Mr. Hill a leading evangelical in Oxford itself. At the time he hosted his Muslim guests, he was about to establish Oxford's first branch of the Church Missionary Society, which would lead England's nineteenth-century attempt to win the Middle East for Christ. Given the fact that a few years earlier Mirza Salih's teacher in Croydon, Reverend John Bisset, had himself graduated from Mr. Hill's college, St. Edmund Hall, it seems likely that it was through Reverend Bisset that the students were introduced to Mr. Hill. The students were making best use of their meager Oxford connections, perhaps little suspecting the evangelical implications of an association with St. Edmund Hall. Nonetheless, their meetings with Mr. Hill were to prove the first of their many encounters with evangelicals, who would see in the Iranians' mastery of Arabic and Persian an opportunity to aid their own agenda for the region. And in being introduced by Mr. Hill to Dr. John Macbride, the two *mirzas* would find themselves placed in evangelical hands that they would have to try to turn toward their own educational purposes.

The Unsettling Opinions of Dr. Macbride

Given the students' previous association in London and Croydon with East India Company scholars of oriental languages such as Sir Gore Ouseley and Professor John Shakespear, it was scarcely surprising that on visiting Oxford Mirza Salih and Mirza Jaʿfar should turn toward its main scholar of Arabic, Dr. John David Macbride (1778-1868). But Dr. Macbride was a very different man from the Ouseley brothers with their fondness and familiarity with the Muslim peoples of Asia. Unlike the Ouseleys, Dr. Macbride had never left England, still less spent years studying with Muslim scholars in Lucknow as Sir Gore Ouseley had in his youth. In the margins of Mirza Salih's account of these different linguists, we can detect a clash of intellectual cultures. This was not a clash between Iranian and English intellectual cultures, but rather one between different kinds of British scholars, those associated with the universities and with the East India Company. Over the next few pages, we will turn toward this matter in more detail through an inspection of the opinions of the Oxford orientalists who appear in Mirza Salih's diary.

Let's begin with Dr. Macbride himself, the students' apparently affable guide on their tour of the library and the examination halls that we have seen in the extract from the diary. As well-born as his Iranian guests, John David Macbride was born in Devon in 1778 as the son of John Macbride (ca. 1735–1800), an admiral and erstwhile member of Parliament for Plymouth. As an undergraduate, this stern son of a naval officer studied at Oxford's Exeter College, where in 1800 he was made a fellow. Given that as early as 1797 his name appeared among a short list of subscribers to Sir William Ouseley's journal *The Oriental Collections*, it is clear that his interest in oriental languages dated as far back as his undergraduate days, perhaps inspired by his father's sea journeys to the east. Despite a period of legal studies during his thirties, in 1813 Dr. Macbride was appointed Lord Almoner's Reader in Arabic, one of Oxford's two endowed positions in the language. The two *mirzas* would have been unable to meet Mr. Laurent, the other main Arabist at Oxford, since (as reported in the *Oxford University and City Herald*) in the autumn of 1818 he was traveling in Greece and

Turkey and not due to return till November. But with Dr. Macbride they had found the more influential figure. For as the *Oxford University Calendar* for that year reveals, by the time of their meeting with him, he was a senior member of the university: he had recently added to his post as Lord Almoner's Reader in Arabic a series of other appointments as principal of Magdalen Hall, university assessor, perpetual delegate of the university press, and perpetual delegate of privileges.

Although in his diary Mirza Salih mistook Dr. Macbride for a fellow of New College—probably due to the fact (revealed in his remaining papers) that he was in the habit of keeping his horse in New College's larger stables—Dr. Macbride's main source of prominence was as the principal of Magdalen Hall. If it was through their Croydon teacher Mr. Bisset that Mirza Salih and Mirza Ja'far were introduced to Mr. Hill of St. Edmund Hall, they may have been introduced to Dr. Macbride through Mirza Salih's London teacher, Mr. Belfour. For the latter appears to have been the same Francis Belfour who was at this time a nonresident member of Magdalen Hall, his interest in Persian nicely complementing his college principal Dr. Macbride's interest in Arabic.

As one of the few remaining "halls" of the medieval university, Magdalen Hall was already a college in all but name and was being steered by Dr. Macbride toward its eventual refoundation as Hertford College with the financial aid of the Barings banking family. Magdalen Hall had a proud history as a center of Puritan intellectual life in the sixteenth and seventeenth century, an ethos discernible in its most illustrious alumnus, the philosopher Thomas Hobbes (1588–1679). The Hall was also an early supporter of Arabic studies, behind which lay an axiomatically Protestant promotion of scriptural scholarship that saw Arabic as a supplement to Hebrew. Hence, over the previous two hundred years, the Hall had played a distinguished role in the development of the "Arabick interest" in England, having been the college at which the main founder of Oxford Arabism, Edward Pococke (1604–91), had matriculated in 1619. Another early member of Magdalen Hall was Henry Lord, who in 1624 became chaplain to the East India Company in the Indian port of Surat.

If Oxford was not nearly so receptive to Islamic learning as the colleges of the East India Company, then of all the university's several dozen colleges the Iranians had managed to associate themselves with the principal of the one college with a strong interest in the expertise they could offer in exchange for their entry to Oxford: the languages of Islam. Once again, we can see a good deal of strategy and planning behind their movements in England, strategizing that echoed the tenacity and tact they had used to gain lessons in Croydon and London. But however sympathetic a host Dr. Macbride may have been to Mirza Salih and Mirza Ja'far—and Mirza Salih's diary suggests that he was—his interest in Arabic was anything but a sign of sympathy with their religion, Islam. For he was transforming Magdalen Hall into the headquarters of Oxford evangelicalism.

We know that Dr. Macbride had already devoted himself to the "conversionist" creed at the heart of the evangelical movement by the time he met the Iranian students. For a letter in his hand survives from three years earlier in which he urged the undergraduates of Magdalen Hall to devote their lives to the spread of Christianity, a career he saw as the most important that a graduate could aspire to. And he was clearly a persuasive man, for under his leadership Magdalen Hall educated four future bishops who devoted themselves to the Church Missionary Society.

It was to such missionary purposes that Dr. Macbride's own study of Arabic was dedicated. For despite his position as one of Oxford's two endowed scholars of Arabic, like many of his predecessors he was far more interested in Christianity and Hebrew. Insofar as he was concerned with the study of Arabic and Islam, it was not as a means of study in its own right, but as a means to better know the enemies of Christ. As he declared during a lecture to the undergraduates at Magdalen Hall around this time (and that he printed a few years later), "the conversion of infidels should be our object in our explanation of the Bible." Clearly, this was not the kind of syllabus that the students expected to find in Oxford, which they had assumed was the fountainhead of the scientific new learning. On closer inspection, matters now looked very different; and a disappointing closer inspection it must have been.

Although Dr. Macbride published a considerable number of sermons and other works on Christian doctrine, the only substantial work in which he put to use his studies of Arabic was *The Mohammedan Religion Explained: With an Introductory Sketch of Its Progress, and Suggestions for Its Confutation.* Here he showed himself as a supporter of a specifically Christian approach to empire. Spelling out his evangelical vision of a strictly Christian imperialism, he admonished the tolerant policies of the East India Company: "While our rulers tolerate false religions, may they imbibe the spirit of the Bible, and reestablish our Government on Christian principles. . . . We know that in God's appointed time Islam must, like all false religions, fall." If nothing else, *The Mohammedan Religion* is a startling testament to the evangelicals' bombastic style of writing. As Jane Austen wrote after reading an evangelical tome she had been sent by her sister, "My disinclination for it before was affected, but now it is real." Learned as it was, Dr. Macbride's *magnum opus* was no more than a manual of anti-Muslim slander. We can only wonder whether he tried out his oratorical techniques of doctrinal confutation on his unfortunate Muslim guests.

Although Dr. Macbride published his *Mohammedan Religion* decades after meeting Mirza Salih and Mirza Ja'far, his writings from the years surrounding their meeting show that he was already a fervent evangelical who was devoting himself to the conversion of Muslims. Mirza Salih would not find in him the kind of sympathetic scholar of Islamic languages that he had found in the Ouseley brothers. But in England's two universities, Dr. Macbride's fervor was far from unusual. By the early nineteenth century, the study of Arabic was mainly being supported at Oxford and Cambridge for missionary purposes. While Dr. Macbride was Lord Almoner's reader (and later, professor) in Arabic, his fellow evangelical Stephen Reay (1782–1861) acquired Oxford's other endowed chair in Arabic, the Laudian professorship, a few years after Mirza Salih's time at the university. Moreover, in the very year that Mirza Salih and Mirza Ja'far were there, under the pseudonym Pileus Quadratus, Dr. Reay published a tract that championed the work of the Church Missionary Society in Asia. As we will see in later chapters, such varsity men would be far from the last members of the new missionary societies that the Muslim students would encounter.

The Libraries of Oxford

Despite walking into the evangelical lions' den, the two *mirzas* still found Oxford could offer them places of interest, even pleasure. By inclination as well as upbringing, they were *ahl-i qalam*, "men of the pen" who had for centuries made up the bureaucrats who served, usually father-to-son, in the chanceries of Iran and India. It was in response to this background that Mirza Salih had arranged their educational program in London and Croydon in a manner that befitted the traditional expertise of such men of the pen by studying what he saw as an equivalent curriculum of English, Latin, and history. Although the students were seeking knowledge that was modern, unlike his companions who were studying subjects like engineering and medicine, Mirza Salih had so far stayed within the traditional parameters of an Iranian bureaucratic education in languages, history, and to some extent natural philosophy. In other words, it was a gentleman's education and as such one that had, so far, enabled him to share the cultured interests of his English gentlemen friends. It must then have been with some excitement that, on reaching England's Parnassus at Oxford, he was finally able to access the great libraries where his passion for learning, and for books in particular, might be sated. Despite his focus on engineering and mapmaking, Mirza Ja'far must have been similarly excited.

Mirza Salih's enthusiasm for Oxford's Bodleian and Radcliffe libraries reflected his more general bibliophilia, for his diary describes his visits to several other major libraries, including that of the Royal Society in London, an institution that, he noted with approval, examined every new book that was printed in England. His appreciation for England's libraries was therefore by no means limited to those with collections of oriental manuscripts, even if these were what his hosts often showed him. For as his English improved, Mirza Salih became a voracious reader of history books in particular; and not only by David Hume, for his diary shows him spending many evenings devouring histories of Greece, Rome, Turkey, India, and Russia as well as Britain and the United States. He also mentioned reading histories of Iran, the most likely of which would have been the *History of Persia* written by his friend Sir John Malcolm which had been published a few months before he had reached London.

This interest in books was not unique to the students. If Ambassador Abu'l-Hasan was undoubtedly of less studious character than Mirza Salih, he too had an interested in books. His London diary of 1810 contains a series of descriptions of the public and private libraries

he visited, including that at the home of Sir Gore Ouseley near Bea-
consfield in Buckinghamshire. There Abu'l-Hasan inspected the fine
collection of Persian manuscripts that Sir Gore had assembled, which
included gold embossed calligraphy from Iran, India, and the Ottoman
Empire. This is not to say that all early Iranian travelers to England
were men of culture. For when, a decade after Mirza Salih's departure,
his acquaintance James Fraser escorted two Iranian princes on a visit
to Windsor Castle, he noted that for all the extraordinary wealth of its
holdings, "the library gave them little pleasure." But Mirza Salih and
Mirza Ja'far were much more scholarly types than the visiting princes
and an interest in books—and in manuscripts in particular—was a preoccupation that they and Abu'l-Hasan shared with their mutual
friends, the Ouseley brothers. Even before the Ouseley's ambassadorial journey to Iran in 1810, both brothers had expended large sums of
money in collecting Persian manuscripts (mainly from India, whose
royal libraries were being disbanded as a side-effect of the East India
Company's rise to power). The sheer scale on which such Persian manuscripts were purchased reflected the wealth that these empire build-
ers were acquiring in India. Sir Gore Ouseley was himself a good example, for after several years trading as a merchant in Bengal, where
he first developed his interests in Persian and became an acolyte of Sir
William Jones, in around 1795 he moved to the Nawwab's Muslim
court at Lucknow, a flourishing cultural center at the time. In Lucknow, Sir Gore (albeit back then an unknighted jute trader) furthered
his knowledge of Persian literature by spending his spare time studying with the city's finest Muslim scholars. When in 1810 Abu'l-Hasan
later complimented the standard of his Persian in London, he was impressed to hear that Sir Gore had learned it in Lucknow, a city whose
learning was famous even in Iran. In what was at this time the most
important center of Persian manuscript production in North India, it
was also in Lucknow that Sir Gore began to purchase manuscripts of
the highest quality that fifteen years later would be admired by the
Iranian Ambassador. Many of these manuscripts would later find their
way to Oxford.

For his part, Sir William Ouseley assembled a similarly large library
of Persian works, which he used to enable his own researches in a
period in which the very first printed books in Persian were only just

appearing from the East India Company's presses in Calcutta. Aside from the studies Sir William wrote on Persian poetry, history, and geography, his familiarity with the different Persian scripts used by manuscript scribes led him to write his *Persian Miscellanies, An Essay to Facilitate the Reading of Persian Manuscripts.* As an orthographic guide, it has hardly been surpassed two centuries later. By the time Sir William offered his collection for sale in 1831, it contained 724 manuscripts of note, some of whose places of purchase (including Mirza Salih's home city of Shiraz) were noted in its descriptive catalogue. The collection was purchased for the Bodleian Library at Oxford, and though this was after the Iranian students' visit there in 1818 it adds a pleasing symmetry to the praise that Mirza Salih showered on the Bodleian's Persian and Arabic manuscripts. This is not least the case because the two unique manuscripts of the works that Mirza Salih had earlier written for Sir William—the travelogue on Iran and the Persian dialogues—were also to find their way into the Bodleian Library that Mirza Salih visited with Mirza Ja'far on October 12, 1818. The manuscripts remain a part of the Bodleian's collection to this day, so that Mirza Salih's own handwriting could be read beneath the portrait of Sir Gore that until recently hung in the Oriental Reading Room in the heart of Oxford.

By peculiar coincidence—if such it was—the Bodleian Library was also presented with a gift of Persian manuscripts around the time of Mirza Salih and Mirza Ja'far's visit. According to the handwritten record book known as the *Annals of the Bodleian Library,* a few months before their visit to the library in the company of Dr. Macbride, the Bodleian received a donation of six unnamed Persian manuscripts. The donor is listed in this accessions book as none other than Dr. John David Macbride, the very person who guided the students around the library just two months after the donation. Despite his work with Arabic, Dr. Macbride had no expertise in Persian and so it is hard to know what to make of his possession of these manuscripts just two months before the students met him. But given the fact that, as Mirza Salih's diary shows, that summer of 1818 was the period in which he and his London supporters were doing their best to make arrangements for him and Mirza Ja'far to study at Oxford, it seems possible that there was some connection between the students and the mysterious Per-

Fig. 11. The Evangelical Arabist: *Portrait of Professor Macbride* by Thomas Goff Lupton.   Source: © National Portrait Gallery, London.

sian manuscripts. Of course, we do not know how long Dr. Macbride had the manuscripts in his possession before he passed them on to the library. But it is passing strange that his sole association with Persian during his seven-decade career at Oxford should occur so shortly before his meeting with two Iranian would-be Oxonians.

It would be nice if the manuscripts themselves offered some confirmation, but an examination of them shows that they are all of Indian rather than Iranian provenance. Since we know very little about the extent to which Indo-Persian manuscripts were circulating in Iran during the early nineteenth century (when, as we have seen, many of them were being plundered from Indian libraries), it is impossible to say with certainty whether the students brought these manuscripts with them from Iran as a form of transferable capital in the same way that Mirza Salih imported the shawls that he sold for profit in London. It is certainly a possibility. Another possibility is that the manuscripts were sent to Dr. Macbride by one of the students' London patrons, perhaps in an attempt to awaken a Persian interest in the scholar of Arabic that might work to their advantage. The likely suspect in this case would be Sir Gore Ouseley, whom Mirza Salih's diary describes as making as much effort as possible in the spring and summer of 1818 to find them a place at Oxford. Sir Gore's own collection certainly contained many such Indo-Persian manuscripts, which he had bought in abundance during his years in India. A closer inspection of the manuscripts suggests the link to Sir Gore as the more likely possibility, for none of them were particularly rare and of the two finer ones— copies of the *Tuhfat al-Ahrar* ("Gift to the Noble") of the poet Jami of Herat and the *Tarikh-i ʿAlam-Araʾi-yi ʿAbbasi* ("History of the World-Ornamenting ʿAbbas") of Iskandar Munshi—there were already better specimens in the Ouseley brothers' collections. The other manuscripts comprised a lone second volume of the *Ashiʿ ʿat al-Lamaʿat* ("Gleams of the Flashes of Light"), a commentary by Shaykh ʿAbd al-Haqq of Delhi on an earlier work on the deeds of the Prophet (its flyleaf bearing seals suggesting it belonged previously to the Mughal imperial library); another lone volume of a history of the Sikhs titled *Nuskhat-i Ahval-i Sikhan*; a copy of the well-known history of Gujarat, *Mirʾat-i Sikandari* ("Alexander's Mirror"); and an undated manuscript of the even better-known Persian sixteenth-century history of India by Firishta. Were these, then, the overspill of Sir Gore Ouseley's collection, a respectable academic bribe that he sent to Oxford in an attempt to cultivate Dr. Macbride's interest in Persian, and in two young Persians in particular? We will never know for sure. But even if we cannot directly link the manuscripts' arrival in the Bodleian to Mirza Salih and Mirza Ja'far's visit there two months later, the fact that they were donated by Dr. Macbride does at least shed light on the momentary Persian interests of the man who became the students' main Oxford associate.

Alternative Interests

In the early 1800s, the number of English collectors and translators of Persian manuscripts was still very small. Between the Ouseleys brothers, William Price, and Professor Shakespear, the Iranian students knew four of the most important men whose efforts were opening Persian learning to a British audience. Once again, we see the mutual character of learning between the Iranian and English sides. For this was by no means a one-way traffic in knowledge, as Iranian intellectuals, at home and abroad, were seeking access to the intellectual assets of *Inglistan*. Their new way of doing this was to send students directly to England in the hope of accessing the scientific new learning. Yet as we have already seen with regard to the mathematical religiosity of the students' math teacher, Dr. Gregory, Jane Austen's England was a place where the scientific new learning made curious submissions to the demands of Christian theology. We see this again in the case of the one Oxford-based scientist whom we know the students encountered. This was the Reverend William Buckland (1784–1856), the renowned geologist and churchman who in 1814 began to deliver his famous series of lectures on geology (and the as yet unnamed science of palaeontology) at Oxford's Ashmolean Museum. Although we have no evidence that Mirza Salih or Mirza Ja'far came into contact with Reverend William Buckland on their visit to Oxford in 1818, we do know that their fellow student Hajji Baba visited Buckland shortly before the other students arrived in England in the autumn of 1815. We know this through the existence among Hajji Baba's possessions of an English translation of a geological textbook by Georges Cuvier (1769–1832) that Buckland inscribed to Hajji Baba in Oxford on June 12, 1815. In line with the revolutionary sentiments of the France in which Cuvier rose to fame in the 1790s and 1800s, he was a strong supporter of the notion of catastrophic geological revolutions. Given the date of the gift to Hajji Baba in 1815, the book must have been Robert Kerr's translation of Cuvier's *Discours sur les révolutions de la surface du globe*, which was published in Edinburgh and London in 1813. Given the linguistic and intellectual expertise Hajji Baba gathered during his seven years' residence in England, we have no reason to doubt that he read the treatise. As such, it is important evidence for the transfer of the latest scientific ideas from Europe to Iran. At the same time, the context of the gift reminds us that the new discoveries of Cuvier and his supporters posed quite as many problems for European Christian intellectuals as they may have done for Muslim thinkers in Iran. For although William Buckland was happy to present his Iranian visitor with Cuvier's book, in his own career he carefully publically distanced himself from the Frenchman's almost atheistic claims. In Buckland's inaugural lecture as reader in geology at Oxford in 1819, for example, he presented an apologia for the lectures he had been delivering at the university for the past five years and made it punctiliously plain that "geology coincides with the records of Sacred History." Showing himself an orthodox Anglican Christian supporter of the natural theology of William Paley against Cuvier's "infinite series of revolutions," Buckland used his lecture to argue that "geology contributes proofs to Natural Theology strictly in harmony with those derived from other branches of natural history." What this implied was that geology—and geologists—presented no threat to the establishment ideology of universal (and thence social) harmony, a political ideology that the loyalist Christian university passed on to the squires and clergymen it trained to rule over England. Such conservative intellectual discretion eventually landed Buckland the canonry of Oxford's Christ Church and then the deanship of Westminster. So it was that even the one Oxford scientist that any of the students met raised the claims of theology and faith over science and reason.

What becomes clear from all this is that even when the Muslim students were able to meet with representatives of the new sciences at England's universities, they were still encountering a society in which the scientific new learning had not yet freed itself from the shackles of religious orthodoxy. There was no innate pattern that some today would project back into the past of a "rational," "scientific" Europe and an "irrational," "religious" Middle East. Back in Oxford in October

1818, as students dispatched from halfway across Asia to acquire the newest forms of learning, Mirza Salih and Mirza Ja'far were not primarily interested in Bodleian's Arabic and Persian manuscripts that Dr. Macbride was showing them. While to Dr. Macbride, these seemed to be the obvious things that would interest the two young Muslims, they were far from the types of text that they had traveled so far to find. Instead, the young Iranian modernists were more interested in works on mathematics, engineering, and medicine, or in recent historical works that would help them understand how European nations had been transformed into industrial and imperial powerhouses. Compared with the diaries of other Persian-writing travelers of the period, the relative lack of poetic quotations and embellished prose in Mirza Salih's diary suggests that he had even come to reject the traditional forms of writing represented by the old manuscripts of Jami and Firishta that he was shown by Macbride. As an *ibn al-waqt*, "a man of the moment," Mirza Salih was far more interested in new, rationalized forms of writing, and he would not find these among the texts he was shown by the evangelical Dr. Macbride, be they in Persian or English.

On the contrary, like Ambassador Abu'l-Hasan a few years before him, Mirza Salih was more interested in the large number of newspapers he saw being printed in England. We need to bear in mind here that when the students reached London, their homeland had never printed a single book, let alone a newspaper. Unsurprisingly, the sight of the latest news and scientific findings being published every day was one that fascinated Mirza Salih. In his diary, he placed the number of newspapers printed every year in Britain at twenty-five million, a figure that must have seemed staggering for someone from a country that had never printed a single page. Keen to note the usefulness of these newspapers, he recorded the way in which up to sixty "advertisements" were at times printed alongside news and information. The sheer novelty of this idea can be gleaned from the fact that he had to borrow the English word "advertisement," spelled out in Arabic letters. As a good servant of the state, he also noted that such advertisements gave the English government extra income by means of a special tax, so providing a financial lesson that might be learned back home. We can guess at the kind of ads that caught Mirza Salih's attention: one ad published in the *Oxford University and City Herald* on the very day that he and Mirza Ja'far took the coach to Oxford announced a sale of fine oriental rugs by Messrs. Clarke and Stokes of Oxford. But even if the university city had its newspapers, overall the varsity had come as a disappointment to the two Muslim visitors. After comparing its colleges and libraries with what they had seen during what were by now almost three years' residence in London and Croydon, they recognized that the university stood nowhere near the forefront of the new learning transforming England into the world's first industrial nation. Oxford's colleges were indeed *madrasas*, as Mirza Salih described them: they were theological and legal colleges equivalent to the traditional Muslim *madrasa* schools of Iran. If he and his friends sought the secrets of more modern forms of knowledge, they would have to look elsewhere.

A Botanic Interlude

Yet the visit to Oxford was not only a time of disillusionment. The chief delight that Mirza Salih and Mirza Ja'far took in their time there was in a tour of the botanic garden (or Physic Garden, as it was then still sometimes called). To gain a sense of the pleasure they took from the garden, it is worth quoting again from Mirza Salih's diary:

> This is a garden where they grow trees, flowers, herbs and spices that have been brought from all over the world. Every herb that comes from a warm climate is kept in rooms whose roofs and walls are made of glass, so the climate there is kept warm to the degree necessary for the plant to grow. Any plant whose nature requires water is kept in water so that it flourishes. Yet it is a very costly enterprise, for there is always a large group of farmers and gardeners busy working there. There are examples there of all the trees and plants of the world! Anyone who is a physician or apothecary, or who is a student, can go there to examine the plants, and in this way its maintenance becomes expensive.
>
> From there we went to the gardens at Christchurch, which is a grand place full of trees and water channels. Every day the students go there to wander the avenues that cross the garden so that their brains

do not burn up with the effort of their studies. In all truth, it is a place like paradise.

The students' tour of the garden occurred immediately after they attended the degree ceremony, and given their feelings of being slighted by the ceremony's grandees, they may have retired to some shady corner in wounded consolation. In any case, they were clearly heartened and impressed: Mirza Salih extolled the trees, flowers, and spice plants carried there from all over the globe. Noticing the technological novelties that could be seen at work even amid England's nature, he praised the ingenuity of greenhouses that re-created the sultry climate of the Indies. Recognizing the difference between this university garden and the pleasure gardens of London, he remarked on the expense of maintaining it so as to aid the studies of Oxford's apothecaries and physicians. His observation was quite correct. Although the botanic garden had been founded for "the improvement of learning" on the site of the old Jewish cemetery almost two centuries earlier in 1621, it was only from the early nineteenth century that it entered its heyday as a center for the new botanical sciences. At the time of the students' visit, it was kept under the supervision of Dr. George Williams of Christ Church, who was professor of botany at the university between 1795 and 1834. However, in the years running up to the *mirzas'* arrival, it was effectively Sir Joseph Banks (whom Mirza Salih had already seen presiding over "the philosophers of London" at the Royal Society) who was responsible for the garden's orientation toward new scientific purposes, "botanic" rather than "physic." As a result, the reign of George III saw the importing to the Oxford garden of no fewer than seven thousand species of exotic plants. In 1789 alone, the primogenitors of all modern chrysanthemums and roses arrived there via London's dockyards, living plants that would complement the seventy-four volumes of specimen books earlier bequeathed to the garden by Charles Dubois, the erstwhile treasurer of the East India Company.

Whether Mirza Salih and Mirza Ja'far ever inspected such drawings we do not know, though their architect friend Robert Abraham was married to the flower painter Eliza Brown (herself the daughter of the celebrated botanical artist, Peter Brown). Since Mirza Salih knew Mr.

Abraham's sister, there is no reason why he should not also have been introduced to his wife when he traveled with him through his native Devonshire. We do know that Mirza Salih was being exposed to the new ways of studying natural phenomena, for as we have already seen, Mr. Garrett in London had given him lessons in the natural sciences that he had himself studied for his degree. There were also more direct connections between the Iranians and great botanist Sir Joseph Banks. Not only had Mirza Salih recorded seeing Sir Joseph in his diary, but while he and Mirza Ja'far were visiting Oxford, Sir Joseph was in London putting together a collection of seeds to be sent to the shah of Iran. Given that several of the students—namely Mirza Salih and the medical students Hajji Baba and Mirza Riza—studied the natural sciences, there is a good chance that it was to one of them that the seeds were entrusted when they set off home. In a letter written to the foreign secretary Lord Castlereagh (who as we have seen had by this time taken a close interest in the students), Sir Joseph stated that he had collected seeds for the shah from the Royal Botanical Gardens in Kew and had stored them at his house on London's Soho Square. Since Sir Joseph's address at 32 Soho Square lay a short walk from where several of the students were living by 1818 on Soho's King Street, there is every chance that the garden in Soho Square was one of the garden squares that Mirza Salih described visiting in his diary. And why not? For in Soho Square's gardens, Sir Joseph had introduced various exotic flora, including almond, peach, and rose trees, along with fragrant lilacs and jasmine. It was the sweetest smelling square in an increasingly smoky city.

With his studies with Mr. Garrett and his awareness of Sir Joseph's new botanical science, Mirza Salih may have appreciated the recently collected oriental trees that were also growing in the Oxford botanic garden at the time of his visit with Mirza Ja'far. These included a Chinese white mulberry (or "silkworm") tree that had been planted there in 1800; a Pagoda tree in 1817; and, in the same year of their visit, a Himalayan Spruce. Perhaps these very trees were "the trees and plants of the world" that he wrote of in his diary. Even so, the two students arrived a decade too early to see the collection of over two thousand plants from Iran that were presented to the garden by Pierre Martin

Remi Aucher-Éloy (1792–1838) in the 1830s before his death in Isfahan, near Mirza Salih's home city of Shiraz.

Mirza Salih's reaction to the enclosed botanic garden was therefore one of scientific as much as aesthetic delight, distinguishing his reaction from the traditional Iranian notion of the walled garden or *chaharbagh* as above all a place of love, wine, and song. Such attitudes were by no means alien to Oxford, and a century before the students' visit the botanic garden was lauded in panegyric verse:

> All Plants which Europe's Fields contain;
> For Health, for Pleasure, or for Pain;
> . . . By Danby Planted, Bobart Till'd,
> Delightful scientifick Shade!
> For Knowledge, as for Pleasure made.

But as Mirza Salih and Mirza Jaʿfar realized, they were now not so much in the age of the poetic garden as that of the scientific garden that had been celebrated in the famous poem, *The Botanic Garden*, by Erasmus Darwin (1731–1802). Whether through the Royal Botanic Gardens at Kew (established in 1759) or Calcutta's botanic garden (established in 1787), it was an age in which gardens became storehouses for the horticultural plunder of empire as new seeds and cuttings were carried there by the thousand for investigation. As the students recognized, the garden was being transformed from the setting of poetry to the setting of science.

This is not to say that pleasure gardens were not an important aspect of England's imperial expansion during the nineteenth century, and one of the first things that Sir Gore Ouseley had done on reaching Tehran in 1812 was to establish such a garden, known as the *bagh-i ilchi*, or "ambassador's garden." In line with Sir Gore's cosmopolitan style as a man between worlds, "the smaller garden . . . was laid out in an English style, with paved walks and formal flower beds, the larger garden across the street was in a more traditional Persian form, a double row of cypresses in the shape of a cross, with fruit trees, pomegranates and plane trees, interspersed with vegetables and melons."

Even so, Mirza Salih and Mirza Jaʿfar could recognize that the Oxford garden represented something new and out of step with the traditional gardens of their homeland that during the nineteenth century continued to be built under its Qajar rulers at the Bagh-i Fin outside Kashan and the Bagh-i Shahzadah outside Kerman. Although Iran had a long tradition of physic gardens and pharmacology—and as late as the seventeenth century the medical writings of the medieval Muslim philosopher Ibn Sina were still being taught at Oxford in Latin translation—the new botany that Mirza Salih and Mirza Ja'far learned of was distinct, more like the new science that they and their fellow students were seeking. We do not know whether Hajji Baba and Mirza Riza also inspected the garden (they were studying medicine in London but visited Oxford at least once). It seems likely that they did. In any case, for Mirza Salih and Mirza Ja'far, the botanic garden was no less interesting than it would have been to their medically minded friends. Even so, while they recognized that the garden was a place of scientific study and no mere place for idle pleasures, Mirza Salih's primary agenda remained that of learning languages and history. Though their visit to the garden provided some consolation after the pompous pretensions of the degree ceremony at the Sheldonian Theatre, it would not change the course of their studies. The excitement of exposure to a new way— or rather, infrastructure—of knowledge would have to wait until they left Oxford and traded the academic town for the industrializing country.

From the Garden to the Watermill

Fortunately, on leaving Oxford, Mirza Salih and Mirza Ja'far did not have to look far for the new and more practical form of science. For at the end of their visit to Oxford, they made an excursion to an innovative mechanized paper mill that they had heard was operating in a village to the north of the city. Mirza Salih had already made a brief visit to a paper mill near Exeter during his tour of Devon and so the presence of more mechanized mills near Oxford gave him and Mirza Ja'far the opportunity to take a closer look at the ways in which machines were changing the textual production of knowledge in a way that had not yet happened in their home country. In the weeks after leaving Oxford and its libraries, the young Muslims became aware of the technological infrastructure that underpinned Britain's ability to

Fig. 12. Education Industrialized: Fourdrinier's Papermaking
Machine as Seen at Hampton Gay. Source: *The useful arts and
manufactures of Great Britain* (London, 1846).

issue so many of the books and newspapers that they had come to
admire. As Mirza Salih in particular had come to realize, there can be
no books and newspapers without paper, and so a nation's ability to
produce—and mass produce—books, and thus knowledge, was only as
good as its ability to produce paper. As they set out from Oxford, their
consciousness was changing as these gentlemen students raised among
the courtly classes of Iran came into a new recognition of the merits of
the artisan—the skills, that is, of their companion the *ustad*, or "master
craftsman," Muhammad ʿAli. For in the visit to the paper mill outside
Oxford came a turning point in the trajectory of Mirza Salih's studies.
While he would never abandon his involvement with the study of languages and history, and Mirza Jaʿfar would not change the program set
up for him at the Royal Military Academy, from this point on Mirza
Salih's educational program took an entirely new turn. It all began
with the tours he made of factories, the discussions he held with their
managers, and the new industries (including coal mines) that he described in his diary after leaving Oxford.

Ascertaining which industrializing village Mirza Salih and Mirza
Jaʿfar visited is not an easy task, for at the time there were no fewer
than nine paper mills operating in the villages around Oxford. In one
edition of Mirza Salih's diary, his Arabic letters spell the village's
name as "Weston Lea," but no such village does or ever did exist in
Oxfordshire. One possible contender is the village of Weston-on-the-

Green, which lies around ten miles to the north of Oxford. However, along with other evidence, a closer look at the village name's original spelling in the original manuscript of the diary makes it clear that the village they visited was Hampton Gay, where there was indeed a paper mill. Moreover, it was owned by a man whom Mirza Salih specifically described meeting there: a papermaker by the name of Charles Venables. The confusion in the place names probably originates in Mirza Salih's own misrecollection, conflating the name Hampton Gay with that of the neighboring village of Weston-on-the-Green through which they may have passed on the way. Whatever the reason behind the confusing spelling, Mirza Salih's mention of Charles Venables as the papermaker there confirms beyond doubt the village's identification as Hampton Gay.

At the time, Hampton Gay lay six miles to the north of Oxford; they reached it by post-chaise, Mirza Salih noted. Today it still lies in deep country, and a signpost for Hampton Gay points toward a single-track lane that ends, after a mile or so, at the gateway to a field with no village in sight. Across the field lie the ruins of a long deserted village, of which only the church and the ruined manor house remain in open land dotted with a few outlying farmsteads. The buildings of the paper mill that the students visited have long since disappeared, after it closed down in 1887, an event that brought the loss of the villagers' livelihood and village's subsequent demise. But in 1818, before it fell victim to the great rural exodus of the nineteenth century, Hampton Gay was important enough for our two travelers from Iran to make a special journey there. Their detour was no mere caprice, and the students spent time in deep conversation with the mill-owner. Mirza Salih in particular learned about methods of producing paper suitable for printed books and not only for the handwritten manuscripts that were still being produced in Iran. For the paper mill provided much of the raw material for the publishing industry that disseminated the learning of the nearby university. Today both the mill and village are forgotten by all except county antiquarians. But Mirza Salih deemed the village important enough to record in a diary intended to be read back at court in far Tabriz. There is no record of the visit elsewhere, and today the main other testament to Mr. Venables's papermaking fortune is an engraved cenotaph in the village's abandoned church. Yet in the depths of the Oxfordshire countryside at Hampton Gay, a meeting took place that connected distant Iran to the insular rural England of Jane Austen. Yet such connections are not part of the conventional history of either nation and lie as neglected as the ruins of Charles Venables's mill.

All that remains of the mill today are its two great millstones, just visible through the waters of the river Cherwell; its sluice gates, now wrapped in reeds; and the remnants of the brick casing that once contained the hearse frame for a large water wheel. Still, as the parish records show, for all the rural silence of its modern setting at the dead end of a single-track lane, Hampton Gay was not an agricultural village but a rural industrial center in which the main source of employment was not in farming but in Charles Venables's great mill. As early as 1681, a medieval mill on the river Cherwell was modified for the production of paper by the village's first papermaker John Allen, a shift toward industrialization that generated new wealth in the village, eventually leading to the rebuilding of its Saxon church in 1767 and the increase in its population to eighty-six people by that year. Even then, the presence of the university press at nearby Oxford meant that demand for paper was high. By the time the two students arrived in 1818, some eight other paper mills were active in the villages around Oxford in addition to the one at Hampton Gay. Of these other paper mills, by far the best known was that at Wolvercote, which affords a clearer picture of the forces shaping the paper industry around Oxford at the time of Mirza Salih and Mirza Ja'far's visit. Although Wolvercote had been producing paper since the middle of the seventeenth century, when the university printer Dr. John Fell commended its suitability for his publishing endeavors, it was the half century either side of the *mirzas*' visit that saw Wolvercote mill reach the height of its importance. Given the nature of their interests, they might also have visited the Wolvercote as well as Hampton Gay, since in 1811 a new coal-fed steam engine was established there, an adaptation of the mechanistic new learning for the intellectual ends of book production that would have appealed to Mirza Salih. Yet the students were clearly well-informed as to which mill they should visit and whom they should meet. For having taken over the Hampton Gay mill in 1815, their host

Charles Venables was one of the most important figures in southern England for the industrialization of paper-making.

Though Venables was a keen advocate of mechanization, he was also a staunch defender of the rights of employers over their workers; on several occasions, he wrote to *oppose* the abolition of child labor! His son George was made of no softer stuff. A report in the *Windsor and Eton Express* from 1827 recorded how

> Richard Goodchild, a lad aged 14, was placed at the bar, and arraigned on a charge of having stolen a piece of brass, part of a vat, the property of Mr. George Venables, a paper maker. . . . [It was] ordered the offender to be placed in solitary confinement for one week and whipped.

With Venables and Son, the students' search for the technological foundations of modern knowledge had brought them face-to-face with a proto-Marxist epitome of the capitalist mill owner.

The Hampton Gay parish register and other documentary sources of the time tell us more about the capitalist and his villagers. Charles Venables had married his wife, Sarah, only a few months before meeting the students. Three years later, Sarah gave birth to a son, the aforementioned George, who in classic Victorian fashion later added respectability to his manufacturing background by serving as the church rector at Burch Castle in Norfolk. The parish records also tell us something about the families of rural proletarians, such as Thomas and Sarah Parrot, who were working at the mill when Mirza Salih and Mirza Ja'far made their tour of inspection. It is tempting to identify this Thomas Parrot with the "Mistar Parkat" whom Mirza Salih described as being sent from the mill to escort them to Hampton Gay from Oxford. But as ever, the working classes remain a shadowy presence in history, and to reach for "Mistar Parkat" is perhaps to clutch at a proletarian phantom.

It was in any case not in working men but working machines that the visitors were most interested. The two Muslims were no incipient socialists, for all the tough times they had seen. And they were in luck. For the mill at Hampton Gay was one of Oxfordshire's largest industrial enterprises. Due to the installation of the cogs and rollers of a large steam-powered Fourdrinier machine when Charles Venables took over the mill in 1815, by the time the Iranians toured the mill three years later, it was producing between eight and ten tonnes of paper per week. With Mirza Salih's keen interest in what he described as England's vast print-runs of newspapers—again, no country in the Middle East had any newspapers at this time—it is possible that the Fourdrinier machine motivated his interest in Mr. Venables's mill. For one of the great advantages of the Fourdrinier machine was its ability to produce the continuous rolls of paper that enabled the massive expansion of English newspaper production in the early nineteenth century, seeing the foundation of such politically important newspapers as the *Manchester Guardian* in 1821. Since Henry and Sealy Fourdrinier's papermaking machine only received its British patent in 1801, by the time Mirza Salih and Mirza Ja'far saw it in action in Hampton Gay, the machine had only recently been modified into the second- and third-generation versions that made industrial-scale production reliable. By 1813, fewer than twenty Fourdrinier machines had been made anywhere in Europe, and by the time the students saw one five years later, the total number in existence was still no more than around thirty.

The existence of the Fourdrinier machine at Hampton Gay is rare precise evidence of early Iranian exposure to European industrial technology, almost half a century before the pioneering industrialist Muhammad Amin al-Zarb (1834–98) took note of steam technology during the Mediterranean leg of his pilgrimage to Mecca in 1863. As deliberate as ever in their choice of visitations, Mirza Salih and Mirza Ja'far had chosen well in beating a rural retreat from Oxford to take in Mr. Venables's paper mill. With their inspection of the machinery there, they placed themselves at the forefront of Muslim exposure to the new technology of knowledge underlying the information revolution that, along with newspapers and scientific journals, also rendered possible large print-runs of novels, including Jane Austen's. With its ability to bring the fourfold process of wetting, pressing, drying, and finishing paper into a single mechanized format, the Fourdrinier machine belonged to a strangely quickened world quite distinct from the lengthy manual performance of these same stages of papermaking performed in slow succession by separate groups of artisans in Iran.

Since the earliest recorded Fourdrinier machine in the United States would not be set up till 1827, in terms of theoretical awareness at least, the Iranians' inspection of the machine a full decade earlier placed their country in an unusually dynamic position compared even to America. But of course, at this point, it only was a theoretical awareness: the Fourdrinier machine was far too large, and too costly, for them to take back to Iran. They were, after all, only students with very limited resources.

Yet there were important lessons here nonetheless, including the unexpected connections between industrialization and religion. For, as with the other paper mills in the Oxford area, the main customer of the Hampton Gay mill was the university press. Its massive demand for print-quality white paper had fueled the reinvigoration of the mills in other suburban villages, such as Eynsham, Sandford-on-Thames, and Wolvercote, whose mills were under the management of Venables's rivals, the Swann brothers, who also possessed such machines. Yet the impulse behind the industrializing knowledge industry that the two *mirzas* experienced came from the vast demand for Bibles drummed up by the British and Foreign Bible Society (founded 1804) and the Prayer Book and Homily Society (founded 1812). For in the early decades of the nineteenth century, nearly half of all of the Bibles, prayer books, and service books produced in England were printed in Oxford. By 1820, the university's Bible Press was producing no fewer than 750,000 Bibles per year. Just as the students' host, Dr. Macbride, was a leading evangelical, so were the majority of Oxford's Bibles printed to serve the work of a new generation of missionaries. Around two-thirds of Oxford's Bibles were purchased by the recently founded British and Foreign Bible Society. The name is worth remembering, for in later chapters we will see Mirza Salih having much more to do with the Bible Society, to use its shorter name.

Fueled by the evangelical demand for the mass production of prayer books and Bibles, it was an odd kind of industrial modernity that the Iranians encountered. But with the religious motivations that were the unexpected power behind its steam engines, the mill at Hampton Gay formed a fitting point of departure for the next leg of their adventures among the industrializing religious communities of the English West

Country. As they were recognizing, divine power and steam power were inseparable in Jane Austen's England. And so, to understand English science, they would also need to understand English religion.

Coming Down

For all their determination, and despite their efforts to cultivate the support of Dr. Macbride, Mirza Salih and Mirza Ja'far were never to study at Oxford. Beyond what we have seen, there seem to have been several factors in this turn of events. As ever there was the issue of finances, though as we have seen, by the time they traveled to the university, they had a circle of wealthy supporters behind them, including Sir Gore Ouseley and even Lord Castlereagh. Despite the challenges of matriculating a foreign Muslim at the university, the idea of sending foreign non-Protestants to study at Oxford was not without precedent. As is so often the case in such matters of principle, financial incentives could often overcome them. It was not the East India Company that provided these earlier incentives for relaxing the rule, but rather the Levant Company, its London-based counterpart that was dedicated to trade with the Middle East. As early as 1699, the Levant Company had attempted to establish a "Greek College" at Oxford with the intention of providing an English education to young Turkish-speaking Greeks from Constantinople. The aim was to teach them enough about the English language and commercial topics to serve the Levant Company as interpreters and middlemen. The scheme did in fact run for a few years till its demise in 1705, and at least ten Greeks from what is now mainland Turkey were sent to study in Oxford. With their upbringing in the culturally "Islamicate" society of the Ottoman Empire, they may be counted as forbears of the Iranian students sent to England a century later. Though the Greeks were of course Christian, they are evidence that despite its ultimate failure, the plan of the two Muslims and their London supporters to study at Oxford was not entirely fantastical. But whatever the possibilities may have been, the attempt to win over Dr. Macbride had not worked. Like many later hopeful applicants to Oxford, they had failed at the interview stage. And like other such failed applicants since, they could console themselves with the thought that the university did not teach the subjects that most interested them.

If their university plans had not worked out, the young Muslims lost none of their ambitions to master the knowledge of the English. Through their visit to the paper mill, they had now developed an interest in mechanical techniques that had not been on their original learning agenda as described in Mr. D'Arcy's letter from Tabriz back in 1815. And despite their earlier conception of England as a place of the *ʿulum-i jadid*, or "new sciences," their time spent with devotedly Christian scholars such as Olinthus Gregory and John Macbride was convincing them of the importance of understanding English religiosity if they were to make sense of England's economical and political achievements, achievements they hoped to transfer back to Iran. Once again making best of their limited options, instead of returning directly to London, Mirza Salih and Mirza Jaʿfar continued westward from Oxford into the uncharted regions of provincial England, leaving their fellow Iranians to continue with their studies in London. In the next chapter, we will follow the two travelers on that next leg of their expedition as they moved away from the varsity's establishment Anglicans toward the remoter towns of England's religious minorities. It would be a journey among the Dissenters.

Faith

3

~

Among the Dissenters

Into Darkest Gloucestershire

After completing their nine months of private language lessons with Reverend John Bisset in Croydon, and ably conversing with the professors of Oxford, Mirza Salih and Mirza Ja'far had by now mastered the English language. Speaking the decorous idioms of the Austenite natives, they were ready to adopt the ethnographer's method for a tour of the West Country. Mirza Salih's diary entries for the following weeks were filled with references to the strange peoples and places they encountered on what was an unprecedented Middle Eastern exploration of the backwaters of Jane Austen's England. On leaving Oxford in the middle of October 1818, they first set off for the fashionable spa town of Cheltenham. They would have left Oxford on the Cheltenham or "Isis" coach, which departed from the Angel Inn in Oxford and arrived in Cheltenham at the Plough Hotel. Advertisements for stage-coaches leaving the Angel (including their running times) were published most days in the Oxford newspapers, particularly the main "town" weekly *Jackson's Oxford Journal*, and so with his keen interest in newspapers Mirza Salih would have found such practical local knowledge easy to gather. Indeed, an advertisement for both the Angel Inn (offering "accommodation inferior to none") and the times of the coaches running from there (including the daily Cheltenham coach) appeared in *Jackson's Oxford Journal* on October 17, 1818 when they were staying in the city.

Once they reached Cheltenham, the students spent a night in an inn, perhaps the Plough itself. Though today less famous than Bath, and less fashionable even then, Cheltenham Spa was one of Regency England's most important little cities for the fashionable and well-to-do. Eighteen months before Mirza Salih and Mirza Ja'far arrived there, Jane Austen had spent several months convalescing in Cheltenham during what was to prove her final illness. The spa town was also fast becoming a haven for Persian-speaking former servants of the East Indian Company seeking to relax or retire on their return from the East. It was fitting, then, that it was in this setting that Mirza Salih described meeting the former envoy to the shah, James Morier, whom he already knew from his journey with the Ouseley embassy and from previous meetings in London. Having been born and raised at Smyrna (modern Izmir) in the Ottoman Empire, where he lived till he was twenty-six, he must have given the travelers a sense of familiarity. Nor was this the first time that Morier had hosted Iranians in England, for he had earlier accompanied Ambassador Abu'l-Hasan on a two-day visit to Bath. Since Mr. Morier would soon become famous as the author of the *Hajji Baba* novels, the encounter with the two students was somewhat ironic, since it led to the literary lampooner of an imaginary Iranian's tours of England himself featuring in the travel diary of a very real Iranian. It is perhaps a pity that Mirza Salih was too fond of the English to write critically of his host, and make a preemptive strike at Mr. Morier. After all, the latter may have based his own "fictional" Hajji Baba on Mirza Salih and Mirza Ja'far's medical student friend, Hajji Baba. And twenty years later, Morier even wrote a novel called *The Mirza*! But the students' call on him had an amicable motive. For around seven years after their original meeting on the Ouseley embassy, he and Mirza Salih were old friends, or at least old acquaintances. They were each interested in one another and would each, in some form, come to write of one another in future years.

Cheltenham was not the only spa town that Mirza Salih and Mirza Ja'far visited on their tour of the West Country; they also, of course, went to Bath. There they reached the mannered epigone of Jane Austen's novels, the city where the novelist herself lived from 1801 to 1806. It was there that Miss Austen set two of her most famous works, *Northanger Abbey* and *Persuasion*; both were first published in 1818, the same year that the two Muslims were visiting Bath. The timing of their arrival was impeccable.

Mirza Salih described the city in his diary:

The city of Bath is in a region called Somersetshire and lies 109 miles from London. It is famous for the fact that, from ancient times to the present day, hot waters flow there that are beneficial for treating illness. Any sick person who goes there gets better. For this reason, people come there from every part of England, and stay there especially during summertime. They have built six *hammams* around the hot waters, and in those *hammams* the hot water flows directly out of the ground. Men and women go together to the same *hammam*. But so that it is not unseemly, the women wear dresses that cover their entire bodies. Bath also has a large and splendid theater. Parallel to it, there are two large halls where the people of the town go to dance and host parties. The entire city is built from the same white stone. When it is brought from the mountain, the stone is still soft so that it can be carved like wood into any shape one desires. All of the streets and houses are built symmetrically and the walkways are also carpeted with stone. Except for Saint Petersburg, I have never seen so fine a city.

It was perhaps not the most eloquent of eulogies, but then, in a letter to her sister Jane Austen had written even more plainly that, "The first view of Bath in fine weather does not answer my expectations." In *Persuasion*, she refracted her dislike into her heroine Anne Elliot, who similarly disliked the city's shallowness. But if Miss Austen had a low opinion of the city, Mirza Salih begged to differ, at least by focusing on its architectural merits. Better traveled as the young Iranian was, he could make a forceful comparison, having passed through Saint Petersburg en route to England.

Still, he and Mirza Jaʿfar were certainly witnessing the key spaces of Miss Austen's recently published novels: his "two large halls where the people of the town go to dance" were the Upper and Lower Rooms, the latter being where Catherine Morland meets Henry Tilney in *Northanger Abbey*. The Muslims were also open to other experiences that the city had to offer, including the peculiar native medicines: Mirza Salih noted how he and Mirza Jaʿfar went to the Grand Pump Room to drink some of the mineral water that made Bath fashionable and famous. They also strolled through the famous Royal Crescent that was the city's most famous architectural feature and tried to take in a theater performance, but found to their disappointment that the "house of spectacles" was closed. It was not "the season."

Fortunately, we are able to supplement Mirza Salih's diary with an extract of a newspaper article that appeared in *The Times* in December 1818 and gave further account of his and Mirza Jaʿfar's time in Bath.

The newspaper report recounts how "accompanied by G. H. Gibbes, Esq., they visited the various buildings, pump-rooms, &c. In the evening, they had a warm bath, and appeared much delighted with the extraordinary phenomenon of the hot-springs." Like European ethnologists later in the century, Mirza Salih and Mirza Ja'far quizzed local experts about various aspects of life outside the capital. They were especially curious about why the waters of Bath were considered so special, a question that they may have posed to the two distinguished physicians they met. For their escort and local informant in Bath was the physician Sir George Gibbes (1771–1851). Until his appointment as the private physician to Queen Charlotte, Sir George served as honorary physician to the Bath General or Mineral Water Hospital and had previously written two learned treatises on the Bath waters. We also know that while they were in Bath the students met Sir James Fellowes (1771–1857), the physician-extraordinary to the prince regent; he later recollected seeing them strolling through the city "dressed in the costume of their country . . . one in a scarlet and gold pelisse, the other blue." While flaunting their exoticism in the Regency's dandiest fashion center, the students were skillful in their choice of precisely which elements of Persian clothing to adopt. For the "pelisse"—as Sir James described their outer garment—was a short fur-trimmed or fur-lined jacket that was extremely fashionable at the time, especially when made with the kinds of rare and foreign pelts that the students' carried from Persia. The letters of Jane Austen contain many references to her own pelisses. Appropriately enough, the same year that the students were in Bath, the pelisse appeared in her *Persuasion*, when the heroic Captain Wentworth declared to Miss Musgrove that he "had no more discoveries to make than you would have as to the fashion and strength of any old pelisse, which you had seen lent about among half your acquaintance ever since you could remember."

Fashionable as they were, the two Muslim students were in much demand in Bath. On December 1, they were invited for dinner at the home of the society hostess and literary patron, Mrs. Hester Piozzi (1741–1821). Since her guests often included the likes of Samuel Johnson and Oliver Goldsmith, her dinner parties were true soirées. The students handled the occasion with élan. In a letter Mrs. Piozzi subse-

Fig. 13. (Not So) Dark Satanic Mills: Belvedere Mill, Stroud Valley. Source: Photo by
Jen Whiskerd.

quently wrote to a friend, she found it "astonishing to see how they
have mastered our language and caught up our European manners."
Indeed, so socially polished was their performance that she declared
them "really a little *better* bred than the rest of the company." Throughout their days in Bath, they were treated as honored guests ("distinguished personages," as the *Gloucester Herald* described them a few
days later). They were received by Bath's most dignified burghers and
elite hostesses, whom they interviewed in turn in their quest for
knowledge about the English.

Like his old friends the Ouseley brothers, whom he had watched as
they noted the behavior of his fellow countrymen on their journey
through Iran, Mirza Salih sought more than a theoretical knowledge
about the life of the Christian English. He sought ethnographic knowledge as well, knowledge of how England's different kinds of Christians
actually lived. For Mirza Salih and Mirza Ja'far were now setting off to
meet the less familiar sects that flourished in the industrializing hill

towns of the rural West Country. As they had already sensed from their inspection of Mr. Venables's mechanized mill, this was a region in which religion and industry were partners.

Millworkers and Moralists

On October 17, 1818, they paid a visit to one of the many silk mills in the valleys around Gloucester. Although Mirza Salih had already looked around a pottery and cloth manufactory during his earlier tour of Devonshire, their significance does not seem to have struck him at the time. But by now, several years into his and Mirza Ja'far's time in England, the economic impact of such factories had become more clear to them, with the inspection of the steam-powered paper mill a few days earlier having especially captured their imagination. From this point onward during their time in England, they would devote more attention to such new industries and technologies, which were increasingly noted in Mirza Salih's diary. In what was perhaps the first ever mention of a train in any Persian text, near one cloth factory they visited somewhere between Cheltenham and Gloucester he briefly described seeing one of the world's first railroads. As he scribbled down in his diary, "all along the route an 'iron road' has been built with a carriage that carries coal and other loads and which moves easily along the iron rails." Since this was just over a decade after the world's first steam locomotive was invented—built in 1804 for the Penydarren ironworks in South Wales by the engineer Richard Trevithick (1771–1833)—it is highly unlikely that the two Muslims saw a steam-powered train. Though Mirza Salih did not expressly say so, as with other early railways, the carriages he described were probably pulled by horses. What he and Mirza Ja'far were seeing, then, was a technology in transition. For through the demand for "warhorse fuel," the Napoleonic Wars had made fodder more and more expensive, creating incentives to find alternative energy sources for the pulling of carts and carriages. So it was that engineers tinkered with Trevithick's invention, leading to tracks for several pioneering steam trains being laid around collieries between 1812 and 1814, albeit mainly in the north of England. The students had not seen one of these steam trains; none at that time could anyway run as far as the distance Mirza Salih described. Even so, the very idea that horses could be made to pull far heavier loads by running their carriages on rails would have appealed enormously to Mirza Ja'far, whose studies with Dr. Gregory were based on the geometrical principles of civil engineering. Even without steam, they were early witnesses to a technology that, though it would soon transform the world, would not reach their own country for more than a century.

Since they would have been traveling on the Gloucester-Bristol toll road that had opened in 1780, and since this road passed through Nailsworth and Stroud, it is likely that it was at either or both of these industrializing villages that they visited the cloth mills described in the diary. Both villages were at this time beginning to mechanize their traditional textile production, and by 1818 Nailsworth alone had six mechanized factory mills. That the two students saw such machines is clear from the diary, where in several places Mirza Salih mentioned them watching the great steam-powered wheels that were their most striking feature. The working of these strange and noisy contraptions puzzled and intrigued them, and we know that in at least one of the cloth factories they visited they spent five hours inspecting its mechanized production methods.

During those years, the remote valleys through which they passed around Stroud were centers of innovation. When the Stroud Valley's King's Stanley mill opened in 1813, it was one of the world's first iron-framed buildings, adopting the fireproof construction methods pioneered slightly earlier at the Ditherington flax mill farther north. They may also have passed Belvedere mill, one of several cloth factories operating in the village of Chalford; at the time, the Belvedere was supplying its hardwearing and weatherproof broadcloth to the East India Company. The mills must have been extraordinary sights; up to five stories high, they were the world's first recognizably modern factories. By avoiding timber entirely, they could be built taller while at the same escaping the fires that destroyed many similar commercial enterprises, especially those that dared invest in coal-burning steam engines. Even so, with the recent loss of the East India Company's trade monopoly over India and amid the post-Waterloo recession, Gloucestershire's mills were suffering at the time of the Iranians' visit, spurring its millworkers into some of the first ever industrial strikes. Pouring fuel on the fires of protest, Nailsworth and Stroud were also Baptist and Quaker centers. The students had finally entered Dissenter country.

The entries written in Mirza Salih's diary during the next few weeks are records of an important moment of discovery and contact. For the period from around 1770 to the Great Reform Act of 1832 saw the Enlightenment principle of religious tolerance becoming a reality on English soil, liberating the Methodists and Baptists, leading to the rise of the Unitarians and, finally, to the emancipation of the Catholics in 1829. In arriving at this turning point in the pluralization of England's religious landscape, the students' timing was impeccable, making them among the earliest Muslim explorers of Christian dissent. Not only does Mirza Salih appear to have been one of the first—perhaps the very first—Muslim to write about such dissenting groups as the Unitarians and Methodists. He was also writing about the minority religious sects of England when only a handful of English savants had even heard of the Shi'ites and Sufis of Iran. Only in 1815, with the publication of his friend Sir John Malcolm's *History of Persia*, had nonexperts first heard of such "Sheahs" and "Soofies." Mirza Salih and Mirza Ja'far's fieldwork among small-town dissenters sets them aside from slightly earlier Indo-Persian travelers to England like the aforementioned Abu Talib and I'tisam al-Din, whose travels were limited mainly to London and Oxford and whose accounts of English religion were generalizing rather than ethnographical. Even Ambassador Abu'l-Hasan had become very quickly bored on his rapid tour of the provinces, leaving his chaperone James Morier to complain that he had sulked his way through the last stops on their itinerary. In this way, Mirza Salih's diary records the other side of an ethnographical dialogue made possible in the early nineteenth century by the reciprocal journeys of Middle Eastern Muslims to England and of Christian Englishmen to the Middle East. Muslims were involved in the creation of the new discipline of ethnography; and, with their notebooks at the ready, they were as keen to describe the Unitarians of rural England as the likes of Sir John Malcolm were to scribble the cryptic mutterings of the Sufis.

It was not until the students entered the religiously diverse countryside around Gloucester that they came into contact with the divisive sects of the West Country. This is no mere hyperbole: the economy and geography of Gloucestershire's steep valleys had combined to rear a culture of independent-minded millers among whom Dissent had long flourished.

Mirza Salih was becoming increasingly interested in England's Christian religion, or rather religions. Having already studied with churchmen such as Reverend John Bisset, by the time he and Mirza Ja'far set off for the West Country, he was well versed in the theological differences between what he termed as the various "sects," or *firqa*, of Christianity. Now he would see those differences in living day-to-day practice. In describing such diversity, he was not blind to the politics of tolerance that enabled it to flourish in England. Elsewhere in the dairy, he wrote in detail about the flight of foreign Protestant refugees to London during the previous century and how they were allowed to settle there. He had also met Catholics during his earlier journey through Devonshire and summarized their beliefs and standing in England as a religious minority. He also penned a brief but accurate summary of the differences between Catholics and Protestants, noting that while Catholics revered statues of Jesus and the Virgin Mary, and even made pilgrimages to places where special statues were venerated, Protestants regarded such practices as forbidden and did not place any such images in their churches. He had read a Catholic catechism and was fully aware that, unlike Protestants, Catholics also believed that the bread and wine of the mass were truly transformed into the flesh and blood of Christ. His exposure to the more relaxed compromises of the Church of England led him to recognize that the English should not be considered fanatical idol-breakers, because they were happy to leave statues intact when they considered them to have artistic value.

After visiting the Quaker-owned mills around Stroud, later that same day in October Mirza Salih and Mirza Ja'far entered Gloucester. They soon made the acquaintance of a "holy and ascetic woman" who belonged to a sect called "Methodists," Mirza Salih transcribing the unfamiliar word phonetically into Arabic script. In view of the fact that till around 1850 Methodists were something of a rarity in the West Country, the Iranians were tapping into what in 1818 was only a nascent movement in Gloucester. The woman they met—a Miss Bleechley—asked the two Muslims to read to her from the Bible in English, an activity they embraced with the ethnographic vigor of the participant-observer. As any fieldworker soon learns, though, the implications of this kind of cultural immersion are all too predictable: from the evidence of Mirza Salih's diary, Miss Bleechley appears to have then attempted to convert the two travelers to Christianity (and of a Methodist kind at that). After what we can imagine were awkward explanations and hurt feelings, she gave up her efforts and instead invited the two strangers to her house for supper in what was perhaps a pioneering instance of proselytizing "flirty fishing." Happily, when they got there, they found themselves in the company of a group of young, unaccompanied women. Happy that the sermonizing was over for the day, they stayed gossiping and laughing till one in the morning. It is one of the most charming images in Mirza Salih's diary, a reversal of the more familiar trope of the European ethnographer among the easygoing maidens of the Pacific.

The next day, Miss Bleechley took her new friends to see the great cathedral in Gloucester. It was a city with whose resonance in English history Mirza Salih was already familiar from the detailed studies of England's history he had redacted into his diary during the summer. With its Anglo-Saxon origins, its carved pagan vestiges by way of green men and unicorns, its place in the ancient mythology of Albion, Gloucester cathedral struck the students' imagination sharply. It was after all a vestige of a very different England from the neoclassical townscapes through which they had largely moved up to this point, a more archaic and autochthonous England than that of the calm Grecian colonnades of Cheltenham and Bath. Observing their pensive perambulation of the cathedral, a reporter for the *Gloucester Herald* wrote that "the sublime and beautiful architecture of the holy pile appeared to impress them with reverence for its pious use." A few years had now passed since the whole student party had visited their first English cathedral at Rochester in the company of Mr. D'Arcy. Since then, Mirza Salih and Mirza Ja'far had gained a much better understanding of the importance of these ancient churches. Mirza Salih noted the fact that several of England's kings lay buried in Gloucester cathedral and that its "bishop" (transcribing the English word into Persian) was one of England's twenty-four such "masters of the faith."

After touring the cathedral, the two fieldworkers fulfilled their ethnographic duties of interviewing its "master of the faith" by being introduced to the Bishop of Gloucester. The prelate in question was the Honourable Henry Ryder DD, *in cathedra* between 1815 and 1824. In reflection of Miss Bleechey's "enthusiasm," Bishop Ryder was the first evangelical ever appointed to an episcopal see. When a branch of the British and Foreign Bible Society was founded in Gloucester in 1812, Bishop Ryder had been one of its chief supporters. We may, then, suppose that he gave his Muslim guests a stern lecture on the superior merits and morals of Christianity. It was, after all, only eight years since the evangelicals had sent Reverend Henry Martyn to Shiraz as the first British missionary to Iran. But Mirza Salih was far from overawed with the hectoring bishop: he described him as a short and mean if at least good-mannered man.

Next Miss Bleechley took the two travelers to the county jail. Here she introduced them to one of the more curious pastimes of the Regency's religious revival by which, from John Wesley onward, born-again Christians made moralizing tours of penitentiaries and prisons. Still, the effect seems not quite to have been as intended: rather than piously pitying the poor prisoners, Mirza Salih was pleasantly surprised by their clean private cells and regular periods of outdoor exercise. Such conditions compared favorably with his own expectations of a criminal's lot. Still, this was more than a newcomer's naïveté, since the previous twenty years had seen a swathe of new prisons built all over England. And though during the depression that followed Waterloo, their proletarian inmates were increasingly interned for common theft, there is no doubt that the reformed prisons were an improvement on the oubliettes and dungeons of former days.

Over the next few days, Miss Bleechley continued to escort the two Muslims through her city and its surroundings. In view of their interests, she agreed to balance the pious tours of prisons and churches with inspections of factories, one of which Mirza Salih recorded as having five hundred workers. The *Gloucester Herald* report identifies these factories specifically: they were the Cloth Manufactory of Messrs. Davis, Beard, and Davis and the Pin Manufactory of Messrs. Durnford and Co. We know that Mirza Salih had by now sold his own Persian shawls in London, though it's unclear whether he and Mirza Ja'far collected specimens of the rainproof machine cloaks of Gloucester. We do at least know that an export report from the Levant Company had lately declared them "very suitable for the Persian winter." Whether they did any shopping or not, the students were entering one of the birthplaces of the industrial revolution, moving among circles of silk and cotton weavers that were hotbeds of Dissent. In the very weeks surrounding their visit, a battle of letters raged in the same *Gloucester Herald* newspaper in which their arrival was itself reported. An anonymous Anglican polemicist condemned the doctrines of local Dissenters and tried to prevent Gloucester residents from sending their children to Dissenter Sunday Schools. It was an assault that the minister of Gloucester's Unitarian chapel, Reverend Theophilus Browne (1763–1835), saw as an attack on religious liberty and penned a series of letters to the *Herald* in turn. Bishop Ryder, the "short and mean" man whom the students had just met, stirred further controversy by publically condemning all who dissented from the Church of England. The two Muslims had walked right into the middle of a sectarian conflict. We can only guess what unintended contribution they made to it by their own "heathen" presence.

Bluestockings and Bible Classes

Taking leave of their female informant Miss Bleechley, the next day Mirza Ja'far and Mirza Salih took a stagecoach to Bristol. There, a world away from the *madrasas* that Mirza Salih had described in Oxford, they spent a long day touring the ironworks and bottle and crystal factories that represented the mechanical modernity they had been sent to England to search for. Here in the West Country, they were finally moving beyond the mannered world of Miss Austen and entering a sootier, more divided England of religious dissenters and factory workers.

Shortly after arriving in Bristol, they were told by their host—Mirza Ja'far's teacher from the Royal Military Academy Dr. Olinthus Gregory who had come from London to meet them—about a learned and religious woman by the name of Hannah More, who lived in the hamlet

of Barley Wood outside Bristol. Clearly, they could not flee evangelicalism for the Methodist factory floor so easily, for Dr. Gregory was
determined to steer their provincial travels toward what he saw as
properly pious ends. Still, there were other lessons to be had. That they
were able to visit Mrs. More deep in the countryside was itself a result
of the dramatic improvement of roads around Bristol that had taken
place since 1816, when the region's large turnpike trust was placed
under the management of John Loudon McAdam (1756–1836). The father of the eponymous material "tarmac," MacAdam had recently pioneered a new technique for laying durable roads more cheaply and
quickly than his better known rival, Thomas Telford. The state of England's toll roads was one of Mirza Salih's favorite subjects, so we might
imagine that along the way he asked Dr. Gregory more questions
about tarmac than the Holy Trinity.

So once again, the students' timing was impeccable, allowing them
to take a comfortable ride in a post-chaise along MacAdam's new
roads to see the wise old woman of Barley Wood. As one of the original "bluestockings," Hannah More (1745–1833) is the most interesting
Englishwoman to appear in Mirza Salih's diary. An habituée of London's theatrical circles in her youth, she turned away from a successful career as a dramatist and poet to write "useful" literature in the
service of girls' education and other good causes. A pioneer educa-
tionalist, along with her sisters she helped establish a successful academy for girls in Bristol as well as the so-called Mendip Schools, which
served as a West Country version of the Sunday School movement
that had originally developed in the north of England. Despite the
social activism of her middle years, Mrs. More never lost the skills she
had developed in writing for the stage, and in addition to her lengthy
tomes on girls' education, conformist "village politics" and matters of
morality, she also produced a vast number of moralizing tracts; one
biographer puts their number at no fewer than 114. At a time when
Jane Austen was publishing her novels anonymously, Hannah More
was a literary celebrity through her authorship of such hugely successful works as her didactic novel *Coelebs in Search of a Wife* (1809).
But she was not without her critics. Although *Coelebs* went through
eleven British editions in less than a year (and soon went through
thirty in America), no lesser a literary contemporary than Jane Austen

Fig. 14. Jane Austen's Nemesis: The Moralizing Hannah More.
Source: "Memoirs of the life and correspondence of Mrs. Hannah More" by
William Roberts (London, 1835).

herself declared of it simply, "I dislike it." For as a close friend of William Wilberforce and the same bishop of Gloucester the Iranians had just met, Mrs. More was a committed evangelical, the kind of enthusiastic Christian that Austen disliked.

Yet Mrs. More was also a pragmatic and above all a *practical* woman, willing to work with High Church Anglicans and outright Dissenters if it meant achieving her tangible goal of bringing a Christian education to the children of rural England. On their trip through what evangelicals saw as the West Country's semiheathen villages, the two Muslims were thus in the company of a promoter of literacy and religious reform. Still, they seem to have admired the form that Mrs. More's zeal took by placing "practical" deeds above the minutiae of theological dispute. It was a time when Iranian Muslims were happy to learn from the faith of English Christians, even if the latter didn't often reciprocate.

For all the religious upheavals that the new Christian missionaries would muster among Muslims worldwide, Mirza Salih's encounters with evangelicals did not push him toward querulous or defensive opinions. His eyes were wide open to the merits of England's Christians. With Mrs. More, he was impressed by a person he considered to be the most capable of women, noting that she had written and published many books of her own and was visited by everyone of importance who passed through the region. He was quite correct. For among other notable visitors, both Wordsworth and Coleridge called on her a few years before Mirza Ja'far and Mirza Salih came knocking. They were treading a distinguished trail to her quiet cottage door.

Describing the visit, Mirza Salih wrote,

> Because she had written a number of books of her own, and printed them as well, everyone—whether foreigners or locals, of high or low standing—came to call on her. She lives in a house twelve miles outside Bristol, set between two mountains and alongside the foot of one of them. It is a lovely setting, surrounded by flowers and odiferous herbs.

This was deep country that was quite literally off the map of Muslim geographical knowledge. In a sense that is no less real than for Europeans in Asia, Mirza Salih and Mirza Ja'far had become ethnographers and explorers of "unknown" terrain which none of their countrymen yet knew.

Accurately estimating her age as seventy years (she was in fact seventy-three), Mirza Salih recorded that Mrs. More lived with her sister (who was to die within months of their visit). He and Mirza Ja'far spent two hours in conversation with her. In model reciprocity, when she asked them about their own faith they explained to her the principles of Islam. They clearly respected her as a woman of learning: "She had a large library," Mirza Salih explained. Then he noted how, when he got up to take his leave, she presented one of her books to Mirza Ja'far and to himself another two-volume book that she had written: "In her own handwriting, she wrote her name for me inside the book." It was on the subject of god-fearing piety, or *taqwa*, he explained; transcribing the words from English into his diary, he wrote down its title, *Practical Piety*.

We are fortunate that Mrs. More also wrote an account of what, even by her standards, was an unusual pair of guests. During the 1830s, the memoir was paraphrased from her now lost diary by her biographer William Roberts. It is worth quoting:

> It was the turn of Persia to be represented at that court [that is, Hannah's cottage], in the persons of two noblemen, who having come to this country with a view to the acquisition of the English language, and an acquaintance with the arts and sciences in which Britain had the fame of superiority, presented themselves at her residence, and were admitted with the respect due to the dignity of their rank and commission. . . . Mrs. More presented her new Persian friends with her work on *Practical Piety*, which they declared they would translate into their language immediately on their return home, and that it should be the first work which should bring into exercise the knowledge they had acquired of the art of printing, and employ the printing press which they were carrying back into their own country. They replied to an interrogatory of Mrs. H. More's, respecting their acquaintance with the sacred volume, that they had read both the Old and New Testament, and that they preferred the books of Isaiah and Job, to any other part. "Then, (replied she,) I presume you feel a special reverence for that person, whose coming is especially predicted in both of these books;" to which they gave a decided assent.

Mrs. More's depiction of the meeting offers a tantalizing contrast to Mirza Salih's, with each confirming the basic details while offering further particulars of their own. Of course, it is by no means certain that the students' offer to publish her book when they returned home was anything more than Persian *ta'aruf* or "politesse" offered to a woman who was clearly an enthusiastic champion of her causes. In any case, no Persian translation or publication of her *Practical Piety* ever appeared. More convincing, though, is the two Muslims' claim to have read the Bible. For despite the fact that they had been sent by 'Abbas Mirza in search of strictly scientific knowledge, the picture we are seeing of the education they were given in England is acquiring a distinctly Christian coloring. For as we are seeing, England was no more the country of pure science that Iranians imagined it to be than Iran was the land of pure mysticism pictured by English readers of Rumi.

In their replies to Mrs. More, the students' choice of the books of Isaiah and Job is an interesting one. Without reading too much into the matter (as Mrs. More herself certainly did!), it does seem possible that their selection of these Old Testament prophets (both also important figures for Muslims) was a strategic answer. It was, perhaps, the kind of equivocation made by many a traveler cornered by a religious enthusiast in a distant land. Most intriguing of all, though, is the choice of Isaiah and the meaning that Mrs. More read into it, smugly assuming that they had chosen this book for the prophecy it made (according to Christian doctrine) of the coming of Jesus as Messiah. What she clearly did not know was that in Muslim tradition, Isaiah 42 is regarded not as a prediction of the coming of Jesus but of the subsequent arrival of Muhammad, the last prophet! In their discussions with this fervent believer who, as a supporter of the Bible Society and other missionary organizations was keen to see signs of Christian faith in her guests, the two young Muslims managed to hoodwink her with a clever answer. It is ultimately up to us how we read their reply. Was it an example of the "pious dissimulation" or *taqiyya* that is permitted to Shiʿite Muslims to protect their faith in difficult circumstances? Or was it just a smart joke about which the two friends enjoyed a good laugh as they wandered away down Mrs. More's garden path?

But before we leave her cottage, Mrs. More's gift of her book *Practical Piety* also deserves our attention, not least because it casts light on the students' readings about "the religion of the English." It is little surprise that it was a copy of this book that she had to hand: *Practical Piety* was one of her most successful works, going through ten editions within the first few years of its publication in 1811. Although like other texts of the Evangelical Awakening, *Practical Piety* emphasized the inward cultivation of devotion over external and ritualistic religion, as its title suggests its main focus was on the "practical" application of piety in the world through the social activism of which Mrs. More was herself a prime example. In her own words from the book, "All the doctrines of the Gospel are practical principles. . . . [Religion] is a life-giving principle. It must be infused into the habit, as well as govern in the understanding; it must regulate the will as well as direct the creed."

In other words, she explained, "Practical Christianity, then, is the actual operation of Christian principles." What was being offered here
was an early manifesto for the "this-worldly" religiosity of social activism that in the course of the nineteenth century transformed not only
much of the Christian world but also, through the foundation of parallel charitable and missionary organizations by Muslims, much of the
Muslim world as well. Mirza Salih's possession of the book—and we
can only presume that his intellectual curiosity led him and perhaps
his friends to actually read it—is evidence for his absorption of new
moral ideas about religion as a practical force for the common social
good. For Iran, which would acquire much more of this ideology
through the Christian medical missions of the later nineteenth century, it is the earliest evidence of its kind.

Yet we should not fall into the trap of seeing the two students as
passive recipients of such Anglican piety. The tenor of Mirza Salih's
diary shows a man determined to acquire on his own terms what was
best and most useful in England's Christian culture. Perhaps Mrs.
More's "practical" personality and book appealed to him through an
elective affinity, for character types are far more recognizable across
different societies than cultural relativity theorists would have us believe. Though there is no sign in Mirza Salih's diary that he or any of
his companions were particularly religious—he does not mention them
praying, let alone fasting or troubling themselves over the light ale
served with every meal—we have no reason to doubt that he remained
a Muslim. Even so, he and his companions were formulating a new
understanding of their faith during their years abroad. And from the
evidence of the diary, it seems to have been a distinctly rationalist one
in line with Mirza Salih's emerging opinions on the harmony of rational knowledge and a just society. In the same way that European religiosity was changing through increasing contact with the wider world,
so the investigations of these thoughtful young Muslims nurtured new
attitudes toward their own faith. If Mirza Salih was impressed by the
writings of Mrs. More, it was not because she convinced him by her
superior arguments but because he felt an affinity between her ideas
and his own.

Though he never committed his private religious opinions to his
diary, we do have evidence for both his and Mirza Ja'far's inclinations

toward the practical kind of piety to which Mrs. More was exhorting her countrymen. For in a newspaper report from *The Times* on December 7, 1818, a month later, we learn that they were not silent observers of English religious life and instead voiced decisive opinions of it: they "observed that the preaching in our churches was wholly mystical; and that in Persia, the reader of the mosque dwelt, in his exhortations to the people, on practical moral duties." On the evidence of our two Muslims traveling and speaking with the English, Mirza Ja'far and Mirza Salih were anything but the stereotypical "mystical Persians" that scores of European scholars would depict through the nineteenth century. On the contrary, in their own reckoning, the mystics were to be found in the parish churches of England.

The students had already been exposed to English religious ideas in the years before their journey through the West Country as a result of their lessons with clergymen such as Reverend John Bisset and the theologically minded mathematician Dr. Gregory. Other newspaper reports help us learn more about the bookish investigations of English religiosity that had preceded their ethnographic journey among the Dissenters. According to *The Times*, "Saleh . . . has read Paley's *Natural Theology*; and both [Mirza Salih and Mirza Ja'far] are curious in their inquiries as to this department of our literature, as well as that of ethics." This is clear evidence of close engagement with Anglican theology, this time not through the writings of a "bluestocking" enthusiast like Hannah More but through William Paley (1743–1805), the man whose ideas lay at the orthodox heart of Anglican doctrine. At the same time as orientalists like Sir William Ouseley were identifying the "sources" and "classics" of Islam, the Muslim students were involved in a parallel intellectual exercise of identifying key works that revealed the beliefs of the English.

Given that for the best part of the nineteenth century, the writings of William Paley would remain at the core of England's university syllabi, Mirza Salih had chosen as good a book as any for unlocking "the English mind." First published in 1802, Paley's *Natural Theology* is now best known for its famous analogy of the universe as a pocket watch, the precision and elegance of whose design inevitably points the rational observer into recognizing an intelligent "watchmaker" rather than sheer chaos standing behind its creation. Building on this claim, in a series of chapters based on observations of comparative anatomy, minerals, muscles, trees and insects, "Watchmaker Paley" constructed his celebrated argument from design to prove that the divine watchmaker was not only an intelligent being, but also a benevolent and personal one. In less than three years between its publication in 1802 and Paley's death in 1805, *Natural Theology* passed through nine editions. It is a perfect example of the religious modernity that in Jane Austen's England sought to fuse rational science with Protestant orthodoxy. Given the fact that *Natural Theology* was not only a best seller but soon also a pillar of the undergraduate syllabus at both Oxford and Cambridge, it would have been an obvious book for the students' tutor in Croydon, Reverend Bissett (himself, as we have seen, an Oxford man), to recommend them. But the book was also the most important English expression of the newly rationalized religion that emerged from the Enlightenment, setting a trend that for the rest of the nineteenth century enabled other thinkers, Christian, Muslim, and Hindu, to formulate new forms of religiosity that could be steered into harmony with science. Mirza Salih's decision to name Paley's book to *The Times'* reporter shows that in the period of his and Mirza Ja'far's West Country journey he was increasingly aware of the importance of rational forms of religion to the industrializing society he saw around him on that trip.

While the writings of Hannah More and William Paley are the only theological works for which we have direct evidence of the students encountering, we can also surmise their familiarity with the ideas (and perhaps the actual writings) of Mirza Riza and Mirza Ja'far's principal teacher, Dr. Olinthus Gregory, who had now joined Mirza Salih and Mirza Ja'far in Bristol. For as well as being a mathematical engineer at the Royal Military Academy, we have also seen that Dr. Gregory was a keen participant in religious debates. Moreover, his ideas were quite distinct from those presented to the students by the Paley-promoting Mr. Bisset in Croydon. For example, in Dr. Gregory's anti-Paleyite *Letters to a Friend, on the Evidences, Doctrines, and Duties of the Christian Religion,* he attempted to fill the widening gap between the new findings of science and the old claims of the Bible with a resolute defense of scriptural authority. He had only just finished writing this book when he took on the Iranian students, so the ideas the book expressed

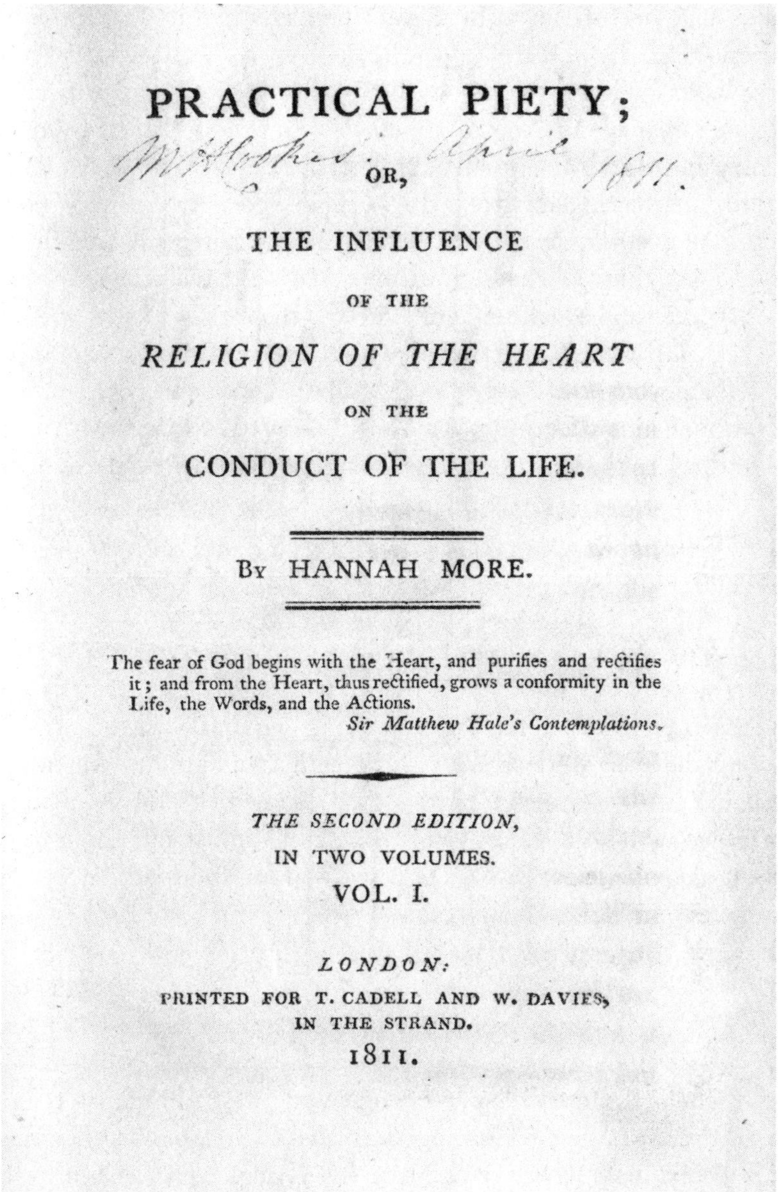

PRACTICAL PIETY;

OR,

THE INFLUENCE

OF THE

RELIGION OF THE HEART

ON THE

CONDUCT OF THE LIFE.

By HANNAH MORE.

The fear of God begins with the Heart, and purifies and rectifies
it; and from the Heart, thus rectified, grows a conformity in the
Life, the Words, and the Actions.
Sir Matthew Hale's Contemplations.

THE SECOND EDITION,

IN TWO VOLUMES.

VOL. I.

LONDON:

PRINTED FOR T. CADELL AND W. DAVIES,
IN THE STRAND.

1811.

Fig. 15. Something to Take Home with You: The Book Hannah More Gave
Mirza Salih.   Source: "Practical piety, or, The influence of the religion of the heart on the
conduct of the life" (London, 1811).

would have been fresh in his mind. We have read in *The Times* how "curious in their inquiries" into theological matters Mirza Salih and Mirza Ja'far were and so it seems likely that they would have discussed with Dr. Gregory his ideas on theology, perhaps on their trip into the countryside to see Mrs. More. Given Mirza Salih's keenness for Paley's *Natural Theology*, a likely subject would have been Dr. Gregory's rejection of Paley's harmonious intellectual accord between faith and science. And why not? Debate is healthy and productive: when nowadays do Christians and Muslims calmly discuss the merits of reason in religion? As *The Times* noted, for their part the students appear to have favored Paley's ideas; they were after all men of science, champions of the rationalist new learning. We can only speculate that as Mirza Salih and Mirza Ja'far rode along those first tarmac roads, they had sufficient courage to counter Dr. Gregory's arguments against their proto-scientific theology.

The picture that is emerging of the students' readings, their opinions about Christianity, and their modernizing sentiments more generally, suggests that it may not be too far wide of the mark to see them becoming religious rationalists themselves. Their "fieldwork" among the Dissenters was helping them form a new religious vision in a similar way that the years their Cheltenham acquaintance Mr. Morier spent in Iran led him to form his own ecumenical universalism. As Morier would later declare, "We are all, great and small, under the direction of God's providence." So it was that, on the road, Englishmen became mystics and Iranians men of reason.

Bristol Religiosa

There would be even deeper engagement with rationalist religion when Mirza Ja'far and Mirza Salih returned to Bristol after their meeting with Hannah More. With Dr. Gregory apparently leaving them alone for much of the time, they spent five days in Bristol in the company of a class of people with whom, after three years in England, they were not yet familiar: the industrializing merchant class. Bristol's merchants had earlier grown rich on the profits of slavery before the evangelicals, in their finest hour, succeeded in abolishing the slave trade eleven years before the students arrived in Bristol. By then, the city's merchants had learned to diversify their interests into the new manufacturing industries. After the medieval quadrangles of Oxford a fortnight earlier, with its newfangled factories, its shipbuilders' docks, its middle-class mansions, Bristol's prosperous modernity appears to have been more to their taste than the ritualistically pompous old varsity. Mirza Salih's notes on Bristol certainly have a verve that was not always present in his diary. We can get a clear idea of the city that he and Mirza Ja'far saw from the 1819 edition of *Mathews's Bristol Guide*: it proudly noted how "the inhabitants of Bristol were very early addicted to trade and manufactures." After their short spell exploring the provincial towns and countryside, the two young men were thrilled to tour a city that was so lively and yet so different from London. They quickly made friends with several merchants and tradesmen, to whom they were introduced through letters of invitation from Miss Bleechley of Gloucester and perhaps also from the Gloucestershire mill owners they had met a few days earlier. Mirza Salih penned a neat ethnographic sketch of the domestic life of the provincial bourgeoisie, describing a house with many rooms of fine furniture, paintings on the walls, and a pretty garden around it. The opportunity came through their invitation to the house of a Mr. Harford. The man in question was a member of Bristol's famous Harford family of Quaker merchants, manufacturers of brassware and former participants in the West African "Guinea Trade." It is likely that the students met the younger John Scandrett Harford (1787–1866), who along with his eponymous father secured the Harfords' admission to the gentry, a social transformation that in religious terms was sealed by John Scandrett's rejection of his simple Quaker roots for the establishment pews of the Church of England. Since the students' factory visits included a tour of a brass works, it may have been Harford's own manufactory—Bristol's leading brass works at the time—that they saw. Mirza Salih noted that "these brass foundries and glass works export their wares throughout Europe and even India."

Describing Bristol in the year the students saw it, the 1819 edition of *Mathews* fills out Mirza Salih's account of their tours of the city's iron and brass foundries, soap factories, and glass works. By 1818, the city's ancient soap industry had expanded to the point of making Bristol the principal supplier of soaps in England. *Mathews also* informs us that there were three significant iron foundries in Bristol at the time, the most important of which was that of John Winwood and Co. And Bristol glass—according to *Mathews,* "the best manufactured in the kingdom"—was being fashioned into many novel shapes. Mirza Salih mentioned in particular a visit to a bottle glass factory, which on the evidence of *Mathews* may have been that of Henry Ricketts and Co. of Cheese Lane, a factory that permitted the public to visit and enjoy the spectacle of glass-blowing. These were by no means the only industrial tours the students made, for as we have seen, a week or so earlier they had inspected one of the new mechanized paper mills outside Oxford and since then toured several cloth mills.

In addition to meeting Mr. Harford, Mirza Salih and Mirza Ja'far received invitations to call on several physicians and other members of the Bristolian bourgeoisie. For their part, the locals were flattered by the Iranians' visit, with an article in a Bristol newspaper seeing fit to describe them as "Persian princes." Once again, a newspaper report helps us fill out the details of Mirza Salih's diary, since it also noted the students touring Bristol's Blind Asylum and its charitable hospital, the Infirmary. At the latter, the report stated that "they seemed affected by the circumstance of a black man being among the patients; and being told that the institution embraced those of every nation and colour, observed that 'this was true charity.'" Whether this "black man" was one of the slaves recently set at liberty in Bristol is unclear, but given the city's key role in the slave trade it seems likely. Perhaps his medical fees were being paid by the one of the "practically pious" Christians who had led the abolitionist movement and who, like Hannah More, expressed their faith in tangible acts of charity. Mrs. More herself spent a good deal of money covering the medical fees of Louisa, "the Mad Maid of the Haystack," at Mr. Henderson's Asylum in Bristol.

Once again, *Mathews* sheds more light on these matters, stating of the Infirmary that "all persons, without regard to country, colour, or dialect, who are accidentally injured, are, on application, immediately admitted, without any recommendation whatsoever." The guide book also relates the purpose of the other charitable institution that the students visited—the Asylum for the Indigent Blind on Bristol's Lower Maudlin Street—as being "to instruct the blind in some useful trade, by which they may be enabled to provide for their own maintenance." Moved by what he saw there, Mirza Salih recorded having a conversation with a blind girl who earned her keep at the Asylum by working as a basket maker. That he was an accurate diarist is confirmed by *Mathews'* note that fine and coarse baskets "are constantly on sale at the asylum."

Mirza Salih and Mirza Ja'far were guided on these tours by a group of men to whom they were introduced by the Gloucester Methodist, Miss Bleechley. For the merchants and tradesmen whose company they kept in Bristol were, like her, members of the growing Dissenter circles of England's new industrial centers. Although the history of Bristol Dissent is less famous than that of Manchester or Birmingham, in the later eighteenth century its religious Dissenters had risen to prominence among the new manufacturing elite. After the students' familiarity with establishment Anglicans like Dr. Gregory and Reverend Bissett, and their recent introduction to Methodism through Miss Bleechley, it was now the turn of the Unitarians to widen their understanding of England's diverse religious life. But first they were to be distracted by a most peculiar sight that temporarily turned their thoughts from the Holy Spirit back to the grosser elements of iron and coal.

A Dockyard Distraction

According to Mirza Salih's diary, he and Mirza Ja'far were taken to the Bristol dockyards and shown what he described as a large ship made of iron. He explained that it was a copy of another ship that had already sailed to Bristol all the way from America by using only the power of steam such that it had no need for sails. And here is the point of interest. For what could the Iranians have seen at this time?

At the time of their visit in 1818, Bristol had not quite been overtaken by Liverpool as the great emporium of Atlantic trade. We have already seen how its links to the former slave trade found echo in their meeting a black person. With Mirza Salih's growing interest in America, whose history he had summarized in his diary that summer, he was intrigued by the Bristol dockyards that for over two centuries had provided England's chief point of contact with its former American colonies. In wandering round the quaysides, the Iranians had arrived at a turning point in both the history of travel across the Atlantic, for the following year, 1819, would witness the first ever steamship crossing of the Atlantic by the American steamer *Savannah*, sailing from Savannah, Georgia, for Liverpool. Hearing of its manufacture over the course of the previous years, the shipbuilders of Bristol had been spurred into action and in 1818, when Mirza Salih and Mirza Ja'far walked through the city's dockyards, Bristol was, with London, the best place in the world to observe the birth of the steamship. With the later establishment of the Great Western Steam Ship Company in 1834 and the launch of the first regular steamship across the Atlantic four years later, Bristol would hand over to Liverpool its control of the ocean. But back in the autumn of 1818, that had not yet happened, placing the two Muslims on the forgotten high-tech West Coast of Jane Austen's England.

The use of steam technology to power boats had been developing since the late eighteenth century: the launch of Europe's steamship era is usually dated to the inaugural journey of the Scottish boat *Charlotte Dundas* in 1802. By the time the Muslim students reached London, there was already a regular steamship service along the Thames that linked the capital to the estuary town of Gravesend, which we saw them visit during their first week in England. Such river-borne steamships were certainly a feature of their English experience, then. But the use of iron to cover ships' hulls was more recent and had only just begun in 1815, when Joshua Horton from the Black Country town of Tipton for the first time clad a canal barge with iron. Horton's bold idea became more famous with the launch of the *Vulcan* in 1819, though neither this nor Horton's barge were powered by steam. Judging from the time and place of Mirza Salih's description, it is unclear which vessel he and Mirza Ja'far could have seen in the Bristol dockyards. For at the time even the *Aaron Manby*, the first ironclad steamship ever built, was still under construction and that was not a Bristol boat. Named after the owner of the Horseley Ironworks in Tipton, where it was designed, the *Aaron Manby* was finally assembled in London's Rotherhithe dockyards, whence it was launched in 1822. So what ironclad ship it was that the students saw that day remains a mystery. But whatever it was, it was clearly at the sharpest cutting edge of the "new sciences" they had been sent so far to discover.

What connected these new technologies to the religious discoveries of their recent travels was the fact that their tours of Bristol's dockyards and factories were guided by members of the Unitarian and Quaker families who led the city's industrialization. The students were already familiar with the use of scientific reasoning to formulate a vision of "rational religion" through reading Paley's *Natural Theology*. But in moving away from the London and Oxford circles that exposed them to Paley's rationalizing but nonetheless orthodox Anglicanism, in Bristol they were meeting Unitarians who were at the forefront of the notion that the "progress" of religious knowledge was the proper spiritual counterpart to the advance of science. The Iranians were entering a heated debate that lies hidden in the establishment Anglicanism of Jane Austen's novels. For while Unitarians were championing the religious paramountcy of reason, the evangelicals were defending the literal word of the Bible's claims to the miraculous flouting of scientific laws. As we have seen, among such literalist defenders of scripture was the students' teacher, Dr. Gregory. Nor were the evangelicals alone in rejecting the brave new world being built by mechanical devices and scientific queries. For the year of Mirza Ja'far and Mirza Salih's visits to Bristol's steam-powered factories was also the year that saw the publication of literature's most famous fable of scientific over-reaching: Mary Shelley's *Frankenstein, or the Modern Prometheus*. As Mrs. Shelley voiced new fears and moral attitudes among the lettered classes toward science, the two Iranians stood at the crest of a wave before which the next generation of Muslim modernists would commit themselves to the *taraqqi* or "progress" of scientific knowledge. Through his observations of the rationalist new creeds emerging from the Dissenting factory yards of Bristol, Mirza Salih was at the genesis of the rationalizing age of Islamic history that in the nineteenth century tried to re-create Islam into a religion in harmony with the discoveries of science. As they moved from the dockyards to the neighboring Unitarian chapel, he and Mirza Ja'far were about to learn about the rationalist Unitarians.

Meetings with Mystics

Their first encounter with the Unitarians seems to have occurred in Bristol on October 23, 1818, when they were taken to visit what Mirza Salih termed a Unitarian *kalisa*, or "church." On entering the church, he described how he saw a man walk up to the pulpit and preach a sermon, to which he and Mirza Ja'far listened, before then being invited to speak with the preacher. Mirza Salih transcribed the preacher's name as *mistar row*, and it seems clear that this was the Unitarian minister John Rowe (1764–1832). Having been brought up in Devon, John Rowe had settled in Bristol in 1798, taking up a position at the Lewin's Mead Chapel beside the hustle-bustle of the quays. As the main Unitarian meeting place in Bristol, Lewin's Mead was the church at which Mirza Salih heard him preach. Since the earliest mention in the chapel records of Lewin's Mead being a Unitarian rather than a Presbyterian meeting place occurred only in 1816, the Iranians were visiting it early in its transformation into an openly Unitarian meeting place. This reflected the fact that it had only been five years earlier, with the passing of the Unitarian Relief Act of 1813, that it had become legal to publicly reject the Anglican doctrine of the Trinity as the Unitarians (as opposed to Trinitarians) did. Just as Sir John Malcolm visited Iran during the years when the "Soofies" were being suppressed, events he described in his 1815 *History of Persia*, just a few years later his Iranian friends were similarly experiencing an England going through its own religious upheaval.

Unlike the downtrodden "Soofies," the Unitarians were on the upswing. When Mirza Salih and Mirza Ja'far visited the Lewin's Mead Chapel in 1818, it was an impressive public symbol of Unitarian pride. Fronted by four Ionic columns, its lofty pediment framed a portico that led into broad interior galleries supported by ornate cast-iron pillars (the latest fashion) and lit by gas-burning lamps (the latest technology). According to *Mathews*, it was "a large, elegant, and costly place of worship, and may be ranked among the principal public buildings" of Bristol. Although the Iranians appear to have been warmly welcomed there by the Unitarians, from the evidence of John Rowe's publications and sermons their host was rather less open-minded than later Unitarians would become through their exchanges with non-Christians. Two years earlier in 1816, Rowe published a tract consisting of *A Letter from an Old Unitarian to a Young Calvinist*, which, though not written by Rowe himself, received his praise in the preface he wrote for it. The *Letter* featured the kind of characterization of Islam that, though common in English writings of the period, is not what one would expect from a Unitarian text. For in no uncertain terms the *Letter* decried the "holy zeal by which the religion of the imposter Mahomet was propagated over one third of the globe, involving mankind in ignorance, superstition, frenzy and barbarism."

Warming to his theme of the superiority of "rational" Unitarians over superstitious Muslims and other denominations alike, the *Letter's* author claimed that,

> By the exercise of our rational faculties, we [Unitarians] have thrown off the farcical, ceremonious and superstitious solemnities imposed upon mankind by the church of Rome, and by the assistance of the best of monitors, we detect the impositions of the pretended prophet Mahomet, treat the fictitious revelation which he has given in his Alcoran with contempt, and adopt the Scriptures as the best guide to happiness.

Since John Rowe published but did not actually write the *Letter*, we can gather a firmer sense of his own religious position from a sermon he preached just a year before meeting the two Muslims. Focusing on the use of reason in understanding scripture, he championed the importance of rationality in religion. Though, if he followed the opinions of the *Letter* he had published, he may not have seen Muslims as fellow rationalists, there is every chance that Mirza Salih and Mirza Ja'far put him straight when they spoke to him after his sermon in October 1818. Though we cannot know what was said, there is good reason to think that Mr. Rowe was restating his favorite Unitarian theme of the religious importance of reason, a theme that we know was by now dear to the two young Muslims.

In the case of the other Unitarian minister whom Mirza Salih and Mirza Ja'far met in Bristol, we are more fortunate with the evidence. This was the Reverend Dr. Lant Carpenter (1780–1840), whom Mirza Salih described guiding them round the city's docks, factories, and ironworks. As the son of a carpet manufacturer from Kidderminster near Birmingham, Dr. Carpenter was in his element leading the foreigners round Bristol's factories, even though he had only moved to the city just over a year before their visit. The Lewin's Mead Chapel, of which (along with Mr. Rowe) he was the custodian, stood just off the quayside and so an additional stroll around the dockyards would have been convenient enough. Showing the proximity of the scientific manufactories of new beliefs and brassware, the chapel was also just near Champion's Brass Works, one of the biggest players in the Bristol metal trade, and so there is a good chance that Champion's was one of the factories they visited. Seeing Christian religion in its muck and brass contexts, this was expeditionary fieldwork indeed.

Although such factories made up the setting in which Mirza Salih described Bristol's Dissenters, he still made sure to gather their actual opinions about religion. Having transcribed the name "Unitarian" into Arabic letters in his diary, he then explained this novel designation by translating the term into Persian as *muwahidin*. He added that these people regarded Jesus as a "messenger" (that is, not as the incarnation of God like other Christians) and that, since Jesus's death, they had worshipped God alone and not worshipped Jesus as an equal beside God. Such "churches" as theirs, he explained, were found all over England and were "especially popular among the wise and enlightened." Though not wholly correct—Unitarianism was a relatively new sect and had certainly not been around "since Jesus's death"—what is most important about this brief description is that Mirza Salih clearly saw a close similarity between the beliefs of Unitarians and Muslims. More on this later!

On the other side of the conversations that day, we know a good deal about Dr. Carpenter's ideas. He published thirty-eight books during his lifetime, works in which he greatly expanded the range and depth of what, by 1818, was still only a nascent Unitarian theology. In line with Unitarianism's rationalizing origins, his writings reflected a new critical spirit toward the historicity of the New Testament, albeit doing so to ultimately confirm the "genuineness" of the Gospels. In the midst of the polemic that the Church of England regularly directed against Dissenters, Dr. Carpenter tried to demonstrate the fidelity of Unitarian doctrine to the scriptures, citing the Gospels as "plain and

Fig. 16. An English *Muwahid*: The Unitarian Minister Lant
Carpenter, by M. Gutenberg, after George Cruikshank, 1871.
Source: Harvard Art Museums / Fogg Museum, Harvard University Portrait Collection,
Gift of Mary Carpenter (eldest daughter of Lant Carpenter) to Harvard College, 1877,
H126. Photo: Imaging Department © President and Fellows of Harvard Museum.

unambiguous" proof that, since "Jesus was not himself truly God," true
Christians should believe that only God (and not Jesus) was to be
worshipped. Unitarianism—worshipping one God intead of a divine
Trinity—was therefore true to the Bible's teachings. Given the precise
parallel between Dr. Carpenter's writings and Mirza Salih's description of Unitarian doctrine, their conversations seem to have laid the
basis of the Muslim's understanding of these Christian *muwahidin*.
Since Mirza Salih also recorded him and Mirza Ja'far receiving gifts of

books from Dr. Carpenter and the other Unitarians when they left, Dr. Carpenter may have presented them with some of his own books, just as Hannah More had a few days earlier.

If Mirza Salih's diary shows the impact of his meeting with the Unitarians on his changing understanding of faith, Dr. Carpenter's own letters from the time show the reciprocity of the process. The letters also show the degree of interest that Mirza Ja'far had by now developed in Christian Dissent. For one of the letters shows Mirza Ja'far actively engaging in debates with the Unitarians that were to result in them modifying their own "practical piety." As Dr. Carpenter wrote to a local friend a few years after the students' departure,

> When one of those distinguished Persians, whose visit, in 1818, we all remember with different degrees of interest, inquired into the institutions connected with our congregation, and its different plans of benevolence, he expressed great surprise that that we had no Sunday School, and was fearful that the religious denomination to which we belong, are deficient in our efforts in that direction. I was able to correct him in the last point. I could point out to him the congregations further north, having noble institutions of the kind,—some of long standing and extensive influence,—others less striking, but in their extent not less useful; and I was able to tell him that the congregation, with which I was previously connected, had taken the lead in establishing one, when even the Wesleyan Methodists were without one. I was able to tell him,—and I did tell him,—that various objects contributing to the welfare of the congregation, and to the relief of others, were flourishing in it; and that very much was done by it which was honourable, and which was encouraging, and I ventured to express a belief that hereafter we should not be backward here.

What we see here is Mirza Ja'far (named again later in the letter) expressing his opinion to Dr. Carpenter about what was best for the Unitarians: they should open their own Sunday Schools. Clearly, the Iranians were not passive observers, still less simple sounding boards for Christian attempts to indoctrinate them. That Mirza Ja'far seems to have genuinely wanted what was best for the Unitarians, urging them not to fall behind the other Dissenting groups such as Methodists in opening such schools, echoes the sympathy for the Unitarians voiced in Mirza Salih's diary. More than this, the letter is evidence of the Muslims' awareness of the varying activities of different Dissenting groups, showing that they were especially well-informed about the new Sunday School movement of which their acquaintance Mrs. More was a pioneer.

Here we have to recognize the importance of the Sunday Schools that in this period were the only educational option for poor children whose families were either unable to send them to the village school (if there even was one) or children who themselves had to work during the week. Echoing at home the evangelicals' humanitarian drive to abolish the slave trade overseas, the Sunday School movement was the more humane side of the period's religious revival. It was the epitome of the kind of "practical piety" toward which Mrs. More had urged the Iranians by presenting them with her book of that title. Just as in his diary, Mirza Salih was impressed by the Christian practice of visiting prisoners and treating them humanely, Mirza Ja'far seems to have been similarly impressed by the attempts of Sunday School promoters to bring education to even the poorest of the rural poor. Indeed, as Dr. Carpenter went on to explain in his letter, so passionate was Mirza Ja'far about this matter, that whenever it was raised in conversation with the young Muslim:

> His repeated reply to every remark of the kind, was:—"Do have a Sunday-School. The Methodists, the Baptists, the Church, as well as Dissenters, have Sunday-Schools, in which they labour for the welfare of their poorer brethren. Do have a Sunday School!"

Mirza Ja'far was not without success. For on hearing that even a foreign Muslim had seen the importance of Sunday Schools for the Unitarians, a certain "Miss M. Hughes, known to the religious world by her excellent Christian Tracts, commenced the Sunday School, each bringing three children: the numbers by degrees increased, the younger members of the congregation enlisted themselves as teachers, and the institution gradually acquired permanency." Shi'ite Iranians had successfully intervened in how English Unitarians practised and promoted their faith. That it was more than a passing acquaintance that they made during that visit to Bristol we know from Dr. Carpenter's son, who recorded how his father later "received two interesting letters from Jaafar, full of strong personal attachment to him, and expressing veneration and respect to Christ, though still regarding Mahomet as the "wise prophet, who illumined the true way of salvation after the corruption of the Gospel.'"

The students may also have met Dr. Carpenter's daughter, Mary Carpenter (1807–77); she was eleven at the time of their conversations with her father. Even if she did not meet them, given her father's enthusiasm for his two Muslim guests, he would have surely told her about them. Whatever the case, her later life bore many echoes of that childhood encounter of her own or her father's. Not only did she take up with vigor Mirza Jaʿfar's cry "*Do have a Sunday School!*" by founding several "ragged schools" for poor boys and girls. She also befriended another Persian-speaking visitor to Bristol, the Indian Ram Mohan Roy (ca. 1772–1833), about whose death in her home city she wrote a moving memoir. In her late fifties, Mary, former child of the Bristol dockyards as she was, finally fulfilled her ambition of sailing off to the East, a desire perhaps nurtured since the visit of the fascinating foreigners. In India, she met many Hindu religious reformers and, together with them, founded the National Indian Association to further the flow of progressive ideas between India and England. Devoted as she was to education for the poor in both countries, it is hard not to think of her remembering down the decades the passionate cry of Mirza Jaʿfar: "*Do have a Sunday School!*"

Rational Religion

Other Unitarian sermons preached around 1818 in the towns which Mirza Salih and Mirza Jaʿfar visited shed further light on the circles they entered during their travels through the West Country. The most informative are the sermons preached by Joseph Hunter (1783–1861), a former cutler's apprentice from the industrializing northern city of Sheffield who was active in Bath when the students visited. One of the key themes of Hunter's sermons (described by one contemporary as "sterling morality expressed in sterling English") was what we have seen as the defining Unitarian claim to "rational views of religion" and to upholding "civil and religious liberty," a cause that the Iranians'

Bristolian host Dr. Carpenter also championed. Still, despite his own humble upbringing, as with many Unitarian preachers of the period, Mr. Hunter's lofty soliloquies were aimed at a middle-class congregation and he strenuously resisted the evangelical ploy of addressing emotive sermons to the unlearned. His rationalist ideas on religion were also shared by the sermons of other Unitarian preachers, such as W. J. Fox, who in a sermon of 1815 defended the importance of "free inquiry" in matters of religion as of politics on the grounds that such freedom was "the source of improvement in every science, especially in theology." Furthermore, Mr. Fox went on, the promotion of free inquiry would also diminish the religious controversies that divide humanity, for "the bigotry which estranges good men, of different opinions on religious subjects, from each other's esteem and affection, is principally to be attributed to a practical belief in the infallibility of sects or leaders. It will gradually retire as free inquiry advances. The well informed of all denominations are the most liberal." But the differences between Unitarians like Fox and the strident evangelicals whom the students also encountered show all too well that such progressive ideals were far from universally accepted among Christians. As different parties struggled with the implications of the new sciences that Mirza Salih's companions had been sent to acquire, nineteenth-century England had no innate claims to religious tolerance.

The Unitarians' similar connections to the scientific new learning can be seen in a speech that Joseph Hunter delivered to the Bath Literary and Philosophical Association a few years later. He praised Bath's contribution to the progress of science, regaling his audience with stories of such local scientists as Venner, Jorden, Cheyne, Oliver, and the famous astronomer Sir William Herschel (1738–1822), in whom Mirza Ja'far had taken a special interest through his studies of mapmaking at the Royal Military Academy. As Unitarians found ways to accommodate the new discoveries of science to form a similarly "rational religion," through the conversations that Unitarians such as Lant Carpenter and John Rowe had with Mirza Salih and Mirza Ja'far, their values found channels into the Islamic Asia where, in the following decades, many reformers tried to similarly rationalize Islam.

Mr. Hunter's sermons also contained the kind of theological clarifications of Unitarian doctrine that Mirza Salih must have heard from his own Unitarian acquaintances before penning his account of their beliefs. He was particularly explicit about the Unitarian rejection of the Trinity on the grounds that, according to the evidence of scripture, Jesus never mentioned such an irrational idea. In a sermon preached in Bath less than a year after Mirza Salih and Mirza Ja'far's visit to the city, he made a number of references to Islam (or rather, "Mahometanism"). And here again we can perhaps detect traces of the Iranians' presence in the debates that followed their departure. Yet Mr. Hunter's sermon did not involve the polemical disparaging of Islam associated with the evangelicals. Rather, it presented Islam through analytical comparison with Christianity, making precisely the kind of comparative exercise in which Mirza Salih had engaged in his own comparison of Unitarian with Muslim theology. For in Hunter's Bath sermon of 1819, Islam was not presented in the form of the "heathenism" of old, but as a parallel monotheism through which, like Christians, Muslims "came in general to receive the great truths of a Divine Creator and his providence." This equinamous comparison between Christianity and Islam shows the new cosmopolitan thinking that the more connected world of the period made possible. Hunter's unusual acceptance that Islam might also be divinely inspired was possibly an outcome of Mirza Salih and Mirza Ja'far's meetings with his Dissenting acquaintances in Bath and Bristol less than a year earlier. The connection may even have been closer. For in Mirza Salih's account of a second visit he made to Bath, he described a visit to the Unitarian chapel there and a supper to which he was invited at the home of the chapel's "priest," or *kashish*. While one modern Iranian editor of Mirza Salih's diary has transcribed his host's name as *Mistar Hasant*, from the close orthographic similarity in Arabic script between the untenable English name "Hasant" and the common English name "Hunt," and the fact that the only Unitarian chapel in Bath at this time was the same Trim-Street Chapel of which Joseph Hunter was then the incumbent, it seems that Mirza Salih did in fact meet Mr. Hunter and misremembered or misspelled his name as "Hunt." If so, the cultured young Muslim clearly left a good impression on Mr. Hunter, for he then preached one of the era's most positive evaluations of Islam. Once again, such appreciation was mutual, for what Mirza Salih did for the Unitarians in his diary, a few months later Mr. Hunter did for the Muslims in his sermon.

We can only guess what conversations took place over supper that night in Bath between Mirza Salih and Joseph Hunter. From their respective accounts of one another's faiths, we can imagine it as not so much a meeting of minds but of worlds. Mirza Salih was quite explicit in his appreciation of Unitarian teachings. For while Muslims have always accepted the prophethood of Jesus, they have always rejected the notion that Jesus was God incarnate, arguing that an omnipotent deity cannot dwell in flesh and bone. Here the Unitarians and Muslims were as one. Moreover, in writing about the beliefs of the Unitarians, Mirza Salih deliberately chose the term *paighambar*, or "messenger," to describe their attitude toward Jesus, using precisely the term that Muslims used for Jesus and Muhammad. In Mirza Salih's estimation, in revering but not actually worshipping Jesus, the Unitarians were like Muslims in offering worship only to God and in this way not mistaking the deity with his venerable but nonetheless human messengers. In Muslim terms, then, the Unitarians were not under the misapprehensions born of *shirk*, of associating human beings with the deity. Finally, by translating the name of the Unitarians as *muwahidin*, Mirza Salih drew a further correspondence with the Muslim precept of God's indivisible unity or *tawhid*, a term implied in the word *muwahidin* itself. Aside from the fact that the Unitarian English *muwahidin* seemed not to recognize the Prophet Muhammad, to all intents and purposes in Bristol and Bath the students had stumbled upon a sect of true monotheists like themselves!

This echoed the claim of W. J. Fox in his London sermon of 1815 that free inquiry promised harmony between the many good people around the world who found themselves divided by sectarian opinions. As people from different sides of the world like Joseph Hunter and Mirza Salih sought universal principles of religious understanding, in the meetings between the Muslim students and the West Country Unitarians we can see early attempts to find affinities and correspondences between the religious systems that divided humankind. This search for cosmopolitan religious principles had found earlier Muslim expression before the Iranians reached England, most famously in the seventeenth-century attempt by the Indian prince Dara Shikuh to find an equivalent for Muslim metaphysics in the Sanskrit Upanisads of the Hindus. In Dara Shikuh's Persian writings, the term he used to identify doctrines that harmoniously recognized a single universal reality was likewise *muwahid*, or "unitarian." Two centuries later and thousands of miles from India, Mirza Salih used the same term to describe the Unitarians of Bristol and Bath. There was surely something unifying in this.

From Unitarians to Freemasons

In their days spent wandering through the chapels and factories of Bristol, Mirza Salih and Mirza Ja'far had entered a kind of cosmopolitan vortex. It was a magical moment when the whole world seemed to be joined together in unity. Yet the Unitarians were not the only rationalizing universalists with whom Mirza Salih came into contact in England. His diary also records his encounters with the more mysterious Freemasons. With its rationalist and universalist ethos, Freemasonry served in this period as an upper class counterpart to the Unitarian gatherings that Mirza Salih and Mirza Ja'far had seen among the manufacturing men of Bristol. Amid the increasing international exchanges of the early nineteenth century, it brought together people of different creeds through the symbolic language of high ritual. Freemasonry also offered an elite form of sociability into which, whether in London, Paris, or Vienna, diplomats and other high-status visitors were usually the first foreign initiates. By the time Mirza Salih reached England, Freemasonry had already become a significant force as far away as India. The first Freemasons' lodge in Calcutta, the headquarters of the East India Company, was constituted as early as 1730. Over the following decades, other lodges were constituted in the provincial towns of Bengal into which the Company was expanding, as well as Bombay and Madras, where the first lodges were founded in 1758 and 1793. Such was the scale of Freemasonry's expansion in India that by the time the Iranian students reached London there were eight lodges in Calcutta alone.

Since Iranian merchants and diplomats already had contact with the East India Company in Calcutta, by the beginning of the nineteenth century Freemasonry was by no means unknown to the Iranian intelligentsia, as stories of Freemasons were transmitted back to Iran in

Persian. In 1804, the Indo-Iranian traveler Abu Talib Khan claimed to have been "frequently urged" to join the Freemasons while he was in London, but to have declined their offers because their principles did not cohere with his own. Even so, he wrote of them sympathetically, noting that "they do not interfere with any man's religion, nor attempt to alter his faith." This latter point helps explain why Freemasonry soon became so important to elite Muslim visitors to Europe. For having heard of the mysterious temples where the leading men of Europe gathered in sworn secrecy, Iranians and Ottomans of the same social class became fascinated with Freemasonry. As a result, the first Iranian Freemason was Askar Khan Afshar, the ambassador to Paris who was initiated in that city on November 24, 1808.

The first Iranian to become a Freemason in England was none other than Ambassador Abu'l-Hasan, who was initiated shortly afterward, on June 15, 1810. He was given the honorary rank of past grand master under the sponsorship of Sir Gore Ouseley, who six months earlier had himself been appointed as the first "provincial grand master for Persia." In Sir Gore, who had studied at the feet of the greatest Muslim scholars of Lucknow, Abu'l-Hasan found someone whose cosmopolitan sentiments allowed for a level of sympathy that was impossible with Christians of narrower understanding. The Freemason meeting at which Abu'l-Hasan was initiated was presided over by General Francis Rawdon-Hastings, also known as Lord Moira (1754–1826), who in 1813 would become the governor-general of India. While we know not into what "mysteries" Abu'l-Hasan was initiated, nor his motivations for joining the Freemasons, a hint is found in a conversation he had earlier with his sponsor, Sir Gore. For in his diary Abu'l-Hasan wrote of Sir Gore that "so learned he is about all religions that each sect considers him one of their own and conceals none of its mysteries from him." While Sir Gore was not necessarily typical of all Freemasons, the universalist principles that had given birth to Freemasonry in the previous century made their lodges a natural home for such rationalists and cosmopolitans. As such, like Unitarianism, Freemasonry was an important counterweight to the high-minded prejudices of the evangelicals who dreamed of converting every Muslim in the world.

Although Ambassador Abu'l-Hasan was the first Iranian to become a Freemason in England, he was not the first Muslim to do so. For prior to his initiation, in July 1800 Yusuf Aqa Effendi, the first resident Otto-man ambassador to London and his nephew, Yusuf ʿAziz Effendi, had become Freemasons at Prince of Wales Lodge No. 259 in London. With its links to Sir Gore Ouseley and Lord Moira, Abu'l-Hasan's initiation was more closely connected to the role of Freemasonry among the East India Company than the initiation of the two Ottomans. If there is a temptation here to see the initiation as a colonial attempt to co-opt the Iranian ambassador, it is important to recognize what he and other Muslim Freemasons gained from their initiation, not least by way of elite networking and the diplomatic leverage it might lend. Freemason lodges offered a rare opportunity for Muslims and Christians not merely to meet on equal terms but to meet as adoptive brothers sworn to aid and promote each other's interests.

There is no doubt, though, that much of the Muslim fascination with the Freemasons was a product of their secrecy, which served to am-plify their claims to higher knowledge. Although Abu'l-Hasan and the Ottoman ambassador did not renege on their oaths of secrecy, by the middle years of the century, Persian accounts of the Freemasons' ac-tivities did begin to emerge. One was written by an Indian Muslim in British service called Zahir al-Din Munshi. Writing in 1853 after he visited a Freemason lodge in Calcutta, Zahir al-Din described in maca-bre tones the strange rites he had watched the Englishmen perform in what he termed their *jadu ghar*, or "magic house." Such was the allure of Freemasonry in Iran and the Ottoman Empire by this time that even the Sufi brotherhoods began to adopt some of its rituals and symbols. Even as early as 1800, the name given to the Freemasons' lodge in Persian was aiding their mystique, for the Persian near-homonym—*faramush-khana*—lent their gathering places the mysterious label the "House of Forgetting."

Although the Muslim fascination with Freemasonry had yet not reached its peak by the time the Iranian students reached England, associating with Freemasons was already a source of great social ca-chet. By the time he made his tour of the West Country, Mirza Salih had already made the acquaintance of a Mr. Percy, whom he described as holding the rank of master among the Freemasons. Keen to help his new friend, along with Colonel D'Arcy senior, Mr. Percy arranged for Mirza Salih to be initiated as a Freemason. It was, he noted in his diary,

Fig. 17. Masonic Muslims: The Ottoman Ambassador at London's Freemasons' Hall.
Source: "The distinguishing characteristic of Masonry, Charity Exerted on Proper Objects" by Francesco Bartolozzi , after Thomas Stothard, 1802. Courtesy of The Library and Museum of Freemasonry, London.

one of his long-term ambitions. And so, on Mr. Percy's recommendation, Mirza Salih was accepted into the *faramush-khana*, as he called it. His fellow traveler Mirza Ja'far also seems to have been initiated, though Mirza Salih himself made no record of this. True to his oath of secrecy, in his diary Mirza Salih wrote that, other than stating the fact of his initiation, he could divulge no more details of what had happened between himself and the Freemasons. We can only hope it was less macabre than the Freemasonic initiation around this time of the fictional Mr. Verdant Green, who was made to stare in "horror and amazement" at "a human head (or the representation of one) projecting from a black cloth that concealed the neck, and, doubtless, the marks of decapitation."

Given the students' earlier difficulties in England, we might suspect Mirza Salih's (and Mirza Ja'far's) motives as basically instrumental, trying to use their entry into this fraternal association to leverage favors from their influential new "brothers." After all, just a decade earlier the Indo-Iranian visitor Abu Talib had remarked on how all Freemasons "consider each other as Brothers." But there is also good reason to connect their interest in Freemasonry to the appeal that cosmopolitan and rationalist forms of religiosity held for them by this time. Their religious interests were not separate from their interests in the scientific new learning, which they saw echoed in the rational understandings of the divinity offered by Freemasonry and Unitarianism alike.

If most of their dealings with the Freemasons remain a mystery, we do at least catch glimpses in Mirza Salih's diary of the kinds of association that their initiation opened to them. For on the way back from Bristol on November 3, 1818, Mirza Salih managed to talk his way into seeing the coffin of Queen Charlotte lying in state at Windsor, where he bumped into one of his fellow Freemasons in the nave of the Royal Chapel. Describing this Mr. Harris as one of England's most important Freemasons, he recounted how, on having heard that his Iranian brother was departing England a week later (a plan that was actually avoided due to Mirza Salih's protestations), Mr. Harris promised to have Mirza Salih raised to the rank of Master if he came to the lodge in London the next day. Delighted to hear this, Mirza Salih did indeed attend the London lodge the next day and was raised in rank as Mr. Harris has promised: he was now an *ustad*, or "master" of the Craft. But his account of this meeting is no less cryptic than his other references to the Freemasons, and we learn no more from his diary of what went on that day.

Nevertheless, if Mirza Salih was himself reluctant to reveal details of his (and perhaps Mirza Ja'far's) meetings with the Freemasons, it is possible to make certain inferences about their likely setting. Given the high status of their London supporters, such as Sir Gore Ouseley, it seems likely that the Iranians were invited to Freemasons' Hall on Great Queen Street near Covent Garden. Designed by Thomas Sandby (1721–98), one of the founding members of the Royal Academy, Freemasons' Hall was completed in 1776 as a grand neoclassical edifice. Its vast interior echoed the cavernous mysterium of a Roman basilica. A surviving oil painting from 1801 by Thomas Stothard depicts the presence there of the earlier Muslim Freemasons, Ambassador Yusuf Aqa Effendi and his Ottoman companions. Another work by Stothard (in this case a preparatory drawing for an engraving) depicts a meeting of the British and Foreign Bible Society at Freemasons' Hall showing a figure in Muslim costume who has traditionally been identified as "the Persian Ambassador." Such evidence suggests that Mirza Salih and Mirza Ja'far might also have been brought there. With their visits to the opera house and theaters around Covent Garden, the Iranians certainly frequented the area directly surrounding Freemasons' Hall and its adjacent Freemasons' Tavern, where much of the brotherhood's informal networking took place.

However, in being dated to "around 1815," Stothard's drawing does present a puzzle, for in 1815 the Freemasonic ambassador Abu'l-Hasan had already left London, while Mirza Salih had not yet been initiated. With Abu'l-Hasan being initiated in 1810 and Mirza Salih in 1817, the drawing from "around 1815" could represent either figure, or perhaps Mirza Ja'far. For if in the newspaper reports from the West Country Mirza Salih and Mirza Ja'far could be described as "Persian princes," there seems no reason why one of them could not later be mistakenly labeled as the "Persian Ambassador" on Stothart's drawing. Whatever the correct identification of Stothart's figure, what is more clear is the link between Freemasons' Hall and the Bible Society. For as we will see in the next chapter, Sir Gore Ouseley, the former ambassador to Iran and first provincial grand master for Persia, was not only a Freemason but also the vice president of the Bible Society. As we now turn toward Mirza Salih's contacts with the evangelical movement, we will see that his religious dealings also saw him associating with the Bible Society, with Sir Gore Ouseley once again acting as the social linchpin.

In their dealings with the Freemasons as in other aspects of their adventures in England, Mirza Salih and Mirza Ja'far were pioneers who stood at the forefront of trends that would become greatly influential in their home country. They were well ahead of their time, for while the Iranian fascination with Freemasonry would continue to grow over the following decades, the first Freemason lodge in Iran did not open till 1858. Whether as some of the first Iranian Freemasons, or some of the earliest Muslims to encounter the dissenting denominations of Christiandom, Mirza Salih and Mirza Jaʿfar's immersion in England's religious life marked them as pioneering ethnographers and explorers. A lack of sources means that we do not know to what extent the other four students had similar experiences at this time, but there is no reason to think they did not. They certainly all knew Dr. Gregory, who had arranged Mirza Salih and Mirza Jaʿfar's tour of the West Country. In any case, whether the other students stayed in London or also toured the provinces, in Jane Austen's England it was hard to avoid the topic of religion. This was especially true as a Muslim. For as we will now see, this was also the heyday of the missionaries who viewed the Middle East as ripe for conquest by the committed servants of Christ.

4

Evangelical Engagements

A Cambridge Alternative?

The provincial Baptists and Unitarians whom we have seen Mirza Salih and Mirza Ja'far encounter represented only one side of Regency England's tumultuous religious life. This was a time of great religious change that, though hidden in the contented Anglicanism of Miss Austen's novels, was a response to industrialization and empire. For if the Unitarians were the religious offspring of industrial Enlightenment, then evangelicalism was the unhappier child of empire. While the previous half century had seen the East India Company acquire an empire in Asia, in England the response was a crisis of Christian conscience that insisted on finding moral meanings behind imperial conquests. This crisis of conscience was resolved through the goal of converting India to Christianity. This grand evangelical agenda had unexpected linguistic consequences. We have already seen the importance of Persian to the East India Company, whose trainee officers had to study the language before sailing East. In parallel to the administrative agenda of the Company, the evangelicals began to take their own interest in Persian. To them, the mastery of Persian offered the potential linguistic key to India's conversion. For if the Bible could be made available in that language, and if Christian missionaries could preach in it the message of Christ, then India—and neighboring Iran to boot—could be won for Christendom.

In reaching in England in 1815, the Muslim students had arrived at a turning point in the evangelicals' outreach to India. Only two years earlier, in 1813, evangelical sympathizers in Parliament had forced a vote requiring the East India Company to open its territories for the first time to missionary activity. At last, the Protestant missionary societies that had been formed in the past fifteen years—the London Missionary Society, the Church Missionary Society, the Baptist Missionary Society, and the British and Foreign Bible Society not least—would be allowed to expand through the Company's Indian empire. And at the center of their plans lay Persian. For the missionaries' Protestant faith in scripture told them that if only the Bible could be read in a language that Indians understood, then God's message would do its own graceful work to win hearts and minds. Suddenly, expertise in Persian was not only in demand by the members of the East India Company. It was in even greater demand by the preachers and translators of the missionary societies.

We have already seen how, in spite of Oxford's long history of Arabic scholarship, the university had resisted the East India Company's efforts to promote the study of Persian. By scorning the language as the lingo of merchant upstarts, the dons had forced the Company to establish its own colleges at Haileybury and Addiscombe, whose own demand for Persian had lured the students to Croydon. Yet the situation was changing. India's opening to the missionaries in 1813 forced the clerical establishment at both Oxford and Cambridge to think again about the Company's empire and the role that their own moral guidance might now play there. In the following years, during the very period when the students resided in England, Oxford's long-standing expertise in Arabic was turned to the evangelical ends of translating the Bible. It was a task in which none other than Mirza Ja'far and Mirza Salih's Oxford host, Dr. Macbride, played the leading part. While Oxford's evangelicals were willing to rest on their Arabic laurels, their rivals in Cambridge saw an opportunity to do better by making their priority the translation of the Bible into Persian. It was the evangelical circles of Cambridge that reared the Reverend Henry Martyn (1781–1812), the first English missionary to India and Iran whose attempt to render the Gospels into Persian set the bar for a generation of evangelical translators. When Martyn died on his way back from Iran in 1812, it was none other than Sir Gore Ouseley who had pledged to hand his translation to the shah and to oversee its printing when he returned home. Such was Sir Gore's commitment that when he reached London, he accepted the appointment as vice president of the British and Foreign Bible Society, history's most important Bible-printing enterprise that had been founded a decade earlier in 1804. If this seems at odds with what we have seen of Sir Gore's role as an admirer of

Fig. 18. An Evangelical Romantic Hero: Reverend Henry
Martyn. Source: *Pioneer Missionaries of the Church* by Charles C. Creegan
(New York: American Tract Society, 1903).

Persian culture, then we should remember that the translation of the
Bible was seen as an enlightened educational project that would van-
quish superstition by opening access to the simple truths of scripture.
Between Sir Gore in London and Dr. Macbride in Oxford, the students
were already caught between two of England's most committed promoters of Bible translation. Mirza Salih, Mirza Ja'far, and also Mirza
Riza would shortly meet the third.

In the months after his tour of the West Country, Mirza Salih recorded in his diary what was one of a sequence of his, Mirza Ja'far's,
and Mirza Riza's ongoing visits to Cambridge, both together and sepa-
rately. This particular visit was arranged with the help of Mirza Salih's

architect friend, Robert Abraham. Just as earlier in Oxford, a meeting was arranged for Mirza Salih, and probably also Mirza Riza, with Cambridge's leading scholar of Islamic languages, Professor Samuel Lee (1783–1852). In Miss Austen's elegant era, their introduction would not be the most decorous one. Far from immune to the comedy of the scene, Mirza Salih recorded the fiasco in his diary. He was traveling to Cambridge on an uncomfortable stagecoach from London. Just as it entered the varsity town after several delays and changes of horses, the coach suffered a crash so calamitous that a crowd quickly gathered round the overturned coach and whinnying horses. The women seated beside Mirza Salih were thrown around the cabin by the impact, and as he struggled to regain his senses, Mirza Salih heard one of them wailing that her body was hurting all over. Turning to help, he looked up to see the woman standing above him and since "Englishwomen wear nothing under their dresses, I looked up to see that she was wearing nothing at all from her knees to her waist; it was not a pretty sight!" The shock of this intimate introduction was only the beginning of his embarrassments. As the crowd grew around the coach they started to lift out the passengers, expecting to find dead bodies. When they instead found Mirza Salih lying there in his bright silk robes and Persian fur hat, their fears dissolved into laughter. Alarmed by the attention, he struggled to break free from their clutches. As it happened, the man he was due to meet in Cambridge, Professor Lee, was standing nearby and guessed that the strange figure in the midst of the commotion must be his Muslim visitor. But when Mirza Salih spotted his host in turn, in his relief he lost his concentration and slipped as he stepped down from the upturned coach. Giving more mirth to the mob, he fell flat-faced onto the muddy road below. Hoping to hide his embarrassment till the crowd lost interest, he limped into a nearby shop. But he could still hear the shrieks and guffaws from outside as his dramatic entry into town was explained as the arrival of the King of Hell, of the Queen of Pain, of a monstrous merman, or a coach-riding courier of the Angel of Death!

After every wisecrack, he later recorded in his diary, three hundred people burst into laughter. It was obviously a painful experience and one that points to more than a modicum of mob xenophobia. There is surely no doubt that he must have faced prejudice at times, even if he chose not to highlight it in his diary. Instead, sitting in the shop and recuperating with a cup of coffee from Professor Lee, who had followed him inside, Mirza Salih felt able to share with the professor and shopkeeper the funny side of the incident. Even so, he was concerned at the threat the ridiculous scene posed to his reputation. He should not have worried too much, though. Such accidents were common enough for Jane Austen to use an overturned stagecoach as the opening plot device for the novel *Sanditon* that she left unfinished when she died in 1817, not long before Mirza Salih's own accident. As art resembled life, and vice versa, both the real and the fictional crash led to sympathetic introductions to new friends: in the novel, to the meeting of Mr. Parker and the Heywood family; in the diary, to the meeting of Mirza Salih and Professor Lee. So it was that the professor took the shaken Muslim to the quiet retreat of a room at Queens' College. There, Mirza Salih penned a letter to the local newspaper requesting the editor resist the temptation of spreading news of the comical incident more widely. In an ironical but thankful aside, he later noted his relief that the editor agreed.

Later that evening, Mirza Salih wrote in his diary a short biography of his host, Professor Lee, whom he described as being around forty years of age (he was actually thirty-five). Clearly taken by what he was told of the professor's life story—for he recorded no similar biographies of the other people he met—Mirza Salih explained how Professor Lee was the son of a carpenter who worked as a carpenter in his own youth before, at the age of seventeen, beginning a program of self-education in the evenings after his labors. Starting by learning Latin—rather like Mirza Salih had done in Croydon—Lee moved on to French, and then Greek, until soon he had "learned the languages of the whole of *Farangistan*," as Mirza Salih called Europe. On meeting an Indian, the young Sam Lee then began to learn "Hindustani" Urdu from him (which according to Mirza Salih he spoke with fine accent and pronunciation), before finally commencing with Arabic and Persian as part his lifelong mission of translating the New Testament into those languages as well as Hindustani. On the basis of its coherence to Lee's own account of his early life, which he recorded in a letter to his early mentor, the orientalist Jonathan Scott (1735–1807), Mirza Salih's biography appears to have been highly accurate. We can only assume that the self-made Sam Lee was not averse to recounting this rags-to-respectability tale, not least to the young Muslim in search of an education. And as a language student who had faced his own travails on the path of learning, it seems that Mirza Salih similarly warmed to Professor Lee and, moreover, respected his skills.

Lee was certainly something of an outsider to the privileged circles to which the Iranians had by now been introduced by Mr. D'Arcy, Dr. Gregory, and Sir Gore Ouseley. Raised far from the mannered combination rooms of Cambridge, he had spent his youth as plain Sam Lee the Shropshire lad. The youngest child of a family of eleven children, his early years were confined to the small village of Longnor, where he was lucky—because by then some of his five elder brothers were already working—to be sent to the charity school attached to the little medieval church of St. Mary in his home village. The emerging cast-iron industry in nearby Coalbrookdale was making Shropshire another of the birthplaces of the industrial revolution, its skilled iron puddlers earning some of the best workers' wages in the land. But while Coalbrookdale lay fourteen miles to the east of Shrewsbury, the Lee family's village of Longnor lay eight miles to the south. Theirs was still a world of rural poverty and custom. After being taken out of charity school at the age of twelve, young Sam was not sent to study the profitable new skills of the blast furnace but shackled instead to that oldest of village trades as a carpenter's apprentice.

Yet there was clearly something special about the boy. As Mirza Salih heard from the mouth of the man he became, in the evenings after a hard day's woodwork, young Sam started to teach himself the foreign languages that would later make his name. It all began by using his meager apprentice's earnings to buy old copies of Latin schoolbooks. Little by little—or more likely, with one great stride after another—he took up other languages for which he could find textbooks. Though born that bit too distant from Coalbrookdale to share in the iron revolution just over his rural horizon, Sam Lee was lucky in that Longnor's closest town was home to one of provincial England's oldest schools, the eponymous Shrewsbury School. Founded in

1552, by the time Professor Lee was regaling Mirza Salih with the tale of his education, the school had as a pupil no lesser a future luminary than that other Shropshire lad, Charles Darwin. Though the carpenter's apprentice was never able to study there, he was able to take advantage of the surfeit of textbooks that found their way onto the local market. And so, like a living version of Thomas Hardy's Jude the self-taught stonemason, Sam the young carpenter managed to teach himself Hebrew, Greek, and French. Having then found an old primer of Hindustani, and met a traveling Indian, he turned to Asian languages while he was still a teenager. After making rapid headway, he wrote the letter mentioned earlier to the orientalist Jonathan Scott, recounting his hard won path to learning and asking for advice and, perchance, preferment.

Since Sam had no social connections, as a former officer of the East India Company and as Shrewsbury's most noted orientalist, Mr. Scott was his best shot. Fortunately, the letter worked; Scott immediately recognized the linguistic genius of this local child of nature. And in a way that closely echoed what that other orientalist Sir Gore Ouseley would do for Mirza Salih, Mr. Scott turned to the charitable offices of the evangelicals by introducing Sam Lee to the Reverend Claudius Buchanan (1766–1815), the retired vice provost of Calcutta's Fort William College. The widely traveled reverend would have been no pushover: at Fort William College he had overseen the teaching of Hindustani and Persian to hundreds of young Britons. But the talents of Mr. Samuel Lee of Longnor, as he was introduced, stood out clearly. Confessing himself astonished by the lad's gifts, in 1814 Buchanan arranged for Samuel Lee—by now aged twenty—to matriculate at Queens' College, Cambridge. Not only was Queens' Buchanan's own *alma mater*, it was also the most evangelical of all the university's colleges, being closely connected to the Church Missionary Society. The latter's governors were particularly impressed when the twenty-year-old Lee showed them a translation he had already made of a missionary tract into Hindustani. Sensing an investment opportunity, the Church Missionary Society awarded him a scholarship to pay for his studies. It was a sensible bet. Professor John Shakespear, the distinguished language teacher at Croydon's East India College and erstwhile teacher of Mirza Salih, was also a humbly born country boy, such that Buchanan and the missionaries must have seen their recruiting of Samuel Lee as a victory for Christ over the East India Company. And indeed it was. For the price of Samuel Lee's education—and his rescue from a life carving ploughs and barn beams—was a debt that he would never forget.

Mirza Salih recorded that he found Professor Lee a hospitable and affable host, as he had Dr. Macbride at Oxford. And why not? We must not forget that the evangelicals were often very sympathetic people; they had, after all, recently campaigned to abolish the slave trade. But evangelicalism was not all brotherly love, especially when it came to talk of other religions. Given the fact that Lee became an even more fervent evangelical than Macbride, we can only wonder to what extent good manners led them to conceal their true opinions of Mirza Salih's Muslim faith. But after his own educational travails, Mirza Salih clearly felt a good deal of empathy with the prodigious Shropshire lad who before he had turned twenty-five had mastered Hebrew, Greek, Chaldean, Syriac, Samaritan, and Hindustani, as well as Persian and Arabic.

Professor Lee was a churchman as well as a scholar, so as well as occupying several livings in the Anglican Church, he spent much of his time writing polemical tracts and sermons. Even more than Dr. Macbride, he placed his knowledge of Islamic languages toward missionary ends by channeling his redoubtable linguistic genius into a series of translations (and improvements to existing translations) of scripture, whether of the New Testament, the prayer book, or the psalter, whether in Persian, Arabic, Hindustani, or even Malay.

Since 1814, then, the self-taught country carpenter had been a member of Queens' College, Cambridge, until, during the period when he was spending time with Mirza Salih, he was appointed to the lofty position of Sir Thomas Adams professor of Arabic. (In 1831, he would rise still further to become Regius professor of Hebrew.) In order to trace his spectacular rise to one of the most prestigious academic posts in the land, and to trace the students' role in that rise, we will first have to turn to the emergence of the evangelicals among whom Mirza Salih now found himself at Cambridge and of their ambitions to win India and Iran for Jesus.

The Ascent of the Varsity Evangelicals

As we saw in chapter two, through the influence of Dr. Macbride, the main early center of evangelicalism was not Cambridge but Oxford. It was there that the new cause of "conversionism" found its first outposts at St. Edmund Hall and then at Dr. Macbride's Magdalen Hall. As we have seen, the circles of the godly had already closed around Mirza Salih in Oxford for it was at "Teddy Hall" that his Croydon teacher Reverend John Bisset had been educated, while his co-host in Oxford, Mr. Hill, was the college's vice principal. It had been through the efforts of its principal Isaac Crouch (1756–1835) that St. Edmund Hall had emerged as the evangelicals' first varsity outpost, so much so that evangelicalism earned the nickname of the "religion of Teddy Hall." In 1807, Crouch had been succeeded by his pupil and protégé, Reverend Daniel Wilson (1778–1858), himself a close association of Mirza Salih's host Mr. Hill. Before quitting the university in 1812 to evangelize the empire in India, Wilson helped place the evangelical agenda on a surer curricular footing in Oxford. It was, incidentally, during the tenure of Crouch and Wilson between 1803 and 1808 that the Iranians' Croydon teacher Reverend John Bisset had pursued his theological studies at St. Edmund Hall, suggesting that their first exposure to evangelicalism may have taken place as early as their time in Croydon in 1817. Be that as it may, it was during the visits to Cambridge of Mirza Riza, Mirza Ja'far, and Mirza Salih that the students became most closely involved with the evangelicals, as we will see when we return to Mirza Salih's diary.

For Cambridge was following Oxford in becoming an evangelical outpost. Almost a decade before Reverend Claudius Buchanan, the vice provost of Calcutta's Fort William College, helped the Shropshire linguist Samuel Lee enter Queens' College, Cambridge, he had made a strategic endowment of £1,000 for two essay prizes, one at Cambridge and the other at Oxford. Whichever two undergraduates wrote the finest essays on "The probable Design of divine Providence in subjecting so large a Portion of India to the British Empire" would be awarded a large cash prize. In this way, the essay prize motivated bright young minds to consider the evangelicals' vision of empire as a religious rather than a commercial enterprise. As the politics of university endowment go, it was a brilliant maneuver.

Buchanan had not stopped there. His goal was to direct the university's hundreds of divinity students into the greatest of all evangelical projects: "translating the Scriptures into the Oriental languages." In 1806, he had used his educational high office as vice provost in Calcutta to take his case directly to Cambridge's vice chancellor, who was the effective head of the university, since the post of chancellor was merely an honorary one. In 1805–6, the vice chancellorship was held by the Reverend Joseph Turner, a sixty-year-old son of the establishment who was also master of Pembroke College and dean of Norwich cathedral. The reverend Mr. Turner was no match for the pushy Buchanan. Resorting again to the lure of pious lucre, Buchanan offered Turner thirty guineas to grant to any varsity man willing to preach sermons at the University Church on translating the scriptures. So it was that Cambridge's age-old Christian learning was finally turned toward Asia. And the forceful tactics of Buchanan's evangelicals worked well: in 1809, the evangelical president of Queens', Isaac Milner (1750–1820), took over as Cambridge's vice chancellor.

Although Milner was the highest ranking Cambridge evangelical, he was not the most celebrated in the wider world. That was Reverend Henry Martyn, who tried to translate the New Testament into Persian before dying in eastern Turkey in 1812 on his return from Iran. Before taking up his evangelical calling, Martyn had been an undergraduate and then a fellow of St. John's College, Cambridge. He then left the university to take up a post as chaplain with the East India Company. It was during his years in India that he made his first Persian translations of the Gospel. However, when Martyn sailed from Calcutta to Iran and set about spreading the Word of Christ in Mirza Salih's home city of Shiraz, it quickly became apparent that his Gospel translations were so faulty as to be almost unintelligible. As an account of Martyn's efforts in the *Christian Observer* delicately phrased the matter in 1820, this initial translation "though suited to the classical eye, had too large an infusion of the Arabic idiom to render it well adapted for general circulation." But there was more to it than this. In Shiraz, local Muslims had made a mockery of Martyn's translation by pointing out that if Jesus was the Lamb of God, then they were better off following imam 'Ali, who as everyone knew was the Lion of God (*shir-i khuda*). Aided by letters of introduction from Sir John Malcolm and Sir Gore Ouseley, Martyn nonetheless settled down at the house of Ja'far 'Ali Khan, the representative of the East India Company in Shiraz. Ja'far 'Ali introduced Martyn to his brother-in-law, Mirza Sayyid 'Ali Khan, who then helped Martyn make a revised version of the Persian New Testament, the manuscript of which Sir Gore later had printed in Saint Petersburg. But the new translation that resulted from Martyn's collaboration with Sayyid 'Ali Khan was a Gospel transposed into a Persian idiom that, far from soothing the soul, had incongruous Persian phrases describing the washing of sins in the Lamb of God's blood that were unsettling and jarring. Even though they were fascinated by the novelty of the printed version imported from Saint Petersburg, few Iranians were attracted by its foreign Christian message and peculiar phrases.

Although back in Cambridge, the evangelicals poured praise on the activities of their godly alumnus Henry Martyn, it became clear that even his revised translation of the Gospels was inadequate. They could not but recognize his failure. But it was just then, less than two years after Martyn's death, that the linguistic prodigy from Shropshire entered Cambridge with the aid of the Church Missionary Society. Samuel Lee was determined to follow in Martyn's footsteps and place his remarkable skills at the service of the same mission to translate the Bible into the languages of Iran and India. For with Henry Martyn's death in a distant land at the age of twenty-nine—the same age as Shelley when he drowned off the coast of Italy a few years later—he had become the evangelicals' own Romantic hero.

The evangelical vision of turning the East India Company's commercial empire into a vast assembly of preachers was at the forefront of public debate when Mirza Salih reached Cambridge. It regularly featured in the newspapers that he and his companions read. During the time of the students' visits to Cambridge, the evangelicals were the talk of the town. Even so, not everyone was convinced by them. As Jane Austen stated plainly in a letter to her sister, "I do not like the Evangelicals." Though Miss Austen herself came close to marrying a Cambridge reverend called Samuel Blackall, whose Emmanuel College was little more than five minutes walk from Samuel Lee's Queens' College where Mirza Salih stayed, she had no time for evangelical zealots. Anxious as the Muslim students were to make connections in the closed world of English learning, they had fewer options. As they had for Mirza Salih and Mirza Jaʿfar at Oxford, at Cambridge too the evangelicals acted as the varsity's gatekeepers.

Conversing with Conversionists

Aside from Mirza Salih's diary, two English accounts survive of the Muslim students in Cambridge, which show that they made at least two visits to the university. While Mirza Salih's diary describes one of these trips, which he made alone and which began with the crash of his stagecoach, an account of an earlier visit to the university was published in the *Cambridge Chronicle* a year earlier. Mirza Salih does not appear to have been present on this trip, which was made by Mirza Jaʿfar and Mirza Riza. Given their keen interest in the vast number of newspapers that Mirza Salih described being printed in England, it is fitting that the article should have first appeared in a local paper. It is worth quoting in its entirety:

> On Saturday, Meerza Jaaffar and Meerza Riza, two Persians of distinction, accompanied by Dr. Gregory of the Royal Military Academy, Woolwich, inspected King's Chapel, Trinity Library, and several of the Colleges in this University; and on Monday finished their examination by visiting the Fitzwilliam Museum, Public Library, Senate House, &c. They were sent into this country by the ruling Prince of Persia, to whose Court they are attached, for the purpose of gaining an acquaintance by actual study and inspection, with the language, institutions, arts and sciences of England, with a view to the improvement of their own country. With the concurrence of our Government various masters have been assigned to them for their instruction. They appear to be quite alive to their object, and were consequently much interested in their examination of our colleges, and with the accounts they received of the modes of education adopted in them. They speak the English language with considerable fluency, and in general correctly. They are in the habit of reading our best authors; and are capable of

appreciating many of their excellencies. On visiting the garden of Christ-college, one of them Meerza Jaaffar, who is a warm admirer of Milton, took away, with an intention most carefully to preserve them, some leaves from the mulberry-tree said to be planted by that immortal poet. On taking their leave, they expressed in strong terms the gratification they had received from their visit to this illustrious seat of learning. They were inhabited in the splendid costume of their country and their rank.

The report offers a fascinating glimpse of the students' activities at the varsity. Though their chaperone was the evangelical mathematician Dr. Gregory, their own interests drew them to the university's museums and libraries, and particularly into taking a memento of John Milton from the mulberry tree planted in 1608, when the poet was born, and under which he supposedly later sat to write *Lycidas*. It is touching to think that Mirza Ja'far may have stood there reciting to himself a few of Milton's mighty lines. Perhaps he had these in mind, from book ten of *Paradise Lost*:

> As when the *Tartar* from his *Russian* Foe
> By *Astracan* over the Snowie Plaines
> Retires, or *Bactrian* Sophi from the hornes
> Of *Turkish* Crescent, leaves all waste beyond
> The Realm of *Aladule*, in his retreate
> To *Tauris* or *Casbeen*.

After all, here Milton evoked villianous Russians, the enemies of Mirza Ja'far's master 'Abbas Mirza, along with the city of Qazvin ("Casbeen"), so close to his home city of Tabriz. Indeed, Milton's Tauris was the old English name for Tabriz. The newspaper report reveals more generally how the students were received in Cambridge. There was no sense of the inferiority of these Muslim strangers of the kind that arguably developed as England became a truly colonial power. Instead, there was a respect and even a fascination with the dignity of their difference. For all the reporter's pride in his varsity and his Milton, he recognized the Muslims' capacity to assess and pass judgment on the merits of English life and letters. He was strangely flattered by their attentions.

Mirza Salih's own account of the university lends further insight into the students' perceptions of English academe and, moreover, of the ways in which evangelical dons sought to manage their access to it. For if in the visit described in the newspaper, Mirza Ja'far and Mirza Riza were chaperoned by Dr. Gregory, during Mirza Salih's visits to Cambridge he spent most of his time in the evangelical circle of Professor Lee. Given the nature of the students' interests—Mirza Riza and Mirza Ja'far in mathematics, astronomy, engineering, and mapmaking and Mirza Salih in history, languages, and increasingly the mechanical arts—it is striking that at neither Oxford nor Cambridge were they to meet scholars who specialized in the subjects that most interested them. Instead, at Cambridge as at Oxford, they met the university's foremost evangelical language expert. Rather than an excursion arranged around Mirza Salih's own interests, it seems likely that his visit to Cambridge was the result of a specific invitation from Professor Lee. For as we will see, at the time of the Iranians' visits to Cambridge, Lee was involved in several translation projects through which he was trying to realize Reverend Henry Martyn's dream of rendering the whole Bible into Persian.

After Mirza Salih's embarrassing introduction to Samuel Lee amid the jeering crowd that greeted his emergence from the overturned stagecoach, the professor had escorted him to the tranquil Elizabethan courtyard of Queens' College. On that first evening at Queens', Lee took him for supper in the company of several senior members of the college. Queens' was at the time a zealous coterie of evangelicals who gathered there under the aegis of the college president, Isaac Milner. As we have seen through the circumstances of Lee's own arrival at the college, Queens' kept close contact with the Church Missionary Society. Much of this came through the Venn family, many of whom were students or fellows of Queens'; Henry Venn, for example, was already a student there when Mirza Salih visited and was elected as a fellow the following year before going on to become honorary secretary of the Church Missionary Society. But it was Isaac Milner who ruled the roost. As we saw earlier, Milner had already served in the university's highest office as vice chancellor. A no-nonsense Yorkshireman, like other heads of Cambridge colleges after him, Milner was an imposing figure, at once massively fat and magnificently grand. Yet he was more than an unusually hungry hound of God. Gourmand and churchman, Milner was also a celebrated conversationalist and pioneering chemist. Having conducted experiments alongside no lesser "natural philosophers" than Sir Humphrey Davy and Sir Joseph Banks (the latter being the president of the Royal Society whose high standing Mirza Salih had noted in his diary), Milner filled the President's Lodge at Queens' with chemical jars and crucibles. Nonetheless, he still found much time to energetically promote the evangelicals.

The Cambridge evangelicals were a tight, committed circle. Milner was a close friend of their other early leader, Charles Simeon (1759–1836), the founding member of the Church Missionary Society whose example had inspired Henry Martyn to evangelize the Muslims of India and Iran. In 1811, Milner and Simeon formed the first undergraduate branch of the British and Foreign Bible Society at Cambridge. Closing the evangelical circle that awaited Mirza Salih at the varsity, back in 1796 it had been Milner's support that had won his protégé Claudius Buchanan the office of chaplain to the East India Company, before, as we have seen, Buchanan in turn found a place for Samuel Lee at Queens'. Passing on the patronage, Professor Lee was now introducing Mirza Salih to the same college. It was largesse in the hope of a conversion.

In his usual laconic manner, Mirza Salih described his arrival amid that conversionist circle:

> After breakfast, I went to the house of Mr Mandell. After talking for a while, he took me on a tour of the *madrasas* of Cambridge. Then, at three o'clock, we went to see Mr Lee at Queens' College. There, I dined with Mr Mandell, Mr Jee and a party of others, who then took me for a stroll around the gardens that are attached to the colleges. Of the many churches I was shown, there was one called "King's Chapel" that needs no columns to support it. In craftsmanship and size, it is one of the most famous churches. After inspecting it, I came home. I stayed at Queens' College where, in a little cell of a room, I finally fell asleep.

He would not be the last foreign visitor to be dismayed by the dinginess of Cambridge guest rooms. But at least the company was of interest. The college fellows with whom he dined on that first night at Queens' included the bursar Mr. Jee and its "priest" (or *kashish*), Mr.

Mandell. The former was the Reverend Joseph Jee, a fellow of Queens' between 1814 and 1829 who later served in the high office of Proctor of the University. As for Reverend William Mandell, at the time of Mirza Salih's visit he was already one of the varsity's leading evangelicals, an influential fellow (and dean) of Queens' who later served as its vice president. When the great inspirer of Cambridge missionaries Charles Simeon died in 1836, it was Mandell who preached his funeral sermon in King's College Chapel. While his dinner conversation with his Muslim guest has been lost in the winds of time, we can guess at its tone from his oratorical style: a sermon he preached on the death of King George within a year of meeting Mirza Salih hardly lends the impression of an enticing dining partner. For in classic evangelical mode, Mandell began with a gory reading from the Book of Revelation before expounding in detail the importance of making England a nation of "sincere Christians."

Messrs. Mandell and Milner of Queens' were far from alone in this wish, because the evangelicals and their organizations were by then as busy at home as they were overseas. Just as Milner had attempted to found a branch of the Bible Society in Cambridge, just over a year before Mirza Salih dined at Queens', Jane Austen's cousin, Reverend Edward Cooper, tried to found another branch in the quite different setting of industrial Wolverhampton. Hoping to bring light to the benighted minds of the Midlands, in 1816 he published *Two Sermons Preached in the Old and New Churches at Wolverhampton, Preparatory to the Establishment of a Bible-Institution.* His literary cousin Jane was no fan of fanatical "enthusiasm" and confessed that she did "not much like Mr. Cooper's new Sermons." Miss Austen found cousin Edward's preaching to be, like the sermons of Mirza Salih's hosts, "fuller of Regeneration and Conversion than ever—with the addition of his zeal in the cause of the Bible Society." When defining the place of religion in their past, Britons today like to look back to John Locke's *Essay on Toleration* from 1667. But a century and a half later, in the England of Jane Austen, intolerant religion was still a potent force.

William Mandell was therefore hardly the ideal host for a Muslim such as Mirza Salih. Yet he was typical of the scholars with whom the students had to deal on their quest for a scientific learning that, as we have seen, was as yet unseparated from Christian concerns. And from imperial concerns too. For from the small but dedicated circle at Queens' College, there emerged an evangelical vanguard that in the course of the nineteenth century transformed the relations between the British Empire and Islam. In the dining room above Queens' dainty Tudor courtyard, Mirza Salih had entered the evangelical lions' den.

Even so, his dinner that first evening does not seem to have been an unpleasant affair, for Queens' laid out famously lavish spreads. Presided over by the college president Isaac Milner—with his awesomely protuberant belly, one of the most renowned gastronomes of the Regency—it was said at this time that Queens' "public dinners were very merry, but the private ones were quite uproarious." Here, we glimpse another side to the evangelical professors to what they recorded in their tracts and sermons; dining in their jovial midst, it was perhaps this side that they revealed to their Iranian guest. For Mirza Salih depicted his Cambridge hosts as kind and welcoming. It is not altogether surprising. The evangelicals were often passionate, humane, and even humorous men, never more so than in their cups. If Mirza Salih described the colleges of Cambridge and Oxford as *madrasas*, then they had one important difference from the theological seminaries of Iran: the abundant supplies of booze in their cellars. By 1818, the hard-drinking at the heart of the Regency varsities was reaching its zenith, or nadir. Mirza Salih may have been entertained to hear that the universities' most popular alcoholic cups had ecclesiastical names. Even clerics might round off their suppers with a potent cup of Pope, Cardinal, or Cider Bishop (the latter a more devilish than godly concoction of brandy, cider and "two glasses of calves-feet jelly in a liquid state.")

After supping with the reverends Jee and Mandell, Mirza Salih was taken on a tour of the other colleges nearby, including Trinity, which he excitedly described as the place that reared Sir Isaac Newton—"a philosopher," he wrote, "who was both the eyes and the lantern of England." This was the Cambridge he had come looking for and he stood quietly gazing at the statue erected in Newton's memory. With his usual attention to detail, he noted that Trinity College was home to a hundred and eighty students and possessed a great library, a reference to the gorgeous gallery library designed by Sir Christopher Wren. Mirza Salih didn't mention Wren's earliest commission, the college chapel at Pembroke, but then he was always more interested in books.

After his tour of Trinity, he spent the night at the house of Professor Lee and his wife; it lay around a mile and a half outside Cambridge, he recorded. It is not clear from the diary how long he spent at Lee's vicarage (it may have been a few weeks), but his next entry described him again meeting the evangelical Mr. Mandell of Queens'. In the latter's company, he made a further tour of the colleges before returning to Queens' for dinner with the godly trio of Lee, Jee, and Mandell. It was a repast that they would have taken in the college's fifteenth-century wooden hall, a setting that may have struck our Iranian seeker of modernity as a peculiarly dated setting for England's new learning.

The next entry in the diary saw Mirza Salih taking luncheon at Mr. Mandel's house. Cambridge's would-be convertors of Iran were certainly keen to learn about his heathen homeland. No doubt needing a breath of fresh air, Mirza Salih took what his host perhaps liked to call a "postprandial perambulation" by way of a stroll through the botanic garden. "Like the Oxford garden," he noted later, "this one has flowers from all over the world growing there," as well as all kinds of vegetables and herbs. Later that day, he met with a Mr. Lambert of Trinity College, almost certainly James Lambert, the former Regius professor of Greek and a fellow of Trinity between 1764 and his death in 1823. Given that Lambert was a strong supporter of the educational reform of the university, and of Trinity in particular, he was precisely the kind of company that Mirza Salih would have been most interested in meeting. Their encounter suggests that he was able to balance his time in Cambridge between helping the evangelicals and meeting scholars of more interest to himself. Later that evening, he dined with Mr. Lambert and other dons of the far from evangelical Trinity College, before being taken on another "postprandial" tour of its gardens.

Since Mirza Salih briefly mentions several other trips to Cambridge in his diary, we can assume that he came to know the university quite well. Indeed, in the final Cambridge section of the diary, he wrote a kind of brochure detailing the various qualities of the sixteen colleges and four halls that made up the varsity as a whole. In his usual systematic way, he emphasized their libraries (one of which contained thirty thousand books) and the Fitzwilliam Museum (only just founded in 1816), adding statistics on the town's population and the representatives it sent to Parliament. As ever, learning and liberty were the things he most admired about England. Alas, most of his Cambridge hosts had different ideas about England's glory, ideas that revolved instead around Albion's service to a world-conquering Christ.

Translate, for Christ's Sake

Although Mirza Salih had some opportunity to follow his own interests in Cambridge, his visits there were enabled by Professor Lee's project of translating the Bible into Arabic and Persian. Since Mirza Salih, and also Mirza Riza and Mirza Ja'far, found themselves drawn into this venture, it is worth looking more closely at the professor's great project. Soon after his arrival in Cambridge from Shropshire, Lee had begun to repay his part of the bargain he had made with the Church Missionary Society, who had funded his studies as a poor boy from the country. So it was that, fulfilling the dreams of Claudius Buchanan whom we have seen trying to persuade the vice chancellor to turn Cambridge into a scriptorium of Bible translators, Lee embarked on the multilingual cycle of scripture translations that continued for the rest of his life. Soon after settling into Cambridge in 1814, he had translated an evangelical tract titled *The Way of Truth and Life* into Arabic and Persian; the Persian version was printed by Scottish missionaries in the Russian port of Astrakhan and shipped south across the Caspian to Iran. The students' home country was no stranger, then, to Samuel Lee. After receiving his BA in 1817, through the grace and favor of Queens' College he was granted the position of curate at Chesterton, the village near Cambridge where Mirza Salih stayed as his guest. Though the evidence is less clear, there is good reason to think that on other occasions Lee hosted Mirza Riza and Mirza Ja'far there for the same translating purposes.

During his subsequent career, Lee trained several generations of British students in Islamic languages, funneling through Queens' a regular supply of young linguists to the Church Missionary Society. But it was ultimately in employing his own abilities that he made his name. And it was here that his expertise coincided with that of the students. For Professor Lee had dedicated himself to no lesser an ambition than translating the entire Bible into Arabic, Persian, and Hindustani in the high Protestant hope that personal access to the Word of God would waken in Hindu and Muslim hearts a sincere love of Christ. And if scripture itself somehow failed to do that, then more obstreperous infidels could be cajoled into conversion by the many polemical tracts he also translated. Like all grand ambitions, Lee's won admirers and detractors. When he had the temerity to publish an "improved" edition of the *Grammar of the Persian Language* composed by the great East India Company (and Oxford) orientalist Sir William Jones, Lee's critics seized their chance. Far from demonstrating his superiority to "Oriental Jones," they declared, the lesser Mr. Lee had only shown his command of grammar to be unfit for one who dared wrangle with the Word of God.

Fortunately for Professor Lee, in the face of such criticism he knew people who could testify to his skills in Persian and Arabic—he knew a group of native experts: the Muslim students. For Lee's rapid rise to prominence closely coincided with the students' years in England. He began studying at Cambridge only shortly before the Iranians arrived in London to begin their studies. And a mere two weeks before Mirza Salih and Mirza Ja'far made the visit to Oxford we saw in chapter two, the *Oxford University and City Herald* published a panegyric puff piece on Lee's accomplishments. He held command, it declared, over eighteen languages—not only Arabic and Persian, but also Coptic, Samaritan, and even Malay; these were languages whose sway stretched far across the infidel world! The timing of the article was no coincidence: it was published amid the campaign to elect him as Sir Thomas Adams professor of Arabic, still today the university's grandest position of its kind. So Lee had his supporters (evangelical, not least) as well as his detractors. Although the chair had sometimes been held by humanist scholars of Arabic literature, its original terms of endowment included in its purpose the desire that the incumbent should help propagate Christianity "to them who now sit in darkness." Lee's evangelical credentials certainly qualified him for that.

And so it was that in late 1818, as perhaps the only educated native speakers of Persian in England at the time, Mirza Salih and his companions were drawn into the campaign to elect Samuel Lee as Sir

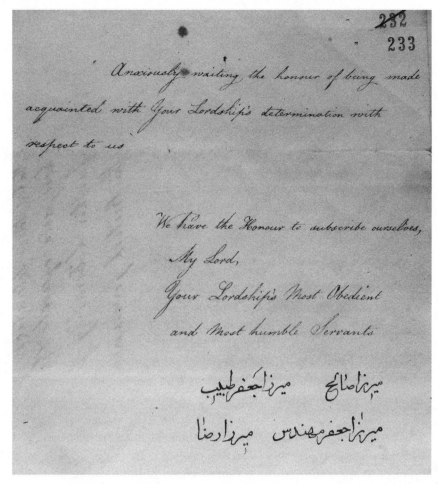

Fig. 19. Testifying to Greatness: The Students' Signatures. Source: Courtesy The National Archives. FO 60/12 (233).

Thomas Adams Professor of Arabic. As his daughter Alice Lee later recorded in her father's biography, "four native Persian gentlemen at that time residing in London . . . testified to his thorough acquaintance with the idiom and pronunciation, as well as the grammar of that language." Lee had to acquire these testimonials not only because of his critics. The more pressing reason was a consequence of his unconventional background as a working man who had married and had children before he matriculated at the university: for all his accomplishments, marriage disqualified him from becoming a fellow of Queens' or any other college and such a fellowship was a basic precondition of promotion to professor. But since Lee's gifts were so self-evident, when he graduated with his BA in 1818 the university sought to immediately appoint him to the professorship of Arabic by finding a way around the regulations. It was then pointed out that a professorship also required Lee to be at least a Master of Arts, for which status he would have to wait several more years after graduating as a Bachelor. As a way around this, his evangelical supporters then proposed that he be made an MA by Royal Decree, and it was in order for such a decree to be passed that the special testimonials were required. As the most obvious referees for his language skills, the Iranians were duly contacted.

In their letter of recommendation, now kept in the university archives, Mirza Salih and his companions phrased the matter like this:

> The object of writing these few lines is this: a person has this day requested the writer of this page, Mohammed Saulih, of Sheeraz, in the particular of information and attestation of this humble [person] as respects the learning and accomplishments of Mr. Lee, in the Arabic and Persic [sic] languages:—and was then desirous that he should write his belief, in this particular, on this page. Mohammed Saulih, of Sheeraz, therefore represents, that, having occasionally met Mr. Lee, and having seen both his Arabic and Persian writing, the above mentioned, in both the pronunciation and writing of Arabic, is eloquent and perfect; and in like manner, he is perfectly learned in the Persic. Upon the whole, this being the entire persuasion of your servant:—and in like manner the belief of all his [Iranian] companions, who have spoken with the above-mentioned [Lee] is this, that Mr. Lee, both in Persic and Arabic, whether as regards pronunciation, or reading, or writing, is learned and perfect.
>
> Upon the whole, this being the entire persuasion of your servant, and in like manner the belief of all his companions, who have spoken with the above-mentioned Mr. Lee, both in Persic and Arabic, that, whether as regards pronunciation, or reading, or writing, he is learned and perfect.

Given the help that we have seen Mirza Salih seeking from such friends as the Ouseley brothers and Sir John Malcolm, the testimonial letter is important proof of the reciprocal role the Muslim students played in the professional advancement of their Christian counterparts. The letter also shows that Lee had dealings with the other students as well as Mirza Salih, for Mirza Salih wrote the letter in the name of "all his companions, who have spoken with the above-mentioned Mr. Lee, both in Persic and Arabic." Given Lee's single-minded interest in the students for his translation projects, the fact that they had the opportunity to assess his Arabic and not only to speak with him in their Persian mother tongue suggests that, like Mirza Salih, they too worked with him on his Bible translations. This would help explain why Mirza Riza accompanied Mirza Salih on at least one of the several visits to see Professor Lee that he mentioned in his diary.

Ironically, the Iranians' testimonial was crucial to the rise of an evangelical to the highest echelons of England's intellectual establishment, helping the country boy Sam Lee surmount the last obstacles he faced as the legacy of his background. Although in his new salaried position, Lee had to sever his formal connections to the Church Missionary Society, he was committed to his Bible translations and so turned instead to the British and Foreign Bible Society. Here again Mirza Salih, and probably Mirza Riza and Mirza Ja'far, proved helpful. For this was the great irony at the heart of the evangelical enterprise: the help of native language speakers was a prerequisite for converting their fellow Muslims. Since educated Middle Eastern travelers to England were a scarce commodity in the early 1800s, they had tremendous value for those involved in translating scripture, tracts, and polemics. So it was that our little group of students found themselves drawn into the evangelical enterprise.

We know from dates in the diary and the testimonial letter that Mirza Salih visited Professor Lee several times in late 1818 (and on into 1819). Mirza Salih clearly knew him well enough to stay at his house. It is not clear from the diary how long Mirza Salih spent at Lee's vicarage; from the dates provided during one visit, he may have stayed up to two weeks at a time. If this was the case, then we can deduce that he spent this time working with Lee on his Persian Old Testament. For according to the memoir written by Lee's daughter, in around 1818 he was helped by "a learned Persian" to prepare a translation of the Old Testament to complement the Persian New Testament that we have seen being prepared by Henry Martyn a few years earlier. According to information in a contemporary newspaper report, it seems that Lee's main helper with the translation was the Indian Mirza Khalil, the Persian instructor at the East India College at Haileybury. As the newspaper noted, "Mr. Lee has in hand a new translation of the Old Testament into Persian, in conjunction with Mirza Khaleel." But given the close contacts between Lee and the students, and the time that Mirza Salih was spending as a guest at his vicarage, the professor also surely availed himself of the rare opportunity of help from a native speaker of Persian. After all, Mirza Khalil was an Indian and not an Iranian, and it was explicitly a "Persian" helper that Lee's daughter remembered.

Another detail further clarifies the matter. For shortly before Mirza Salih paid one of his visits to Professor Lee, Mirza Khalil's arguments with the governors of the East India College forced him to return to India, leaving Lee in dire need of a replacement helper. As we have seen, in the testimonial written by Mirza Salih, he declared that he had read several of Lee's Persian and Arabic works. Since all of Lee's Arabic and Persian works were either Bible translations or evangelical tracts, this means that Mirza Salih had read these works carefully enough to attest to their grammatical correctness. We have another confirmation of the students' exposure to Lee's evangelical writings from a few years later, when Lee isued his "improved" edition of Jones's *Grammar of the Persian Language*. In its preface, he acknowledged the "the opinions of intelligent and learned Persians whom I have had the opportunity to consult." Aside from Mirza Ibrahim of the East India College at Haileybury and Ambassador Abu'l-Hasan (whose own diary nowhere mentions Samuel Lee), the Iranian students were the only educated native speakers of Persian in England during the years when Lee was revising the *Grammar*.

The students surely had their own objectives in helping him: he enabled them to meet other Cambridge scholars, and enter college libraries, in which they had more interest. But the basic fact remains that the visits to Cambridge made by Mirza Salih, Mirza Riza, and Mirza Ja'far were all made possible by Professor Lee's need for the advice of native speakers in preparing his Persian *Grammar* and Old Testament. After all, their meetings with Lee fitted into a preexisting pattern that defined the students' access to the universities: he was the

Fig. 20. The Evangelicals Enthroned: Samuel Lee in His Professorial Regalia.
Source: Courtsey Trinity College Cambridge, the Master and Fellows of Trinity College Cambridge.

Cambridge counterpart (and close collaborator) of Professor Macbride, whom we saw hosting Mirza Salih and Mirza Ja'far in Oxford. Both professors were at this time devoting themselves to translating the Bible into Arabic and Persian, the two languages in which the students had been educated back home. Although Mirza Salih's diary contains no direct statement of collaboration on these Bible projects, his and Mirza Ja'far's visit to Oxford also coincided with Macbride's work on his Arabic New Testament. Mirza Salih would never have mentioned such assistance of Christian missionary efforts in a diary destined to be read by his Muslim sponsors back in Tabriz, where Shi'ite clerics held considerable influence at court. And it is hard to imagine Samuel Lee resisting the temptation to test his translations on all-too-rare native speakers. After all, the stakes of making a correct translation of Holy Scripture were incredibly high. In a period of virulent public polemics about the varsity orientalists' language skills, the reassurance of educated Iranian men of the pen was a tremendous bonus.

Overall, then, the evidence points strongly to Mirza Salih, and probably Mirza Riza and Mirza Ja'far, helping Samuel Lee in the translations he was making for the Bible Society. If this was a strange turn for a group of Muslims sent to England in search of scientific learning, then we should remember that their encounters with England's Christians were not wholly dominated by the interests of evangelicals. In the case of Mirza Salih at least, such "collaboration" will become more understandable as we now turn to what he gained in return.

A Persian Printer on Fleet Street

In order to partake in the modernizing 'asr-i jadid, or "new age," that his master 'Abbas Mirza sought to initiate in Iran, Mirza Salih had come to recognize the interdependence of knowledge and technology. The most important element of this was printing, though this interdependence had also become clear through his inspection of the mechanized paper mill near Oxford and the factory-based knowledge industry in Bristol. By the time he was helping Professor Lee in Cambridge, Mirza Salih had abandoned his hopes of studying at Oxford, whose pompous rituals he had scorned a month or two earlier. While he did not explain the decision, it is clear that he reached it for a variety of reasons. Not least of these were that the university didn't teach the new mechanical sciences in which he had become increasingly interested and that its evangelical professors were more interested in converting Muslims than helping defend their countries from Russia. Despite the realization that he would never study at either of the two varsities, he knew that his time there had not been wasted. As we have already seen, both he and his companions owed both their educations to the contacts they made with influential men and the institutions they controlled. And the evangelical professors with whom they spent time at the universities and even helped in their translation work formed part of this pattern of winning patrons. For Professors Lee and Macbride held sway over another important institution that would now prove central to Mirza Salih achieving his educational aims. That institution was the British and Foreign Bible Society, the most "establishment" of the period's many evangelical groups.

Even so, keeping company with the academic associates of the Bible Society was all very well when there still lurked in the background the practical matter of money. Despite the previous interim settlement of the students' affairs, in May 1818 Mr. D'Arcy was again writing to the Foreign Office to request further funds that would allow them to complete their education. This time, following the diplomatic advice of the foreign secretary Lord Castlereagh, the government was easier to persuade. Within a few weeks, Mr. D'Arcy was writing back to Joseph Planta at the Foreign Office to acknowledge the receipt of £800 (today around £61,000 or $100,000) for the students, who he attested (now that the money was flowing again) were still "under my charge." If this financial turn in their fortunes was partly down to the investment that the canny Lord Castlereagh made in their education, it also had much to do with the students' relationship with Sir Gore Ouseley. For in the months prior to Mr. D'Arcy's letters to the Foreign Office, it had been Sir Gore who, as former ambassador to Iran, had written to Mr. Planta to praise the young Iranians' commitments to their studies. "I have taken pains to ascertain the progress which the Persians have made," wrote Sir Gore, "And find it, *consideratis considerandis*, astonishingly great, so much so that I suppose a year or two more would finish their education." Turning toward the matter of money that had always been the root of their problems, Sir Gore added delicately that, "it would therefore be a pity to send them back for such a *trifling* difference as their staying a little longer might make." His tact won the day. The students no longer had to worry about funding their education, and for his part Mirza Salih was able to turn to the new subject he had now decided to master: the mechanical art of the printer.

Shortly afterward, Mirza Salih described how he was introduced to a printer in London who allowed him to attend his workshop daily where he would be taught to print books. The introduction to the printer came through his acquaintance with several prominent associates of the Bible Society, the most important of whom were its vice president Sir Gore Ouseley and its professorial advisors, John Macbride and Samuel Lee. Having reached London as a gentleman *mirza*, the young Muslim was now ready to transform himself into one of the revolutionary tradesmen of the nineteenth century. He was finally abandoning his aspirations of studying beneath the dreaming spires of Oxford for a more practical vocation in the smoky workshops of London.

It cannot have been an easy decision. For in Iran as in England, artisans were looked down on as the social unequals of *ahl-i qalam*, "men of the pen," like himself. Such social distinctions were no less clear among the students themselves. All but one of them held the esteemed "men of the pen" title of *mirza*, leaving their companion Muhammad ʿAli with the lowlier title of *ustad*, which though meaning "master craftsman" still denoted his lesser status. Such differences of rank had been apparent ever since the students left Iran: on their departure, Prince ʿAbbas Mirza had assigned only £100 to Muhammad ʿAli after assigning between £250 and £300 to each of the other students. Muhammad ʿAli's separation from the other students had continued throughout their time in England. He was the only member of the 1815 party to live apart from his companions when they all went to live in Croydon, leaving him behind—and perhaps ostracizing him— as he labored in London as a tradesman's apprentice. While Mirza Salih and the other *mirzas* visited the universities and studied with the gentleman officers of the Royal Military Academy, Muhammad ʿAli was instead acquiring artisan skills in the workshops of James Wilkinson & Sons, Gunmakers to His Majesty, at 12 Ludgate Hill and Alexander Galloway, Machinist and Engineer, at 69 High Holborn.

While Messrs. Wilkinson and Galloway were both distinguished craftsmen, their workshops were hardly the type of places which a *mirza* would frequent, other than perhaps as a customer. It must, then, have taken considerable courage for Mirza Salih to take up a similar apprenticeship to that being pursued by the humbler *ustad* Muhammad ʿAli. Given the socially sensitive character that his diary, with its many mention of slights and indignations, reveals him to have been, it was surely a daunting decision. Yet, as he recognized, these were revolutionary times, and he had lately come to see mechanical (if perhaps not manual) work in a new light. In this, he may have been influenced by the activities of the other *mirzas*. For the Military Academy students Mirza Riza and his close friend Mirza Jaʿfar and the medical students Hajji Baba and the other Mirza Jaʿfar, were all learning to conduct various "manual" operations—chemical experiments, bodily dissections, trigonometric observations. In the same months that Mirza Salih began his placement with the master printer, Mirza Jaʿfar went to Paris to spend several weeks "devoted to professional and scientific enquiries" that involved various practical experiments. With the other *mirzas* getting their hands dirty in manual procedures that were dignified with the label of "science," Mirza Salih may have chosen to see his new activities as having more in common with the scientific ventures of his fellow *mirzas* than the craftsman's apprenticeship of the humbler *ustad*. After all, in operating one of the new mechanical printing presses, his activities did have elements in common with the other *mirzas'* experiments with chemicals and theodolites. So it was that as the autumn of 1818 turned into winter, Mirza Salih finally decided to learn the art of printing that, when he left Iran three years earlier, none of his fellow countrymen had yet mastered.

His decision was a sensible one. We have already seen his fascination with books and newspapers, and his recognition of the role played by industrial technologies in the mass-production of paper. Such recognition would have been all the more piquant for knowing that the printing presses and papermaking machines behind England's book and newspaper trade did not exist in his homeland. Since, with their diplomatic and military backgrounds, none of his English friends belonged to the mercantile circles where he might learn the skills of the printer, it was through the help of Sir Gore and the evangelical professors that he gained his introduction to that great and godly consortium of book printers, the British and Foreign Bible Society (or for short, the Bible

Society). The other person who helped him was a "Mr. Butterworth of Bedford Square," who the students later thanked in a letter. A legal bookseller by profession, Joseph Butterworth (1770–1826) ran a bookshop on Fleet Street within a few minutes walk from where Mirza Salih was about to learn the printer's art. Yet even Mr. Butterworth connected him back to the evangelicals through his role as one of the founding figures of the Bible Society. Indeed, a few years earlier, Butterworth pledged £50 per year (today around £3,800, or over $6,000) over a period of seven years to support the Bible Society's revised translation and reprinting of the Polyglot Bible. The gift was specifically earmarked to aid the efforts of his brother-in-law, the Methodist Adam Clarke (1762–1832), in retranslating the Polyglot's sections in Persian.

So it was that between Messrs. Lee, Macbride, Ouseley, and Butterworth, Mirza Salih was about to be directed toward the greatest publisher on earth. For the Bible Society worked on a scale that rendered insignificant even the print-runs of Jane Austen's best-selling novels. To Mirza Salih, it formed the crucial link between the evangelical circles he had entered in the universities and the mechanical circles of London toward which he now wished to turn. In the fourteen years since its foundation in 1804, the Bible Society had already entirely transformed England's publishing industry by adapting new production technologies and distribution methods that enabled it to print books on a scale that England (or the world) had never seen. Despite first being set up to supply the poor people of Wales with Bibles in their own language, the Bible Society soon garnered the larger ambitions signaled in its title of the British *and Foreign* Bible Society. As we have seen, in the background to Jane Austen's stories of country parsons, in the opening decades of the nineteenth century there emerged many new missionary organizations seeking to bring Christianity to the "heathens" of England's growing empire. In 1795 the London Missionary Society was founded, followed in 1799 by the Church Missionary Society, with which we have already seen Professors Lee and Macbride closely connected. Founded five years later, the Bible Society saw itself as a more theologically mainstream organization, less prone to the zealous "enthusiasm" of the missionary societies proper. For the Bible Society was not concerned with dispatching missionaries to foreign lands. Instead, its sole concern was in translating, publishing, and distributing the Bible, believing that direct and unmediated access to the word of God would do its own work in winning hearts and minds for Jesus.

At heart, the Bible Society was as much an educational organization as an evangelical one. It saw an expressly Christian education as the key to human progress: a literate and learned faith would dissolve the superstitious and fanatical darkness in which much of the world was shrouded. These were, after all, the years in which progressive evangelicals had used scriptural arguments to force the abolition of the slave trade all across the British Empire. Given that slavery was still very much alive in Iran, which like the rest of the Middle East continued to import slaves from Africa, we can sense the appeal of this Christian humanism to educated Muslims like Mirza Salih. As *The Times* in London had reported after he inspected a Christian charitable hospital during his trip to Gloucester a few months earlier, Mirza Salih "seemed affected by the circumstance of a black man being among the patients; and being told that the institution embraced those of every nation and color, observed that 'this was true charity.'" Even though it was distributing the Bible and not the Quran, Mirza Salih may therefore have been sympathetic to the educational and charitable aims of the Bible Society. And even if he had no such sympathy for its aims, he surely realized that, as England's largest publisher, the Bible Society had skills in which he had great interest: the skill of printing books.

Yet it was not so much the general matter of printing that interested Mirza Salih. It was the Bible Society's increasing specialization in printing in Persian and Arabic. This turn from its original interest in Welsh to the learned languages of the Middle East and India owed much to the influence of its first president, Lord Teignmouth (1751–1834). As the most "establishment" of the period's many evangelical societies, the Bible Society had close contacts with the expanding empire's elites: Lord Teignmouth was the former governor-general of India. Having overseen the East India Company's administration at a time when its official language was still Persian, Lord Teignmouth—or Sir John Shore, as he was formerly known—was all too aware of Persian's importance. Indeed, he was a considerable scholar of Persian and Hindustani in his own right, well versed in the classical poetry of Sa'di, Hafiz, and 'Attar, which he could quote from memory. After he retired from Calcutta to take up his position at the Bible Society, he was still able to speak Persian with considerable fluency and had conversed with Ambassador Abu'l-Hasan on numerous occasions during his stay in London from 1809 to 1810. During his years of service with the East India Company, he had witnessed in Calcutta Asia's earliest attempts to print books in Persian. In a letter he had written back in 1783, he had not felt confident about the prospects of printing books in Persian, noting that "the expense of printing them is so enormous, and the reputation derived from the labours of translating them so little, that few attempts more will be made." But by the time he was at the helm of the Bible Society in London thirty years later, the prospects of printing Persian—as well as Arabic and Hindustani—were looking rather different. This was not least due to the economies of scale that the Bible Society's vast resources could bring to the task.

The mere fact that Mirza Salih knew Messrs. Ouseley, Lee, and Macbride may not have been enough to persuade them to help him learn the printer's craft. After all, this was a time when an apprenticeship to any craftsman was a formal undertaking that usually required not only a commitment of around seven years of service but also the payment of fees. But given what we have seen of his help with the translations Professor Lee was then making for the Bible Society, there is good reason to think that he was expected to help with its scripture printing activities in return for his training. We will see more evidence for this later. There may have been even more to the matter than this, for in his meeting with the evangelical bluestocking Hannah More during his tour of the West Country with Mirza Ja'far a few months earlier, Mirza Salih had made an extraordinary pledge. According to the diary in which Mrs. More penned her record of the meeting, she stated that when she presented Mirza Salih and Mirza Ja'far with her book *Practical Piety*, "they declared they would translate [it] into their language immediately on their return home, and that it should be the first work which should bring into exercise the knowledge they had acquired of the art of printing, and employ the printing press which they were carrying back into their own country."

In other words, the two Muslims had pledged to translate and print an evangelical Christian text on their return to Iran. The evangelicals were certainly keen to acquire "on the ground" helpers in the regions they sought to convert. Cambridge's Reverend Henry Martyn had employed Arab and Iranian assistants in Calcutta and Shiraz, and the same years that saw Mirza Salih learning printing in London saw other Iranians help translate and print the Bible at the Scottish and German missions in Astrakhan and Shusha just over the border from Iran in Russian territory. We do not know whether Mirza Salih made similar promises to Sir Gore Ouseley or Professors Lee and Macbride to the one he made to Mrs. More. But given the combination of pressures he was under—from the evangelicals on the one hand and his Iranian royal master on the other—a few equivocal promises would have been a small price to pay to finally access so important a technology as printing.

London's Typographical Bazaar

Long before taking up his apprenticeship, Mirza Salih had learned of London's experiments in printing Persian through his associations with various orientalists. From his time with the British embassy to Iran in 1811, he knew Sir William Ouseley, who through his journal *The Oriental Collections* served as an impresario for printing Persian. We have also seen how in Croydon, Mirza Salih briefly studied with John Shakespear, who in 1817 published his *Dictionary, Hindustani and English* with Persian fonts cast in London. Then there was Cambridge's Professor Lee, who we know from a newspaper report was designing a new Persian type for his Bible translations just prior to meeting Mirza Salih. As reported on September 26, 1818, "Mr. Lee has moreover made a new fount of letters for Hindostanee and Persian printing."

Before the turn toward Persian, England had an earlier history of printing Arabic: by the second half of the seventeenth century, there were already half a dozen Arabic presses operating there. With the study of Arabic established at Oxford by that time, much of the demand came from university men like Edward Pococke, the first holder of the Laudian professorship at Oxford. Early attempts to establish Arabic printing in Oxford itself were made by Dr. John Fell (1625–86), the bishop of Oxford. He established the university press in the Sheldonian Theatre, where such books were still being printed when Mirza Salih and Mirza Jaʿfar visited it earlier in 1818.

By that time, a combination of the political interests of the East India Company and the intellectual interests of several of its employees had led to the adaptation of those Arabic printing skills to print Persian as well. Many of the early fonts were clumsy, though—their appearance an affront to the keen orthographic tastes that English orientalists acquired from their Indian *munshi* teachers and the ornate manuscript culture on which they were reared. It was therefore in Calcutta rather than London that the most important breakthroughs were made in Persian typography. There in 1781, the first Persian book was printed in India through the efforts of the Company employee and oriental scholar, Francis Balfour. Alongside him, Calcutta's other key promoter of Persian printing was his collaborator Charles Wilkins, who had been experimenting with Asian language fonts since 1778. After Wilkins returned to London in 1786—more specifically after 1800 when he became librarian at East India House, where he may have met Ambassador Abu'l-Hasan on his tour of its library—he helped direct the emergence of London's Persian printing industry.

In 1799, Sir William Ouseley published a notice in his journal *The Oriental Collections* that "a fount [*sic*] of Persian types, in imitation of the *Talīk* character generally used in manuscripts has been lately cast by Mr. Vincent Figgins, for the use of the Oriental Press." Over the next few decades, Vincent Figgins (who died as late as 1861) became the East India Company's most important supplier of "exotic type," winning particular fame for his delicate Persian fonts. Due to demand from the East India Company (including its two colleges), several other London typecasters learned to produce Persian type. For example, rather than Figgins, Charles Wilkins favored the fine printer William Bulmer (1757–1830), who used the "elegant orientals" cast by the Birmingham-born type-founder William Martin (d. 1816), who won a good many East India Company commissions. Martin's foundry was located on Duke Street in Piccadilly, while Vincent Figgins's workshop was found on 17–18 West Street in Smithfield, somewhat closer to East India House. From these early entrepreneurial workshops, Jane Austen's London soon grew into the world's biggest center of both Persian and Arabic printing.

Despite all of the business supplied by the East India Company, none of these printers could match the scale on which, from around

1810, the Bible Society began to print in the many languages that used the Arabic script. Just as it transformed the publishing of books in English, the Bible Society utterly transformed every aspect of publishing in Islamic languages. Its *Annual Reports* detail the scale of its investments in Arabic-script printing, including Persian. During the students' years in London, the average print-run for such books was 5,000 copies: this was the number of copies they printed of their Arabic Bible, Arabic-script Malay Bible and Arabic-script Hindustani New Testament. This was also the print-run for the Persian and Turkish New Testaments, which the Bible Society arranged to have printed through its overseas agencies in Saint Petersburg and Paris. A few other works were issued on different scales, with its 1819 Arabic Psalter running to only 2,000 copies while its 1821 Arabic-script Malay New Testament ran to a massive 10,000. When these print-runs are compared with those of books produced for the East India Company in Calcutta and London, they show that the Bible Society was printing on a far larger scale.

By the time Mirza Salih decided to take up his printer's apprenticeship, the evangelical desire to convert Asia to Christianity had therefore turned London into the global center of typographical innovation. No city in the world at this time printed more books in the languages of Islam, albeit a narrow range of books devoted to the cause of Jesus. In switching his interests toward the study of printing, Mirza Salih had made a wise and informed decision. For aside from a few earlier Ottoman experiments, printing had not yet spread to Muslim hands anywhere in the Middle East. The stakes were high enough to encourage him into an unusual move for a Muslim: to become an evangelical apprentice.

The Evangelicals' Apprentice

The master printer under whom Mirza Salih began his apprenticeship can be identified as Richard Watts (d. 1844), a printer and type-founder who worked very closely with the Bible Society. Before moving to London, Watts had gained his reputation as a printer in Cambridge, where from 1802 to 1809 he held the influential office of university printer. It was in 1806 in Cambridge, where we have already seen evangelical causes gain momentum, that Watts and his colleague John Smith printed a cheap edition of the New Testament in Welsh. As a demonstration of what could be accomplished through linking linguistic and printing skills with the new economies of scale afforded by industrially produced paper and mass-produced copies of a single book, the Welsh Bible became the launchpad for the Bible Society's venture of printing the Bible in every language on earth. It was little surprise that the success (and further potential) of the Welsh Bible project brought Watts to the attention of Professor Lee. For as the professor already knew, Watts was renowned for his ability to cast type in the variety of scripts used by the varsity's Bible scholars , such as Syriac and Greek. And so it was that, though Watts knew no foreign languages himself, his reputation as a typecaster and his meticulous work in printing the Bible in Welsh saw Professor Lee and the Bible Society fund him to cast many new fonts, eventually leading him to produce sixty-seven different type sets. Crucially, these included many Arabic-script fonts, including several specially made for Persian, which has four more letters than the basic Arabic alphabet.

After leaving the university press, in 1816 Watts arrived in London and established a spacious new workshop on the continuation of Fleet Street known as Temple Bar. It was a shrewd business move, for his new premises were just a few minutes' walk from Bible House, the headquarters of the Bible Society whose insatiable desire to print foreign-language Bibles made them Watts's chief customer. Among the many Arabic-script projects that he took on for the Bible Society and other evangelical groups, in 1818 he deployed his newest Persian type to print for the Homily Society the Anglican *Book of Common Prayer* that Cambridge's Henry Martyn had translated into Hindustani. It may well have been this project, heard of through his extensive dealings with Professor Lee that year, that first attracted Mirza Salih to Watts's workshop.

However the introduction exactly came about, it is clear that of the several hundred printers working in London at the time, Mirza Salih was in contact with someone from the same small circle of committed evangelical Christians he knew from Oxford and Cambridge. In his diary, he noted that Mr. Watts had already printed the New Testament

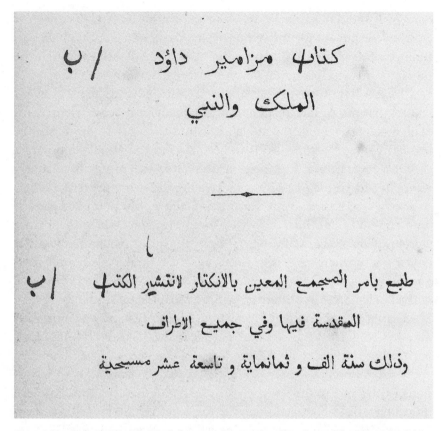

كتاب مزامير داؤد   ب /

الملك والنبي

ا

طبع بامر المجمع المعين بالانكتار لانتشير الكتب   ب /

المقدسة فيها وفي جميـع الاطراف

وذلك سنة الف و ثمانماية و تاسعة عشر مسيحية

Fig. 21. Fresh from Watts's Workshop: Arabic Books of Psalms with Dr. Macbride's Corrections.   Source: Published with permission of the British and Foreign Bible Society, Cambridge.

in Persian, Arabic, Hindustani, and Syriac, as indeed he had. As chief oriental printer to the Bible Society, the Church Missionary Society, and the Prayer Book and Homily Society, Watts issued thousands of Arabic-script books from his presses every year.

During the very year in which Mirza Salih was learning to print, Watts's workshop took on a large contract for the Hindustani New Testament, for which he deployed an expanded set of his Persian font. The project's supervisor was none other than Professor Samuel Lee. Also being printed in Watts's workshop that year was an Arabic translation of the Book of Psalms, whose supervisor, with perfect symmetry, was Oxford's Dr. Macbride. Both projects were funded by the Bible

Society. Around this time Watts was also printing an Arabic version of the New Testament for the Bible Society, the supervisor of which was again Professor Lee. Although when it was finally seen through the press, the Arabic Testament bore the date 1821, since such large projects took a long time to pass through Watts's hands there is every chance that the Arabic Testament was already in process when Mirza Salih was working in Mr. Watts's workshop. On a day-to-day basis, the learned young Muslim's skills in both Arabic and Hindustani would certainly have been a huge help, since Watts's two professorial supervisors lived a whole day's journey away in the two university towns.

The two professors were not Mirza Salih's only points of contact with Mr. Watts. For the latter was also closely associated with Sir Gore Ouseley, who as the Bible Society's vice president maintained regular contact with their printer. In Mr. Watts's Oriental Type-Foundry (to give his workshop its proper name) Mirza Salih was clearly surrounded with people he knew. Moreover, with its location on Temple Bar at the junction of the Strand and Fleet Street, the workshop was only five-minutes' walk from the premises of Alexander Galloway on High Holborn, where Muhammad 'Ali was pursuing the second part of his own apprenticeship. At the time, Temple Bar was filled with talk of inventions, with a mix of the latest gossip and revolutionary ideas. For with its centuries-old connections with the legal profession, it was now becoming the pulsing heart of English journalism that flourished on the adjoining Fleet Street. It was here that England's coffeehouse culture had begun, where ideas and newspapers came free with a steaming cuppa. For someone with Mirza Salih's interests in constitutional history, Temple Bar was a fascinating place to be. The winding alleyways that led off Temple Bar to the courtyard legal offices of the Inner and Outer Temple were filled with such history. Down one alley were the rooms where the great constitutional lawyer and founder of England's liberties Sir Edward Coke had studied two centuries earlier; down another alleyway was the house where in the 1770s Dr. Samuel Johnson had produced his outspoken journal *The Idler*; another gulley led to the house where England's finest journalist essayist, Charles Lamb, was raised. Fleet Street, and Temple Bar, was where the working man met the thinking man. As he made the shift from *mirza* to artistan, this suited Mirza Salih perfectly.

He did not record much in detail of his day-to-day dealings with Mr. Watts, merely noting that for six months he went each day to learn to print in Watts's workshop. The fact that when he left Iran four years earlier, no one in the entire country knew how to print a book highly motivated him to learn the practical and mechanical dimensions of printing. Overcoming his background as one of the dignified "men of the pen," he grasped the importance of understanding the machinery that was creating an industrializing knowledge industry in the England of the time. There is little doubt that he set himself the oily task of learning to actually operate a press, a task that for all the skills involved was still very much a form of physical labor. The new iron handpresses used by Watts and other commercial printers around Fleet Street were heavy items of machinery requiring muscle and sweat. Anyone who spent time around Fleet Street could spot an experienced printer: the constant labor of pulling the press's lever with their right arms overdeveloped the muscles on the entire right side of their bodies, leaving them with a distinguishing lumbering gait.

If for his part Mirza Salih was dedicated to acquiring these physical machine skills, it is likely that Mr. Watts wanted different services from him in return. As we have seen, during the six months that Mirza Salih worked with him, Watts was seeing through several major contracts involving Arabic, Persian, and Hindustani, all languages his new apprentice knew well. It was a beneficial exchange of skills for both Mr. Watts and Mirza Salih. Although there is no precise evidence that they struck this deal, official documentation in the British National Archives shows that in late 1818, a few months before Mirza Salih came to work for Watts, his companion Mirza Riza was doing translation work relating to the Foreign Office's diplomatic correspondence in Persian. With so few educated native speakers of Persian in England, and with their additional knowledge of Arabic and Hindustani, once again the students had important skills they could trade for their own purposes.

In any case, it would not have been an unusual bargain for Watts to make. In Calcutta, translators and printers of scripture had been using native-speaker asssistants since the evangelicals had begun working there twenty years earlier. Watts would himself later employ other Persian-speaking Muslims, albeit of Indian rather than Iranian background. One of them was Sullivan Law Hyder, a young lad whose father Ghulam Haydar (d. 1823) taught Persian handwriting at the East India College at Haileybury. Also known as Sulman (that is, the Muslim name Sulayman), Sullivan spent a full five years as Watts's apprentice in the mid-1820s. Then, having finished his term, he sailed away to find work in Calcutta, the other great center of missionary printing. Presumably, Sullivan had learned to write Persian from his father (teaching it was, after all, his profession) and so brought to Mr. Watts similar skills to those of Mirza Salih a few years earlier. For as both printer and typefounder, Richard Watts needed proofreaders to scan what he printed for mistakes; and he needed calligraphers to draw the elegant originals of his typefaces. As a traditionally trained man of the pen, Mirza Salih fulfilled these needs perfectly.

Mechanical Motivations

So it was that, after his disappointments at Oxford and Cambridge, Mirza Salih found himself studying in the printing shop of the Bible Society. There seems little point in using the postcolonial framework of "resistance and opposition" to understand his motivations, or invoking the "persuasive means, the quotidian processes of hegemony" theorized by Edward Said in his study of the colonialist underbelly of Jane Austen's era. For high-status Iranians at least, and in Mirza Salih's period, modern assumptions of political and cultural hegemony are easily overstated. The fact that Mirza Salih was an Iranian and not an Indian is significant here: he and his fellow travelers had no experience of English rule in their homelands, and at the start of their journey England was an ally against Russia. As for the evangelicals, it is clear from the tone of his diary that Mirza Salih actually liked his evangelical friends. For all their rhetoric against false religions, in their personal dealings they were humane, god-fearing, and generous people. His diary suggests that it was among evangelicals that he was often made most welcome—in London and the West Country no less than the universities—and if this was partly due to his usefulness to their cause, it probably also had something to do with their charitable dispositions. And in any case, testing as some of his encounters with the evangelicals must have been, they were now paying off a tremendous educational dividend by teaching him what were for an Iranian the unique skills of the printer.

Yet there was undoubtedly a certain reticence in his diary about admitting how closely he had worked with the evangelicals who, after Henry Martyn's public disputes with the mullahs of Shiraz, were already notorious in Iran. So while Mirza Salih did candidly mention that his printing master Mr. Watts had issued many translations of the New Testament, including in Persian and Arabic, he did not explicitly mention that he worked for the missionaries. Perhaps that was implicit enough to be clear. But for someone sent to England to learn skills that would help Islamic Iran confront the invasions of Christian Russia, it would hardly have made a sensible emphasis in a diary destined to be read by his superiors back home. Reticent about the missionaries as he may have been in his diary, after several years of close engagement with the evangelicals, Mirza Salih was well aware of their intentions. Even if it meant teaming up with men who sought to convert the world to Christianity, he recognized the benefits of the skills he could learn from them. Ironic as it may seem, at the time there was nowhere better in the world for a Muslim to study printing than in the back alleys of Fleet Street.

If there were no genteel salons around Fleet Street, it was nonetheless one of the most important literary districts of Jane Austen's London. Indeed, it was at Temple Bar, a couple of doors away from Mr. Watts's workshop, that Miss Austen's first novel, *Sense and Sensibility*, was printed in 1811 by C. Roworth. During the months of Mirza Salih's apprenticeship, he was living with Mirza Ja'far at 8 Salisbury Court, just off Fleet Street. It was a fitting new home, because for centuries Salisbury Court had been the meeting place of London's writers and printers. Samuel Richardson had written his pioneering novel *Pamela* in his house there (and then printed it at number 11); and the satirical printmaker William Hogarth was also a frequent visitor to Salisbury Court. Moreover, it was over many a pint of ale that Dr. Johnson had written his dictionary in Salisbury Court. And now Mirza Salih was sitting there writing his diary, his own unknown contribution to England's literary history.

It must have been a lively time for him and Mirza Ja'far. In their neighboring taverns along Fleet Street, wits and jobbing writers rubbed shoulders every evening at Ye Olde Cheshire Cheese, where Ben Jonson and Oliver Goldsmith had once supped and sung. Mirza Salih mentioned in his diary that each day, after leaving Watts's workshop, he would go to eat supper at a nearby inn, and Ye Olde Cheshire Cheese was certainly the nearest. He would have met all sorts there: men who assailed him in the workers' cant of the Regency netherworld, asking him "How dost do my buff?" Perhaps they inquired what a "swell cove" (fine gentleman) was doing in such a "touting ken" (alehouse) and what "fuddle" (drink) he would like to "guzzle down his gullet." "Flash lingo," "St. Giles Greek," this was an English that didn't feature in the delicate drawing rooms of Miss Austen's novels. But Mirza Salih and Mirza Ja'far would have heard it all the same. For Salisbury Court, Temple Bar, and Fleet Street made up a raucous neighborhood where not only Bibles but slanders, scandals, and satires were also printed. Far from the quiet Christian libraries of Cambridge, it was where the New Testament was just one printing job among many. And that practical spirit suited Mirza Salih just fine.

A neighborhood of buffs and books, then; but also of machines. For in Watts's workshop on the eastern boundary of Fleet Street, Mirza Salih found himself in a place of great technological invention. Just a couple of years earlier in 1814, it had been here that the power of steam was successfully applied to printing for the first time in history. It happened when the German inventor Friedrich König adapted a steam press to print *The Times* newspaper, which Mirza Salih often read and whose huge production numbers he cited. Through fast iron hand-presses, cheap mass-produced paper, and in some cases steam engines, such recent advances had allowed the Bible Society to leap from nowhere in 1804 to become in the short space of a decade the world's largest producer of books in Islamic languages. But Fleet Street was not only a place of innovations in printing and literature. A quite different set of Fleet Street inventions were connected with the other students, Hajji Baba, Mirza Ja'far, and Mirza Riza. Outlining a program of studies for Hajji Baba, the latter's medical teacher Dr. Fromager had written that "there is now making for the American Government by Mr. Troughton, Mathematical Instrument Maker in Fleet Street, a complete and very extensive apparatus for measuring a base and carrying on a Trigonometrical Survey in America, similar to the one carrying on in England . . . under the direction of Lieutenant-Colonel Mudge."

Fig. 22. English Literature's Byways: The Back Alleys of Fleet Street.   Source: Photo by Nile Green.

Since Colonel Mudge was overseeing the education of Mirza Jaʿfar and Mirza Riza at the Royal Military Academy, and Dr. Fromager was one of Hajji Baba's (and perhaps the other Mirza Jaʿfar's) teachers, the new inventions issuing from Fleet Street were also finding their way into the other students' educations.

While Mirza Salih was learning to print books, Mirza Ja'far and Mirza Riza had become excited about learning the new skills made possible by the Military Academy's Colonel Mudge and the mathematical instrument maker, Mr. Troughton. For they had reached London in the middle of a brief but magnficent era in the history of mapmaking and surveying that was based around Mudge's new techniques and Troughton's new instruments. In 1818, that same year, these techniques were deployed to found the Great Trigonometrical Survey of India. It was led by a young military surveyor like Mirza Ja'far and Mirza Riza; his name was George Everest. Under his leadership, for the first time in history the Great Trigonometrical Survey managed to definitively map the subcontinent. Despite his objections, George Everest was later honored by lending his name to the subcontinent's crowning mountain glory. Yet before he found fame, George Everest was a student at the Royal Military Academy like Mirza Ja'far and Mirza Riza, whose names found no such cartographic immortality. Smaller as their part may have been, they too participated in that revolutionary era of mapmaking.

Nor was it only the *mirzas* who were taking part in these technological revolutions. For the humbler *ustad*, or "master craftsman," Muhammad 'Ali was also being introduced to new tools and techniques that would prove no less pivotal. As we saw in an earlier chapter, when the students' educations had finally been fixed up a few years earlier, Muhammad 'Ali was apprenticed to the swordsmith and gunsmith James Wilkinson of Ludgate Hill. By background in Iran, Muhammad 'Ali was a blacksmith. Fittingly, the man under whom he now studied in London specialized in a trade that relied on the improved use of iron developed over the previous few decades. For if the industrial revolution was powered by coal, then it was built with iron. Whether boilers, pipes, and cylinders for steam engines, or girders for bridges and railroads, almost every mechanical and engineering advance of the era was made possible by the improved manufacture of iron. All this had its origins in the relatively simple but revolutionary invention of cast iron, of smelting iron with coal rather than charcoal so as to render it pourable and moldable into an infinity of shapes. First pioneered by Abraham Darby of Coalbrookdale, the casting process turned iron into the plastic of the nineteenth century. For Darby and his heirs, it

brought their Coalbrookdale Company immense riches by mass producing the kinds of iron cooking implements required by every household in the land, rich and poor, and by countless more overseas. By
1779, Coalbrookdale cast-iron girders were used to build the world's
first iron bridge, just a mile or two away from Coalbrookdale itself;
other bridges followed, as did many other architectural uses for cast
iron. Few admirers of Regency architecture realize that the graceful
buildings of John Nash relied on the extensive use of cast iron for both
structural and decorative purposes. Nash even used cast iron throughout the Brighton Pavilion he built in flamboyant Muslim style for the
prince regent. Next time you see a nineteenth-century classical col-
umn, knock it and hear whether it's made of slowly carved stone or
quickly cast iron. It is more likely the latter.

From the Shropshire vale of Coalbrookdale, Darby's new method
spread to the nearby city of Birmingham: the surrounding region
gained the name of the "Black Country" for its concentration of iron
and coal working. The key figure in the spread of iron casting was the
Shropshire blacksmith John Wilkinson (1728–1808), dubbed the "Iron
King" for the vast Bradley ironworks he founded at Bilston in the Black
Country. And though John Wilkinson seems not to have been a direct
relative of Muhammad ʿAli's master James Wilkinson, there were other
connections that linked Muhammad ʿAli's teacher to the iron-based
innovations in the Black Country. For James Wilkinson was the fore-
man, son-in-law, and heir of the Birmingham gunsmith Henry Nock
(1741–1804), who moved to London after learning his trade in Birmingham. In 1768, he established his business in the London district of Holborn, where fifty years later Muhammad ʿAli entered his workshop to
learn his trade. In Nock's time, the concentration of metalworkers in
Birmingham saw hundreds of workshops flourish in the city's Gun
Quarter. As the largest weapons manufactory in the world, Birmingham supplied arms by the thousand for the many wars of the eighteenth and early nineteenth centuries, from America to India and New
Zealand. Mirza Salih himself described its preeminence in the weapons
trade, writing that "Birmingham is a place that is famous for manufacturing weapons of war, including muskets, swords, pistols, daggers,
and other weapons; many workstations and large crowds of people are
busy at work there." Since he never visited the city, it seems likely that

he had learned about it in conversation with Muhammad ʿAli, who would certainly have heard of it from his gunmaking teacher, Mr. Wilkinson.

It was Wilkinson's teacher and father-in-law, Henry Nock, who transferred those Birmingham skills to London. There he took out several patents for his inventions, which included a removal and cleanable rifle barrel that became an industry standard. He also specialized in bladed weapons. In time, Nock won large commissions to supply both guns and bayonets to the East India Company. When he died in 1804, he was succeeded by his son-in-law James Wilkinson: his name is still remembered today by shavers worldwide through the title of the company he inherited: Wilkinson Sword. During the year or two that Muhammad ʿAli studied in Wilkinson's workshop on Ludgate Hill, he learned much about the new uses of iron that had developed in the past few decades, especially the new technique of "rifling" gun barrels. For the mechanically improved guns—some of the world's first rifles—that won James Wilkinson the title of "Gun Maker to His Majesty and the Honorable East India Company" were among the most history-changing machines of their day. They had helped the East India Company win control of Bengal and helped Wellington defeat Napoleon at Waterloo. Learning his craft each day in London, the former blacksmith Muhammad ʿAli hoped those same rifles would defend his home city of Tabriz from the Russian soldiers staring over the border.

If anything, the second apprenticeship that Muhammad ʿAli was serving at the time of Mirza Salih's apprenticeship with Mr. Watts was even more exciting. His master, Alexander Galloway (1776–1847) of 69 High Holborn (a short walk from Watts's workshop), was listed in London's trade directories at this time as a "machinist and engineer." In Galloway's case, what this actually involved was the manufacture of the new steam engines whose versatility was changing every form of industry, from cording cotton to printing news. As Matthew Boulton, the greatest manufacturer of steam engines, proudly told visitors to his Birmingham factory, "I sell here, sir, what all the world desires to have—power." Following in Boulton's footsteps, in London Galloway developed his business in this direction by shifting away from his earlier specialization toward the manufacture of steam engines. Like Boulton, he was also an effective salesman of steam, in the years before he met Muhammad 'Ali writing to magazines to defend the safe use of steam power for wooden-hulled ships. By the time the young Muslim entered Galloway's premises, his workers had built many different kinds of steam engine. While it is unlikely that his Iranian apprentice studied every aspect of their manufacture, Muhammad 'Ali would at least have learned their basic principles, including, with an eye to having one shipped back to his princely master, how to operate them. It was not an outlandish idea. By this time, Matthew Boulton's company had for decades been selling steam engines to the East India Company and shipping them out to Calcutta and Bombay. One of Boulton's steam engines was used to mint hundreds of thousands of coins for the East India Company with ornate Persian inscriptions! By the time of Muhammad 'Ali's apprenticeship, Galloway was exporting his own machines as far as Athens and Alexandria, the Egyptian port with which Jane Austen's sailor brother Francis had many dealings.

Around this time, another Muhammad 'Ali, the ruler of Egypt, began importing steam engines to Cairo via Alexandria; these may have been Alex Galloway's engines. Even so, our Muhammad 'Ali, the blacksmith from Tabriz, was one of history's very first Muslims to learn the workings of the steam engine. He was learning to practically operate machines that Mirza Salih and Mirza Ja'far had only looked at, as on the day they spent hours trying to understand the steam engine at the cloth mill they visited in Gloucestershire. Mirza Salih frequently mentioned the new power of steam, or *bukhar*, in his diary. But it was only Muhammad 'Ali, the lowliest of all of the students, who properly studied the machines that were changing the world.

We can, then, imagine the students' excitement at this time. Finally, in their different ways, they were all accessing the *'ulum-i jadid*, or "new sciences," they had traveled so far to find. Whether theodolites, handpresses, or steam engines, each of the students was absorbed in mastering the new apparatus of the age. Given Mirza Salih's desire to likewise share in this scientific revolution and not only conjugate Latin verbs, his motivation to take the evangelicals up on their offer of a printer's apprenticeship becomes more understandable. Machines and scientific instruments were heavyweight iron symbols of the new learning. And if that meant helping print the Christian scriptures that Muslims anyway considered holy, then it was a compromise that he found reasonable enough. And reason was, as ever, Mirza Salih's guide.

Friendship

5

Diplomatic Friendships

Amicable Allies

By late 1818, the students were finally settled into the varied rhythms of their studies. Mirza Salih described his typical daily routine:

> I wake up at seven in the morning, and remain at the house of Mr. Belfour till ten o'clock, studying French with him. Then, after taking lunch, I set again to my studies and read more French books until two o'clock. Then, after changing into English clothes, I go to the house of the master printer. Until four-thirty, I remain in his printing workshop. Then I go to an inn to eat supper and return home. There I read about the history of Rome, or Greece, or Russia, or Turkey, or Iran, or else read stories in English, and finally write down some pages of translation from French into English.

It was during these months of happy routine that a long-awaited message arrived from Iran. For on September 18, 1818, their friend Mr. Percy informed the students that a letter had been carried for them by Sir Robert Liston (1742–1836), who had just returned from serving as ambassador to the Ottoman Empire at Constantinople. It was a big moment: the students all hoped the letter promised lavish funds for furthering their education. After waiting so long for news about how much money their government would send them for lessons being funded by the English prince regent and the Foreign Office, its contents came as a grave disappointment. The letter only brought bad news: Ambassador Abu'l-Hasan was on his way back for a short visit to England, and when he left the students would all have to accompany him back to Iran. In short, they had only five or six more months to complete their studies. A further letter, written on behalf of Abu'l-Hasan by the Foreign Office, was addressed to Mr. D'Arcy, making the "request that you will immediately take the necessary steps for embarking the five Persian students under your charge, together with Hajee Baba, on board a vessel for Constantinople." As though Mr. D'Arcy needed any more encouragement to rid himself of the youths he felt were a noose around his neck, the letter warned that "no delay may take place."

Yet the matter was not so straightforward. Even Mr. D'Arcy was in a dilemma. In his reply to William Hamilton at the Foreign Office, he appeared keen to avail himself of this unexpected opportunity to be rid of his responsibility. But as ever in his dealings with the students, there was the problem of money. Even if he trusted that Ambassador Abu'l-Hasan would refund him, he explained that he couldn't afford to purchase their passage to Constantinople. As letters were sent back and forth between Mr. D'Arcy and the Foreign Office, it was soon November. With winter approaching, there was only one more ship departing from London for Constantinople before the early spring and that one ship was due to set sail in a few days' time. Realizing that this would be his last chance for some time to rid himself of his burden, D'Arcy decided the financial risk was worth it and set about negotiating a price for the students' passage aboard that last ship of the season. Learning what he was up to and fearing their time in London was about to come to an unforeseen end, the students were devastated. They knew all too well that Mr. D'Arcy would only be too happy to see them go. Their response was to rush as a group to the house of the one man they knew had both the clout and inclination to help them: Sir Gore Ouseley. A few hours later, Sir Gore wrote a letter to Mr. Hamilton at the Foreign Office: "I have just been *invaded* by a tribe of dismayed Persians to whom a sudden order has just been sent . . . to be off in a week to Constantinople & Persia." Using all his influence as a former ambassador to Iran, Sir Gore advised Hamilton that it was far better to allow the students to stay in London eight months or even a year longer to "render them perfect in their respective professions."

Eager not to lose his opportunity, Mr. D'Arcy was meanwhile dashing round London's East India Dockyard seeking the captain of the ship due to sail to Constantinople. While Mr. Hamilton was pondering Sir Gore's suggestions of an extended stay, the impatient Mr. D'Arcy managed to persuade Captain Powell to buy provisions for the students and turn away other passengers on the promise that the full fare for the "Persian gentlemen" would shortly be paid. In the end, it was Sir Gore who held more sway than the lowlier Captain D'Arcy. After Sir Gore pledged to himself persuade his old friend Abu'l-Hasan that the students were better staying longer in London, the matter was decided. In December 1818, another letter arrived from Abu'l-Hasan, who was by then in Paris. The reprieve he agreed to was short: the students could only remain in London till the end of March 1819. After almost two years of relative calm with the students being funded by the prince regent and the Foreign Office, their missing the boat spelled trouble for Mr. D'Arcy. Captain Powell wrote an angrily litigious letter to Hamilton at the Foreign Office demanding compensation for the money he had lost by following D'Arcy's instructions. So the students had found their reprieve at Mr. D'Arcy's expense. Even so, they knew they would be leaving within months. Realizing that another victory over their fuming chaperone was unlikely, they set about completing their studies and making the best of friendships that suddenly seemed sweeter through the thought of separation.

Friendship is the affective union of knowledge and faith: it requires understanding of oneself and of another self; it requires the gamble of faith that the emotions invested in a friend will be repaid and not betrayed. Knowledge is a prerequisite for the kinds of cross-cultural friendships that the students made in England, and the most elementary part of such knowledge is language. As we have seen, their earliest friends in England were speakers of Persian like Sir John Malcolm, and it was only with their growing proficiency in English that they had been able to expand their circle into less familiar quarters. After acquiring the skills in English that formed their first educational task, little by little the students came to understand England's foreign culture. For all its peculiarities and foibles, they learned to safely navigate their way around England, and in turn to trust its people.

Yet the relationships they made were not merely private friendships. They were bonds that laid the basis for the friendship of nations. Three years before their arrival in London, it was a friendship that was made official in the Definitive Treaty of Friendship and Alliance signed on behalf of Britain and Iran in 1812. The students were fully aware of this, and when times were hard it was this larger friendship of nations

Fig. 23. Renting in Theaterland: Muhammad 'Ali's Lodgings on Covent Garden's King Street. Source: Photo by Nile Green.

that they evoked in their pleas for help. In one of the several letters that they wrote to Lord Castlereagh, they explained that even in their darkest hour they were "trusting in the liberality of the British Government and in the friendship that exists between this country and ours." And when Lord Castlereagh had finally decided to intervene in their welfare, the arrangements made to help them were, initially at least, presented as a private act of friendship between the prince regent George and the crown prince 'Abbas Mirza. As Lord Castlereagh had phrased the matter in a letter to Mr. D'Arcy, "the Prince Regent, as a mark of his esteem and friendship for the Prince of Persia, has not hesitated to advance the further sum necessary for their maintenance." Even though the crown prince and the prince regent had never met, their princely friendship had saved the students.

Hoping to build on what was for an Iran facing Russia a vital alliance with the English, Mirza Salih began now to realize that his future lay not only as a printer. The language, cultural, and social skills he had learned could be put to better use as a diplomat. After all, had not Sir Gore used his knowledge of Persian and of Iranian ways to embark on a late career in diplomacy? Although Mirza Salih had latterly turned to the mechanical arts with Mr. Watts the printer, he had mainly studied languages in England, along with the subjects of history and literature that lent a deeper understanding of English life. What he now realized was that if he was to truly master the arts of the diplomat, he would also need to understand the subtle etiquette that encompassed the fine-tuned social rituals of Jane Austen's England. For this was not a time when friendship was seen as a merely natural or organic phenomenon, still less a time when civilized friends let it all hang out. As Miss Austen's novels show so well, friendship demanded rituals and displays; proper manners and flourishes; obligations and limitations; a proper balance of sense and sensibility. As he began to envisage a diplomatic future in his exhausted evenings after toiling in Watts's workshop, Mirza Salih saw that he had to master the codes of conduct by which good relations could be maintained with Europe's Christians. Building on the ethnographic skills he had gained with Mirza Ja'far on their journey through the West Country, during his last year in England Mirza Salih planned to explore the possibilities of friendship across nations and cultures. In an age that saw the birth of modern relations between the Middle East and Europe, he hoped to make a diplomat of himself, a friend of nations.

As conceived by both the English and Iranians at this time, diplomacy was a form of politics built on affection, whether inwardly felt or outwardly acted. This is clear from the language of diplomacy that was current in the early nineteenth century. For the key term in the diplomatic letters carried by Abu'l-Hasan and Sir Gore Ouseley was that of the "friendship," or *dusti,* between England and Iran—more specifically, the personified national friendship of King George III and Fath 'Ali Shah. Such terminology was not merely figurative. For just as Mirza Salih's personal friendships in England developed from the amicable diplomatic relations between England and Iran, so was the friendship of nations built on the individual affinities between such men as Abu'l-Hasan and Sir Gore—or, waiting in the wings, the would-be diplomat Mirza Salih, scribbling in his diary whatever he could learn about English ways of friendship. And so his diary leads us toward what one theorist has called "the politics of friendship."

In an age when ambition remained a dirty word, Mirza Salih's new diplomatic aspirations were not without their risks. As he noted in his diary, one or two of his student companions began to spread rumors that he was planning to seize Ambassador Abu'l-Hasan's position, even writing letters to that effect. There were no doubt rivalries among the group. But in terms of qualifications at least, it was a feasible ambition for, with English and French, Mirza Salih had acquired the chief diplomatic languages of Europe. He had become a Freemason, making him a ritual brother of many other diplomats. And he had met many of the men associated with the "Honourable Company" that governed India. Undoubtedly, he had also come to understand the English far better than Abu'l-Hasan, the only living Iranian who had served as an ambassador to England. Mirza Salih began to sense his calling.

In an age when communications between London and Tehran were still conducted at the speed of the horse and sailing ship, distant foreign nations had to be made present in the fallible flesh of an ambassador. In 1818, diplomacy remained in large part a question of personal friendships and the individual capacity to inspire and reciprocate trust. The collective friendship of nations could be founded on the private friendships of their representatives. Mirza Salih's diary in this way affords us a glimpse into the small scale of history that constituted meetings with such men as Sir Gore Ouseley and Sir John Malcolm that forged Europe's earliest diplomatic relations with Iran. Such personalized politics did not render diplomatic matters any more informal. Codes of conduct remained of the greatest important, for this was a mannered age in which ambassadors and their embassies were surrounded with the ceremonial civility of fanfares, gifts and flattery. In a period when diplomatic relations were only beginning between Iran and England, it was easy to misunderstand the other party. With so much at stake, Mirza Salih decided to carefully study and record English protocol. For things did go wrong. When Abu'l-Hasan had first arrived in London in 1809, he was appalled not to be met by the grand ceremonial of the *istiqbal*, or public reception. But most of all, he was confused: this was the first venture of an Iranian diplomat to England for over two centuries, and Abu'l-Hasan was constantly wrong-footed in entering a culture whose rules of civility he didn't understand. Without knowing the rules, he was unable to play his proper ambassadorial part. Such behavioral wrong-footedness saw him lampooned in the *Adventures of Hajji Baba of Ispahan in England* that we have seen James Morier inspired to write by Abu'l-Hasan and the medical student Hajji Baba. For his part, having already stayed more than twice as long in England as Abu'l-Hasan, Mirza Salih was determined that such mistakes would not be repeated. No one would lampoon him; he would be a safer bet than Abu'l-Hasan for such diplomatic shuffling between worlds. So as the prelude to the making of future diplomatic friendships, with his characteristic alacrity Mirza Salih set himself a final educational task: mastering English manners.

If James Morier felt able to mock his quasi-fictional Hajji Baba for his cultural misunderstandings, then the English were themselves similarly vexed by their interactions with different cultures. One aspect of Persian diplomatic culture that presented them with problems was the giving of gifts, or *nazr*. Presenting a ruler with *nazr*—or "nuzzer," as it was spelled in the English of the period—was the counterpart of the monarch's bestowal of a robe of honor, or *khil'at*. While such diplomatic gifts were by no means unique to the Middle East and India, the older wealth of the courts of Islamic Asia (and their easier access to precious stones) meant that the culture of gift-giving was more developed (and expensive) than in Europe. This became clear very early in Anglo-Iranian relations, when the first English ambassadors from London and Calcutta struggled to provide suitably munificent gifts for the shah. Though English commentators came to increasingly comment on the rapaciousness of these demands for gifts, it is important to recognize the symbolic no less than the financial dimension to the *nazr*. For the giving of gifts was what friends did; as such, the symbolic value of the *nazr* lay in testifying to the affective bonds of friendship. The gift was a visible proof of the friendship between its giver and receiver, the means to display the diplomacy of *dusti* or friendship.

Nowhere was this more apparent than in the gifts that were brought to England by Abu'l-Hasan when he returned to London in 1819. The best example is a gift from the shah that he presented to the prince regent at Carlton House. *The Times* described it as "a gold enamelled looking-glass, opening with a portrait of his Persian Majesty, the object of which was to exhibit, at one view, the portraits of [the] two sovereigns, the one in painting the other by reflection, and around which were poetical allusions." In creating by artifice a mirror into which the prince regent could gaze and see the painting of the curly bearded Fath 'Ali Shah facing him, the gift sumptuously invoked the Persian symbolism of romantic love. For as recounted in scores of Persian miniature paintings and poems, it was the wont of lovers to gaze together into a mirror or *a'ina* at each other's reflections. To maximize the simulacrum effect, the artist had created two such portrait mirrors, one for each prince. These not only allowed the two rulers to gaze into each another's reflections, but also to see their own reflections reflected, and so contained, in each other's image. The effect was a visual conceit, an artist's play on the notion that lovers become absorbed in one another—that they come, as it were, to contain one another. In such ways, Abu'l-Hasan's gift exemplified the playful ingenuity of Persian idioms of friendship.

With all the period's advances in knowledge about Iran, we might imagine that the English could understand the mirror's symbolism. As a report on the gift in *The Times* interpreted it, since "the Persians abound in metaphor, there is no doubt but the [alabaster] material from which the mirror is principally wrought, is intended to signify the stability of the [Persian ruler's] sentiments." This was not far from the mark, for the mirror was an expression of the political amity through which Iran's rulers sought nothing less than the love of their English counterparts. Because above all, love demands loyalty, the greatest asset of any political ally. Despite that layer of *Realpolitik*, the mirror's central suggestion was nonetheless startling: that the prince regent and the shah were not merely friends but lovers! We can only wonder what the prince regent himself thought of the gift. We do know Abu'l-Hasan's response to a gift that George III had earlier sent to him. On receiving a jeweled dagger—itself a classic *nazr* that was second only in popularity to the robe of honor—Abu'l-Hasan was horrified to find that the diamond in its handle was made only of glass. Shocked by the English skinflints, he issued a complaint through Sir Gore Ouseley. Happily, the next day his hurt feelings were appeased when the prince regent in person placed a genuine diamond ring on his finger. If the gesture didn't quite promise a royal wedding, it did pledge a royal friendship.

What this makes clear is that the exchange of "lovers' gifts" was a vital diplomatic ritual that could go terribly wrong by insulting, confusing, or disappointing the recipient. In this period of increasing contact between European and Muslim rulers, Mirza Salih was therefore right to recognize the value of his skills as a cultural middleman. Diplomatic blunders carried high costs, and so his insider's knowledge of Jane Austen's world could help avoid such blunders. Such knowledge was not only a valuable asset, it was also a learnable asset that could be transferred and taught to future emissaries in Iran. So it was that while Mirza Salih's companions continued with their studies of medicine, map making and steam engines, he set himself the final task of mastering the manners and customs of the English. Recording his findings in his diary, he was penning nothing less than an ethnography of amity.

An Ethnography of Amity

A traveler's description of other cultures need not be a project of cognitive domination, an insidious Orientalism or Occidentalism. It can also be a venture of affection and affinity. Among the students' friendships, the Persianate enthusiasms of the Ouseley brothers are the best example. The same affinities and affections for another culture are found in reciprocal measure in Mirza Salih's diary. Like the shah's gift to the prince regent, his Persian diary was a literary mirror of the Ouseley brothers' English diaries from Iran. As an independent trader before he took up with the East India Company, as a young man Sir Gore Ouseley had settled beyond the reach of the Company's power in the Muslim capital of Lucknow in North India. For several years, he studied Persian literature and learning with Lucknow's leading scholars and served as advisor to its ruler, Sa'adat 'Ali Khan, before entering the Company's service. Even though he remained a Christian (just as Mirza Salih remained a Muslim), his attitudes toward Islamic culture were informed and sympathetic. Like Mirza Salih, he was a man fashioned by his travels: even in England his dinner parties served Persian stews and great *pillaus* of rice surrounded by the carpets and paintings he had carried from Iran and India.

If travel was capable of fostering affection for another culture, and writing was in turn capable of transmitting that affection, then when Mirza Salih's descriptions of England's social rituals were read back home they could serve as a guide for the making of friends and allies. He had realized that friendship is a corollary of understanding: the more we understand someone, the more we come to feel affection for them. And after over three years in London, it was his growing understanding of English culture—like Sir Gore's corresponding understanding of Persian culture—that afforded him with the possibility of writing an ethnography of England's customs of friendship. Of all the rituals of friendship in which he took interest, the most basic was the shared meal.

The high table was the forge on which friendships were hammered into shape. In Iran similarly, sharing food was so important a commitment of friendship that the Persian expression *nan u namak khurdan*, "to eat bread and salt," served as shorthand for the bonds of loyalty and friendship that followed hospitality. Mirza Salih had already recognized that commensality, eating together, was as important in England as in Iran. As Sir John Malcolm had told him in London back in 1816, having himself "eaten the salt of the Shah of Iran," he considered himself a servant of the shah who would offer Mirza Salih his advice as though he were his own father. Now Mirza Salih made dozens of notes about the people he dined with and the rituals of dinner. He had come to recognize that such experiences—and the records he kept of the customs he observed—were a vital part of his education. He would leave the "new sciences" to his companions and commit himself to another kind of new learning for which there was as yet no name in either England or Iran: social science.

His ethnographic notes allow us to reconstruct his dining experiences and see how they contributed to his making friends in England, both for himself and for his country. Before turning in the final chapter to the students' individual friendships, we will now look first at the ways in which Mirza Salih especially came to understand the culinary customs around which English friendships were made.

The Rituals of Dinner

It is easy to imagine that Muslim visitors to England faced all manner of ritual injunctions that restricted their dining with Christian hosts. Was wine being drunk at table? Was pork being served? Indeed, was any of the meat *halal*? From a theological reading of Muslim mores, we might imagine that the moveable feast of Regency high society presented Mirza Salih and his companions with religious obstacles to the conviviality of shared food and drink. In practice, this seems not to have been the case. There certainly were Muslim travelers for whom, for example, the difficulty of accessing *halal* meat was a cause of distress, such as the earlier Indo-Persian scholar I'tisam al-Din. But we have no evidence that this was the case with the students. Mirza Salih didn't mention in his diary the issue of *haram* and *halal*, forbidden and licit foods, nor the "problem" of alcohol. He was not alone in this gastronomic liberalism, for the slightly earlier travel diaries of the Indian Muslim Abu Talib and Ambassador Abu'l-Hasan cohere with his attitudes. Of course, the possibility remains that the students prepared more licit foods on their own account, though it is hard to picture them ritually slaughtering sheep in their London lodging houses. Be that as it may, when eating either in public or as guests, both the ambassador and the students joined with the dining customs of their English hosts.

Other Muslims might have behaved differently, and it would have been their right to do so. But the students show that the dietary rules of Sharia were not every Muslim's concern. Although Sharia traditionally accommodates the difficulties experienced while traveling, the diaries of Mirza Salih, Abu'l-Hasan, and Abu Talib do not suggest personalities concerned with such finer points of dietary law. And given the students' exposure in England to the rationalizing theologies of the Unitarians and Watchmaker Paley, they may have come to regard ritual and legal forms of religiosity as less important than the moral dimensions of Islam. In any case, the dinners, dances, and high teas that they enjoyed make it clear that considerations of diplomacy and friendship regularly outweighed the theoretical prescriptions of their faith.

As part of the diplomatic future he was now imagining for himself after his days laboring in Mr. Watts's print shop, Mirza Salih tried to codify his dining experiences into a coherent system that explained the subtle rules of English society. Deploying the ethnographic skills gained on his journey through the West Country with Mirza Ja'far, he now recorded details of quotidian routine, of eating habits and inebriations, of amusements and ettiquettes. The picture he painted of the English was of a surprisingly domesticated people. He depicted the typical Englishman's daily cycle as a happily humdrum affair: he dressed, shaved, took breakfast, went to work (usually, *pace* Napoleon's famous put-down, in a shop!), came home and ate supper (enjoying cheese or sweets for his pudding), before reading and retiring to bed. He was probably correct, for this was not very different from what Miss Austen described as her own family routine in one of her letters: "We dine now at half after Three. . . . We drink tea at half after six. . . . My father reads Cowper to us in the evening." Turning to food customs, Mirza Salih next gave an account of the kinds of food eaten in England. What is striking about it is his vivid awareness of the intersections between food, class, and economics. But by early 1819, he could draw on a good deal of experience. After all, he could look back on eating humble pie at the modest home of his former teacher Mr. Garrett and dining finely at the Belgravia mansion of Sir Gore Ouseley. Linking food with economics, for example, his discussion of English foodstuffs included a section on the Atlantic fishing industry. Transcribing the English term, he described how a certain fish "which they call *haran* [herring]" is usually salted, after which it can be stored away for years. Such is the *haran*'s importance, he added, that in Scotland no fewer than 15,000 fishermen were employed in catching its vast stocks, with many more people working in subsidiary jobs transporting and selling the fish. Many other people in England and Scotland, he added, were kept similarly "busy in catching a fish they call *kad* [cod]," which after being salted was then traded with France, Germany, Italy, and other countries of Europe. Most striking of all is Mirza Salih's awareness of the fact that much of this abundance of cod was ultimately acquired from fishermen operating in the distant ports of what he called *niwfirlund*, that is, Newfoundland, a place for which there was then still no name in Persian. His understanding of English food was in this way connected back to his acquisition of knowledge, in this case geographical. We can imagine the kind of tabletop discussions that led from Mirza Salih asking about an unusual fish into a conversation about the fishing trade of Scotland and the far-off fisheries of the New World.

In a reflection of the social class with which most of the students were mixing, Mirza Salih described not the foodstuffs of commoners but of the gentry. From his diary, Jane Austen's age appears as a carnivorous one in which dinners might comprise beef, veal, mutton, venison or boar, alongside chicken, pheasant, or goose. Detail mattered to Mirza Salih, and he noted with thoroughness England's eating habits, from the times at which they ate to the etiquette they observed while doing so. For example, he described breakfast as consisting of either coffee or tea, along with bread, butter, and a "half-cooked egg." Perhaps more surprisingly, he added that aged cow's tongue ("which is delicious") was also sometimes eaten to start the day. Before the Englishman ate breakfast, Mirza Salih continued, he would dress in clean and dignified clothes that his servants laid out for him. By the time he and his family sat down for breakfast, a knife, fork, and spoon would have been laid out on a table in front of a chair for each person. Mundane as it may now seem, Mirza Salih was astute to note such matters, for this was a method of eating that was quite foreign to Iranian floor-and-hands dining. Aware as he was of the possible *faux pas* of future envoys, he carefully described the customs of cutlery. (We know that the students themselves mastered this technique because one of their society hostesses wrote that they could "manage knives,

Fig. 24. May I Present Mrs. Piozzi? Dr. Johnson's Friend and Mirza Salih's Hostess. Source: *Autobiography, letters and literary remains of Mrs. Piozzi* (London, 1861).

forks and chairs with grace and propriety.") Mindful again of potential embarrassments, Mirza Salih repeated for emphasis that before even arriving at the breakfast table it was necessary to don appropriately elegant dress, to wash one's hands and face and, for men, to shave. However fine the plates and cutlery, he explained, no one was allowed to exchange their utensils with those of another person. Furthermore, it was important to display good manners and make polite table-talk throughout the meal.

Noting the different eating times for workers, artisans, and gentry, he turned next to the manner in which English families always ate together—men, women, and children—no matter how large the family. Though he took special note of it, he did not critique England's form of male-female sociability, whether within the family or beyond it. His aim was to understand not criticize. Not only did women eat with and even sit between men at table. The master of the household also always placed his wife at the head of the table and himself sat opposite her at its foot. This was a radical shift from the Iranian social order of eating with its custom of *bala nishastan* or "sitting atop" by which only male hosts and their chief guests sat at the head of the table. Even so, he explained, the scene in England's special dining rooms was a graceful one, with white tablecloths and clean napkins laid out beside the polished silverware. Dinner itself might consist of a meat broth, followed by fish, chicken, what he described as "kebab" (presumably a reference to John Bull's famous roast meats) and other "exquisite foodstuffs," none of which one was allowed to touch with one's hand. Afterward, servants would bring sweets, then what he referred to by the Persian combination *panir u sabzi,* "cheese and herbs," followed finally by wine served with fruit and almonds. Lest wine-drinking among women seem too shocking to his countrymen, he added that Englishwomen never took more than one or two glasses of wine themselves and that the drunkenness of any guest was seen as a grave offense. The sheer fact that Christians drank alcohol did not render them decadent infidels.

There was reasoning behind this representation. Part formal *safarnama* "travelogues," part personal journals, diaries such as Mirza Salih's were partly intended to be practical works aimed at smoothing the way for future interactions (in Mirza Salih's case, diplomatic interactions). What he discovered and wrote about the English would form the pattern for understanding the other Europeans with whom his Muslim countrymen were coming into contact. A decade later, a parallel Persian description of Russian dining habits was written during the Iranian embassy to Saint Petersburg in 1830, which Mirza Salih accompanied. Served with gold cutlery and crystal glassware, dinner in the imperial Russian capital was presented as a much grander affair than the bourgeois manner of the English. But like Mirza Salih's account of English dining, the account of Russian culinary customs was meant to serve as practical advice for other Iranian travelers, diplomats especially.

Back in London in early 1819, the topic of food next led Mirza Salih to the subject of hunting, another custom around which friendships were forged. In an implicit contrast to the hunting practices of Iranian elites that his friend Sir John Malcolm had described in his account of Iran, Mirza Salih remarked that England's hunters were mostly limited to chasing rabbits, adding that some of the aristocracy also kept deer on their land that they hunted for sport. In contrast to the many animals still found in the mountains and plains of Iran, aside from rabbit and deer, the English hunter had to make do with the humble quarry of rabbits, birds and foxes. When we compare this to the fact that in London Ambassador Abu'l-Hasan liked to begin his days with a ride in Regent's Park hurling javelins at his retainers, the sporting life of John Bull must have seemed tame indeed.

Mirza Salih also wrote about the Regency's emergent culture of consumption by way of tea gardens, coffeehouses, and what he termed public "kitchens," or *ashpaz-khana*. After all, it was as important to understand where the English ate as it was to understand what they ate. While his picture of coffeeshops and tearooms might seem unremarkable to the modern reader, it is worth emphasizing the sheer novelty of the restaurant in Jane Austen's London. For through providing an ostentatious dining setting for those lacking a grand dining room and servants of their own, the novelty of the restaurant signaled the rise of the middle-class that was the most important social development of the era. Even if the "restaurant" as such had not truly developed in the Regency period, the public "kitchens" and "hotels" that Mirza Salih described were nonetheless novel, especially to Iranians. Even so, the culinary worlds of Asia and Europe were beginning to intersect. For by their final six months in London, the students could have eaten many a curry in London's coffeehouses. As Dr. William Kitchiner had testified in his *Cook's Oracle* of 1816, many coffeehouses served curries as their most popular dishes. London's taverns, meanwhile, were selling in abundance the spicy curried bar snacks created by Henry Osborne of Soho Square. Such was the popularity of Indian foods that they spread through the most genteel households. Martha Lloyd, a relative of Miss Austen who lived with the author at Chawton Cottage where Austen wrote most of her novels, left two such recipes from the time. One was for a curry soup "with knuckle of veal"; the other, based on chicken, was "a Receipt to Curry after the Indian Manner." In 1816, when the great French chef Carême was appointed supervisor of the immense kitchens at the prince regent's Indian-style Brighton Pavilion, he too had been expected to add curry to his repertoire. Though many of these dishes bore Persian names—from *biryani* and *pilaw* to *nan* and *roghan josh*—they were not actually Iranian dishes. Through the foods they encountered in coffeehouses and taverns, the students were encountering the culinary cosmopolitanism that was already making London a global city.

The public buildings where they tasted such foods also interested Mirza Salih. While early nineteenth-century Iran did have travelers' inns, or *musafir-khanas*, at which a sojourner might find shelter and even food, it would have to be a needy traveler who did so. When traveling in their own country, Iranian elites typically set up their own camps, attended by their own cooks and servants. The same was true for dining in one's native city, where elite Iranians would entertain at home—whether in the public or *biruni* section of the house or in the pavilion of a private garden—rather than resort to a public kitchen. As yet Iran had no middle class seeking imitation aristocratic dining rooms to show off in public. As a result, the public eating places of Iran were not the showy hotels Mirza Salih saw in London and described as being not only impeccably clean but as serving food with fine plates and silver cutlery. The practice had earlier caught the attention of Ambassador Abu'l-Hasan, who decided to buy an English cutlery set to take home to Iran. Such forks and spoons would gradually change the way people ate in Iran, showing that, then as now, culture is flexible and adaptable.

Now that in early 1819 the students knew their time in London would last no longer than another six months, they decided to accept friends' invitations to enjoy the city to the full. There was much opportunity to explore the countless eating houses, taverns and teahouses of the capital, as well as to attend dinners at the houses of the many friends they now had in London. For Mirza Salih, collecting data on England's dining customs was perhaps also a way of lending purpose to the pursuits of pleasure in which he and his fellow students were involved during their last months in London. Trying to gather useful information from these culinary excursions, he recorded some startlingly specific statistics: each year Londoners consumed 10,000 cows, 210,000 calves, and 800,000 sheep. It was, he added, the finest meat he had ever eaten anywhere. Since mutton would have seemed familiar enough fare to Iranians, he pointed out differences: the English, for example, found it strange that Iranians drank the milk of sheep. But in trying to make English society intelligible to his Iranian readers, he also looked for commonalities with Persian practices. We can gauge the degree of culinary familiarity and difference he experienced through his varying use of either native Persian words or English loanwords to describe what he saw on his tours of London's eating houses. While for tearooms and coffeehouses, he found easy Persian equivalents in the *chai-khana* and *qahva-khana*, for the "hotel" and the "inn" he was forced to transcribe the English words into Arabic script.

In many respects, these were also novelties in England, for improved roads and increasing coach traffic meant that the Regency years saw improved hotels and coaching inns open all over the country. Mirza Salih and Mirza Ja'far had already seen some of these on their travels, perhaps even staying at the comfortable Clifton Hotel that had opened in Bristol in 1811; we know from the diary that they stayed in the smart Star Inn in Oxford. They had certainly sampled different foods during their journeys. Driven by a sense of similarity to the Iranian tradition of sweetmeats, continuing his study of England's eating habits Mirza Salih wrote about the pastry and sweet shops to which he said Englishmen retreated when they felt tired. Though the shops served all kinds of sugary and fruity confections, perhaps these tired Englishmen were also reinvigorated by the young women that Mirza Salih noted working there. To describe the cakes on sale—surely sticky puddings of a very English kind—he drew on his native gastronomic vocabulary, labeling them as *shirini, halva,* and *nakh-band,* sweets that his Iranian readers would feel they recognized at once. Never neglecting his principal interests in matters of learning, he also pointed out that London's coffeehouses were the best places to read *kaghaz-i akhbar* or "newspapers." In such remarks, we can sense the ways in which his exposure to the spaces of English sociability served as a medium for his access to the knowledge he was always seeking in England.

From Foodstuffs to Friendships

This was all the more true for the students' entry to the parties and balls that were so central a feature of Jane Austen's novels. And no less of her life: as she described one such party in a letter from 1811, there was "Syllabub, Tea, Coffee, Singing, Dancing, a Hot Supper, eleven o'clock, everything that can be imagined agreeable." By increasingly socializing with the English during their last months in London, the students won the friendship of their hosts. In some cases, that was incentive enough; in others, it won them help in completing their different projects before their departure. While it would be plainly false to suggest that Muslim visitors were always well treated in Regency England, in the early nineteenth century their presence was still relatively uncommon outside of the dockyards where Arab and Indian "lascar" sailors congregated. For elite and wealthy travelers at least, this rarity lent them an enhanced status. The London diary of the Indo-Persian gentleman Abu Talib Khan from a decade earlier contained striding compliments about English hospitality. "To be hospitable [*mihman-gharib*]," he wrote, "is one of the most esteemed virtues of the English; and I experienced it to such a degree, that I was seldom disengaged. In these parties I enjoyed every luxury my heart could desire. Their viands [*ta'am*] were delicious, and wines [*sharab*] exquisite." Once again, food was part of friendship. The appreciation appears to have been mutual. As though to return the compliment, the students' acquaintaince James Fraser stated that "the fact is that Asiatic notions of hospitality have at all times been far more extended than ours."

In this period of early contact between Muslims and the English, there was still much room for the friendship born of fascination. In an age of fashionable orientalism, after his return to London at the end of 1818 Ambassador Abu'l-Hasan brought the thrill of the exotic to many a party. No mere Muslim mannequin, he was considered both a wit and a dandy. As one English observer phrased the matter, Abu'l-Hasan was such "a fine handsome dark man" that he "was sometimes much annoyed by the insatiate admiration, fixed stare, and intense regard of the British ladies." Such was the prestige of his presence at London's soirées that, at the insistence of his proud hosts, as on his first visit eight years earlier, his attendance at their parties was publicized in the newspapers.

Such society dinners were grand affairs, and although the status of Mirza Salih and his companions as visiting students did not always warrant their inclusion in newspaper gossip columns, there is good reason to believe they attended at least some of the many parties arranged for Abu'l-Hasan that winter season of early 1819. Having all but crept into England in 1815 in the near bankrupt company of the minor officer Mr. D'Arcy, with the return of the enchanting ambassador to London they found themselves in the company of the Muslim darling of high society. Abu'l-Hasan's Persian diary provides some idea of the gatherings they attended, which he found sufficiently strange to adapt the English loanword, "*parti*," to describe them. One such party involved that English custom that continues to confound foreigners to the present day: fancy dress. At this peculiar breakfast (or *brak fas* as he transcribed it), Abu'l-Hasan witnessed scores of Englishmen dressed not only in the familiar standbys of ancient Romans and hoary seadogs, but also in the more fashionably oriental manner of Iranians, Indians, and Turks. Acting as though this was all quite normal, the English consumed "food and drinks and kebabs [*ta'am va sharab va kabab*]" in the host's quaint little garden. Abu'l-Hasan took particular note of a man with a thick false beard made, he said, of goat's or cat's hair (perhaps the Iranian wasn't sure which word he heard). More strangely still, the Englishman claimed to be dressed as an Iranian and to be able to speak Persian. But when Abu'l-Hasan addressed him, he was quickly divested of his pretentions to sartorial no less than grammatical accuracy. Unable to respond to the ambassador's Persian, the cat-bearded Englishman was left *'ajiz va hayran*, "helpless and bewildered." Clearly, he had not been one of Mirza Salih's conversational exchange partners.

In reciprocal recompense for such ineffectual orientalisms, Abu'l-Hasan threw parties of his own that provided more accurate recreations of Iranian life. He hosted them at his lodgings in Mansfield Street, inviting such fellow diplomats and friends as James Morier and Sir Gore Ouseley as well as society hangers-on. Although Mansfield Street was two miles fashionably west of the students lodgings on Salisbury Court and King Street, they were still sometimes invited to their ambassador's parties. On these occasions, Abu'l-Hasan served Iranian food prepared by the domestic staff who had accompanied him from Tehran. According to a newspaper report in the *Morning Post*, one evening he hosted his London friends to "an entertainment, called in the Persian language a *Pillau*; it was composed of rice and fowls stewed together with spices." To give English readers a better sense of the exotic feast, in the same way that Mirza Salih resorted to the familiar language of kebabs and *halva*, the reporter added in plainer terms that "the dish was prepared in the same way as marinaded chickens."

Emulating the arrangements of his ambassadorial Iranian friend, Sir Gore Ouseley had his own kitchen arrangements changed, such that he took to serving Persian food to his guests at his own London home, where the students regularly visited him during those last six months. He had, after all, become their greatest supporter, having recently persuaded Abu'l-Hasan to delay their departure. As 1818 turned into 1819, Sir Gore was living just off Berkeley Square at number 12 Bruton Street, fifteen minutes' walk from the rented residence of Abu'l-Hasan. Sir Gore's home was a splendid Georgian mansion in the heart of London's Belgravia, even then an exclusive neighborhood. His neighbors included lawyers and physicians, esquires, and baronets, with the few shops in the adjoining streets being tailors and perfumers who appealed to the tastes of this elite clientele. Bruton Street would remain an establishment stronghold for many years to come: in 1926, a few doors away from Sir Gore's house, a baby girl called Elizabeth Windsor was born; she would later be better known as Queen Elizabeth II. Back in the days when Sir Gore was hosting his Iranian friends to dinners of kebab and *pillau*, London's increasing trade connections with India were making it easier to acquire the kinds of exotic foods that Sir Gore enjoyed serving. An advertisement in the *Morning Post* from these years describes the availability at Pressey and Co.'s Foreign Warehouse, at 371 Oxford Street (a short walk from Sir Gore's residence) of "Patna rice, per the last ships from India, by far superior to any other rice for whiteness, flavour and general purposes of domestic economy. Bombay and China mangoes and buffaloes' humps, a very esteemed Asiatic table delicacy." Perhaps it was from this very shop that Sir Gore's servants found the provisions for his feasts that winter season at the beginning of 1819. It was a habit of hospitality that he long maintained. A few years after the students regularly dined with him, another foreigner Hermann von Pückler-Muskau was invited to dine at his home. In his German diary, Pückler-Muskau wrote that he ate "some Oriental dishes, and I drank genuine Schiraz [wine] for the first time in my life." Through the foods Sir Gore learned to serve his Iranian friends, their presence vicariously lingered in Berkeley Square

Fig. 25. Join Me for *Pillau*: The Home of Sir Gore Ouseley on Bruton Street.

long after they went home. It was all part of the making of multicultural London.

In such ways, the mutual diplomatic effort to forge friendships created a two-way exchange of English and Persian dining habits. While dating to over a decade after the students' departure from London, the best account of this exchange is found in the diary of the London visit of two Iranian princes written by their official host or *mihmandar*, the students' close acquaintance James Fraser. There we find recorded the following opinions of the Iranians about the food they encountered:

> [W]hen asked what dishes they preferred, the usual reply was, "Oh! anything; just what you English eat." There were, however, exceptions . . . To turtle and lobsters they obstinately maintained their antipathy, refusing to taste them, although mock-turtle soup was one of their favourite dishes; but one day, as a dish of nice scalloped oysters was put on the table at Mivart's, I pressed Timour Meerza to taste a little bit. He confessed that the dish looked very well, and smelt very well; and after a queer imploring look at his brothers, and a glance of irresolution at the morsel, he put it in his mouth. His countenance betrayed that the taste was not displeasing; he asked for another morsel—swallowed it—and then desired the whole shell to be sent to him. This he gobbled up without a word; and then, turning to his brother, said, "*Dadâish*, by your head, it is capital! What fools we have been! Saheb Fraser, pray order that dish of these same oysters be set down at table every day we dine here. *Ajaib-cheezee ust!*—A wonderful sort of thing it is!"

There was certainly an element of teasing, even cruelty, in Mr. Fraser's pushing of the horrid crustaceans, not least in view of their "abhorred" (*makruh*) status in Islamic dietary law (though, again, neither of the princes apparently mentioned this). Even so, as *mihmandar*, it was not Mr. Fraser's task chiefly to pander to the princes' wishes but to safely introduce them to English ways. It was again a reciprocal process, for amid this diplomatic exchange of social customs Fraser described Persian cooking techniques finding their way into the kitchen at James Mivart's famous Claridge's Hotel. As he explained,

> Another dish of which [the Iranian princes] became very fond was a preparation of cream, under the name of Charlotte Russe. The Wali, in

particular, was a great admirer of it, and ate, as he always did when he got what he liked, to excess, making all of the time puns and bon-môts in Persian on the sweetness and fairness of his favourite dish as compared with the living Charlottes of his acquaintance. Still, after they had been for some time in London, they began to long for some of their Persian fare; and, as one of their servants was a cook, by the assistance of Mr. Mivart's artiste the matter was easily managed, and pillaws of various sorts, and sundry stews, mutemjâns, fizenjans, moosommahs, cookoos, and vegetables à la mode de Perse—made their appearance at their table.

This tale of Iranian gastronomy hints at the two-way exchange of English and Iranian dining customs in which the students were also involved. For Mr. Mivart's *fizenjans* reflect the culinary cross-overs that Mirza Salih and his companions encountered in their circle of London friends. We have already seen the rice "pilafs," or *pillaus,* that Sir Gore Ouseley liked to serve them, but their other friend Sir John Malcolm had an even better culinary tie to Iran. Like a latter-day Walter Raleigh, he had tried to introduce Iran to the simple pleasures of the potato and, for a short while at least it, his imported tubers carried the correspondingly mixed name of *alu-yi malkum,* "Malcolm's plums." Still, Mirza Salih had no illusions about the humble status of Malcolm's plums and recorded in his diary that only the Scots and Irish ate potatoes.

These exchanges were not only of foodstuffs, but also of the culture of sharing food. Just as Mirza Salih was studying the social rituals of the English at table, so did the English friends of the students take interest in the cultivated table-talk perfected by their Muslim guests. We glimpse something of this display of word play in Fraser's account of the princes at table, comparing the creamy *charlotte russe* with limpid-skinned ladies of the same name. Memorized, improvised, or parodied, poetry was central to this art, and Persian and Arabic literary tradition preserved countless verses to the joys of the good life that could be evoked at apt moments. When nineteenth-century Christians condemned Islamic morality, it was not as today for their puritan denial of the pleasures of this world but for what they considered the excessive sensuality of Islam. Since educated Muslims expected any man of culture to carry a collection of choice verses or anecdotes in his repertoire, the Iranians' entry to London society led to English attempts at participating in these rituals of table talk. As we have already seen, the desire of London hosts to appreciate this conversational art had led Philoxenus Secundus to publish his *Oriental Recreations* on the correct form of witty *nuqtas* and *latifas*, the *bon-mots* in which Iranians delighted. Now on his second visit to London, Ambassador Abu'l-Hasan excelled in such gallantries. When one Englishwoman, presumably having digested the orientalist extravagances of Lord Byron, asked Abu'l-Hasan if he believed in the powers of talismans, he replied that the only worthwhile talismans he knew were ladies. But not every Englishman was ready to adapt this line of charm and the prince regent took the blunter approach of telling Abu'l-Hasan his own favorite *latifa* about the length of his brother's penis. In the prince's characteristically smutty way, it was a gesture of friendly bonhomie with his Muslim guest.

In an age of sensibility, the more refined conversation of the students had a pleasing effect on their hosts. This was, after all, the age of Austen's Edmund Bertram and George Knightley no less than the prince regent. It is probably no coincidence that the cultivated elites of Iran found a better reception in the mannered society of the Regency than in the more bullish age of the Victorians. As one newspaper wrote about Mirza Salih and Mirza Ja'far, "they will be followed by the good wishes of all who witnessed their friendly and ingratiating manners." For as the students had learned, in Miss Austen's England the art of making friends was all about finding the right balance between etiquette and dash.

By deliberately mastering the delicate arts of friendship, by 1819 Mirza Salih finally began to enter the highest echelons of English society, the spheres he knew he must access and understand if he were to have any hope of becoming a successful diplomat. His (and Mirza Ja'far's) initiations as Freemasons allowed him to meet regularly with these powerful new friends, and while he pledged in his diary not to describe their activities, his occasional mentions of dining with the Freemasons shows that it had been a sociable as much as a symbolic initiation. Since at the time such dinners were usually held in Freemasons' Hall just off his regular haunt of Covent Garden, it was in its grandiose neoclassical hall that he would have attended these gatherings. It seems to have been through his fellowship with the Freemasons that in late November 1818 both Mirza Salih and Mirza Ja'far had been allowed to see the coffin of the queen consort of King George III, Charlotte of Mecklenburg-Strelitz, lying in state at Windsor Castle. At first, Mirza Salih wasn't allowed into Windsor's crowded St. George's Chapel and only Mirza Ja'far was allowed in. When Mirza Salih somehow managed to talk his way past the grenadier guards at the chapel gates, he spotted a friend, Mr. Harris. Here at the heart of the establishment, he had bumped into a senior Freemason and with quiet whispers in the pews arranged to meet him back in London the following day.

That next day, after a visit to the Freemasons' Lodge, Mirza Salih was provided with a proper invitation to the royal funeral that was about to take place now that the queen's coffin had lain for in state for several weeks. While the role of Mr. Harris and the Freemasons in this episode is not entirely clear, they seem to have transformed Mirza Salih from one of the crowded thousands trying to glimpse the queen's coffin into one of the select few formally invited to the actual funeral. However it precisely came about, Mirza Salih was delighted! His enraptured account of the event was no exaggeration, for even the formal official prose of the printed funeral sermon turned purple in recounting the sight of the procession:

> the torches were lighted: the illumination extended nearly a mile, and the rich glow of their scarlet uniforms, together with their splendid helmets and caparisoned horses, gleaming along the funeral line, formed a picture that would at once have excited the transport and baffled the skill of the finest artist.

And there, seated among England's high and mighty, were the two Muslim students. They watched the prince regent, the dukes of the realm, and the highest officers of the land enter the church in black suits and carrying candles, before the funeral service was conducted by no lesser a churchman than the archbishop of Canterbury. From Mirza Salih's detailed description of the ceremony and the trouble to which he described his English friends going to to procure him an invitation, it appears that he and Mirza Ja'far were among the fifty-four select "visitors" allowed to enter the chapel for the actual funeral in addition to the formal high-status guests. A contemporary report stated that, aside from the lords and bishops, only these fifty-four had "a tolerable view of both the entrance of the procession and the solemn concluding ceremony." Since this was the view Mirza Salih depicted in his diary, it seems his attention to the rituals of friendship won him a place among England's high and mighty, one more befitting the status of the diplomat he wished to become than a mere student. Proving the two *mirzas'* presence among this select group of mourners, a newspaper reported that "two 'Persian Princes' are said to have been among those in the organ-loft, who were particularly remarked for the sorrowful interest with which they contemplated the awful scene. (These were doubtless our illustrious and amiable visitors, Meerza Jaaffa and Meerza Saalih.)"

Licit Libations?

By now, the students were living in different parts of London. The two medical students, Mirza Ja'far and Hajji Baba, were living near St. George's Hospital at Hyde Park Corner. Mirza Riza was still staying near the Royal Military Academy in Woolwich. Mirza Salih and his closest companion the military engineer Mirza Ja'far, meanwhile, were living at 8 Salisbury Court, just off Fleet Street where Mirza Salih was still going every day to Mr. Watts's print shop. And a fifteen-minute walk west of Salisbury Court stood the artisan Muhammad 'Ali's lodgings at 36 King Street. This was the home of the Dudley family, who accepted their Muslim fellow artisan as a lodger. Though very much a working-class residence, the house at 36 King Street (it is still there today) had the great advantage of overlooking the Covent Garden piazza. Since being originally been laid out by Inigo Jones in the 1630s, the piazza had come a long way down in the world by 1819 and it would not be till 1830 that Charles Fowler added the elegant neoclassical market building that dominates Covent Garden today. Even more than Mirza Ja'far and Mirza Salih's accommodation at Salisbury Court, Covent Garden was a humble neighborhood, albeit one that, by bordering theaterland, allowed poor market girls to sell their bodies to rich men in their carriages.

Officially at least, though, Muhammad 'Ali's neighbors on King Street were mostly other craftsmen and tradesmen: the parish register from the time shows chandlers, tailors, bootmakers, corn dealers, and victuallers living on the surrounding streets. A few doors away from the Dudleys at 31 King Street lived Mr. Eli Dyer, a carpenter who worked with his hands like Muhammad 'Ali. Since the head of the latter's household, Thomas Dudley, was also an artisan (an ironworking "ornament man" to be precise), we can assume that the dinners that Muhammad 'Ali was eating at this time were less lavish than some of those enjoyed by the five *mirzas*. And they surely comprised a tankard or two of the small beer that in the slang of the day was called "water bewitched." Even if it was not at Mr. Dudley's humble table, the students met regularly for evenings out. Now that their financial troubles were behind them, Mirza Salih and at least some of his companions became regular visitors to Covent Garden. Standing between their different residences on King Street and Salisbury Court, London's most notorious pleasure district between the Strand and Covent Garden became their favorite stomping grounds. Precisely midway between their two residences stood the Lyceum Theatre to which Mirza Salih had been introduced by his friend Samuel Beazley. With many other theaters and taverns in the adjoining streets surrounding the Lyceum and Covent Garden, this was the bustling hub of London's drinking dens and worse, its somewhat euphemistic "theaterland." Less than a minute's walk from the Lyceum stood the house on Tavistock Street where, just over a year after the Iranians walked regularly by in 1819, Thomas de Quincey penned his *Confessions of an English Opium Eater*.

Since we have looked at the students' dining experiences, it is therefore only fair to ask whether they also shared in the more boozy pastimes of Jane Austen's era during the dinners they enjoyed during their final months in London. Whether or not they followed de Quincey into his opium reveries remains a mystery, for though many Iranians did smoke *afiyun*, as they called it, there is no direct evidence that they did so in London. But this does lead us to the bibulous question at the core of the students' social lives: did the young Muslims partake in a wee dram or two? Knowing that his journal would later be read back at the court of 'Abbas Mirza in Iran, where members of the Shi'ite clergy had considerable influence, Mirza Salih was careful never to confess to drinking alcohol in his diary. But we know from other sources that he and the other students were capable drinkers. As the society hostess Mrs. Piozzi wrote of Mirza Salih and Mirza Ja'far after entertaining them one evening, they do "what they ought not to do (for they are Mussulmen), take their glass like an English country squire." In her arch way, Mrs. Piozzi was making a comparison between the students' capable quaffing and that of the Regency's proverbially inebriated churchmen.

Even if wine found only the occasional mention in the dietary knowledge Mirza Salih thought proper to record, there remains a pleasing symmetry to the fact that his travels coincided with the golden age of punches. For punches formed England's most lasting offering to the cosmopolitan drinker. As one Regency drinker's handbook explained, "the liquor called *Punch* has become so truly English, it is often supposed to be indigenous to this country, though its name at least is oriental. The Persian *punj*, or Sanscrit *pancha*, that is, five, is the etymon of its title, and denotes the number of ingredients." Perhaps the students picked up on this strange exchange of words and drinks between Persian and English. But against the befuddled backdrop of the Regency, Mirza Salih was circumspect about referring to alcohol consumption, noting only as we saw earlier that Englishwomen drank little at table and that overtly drunk men were considered a disgrace. While we might take this as an attempt to politely pass over what he considered a reprehensible custom, the more likely answer is that wine drinking in Iran was sufficiently common among elites to be unworthy of special mention. For through his close ethnographic investigations of English table manners, he understood the civilized uses of alcohol for celebrating friendship. It was no less familiar to Miss Austen, who wrote excitedly in a letter that "the Hattons and Milles' dine here today—& I shall eat ice and drink French wine & be above vulgar economy. Luckily the pleasures of Friendship, of unreserved Conversation, of similarity of Taste & Opinions, will make good amends for Orange Wine."

Even so, Mirza Salih knew that back at 'Abbas Mirza's court, confessions of boozing with Christians could do much to discredit him. Such an admission would have been all the more dangerous if he admitted to drinking alcohol with the mysterious Freemasons who were already raising suspicion among Iranian clerics by this time. There is a good chance that he did, though. After all, by now he and his best friend Mirza Ja'far were both Freemasons and the brethren's main informal meeting place was Freemasons' Tavern, on the corner of Covent Garden where they were then spending a good deal of time. A few years earlier, the Indian Muslim traveler Abu Talib described his attendance at a Freemason garden party where it was the custom to call at every table and drink wine with those seated there. "I was therefore obliged," he wrote in Persian, "to take a bumper of wine at each table and having been frequently challenged by some beautiful women to replenish my glass, I drank more wine that night than I had ever done at one time in the course of my life." What a weighty obligation it must have been! And perhaps, *noblesse oblige,* it was one that Mirza Salih and Mirza Ja'far also had to bear. Mirza Salih certainly mentioned attending Freemason dinners.

Given what we have seen of the reasons why he was unlikely to discuss alcohol in his diary, to finally resolve the bibulous fog around their nights out in London we will need to look beyond Mirza Salih's journal. And it just so happens that firm evidence does indeed survive of his wine consumption in the form of a series of letters that he wrote to His Majesty's Customs Office. Though he hoped his sponsors back in Tabriz might turn a blind eye to his drinking, fortunately for us the tax man never misses a trick. For Mirza Salih wrote the letters in an attempt to avoid paying import duty on a shipment of beverages he was importing from France. And a shipment it was, for Mirza Salih expressly testified that the no fewer than seventy-four bottles of champagne and three dozen bottles of brandy and other liqueurs dispatched from Boulogne to his London address had been ordered "for my own use." Like many a latter-day English drinker, he had been caught out at duty free.

It is possible that the students had been granted the same cultural *passepartout* as Ambassador Abu'l-Hasan, allowing the finer points of Islamic dietary law to be overlooked for the higher purposes of making friends among nations. For as Philoxenus wrote of Abu'l-Hasan, "He drank wine at table with the Prince [Regent], because his master had given him permission to conform to the customs of the English on open great occasions." Diplomacy, then, was a powerful motor for the

Iranians' participation in the pleasures of the high table; and alcohol was in turn a powerful motor for making friends. Given that wine consumption was commonplace in the court circles of Iran, it is not clear why such a special dispensation was deemed necessary. Various diplomatic travelers to Iran testified to the scale of alcohol consumption they witnessed there at the time. Writing in 1817 of the Russian embassy to the court of the students's royal sponsor 'Abbas Mirza, Moritz von Kotzebue praised Iranian Muslims as "valiant topers," who he saw on several occasions "drank off a bottle of rum at once, without appearing to suffer any inconvenience from it." Describing a banquet hosted by 'Abbas Mirza himself, von Kotzebue affably remarked that "the wine, at dinner, was very good, and the Persians quaffed it off, as well as the liqueurs, in immense quantities." Whether among 'Abbas Mirza's Muslim elite in Tabriz or around the dining tables of England, wine promoted the same conviviality. At diplomatic dinners especially, wine played the practical role of facilitating communication across barriers of language, loosening tongues to sally forth with foreign verbs and summoning, however transiently, fraternal sympathies. In Persian, this intangible alcoholic élan was summed up in the word *kayf*, a state of mind rather than an ingredient that could be found in the intoxicants of any country. As the Iranian princes in London a decade later liked to ask James Fraser whenever he offered them a new alcoholic beverage: "Has it *kayf*?"

There seems little doubt, then, that the students enjoyed at least the odd drink during their last six months in London. The newspaper reports from the period certainly depict them as a jolly and sociable band. Although their consumption of alcohol was not without its religious contradictions, as individuals with their own moral agency they made their own decisions and compromises. Theology, whether Islamic or otherwise, is an adaptable tool and rather than submitting to the rulings of clerics, the students were making their own interpretations of Islam. Mirza Salih and Mirza Ja'far's strong interest in variant Christian theologies suggests far from dogmatic minds. Other Iranians of the period were similarly thinking their way around the stricter sides of Shari'a law. When the aptly named missionary Henry Stern refused to give one Iranian a bottle of *arrak* on the grounds that it was forbidden in Islamic law, the disappointed Muslim "swore by Ali, and all the 124,000 Mahomedan prophets, that sherab and arrack [wine and liquor] were only interdicted to those who prayed; but as he never prayed, he could not be included in the law." When the students' associate James Fraser later hosted the two Iranian princes in London, one of them kept reminiscing about the wine of Shiraz, crying out:

> Ah! you know the wine of Sheerauz,—and we had the best of it, to be sure: for each of us there was never less than two *jouingees* (glass bottles holding at least half a gallon a-piece); and we thought nothing of him who should leave not a drop of that; ay, and a good bottle of *arrack* (spirits) to boot, perhaps; and we had champagne and madeira also, from [the Iranian port of] Busheer. Ah! those were days of enjoyment!

Judging by Mirza Salih's colossal order of champagne and brandy "for my own use," there is therefore good reason to suspect that, like other students at other times, he and his companions enjoyed a good tipple or two. After all, strolling regularly through Theatreland during those first six months of 1819, they were by now part of the Regency's *beau monde*. They had come a long way since their darkest hours in Croydon.

Ultimately, though, it was the drinking of tea rather than wine that formed the most important culinary ritual that the Iranians and English shared in common. And if Mirza Salih was reticent in his diary on the topic of his champagne purchases, he did describe on many occasions taking tea with his English hosts. As with eating habits, he was interested in the social rituals around this beverage. He noted the widespread serving of tea to guests in people's homes and, pointing to shared social rituals, the special little tea gardens, or *baghcha*, that resembled the shady *chai-khanas* of Iran. As a commodity being traded in vastly increasing quantity in the early nineteenth century, it is finally tea that points us to the interdependence of culinary, social, and diplomatic interactions between Mirza Salih's Iran and Jane Austen's England. For not only did the period see England's role in the trading of tea increase through the East India Company's control of both the Indian and Chinese trade, it also saw a massive expansion of tea-drinking in Iran. Through the same mercantile forces, in both countries teashops replaced coffeehouses as spaces of sociability. Later in the century, the Iranian historian 'Abd Allah Mustawfi would reckon Ira-

Fig. 26. The Beverage That Bonds: Twinings Tea House near Fleet Street.
Source: Photo by Nile Green.

nian tea imports as comprising 1,350 tons of white tea from China and 450 tons of black tea from India. Most of it arrived on English ships.

The origins of this common tea consumption can partly be found in the students' London. For it was there that the great naturalist Sir Joseph Banks—who we have seen Mirza Salih mention in his diary—first suggested to the directors of the East India Company the idea of planting tea in India as a cash crop instead of importing it from China. After experiments in the botanic gardens of Oxford and Cambridge that the students had visited, India's first tea plants were cultivated in Assam. But its first harvest did not take place till 1819, their final year in London. They must have been drinking Chinese tea the whole time.

Whether black Assam or green Longjing, through the interplay of botany, commerce, and consumption, the sharing of tea was becoming an internationalized ritual of conviviality in which the Iranians and their English friends took equal pleasure. Little wonder that Mirza Salih's ethnography of amity focused so much on drinking tea, for it was a custom that his Iranian readers would immediately recognize. One place for tea that Mirza Salih would certainly have recognized was Twinings Tea House on the Strand: it stood just yards away from where, during that winter season in London, he was studying in Mr. Watts's print shop. It was in any case hard to miss, since by the time Mirza Salih was walking past it each day, Twinings's doorway was graced with a grand neoclassical portico surmounted by a colorful coat of arms and two bright statues of Chinese men.

Mirza Salih's repeated references to the eating and drinking habits of the English hinted to his Iranian readers at patterns of sociability, and perchance friendship, that they could share with the distant people of *Inglistan*. What rendered these trivial acts significant was that the students not only consumed English food and drink, but ate it with English people. In so doing, they did not merely adjust to foreign ingredients; they conversed with foreign people. In learning the importance of England's social rituals, the young Muslims took their education beyond the mechanical and bookish knowledge of their formal studies. They came to feel an affinity and even affection for another people.

In evoking for his Muslim readers the commonalities they shared with the distant Christians of *Inglistan*, there was subtle method in

Mirza Salih's decision to talk of tea and use familiar words to describe the English as enjoying kebabs and *halva* (or perhaps he had somehow glimpsed forward through time at a later London of immigrant shops and takeaways). For in the fond prose of his diary, he showed his English friends practising social rituals that corresponded to Iranian ways of friendship. Seen in this way, these were less clashing civilizations than overlapping ones.

Radical Companions

While the more genteel *mirzas* were enjoying the refined pleasures of tea drinking with the likes of Sir Gore Ouseley, their craftsman companion Muhammad 'Ali was mingling with an altogether different circle. If for him there was no tittle-tattle with society hostesses, Muhammad 'Ali was far from shut out from the finer purposes of conversation and among his workmates he found himself among people dedicated to the kind of discussions that Alexander Pope called "the feast of reason and the flow of soul." For in his London workplace, Muhammad 'Ali was meeting the radical heirs of the Levelers. With them during that last season in London, he took part in an altogether different politics of friendship than that learned by the other students at the dinners of the great and good.

So far, Muhammad 'Ali has mostly been an elusive presence in our story. Whether in Mirza Salih's diary, the surviving letters that the students wrote in English, the newspaper reports about them, or the diaries of those they met, Muhammad 'Ali is at best a shadowy presence in the background of his companions. As an *ustad*, or master craftsman, and not a gentlemanly *mirza*, he moved in different—and less elevated—circles than the others. Through both his background and smaller stipend he was unable (and perhaps unwilling) to behave in the way that led English newspapers to call the other students "Persian princes." He was a working man through and through. And as such, from his King Street lodgings to his High Holborn workplace, the London world in which he moved was a very different one. Although few direct records survive about him—he is the subaltern of his otherwise smart set—enough clues remain for us to piece together his social world. And it is worthwhile to do so. For as we will see later, before leaving England he would make the most dramatic of any of their pledges of friendship.

There is no evidence that Muhammad ʿAli ever made the tours of Bath and the university towns enjoyed by the other students. But by the same token, he seems to have been far less exposed to the evangelicals, whether by way of Dr. Gregory or the university professors. Instead, the friendships he made in England were all formed in the working-class districts of London where quite different movements were emerging. As we have seen, his first apprenticeship was served with the gunsmith and bladesmith James Wilkinson, after which he moved on to his second master, the machinist and engineer Alexander Galloway. Situated on Ludgate Hill and High Holborn, these two workshops were very much in London's industrial neighborhoods. Situated to the east of the upper- and middle-class areas near the Strand, to all intents and purposes Ludgate Hill and Holborn were the Regency predecessors of the gritty East End that in Victorian times spread further east. This was a far cry from the neo-Tudor palace of the Royal Military Academy where Mirza Jaʿfar and Mirza Riza were learning to be officers and gentlemen and from St. George's Hospital on Hyde Park Corner where Hajji Baba and the other Mirza Jaʿfar were studying. If Mirza Salih was now a printer's apprentice off Fleet Street, he was spending his evenings hobnobbing with the likes of Sir Gore Ouseley plotting a career as a diplomat. We never hear of Muhammad ʿAli entering such circles. While the other students were enjoying nights at the theater, like other residents of proletarian Covent Garden, the closest Muhammad ʿAli came to the Theatre Royal was the market square outside his lodgings on King Street.

Yet from what is known of his workplaces, we can conjure the outlines of his quite different life, and friendships, in London. The Wilkinson & Sons company had been recently founded by "immigrants" from Birmingham, a city whose residents spoke a very different dialect from Londoners and who saw themselves as a people apart from English southerners. Perhaps being in this circle of outsiders helped Muhammad ʿAli fit in better than he may have done elsewhere. He may have quickly won the respect of these working men. After all, unlike the other students who had nothing to trade but their language skills, Muhammad ʿAli was a master *ustad* whose skilled hands spoke the universal language of craftsmanship. It was a language that allowed hundreds of other foreign craftsmen to settle in Regency London, coming from all across Europe to settle in such districts as Spitalfields, just to the east of Muhammad ʿAli's two workplaces. In such proletarian yet cosmopolitan districts, he was less of an oddity than in other parts of the capital. After all, East London's dockyards hosted thousands of Arab and Indian Muslim sailors each year, most of them loyal seamen on ships of the East India Company.

Perhaps on his evenings after work, Muhammad ʿAli joined his workmates on their daily visits to such watering holes as the Castle Tavern on Holborn, a short walk from James Wilkinson's workshop and a mere hop from Alex Galloway's at 69 High Holborn. A highly popular pub at the time, having been founded in 1543, by the early nineteenth century the Castle was famous for its prize fights. Approached through a long dark passage that led off High Holborn to a glowing red lamp at its end, the Castle was home to the Prize Ring managed by the heavyweight hero Thomas Belcher. A one-eyed boxer from Bristol, Belcher was in his prime at the time of Muhammad ʿAli's apprenticeship. Such was the Castle's fame that, whether to gamble, spectate, or guzzle a tankard of ale, it is hard not to imagine Muhammad ʿAli being taken there by his workmates. After all, as a famous song of the time advertised it,

> You lads of fancy who wish to impart
> The tokens of friendship and soundness of heart,
> To Belcher's repair at the Castle so strong,
> Where he'll serve you all well—and you'll hear a good song.

Such, perhaps, were the proletarian pastimes that Muhammad ʿAli shared with his workmates and the tavernous places in which he learned to befriend the English.

Yet working-class history has always been more than a story of drinking and fighting. For these years also witnessed the birth of working-class radicalism in London. Preceding the more famous communism of Marx's later East End, this new politics tried to forge new ties between working men of all nations. Here lay a different politics of friendship to that of Fath ʿAli Shah and King George, one that instead celebrated the affinities of the lower classes from every land. And it just so happened that Muhammad ʿAli's second workplace was one of the most important hotbeds of such ideas. For his master at 69 High Holborn, Alexander Galloway (1776–1847), known to all as simply Alex, was one of the period's most notorious radicals. He even served time in prison for his convictions. We know that Alex Galloway had lost none of his beliefs by the time he took on Muhammad ʿAli because in 1818 he was raising money to help fellow radicals still held behind bars. As a leading member of the London Corresponding Society (LCS), much of his energy was devoted to parliamentary reform, a cause through which he sought more representation for working people in Parliament. Founded in 1792 in a pub off the Strand, the LCS has often been seen as the first mass political movement of the working classes. Alex Galloway eventually became its president, bringing him into contact with the many thinking artisans who made up its membership. Some of these men were immigrants like Muhammad ʿAli: the most famous of them was the African former slave, abolitionist, and autobiographer, Olaudah Equiano (ca. 1745–97). Alex Galloway was used to mixing with such men on equal terms, and, being a radical internationalist by conviction, he was the ideal person to take on a Muslim apprentice. In any case, many members of the LCS, and perhaps Galloway himself, were Deists, rationalist believers in a universal God who lay hidden behind the divisive doctrines of conventional religions. If, unlike Mirza Salih and Mirza Jaʿfar, Muhammad ʿAli was unable to join the Freemasons or visit the broadminded Unitarians of Bristol, in London he found a similarly tolerant circle who toiled lower down the social ladder.

Although the LCS was declared illegal and disbanded fifteen years before the students set foot in London, as an informal social network it remained strong, attracting gatherings of radical, Deist artisans to such bibulous haunts as the Angel Inn and Green Dragon. One of their meeting places, The Fleece at 27 Little Windmill Street, was just a short walk from Muhammad ʿAli's digs on King Street. Perhaps he sometimes joined his fellow artisans there, debating a different future for working people worldwide. That Muhammad ʿAli was accepted by his master and colleagues is not only suggested by Alex Galloway's political views but also by the way Mirza Salih was treated by his own apprenticeship master, Richard Watts, a few streets away. As he wrote about Mr. Watts in his diary, "from the path of goodness, and through his own good nature, charitableness and honest dealing, he always treated me well." As a former apprentice himself, such were Alex Galloway's sympathies with junior craftsmen that, four years before Muhammad 'Ali first came to his workshop, he led a campaign to abolish the apprenticeship clauses in the Statute of Artificers with the hope of improving the conditions and pay of apprentices. Sympathizing with his junior workers, Alex—always Alex—Galloway mixed easily with his fellow workmen.

There is a curious coda to the tale of Muhammad 'Ali's apprenticeship. For during the year or more that he spent at Galloway & Sons from 1818 to 1819, the young Muslim would have worked beside Alex Galloway's son and employee, Thomas. In a strange turn of events toward the end of their time together, the twenty-year-old Thomas decided to sail away from London bound for Cairo. What motivated this strange move is a mystery. But it just possibly came as a result of hearing Muhammad 'Ali talk of his ambitions to take modern machinery home to help his Muslim homeland progress. For what young Tom Galloway did when he reached Cairo was enter the service of another Muhammad 'Ali, the ruler of Egypt, who sought similarly to bring steam power to the people of Islam. Such were Tom Galloway's services to that other Muhammad 'Ali that he soon became Egypt's engineer-in-chief and won fame under an adopted Islamicized name: he became Galloway Bey. We will never know for sure the cause of Tom Galloway's abrupt departure for Egypt, nor what else came of the friendships between the *ustad* Muhammad 'Ali and his radical companions. But they surely shared with him their vision of an egalitarian world for which working men of all backgrounds should struggle in common cause. As the motto of the LCS had declared, "Unite, persevere, and be free." It made a fine toast.

6

The Love of Strangers

Foreign Friends

In the final months of their studies in 1819, the students were at ease in their adopted country, fluent in both its language and social customs. Such sentiments well over from Mirza Salih's diary, where over and again he showed himself to be a friend and admirer of the English. For later Iranian intellectuals, this was his greatest weakness: he was too impressed by "the West"; he was *gharbzada*, "Westoxified." Yet such concepts— "Westoxification," indeed, the very notion of a coherent "West"—did not exist in Mirza Salih's day. His opinions were based not on airy ideologies but on concrete encounters with real people, encounters from which he had built his personal ethnography of amity. If he and his companions were guilty of anything, it was the virtuous crime of xenophilia: the love of strangers.

In Europe no less than the Middle East, it is now more fashionable to critique than to admire and to detract than to praise cultural "others." But Mirza Salih and his friends were no ideologues, and their attitudes have much to teach us. As young men they had entered London without any preconceived ideas about Europe's inherently colonialist culture or the incompatibility of Muslim and Christian ideas. They had traveled to England in search of knowledge, and pursued it even as it took them to unexpected people and places. And in its pursuit, they had made many friends. Since the story of Middle Eastern relations with Europe is too often told as a tale of enmity, the unfolding of those friendships are important testimony to the shared humanity of both the Iranian Muslims and their Christian friends. On the human scale of world history, the sincerity of those friendships offers a corrective to ideas of the inevitable clash of cultures. While never neglecting his duty to his princely master, Mirza Salih saw no contradiction in serving his own country while also loving another people. The English, he wrote fondly, were both a disciplined (*qaʿidadan*) and polite (*muʾaddab*) people, who were much given to the intimacy or friendship that he labeled with the Persian word *ulfat*. Yet Mirza Salih was no dupe, no *gharbzada*; he was developing as canny a diplomatic mind as any Iranian of his generation. He knew full well that his genuine affection for the English, and the relationships that this opened up for him, allowed him to serve his own people as well.

From the day they disembarked in Great Yarmouth, friendship had been crucial to the students' public success and private solace. Now that they knew they would shortly be departing for Iran, their friendships in England seemed all the more valuable and developed toward a late blossoming. Although Ambassador Abu'l-Hasan had only agreed to let the students remain in London till the end of March 1819, as matters turned out, Sir Gore Ouseley was again able to intervene on their behalf. He persuaded Abu'l-Hasan to allow them to remain throughout the summer as well. Even so, it was clear that by autumn they would be on their way. Having missed the last eastbound ship of the autumn season in 1818, they would not be allowed to miss another opportunity to be returned to the homeland where their newfound expertise was so needed. They had one last spring and summer to not only complete their studies but also make the most of a London that was by now full of friends.

Though the students' friendships with people such as Sir Gore were not separate from their mission, they were no less sincere for that. It was only through their first, often tentative, friendships in England that they had been allowed into the social circles in which knowledge and education were confined. Time and again, friendships formed the means by which they were able to navigate the elaborate social networks of Jane Austen's era. In this way, knowledge and friendship were tied to each another from the beginning to the end of their journey. So it is fitting that, as we move into their last months in England, we will focus now on the relationships that underwrote their passage through the knowledge and faith of the English toward friendship with the English themselves.

As Mirza Salih's diary makes clear, the four years that his companions spent in England were years in which their attitude toward the Christian English changed considerably. Even though before Mirza

Salih even reached England he had spent time with the Ouseley brothers in Iran, these were men who spoke Persian and the setting was still very much Iranian. In the case of the other five students, there is no similar evidence of them meeting English people before they left Iran in 1815. Their months of travel from Tabriz to Great Yarmouth were similarly in the company of the Persian-speaking Mr. D'Arcy. Being then suddenly flung into English society, where they were the only Iranians in the entire country, had been bewildering in all kinds of ways. As we have seen, their early months were a time of disappointment as much as excitement, months when they realized that Mr. D'Arcy was unable or unwilling to find and fund teachers for them. It had been an altogether unpromising start to their relationships with the English, as the man who had sworn to their crown prince that he would help them turned out to be unreliable. Many values of the English were different from those of the Iranians, and while the characters in Jane Austen's novels spoke much about honor, this rarely stretched toward facing bankruptcy to fulfill a forced promise. As both parties drew on the moral expectations of their backgrounds to justify their different positions, there was much divergence, both subtle and gross, between what the students and Mr. D'Arcy felt was the proper response to that promise to the crown prince. The sum of it all was that the students' relationship with their first English friend had proved to be a great disillusionment. It was a theme that came up again and again in Mirza Salih's diary.

It was, then, a far from promising start. And as a result, it was only gradually that the students learned to trust the English and, through their journey through knowledge and faith, come to regard them as both a friendly nation and a nation of friends. Faced with the bewilderment of their new surroundings and their disappointment in Mr. D'Arcy, like many later immigrants they had then turned to a fellow countryman for help. So it was that their earliest true friend in London was Hajji Baba, the medical student with whom several of them lodged in Camden Town after their frustrations with Mr. D'Arcy led them to flee his house on Leicester Square. It had been from Hajji Baba that they had taken some of their first lessons in the language and ways of the English. Since, as one of the earlier pair of students sent to England in 1811, Hajji Baba had by then already been in London for four years, he may also have shared with them the basic premises of the scientific learning he had already acquired. As we have seen, Hajji Baba had also adopted the dress of an English gentleman. It was through their friendship with this Anglicized fellow Iranian that the other five young Muslims had made their vicarious first steps toward the knowledge of the English that would pave the way for fuller relationships with English people. It was only after several months living under Hajji Baba's tutelage that they had felt comfortable enough to swim unaided through the currents of English life and leave his north London lodgings for the small town of Croydon.

It is perhaps surprising that in their first year in England, they had socialized mainly with Persian-speaking Britons such as Sir Gore Ouseley and Sir John Malcolm. As recent migrants, it is natural that they should have been inclined toward Sir John. His familiarity with Iran was not only limited to its language. For as a traveler to Iran as well as a historian of the country, his familiarity also extended to its religion and culture. On one occasion when Mirza Salih and Mirza Ja'far came up from Croydon to see him in London, Sir John had reiterated the pledge he had made on their first meeting. "Because I myself ate the salt of the shah of Iran, and so see myself as his servant," he had declared to them, "I will give you the same advice as though I were your father." Unlike the many retired East India Company employees who had, to varying degrees of fluency, studied Indo-Persian, Sir John had learned the idioms and pleasantries associated with the royal courts of Fath 'Ali Shah and 'Abbas Mirza in Iran—that is, the students' home milieu. Having been in Iran only a few years earlier, there is also a fair chance that he had met people whom the students knew back home, a single degree of separation that always aids new friendships. However, it had turned out to be a friendship that did not last, for just as they were settling into their regular routine of visiting him, in October 1816 Sir John had been recalled for duty in India. With Mirza Salih's growing interest in newspapers, he could have easily kept up with news of their friend through the regular reports that were printed on Sir John's expeditions against the Marathas in central India. But from this point on, it would be a vicarious and remembered friendship: Sir John would not return to England till after the students' departure.

The six students were the only Iranians in London at this time, making up Europe's first group of Muslim students. Even so, there were already Indians residing in London, and although they were not students they did include several Persian speakers. Some of these Indians were short-term residents, staying in England for shorter periods than the students; others spent many years living there and were even more versed in England's ways than Hajji Baba. We have already seen how the students' arrival in Croydon had coincided with the departure of Mir Hasan ʿAli, the Indian teacher of Persian at the East India College. While there is no evidence that they crossed paths, the students would certainly have known of the presence of Indian Persian-speakers, some of whom advertised language lessons in the newspapers with which Mirza Salih eventually became so enamored. But the Persian spoken by Indians and Iranians had sufficiently diverged by the nineteenth century that its speakers felt they were conversing with foreigners rather than compatriots. In the preface to the book of Persian dialogues that Mirza Salih originally wrote with William Price back in Iran and that Price subsequently published in 1823, Mirza Salih was quoted as being "disgusted with the style" of Persian used by Indian teachers of Persian, because they favored "pedantic phrases and obsolete words." Though far fewer than his mentions of English friends, Mirza Salih did nonetheless mention in his diary a few encounters with Indians in London, including in 1819 Shaykh Muhyi al-Din and Mir Afzal ʿAli, the emissaries of an Indian prince sent to protest the East India Company's seizure of royal revenues. Although Mirza Salih tried to help the Indians in this hapless venture, their friendship only developed during the students' last months in England. Up until then, for most of their four years there, they had been forced to befriend the natives.

By their last summer in London, they counted not only older teachers and patrons like Dr. Gregory and Sir Gore as their friends, but also younger gentlemen of similar age to themselves. One was the theatrical architect Samuel Beazley, the relative of Sir John Malcolm to whom Mirza Salih had been introduced at one of Sir John's dinner parties three years earlier. He would have been just turning thirty when he met his Iranian friend. By 1819, Mirza Salih had spent many an evening with Sam Beazley, frequenting the theaters around Covent Garden where Beazley's own English Opera House was located. Together they explored much of booming Theatreland, which Mirza Salih came to know well. Describing London as having no fewer than ten major theaters, he clearly passed enough time in them to learn their seat prices (three shillings for a seat in the stalls, seven shillings for a box seat) and to pen an account of the most famous actors of the day. Since during that final spring and summer season, Mirza Salih (and perhaps the other students) was spending many an evening around Covent Garden, it is worth taking a better look at the environment in which they socialized.

Mirza Salih described the interior of Covent Garden's opera house in detail, with its five stories of private booths, each with its own lantern; its stage fronted with a great arch and lit with many chandeliers that reflected light through the diamond-like glass decor on the surrounding walls; and the various types of musicians who sat beneath the stage. He appears to have been describing Covent Garden's second Theatre Royal that had replaced the first one, which was destroyed in a fire. It had opened only a few years earlier in 1809 and was built to the designs of the Greek Revival architect Robert Smirke (1780–1867), who a year after the students' final London summer redesigned the British Museum that Mirza Salih so admired. As well as opera proper, the Theatre Royal hosted ballets, musical comedies, variety acts, and even clowns. It also helped raise the status of the quintessential English art of pantomime. Such palaces of pleasure were fine places for making friends. Whether with Sam Beazley or with the other pals he had in London by the spring of 1819, Mirza Salih knew many of London's theaters and other places of distraction, such as the famous Vauxhall Gardens to which we will turn shortly. He and Sam Beazley also spent time in the Covent Garden pleasure district adjacent to Beazley's theater. Evidence we will see of the other students' winning female admirers from high society suggests that they too shared these nocturnal tours, gaining friends, acquaintances, and even lovers along the way.

In that spring of 1819, as the young Muslims neared the prescribed end of their studies, Mirza Salih wrote that he was working hard every day except Sunday and only going once per week to a theater or party. Perhaps this was true, and perhaps it was not. His diary had to justify the debts Iran had incurred to the British Government for the costs of his education and for the extension granted to remain in London past the already extended deadline of March 1819 set by Abu'l-Hasan.

Whether or not during those last months Mirza Salih resumed his prior routine of more regular theater visits with Sam Beazley we cannot know. But it is clear that by 1819, he had come to know the area around Covent Garden well, not least because Muhammad 'Ali's lodgings at 36 King Street overlooked the Covent Garden piazza.

We do not know whether the theatrical Sam Beazley's interests also stretched to the scientific institutions that Mirza Salih described himself visiting, such as the Royal Society and the British Museum, though it was clearly by means of Mirza Salih's acquaintances if not his friends that he was introduced to such places. Friendships were after all the means by which the students made their way in England, webs of obligation and duty by which they were able to simply get things done. Judging by the evidence of Mirza Salih's own words, the main figure in helping the students make their connections with London's learned societies seems to have been Dr. Olinthus Gregory, the mathematics professor at the Royal Military Academy, who Mirza Salih described on several occasions introducing them to learned societies and individuals. Over the years, Dr. Gregory and Sir Gore Ouseley had served as their most important senior friends and advisors, introducing them to people or institutions that had furthered their search for knowledge. By their last season in London, the importance of Sir Gore's friendship was clear to them all. In a letter that Mirza Ja'far wrote to Mr. Planta at the Foreign Office around this time from his lodgings with Mirza Salih on Salisbury Court, he declared "that we have not lost *all* the time we have been in England we owe principally to the disinterested friendship of Sir Gore Ouseley and Mr Butterworth of Bedford Square, who so felt for our deplorable situation & kindly exerted themselves to get the arrangements made for the instruction of every one of us." As we saw earlier, "Mr. Butterworth of Bedford Square" was the Bible Society supporter Joseph Butterworth, whose bookshop on Fleet Street was close to where Mirza Salih was studying printing and who was by Christian vocation a supporter of educational causes. Such Christian commitments did not prevent him from helping the Muslims. Mr. Butterworth was, after all, one of the greatest philanthropists of the period. And had not the evangelicals already performed the great humanitarian service of ending the slave trade of their African brothers? Perhaps Messrs. Ouseley and Butterworth saw their help to the abandoned Muslim students in similar terms.

Not forgetting their other helpful friend, in his letter Mirza Ja'far also praised "Dr Gregory, who has shown himself our friend as well." As the students' time in England was drawing to a close, it was Dr. Gregory who wrote Mirza Salih and Mirza Ja'far a letter of introduction to meet the famous astronomer Sir William Herschel (1738–1822) and his son, Sir John Frederick Herschel (1792–1871). Like a social key, Dr. Gregory's letter opened the door for the students to the discoveries of those knights astronomical. For in his letter, Dr. Gregory specifically asked Sir William and his son to show the two *mirzas* how to operate his telescope. Through Mirza Ja'far's studies of surveying and map-making, he had already learned not only of the discoveries being made by Sir William but also of the importance of the new scientific equipment on which such discoveries were being made. When the two Muslims went out to visit Sir William at his house near Windsor in the spring of 1819, Mirza Salih declared his astonishment that his telescope was no less than forty feet long. It must have been an extraordinary sight, reaching for the heavens through the roof of a special wooden shed in Sir William's garden. After the latter explained the nature of his discoveries to the Iranians, his son Sir John showed them how to operate the giant telescope. In his diary, Mirza Salih called it a *durbin*, or "far-seer," a literal translation of the Latin term "telescope" that the two students would have understood from their Latin classes with Mr. Bisset back in Croydon.

Though then less famous than his father, it was Sir John who seemed to be the more useful contact, for as a gifted lens-grinder as well as an astronomer, he presented the possibility of helping the students acquire one of the latest telescopes to take back to Iran. It would be an important coup, for astronomy was one of the branches of the "new learning" that most interested their princely patron, 'Abbas Mirza. Yet the prince's keenness for studying heavenly bodies remained rooted in Iran's cultural soil. In his memoir of the Ouseley embassy of 1812, Mirza Salih's friend William Price had recorded that:

> Prince Abbas Mirza consults his astrologers, and they consulting the planets, discover that if he signs the definitive treaty before the next

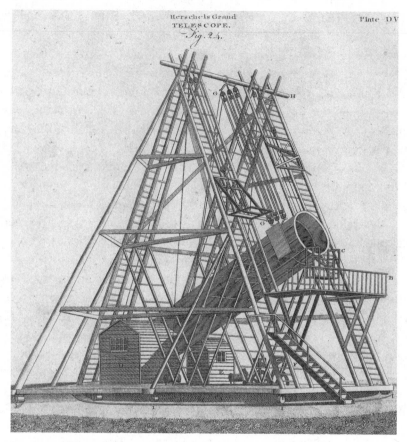

Fig. 27. Sharing the Same Heaven: The Herschel Telescope Shown to Mirza
Salih and Ja'far.   Source: Collection of the author.

conjunction, evil may attend it; therefore the signing of the treaty is
deferred till the lucky day arrives; consequently Sir William Ouseley
and myself are detained from setting out for England with the treaty.

Price's observations show that 'Abbas Mirza and his court astrologers still understood the planets in terms of the ancient Ptolemaic system that laid the basis for Islamic astrology (known as *ahkam-i nujum*).
What this in turn shows is just how far Mirza Salih and Mirza Ja'far
had moved ahead of even their most scientifically enlightened compatriots. Through their studies and visits to museums and learned societies, they well understood that the Herschels' telescopes were not sim-

ply new tools for old astrology, for *ahkam-i nujum*. They realized instead that these were revolutionary instruments, enabling European scientists to rewrite the traditional map of the heavens used by ʿAbbas Mirza's astrologers. As Mirza Salih jotted in his diary, even as far back as 1781 Sir William had used his telescope to discover what he had first thought was a comet. What Sir William soon realized he had discovered was far more startling than a shooting star: it was a planet previously unknown to humankind. Today we call it Uranus, but, in honor of King George II, Sir William named it *Georgium Sidus* ("George's Star"). It was this Latin name that Mirza Salih transcribed into the Arabic script of his diary. This had been the first time since antiquity that a new planet had been discovered and the first time ever that a telescope had been used to do so. Now, through Mirza Salih, Muslims were also learning of this heaven-changing discovery.

By talking to the Herschels and peering through their telescope, in the spring of 1819 Mirza Salih and Mirza Jaʿfar stared up into a whole new universe, one of which their contemporaries back home had as yet no inkling. Partaking in Europe's scientific revolution, by their final months in England they reached a level of immersion in the new learning of the age that no one in their home country could match.

Sir John Herschel was keen to spread his science far and wide and agreed to make a telescope for Mirza Salih to carry home to Iran. It was not the only item of scientific apparatus that the students' friendships helped them acquire. With their departure now set for late summer, they began making arrangements to take home with them all manner of equipment, whether for themselves or their princely patron. In an earlier chapter, we saw the botanist Sir Joseph Banks gathering a collection of seeds from the Royal Botanic Gardens at Kew: the students would now deliver them to Fath ʿAli Shah, the ruler of Iran. And it was not only seeds and telescopes that they planned to export. The craftsman Muhammad ʿAli ordered from his apprentice-master "four cases purchased of Mr. Galloway for his own use." While we do not know what was in these cases, since the radical Alex Galloway was listed in the London trade directory that year as a "machinist and engineer," they may have contained one of the steam engines in which Galloway specialized and which he was already exporting to Egypt. Through Muhammad ʿAli's earlier apprenticeship to the gunmaker James Wilkinson, he also placed an order for King Fath 'Ali Shah of a long list of rifles and shooting equipment, including sights, leather slings and silver mounts. In an intriguing hint at Muhammad 'Ali's role in making these items for his king, the order specified that the rifles should have "barrels inlaid with gold Persian characters." If such dandy weaponry wouldn't help Fath 'Ali Shah defeat the Russians during their next war with Iran in 1826, then his side could at least go down in style.

While Iranian royals were therefore not entirely practical in their choice of equipment, after four years of studying the "new sciences" the students had a far better idea of what to take home with them. The medical student Hajji Baba used his connections to place orders for medical books and "mathematical & surgical instruments and tools and medicines," for example. He ran up the large bill of £367 (over £27,000, or $42,000, in today's terms), which he was confident would be paid by Ambassador Abu'l-Hasan. Not to be outdone, the other medical student Mirza Ja'far sought help from his teacher Dr. John Shaw in acquiring surgical equipment. A surviving letter that Dr. Shaw wrote Mirza Ja'far in response advised him that "the most useful thing for you will be good drawings and coloured casts of the different parts" of the body. These were specialist items, he added, which "I fear will be very expensive." Recognizing the importance of proper equipment for putting into practice in Iran the skills he had learned in London, Mirza Ja'far was not to be discouraged. A subsequent surviving memorandum details the various items he then ordered to carry home with him. They included books (costing £100, 1 shilling); surgical instruments (costing £54, 16 shillings, and 6 pence); chemical apparatus (costing £16, 15 shillings, and 6 pence); and medicine (costing £27), the latter coming from the very best medical supplies of London's Apothecaries Hall. It at least added up to a smaller bill than Hajji Baba's. As the students' departure grew closer in the spring of 1819, Mr. Planta at the Foreign Office further authorized Mr. D'Arcy to "make such a selection of these articles as your knowledge of Persia, and of [the students'] different professions, shall suggest to you to be the most useful," providing him to cover these final purchases the considerable sum of £500 (today around £37,000, or almost $60,000). When the students departed, they would be carrying not only ideas with them, but also the tools and machines of the scientific revolution.

An Education in the Arts

Even so, it was not only telescopes and scalpels that captured the students' interests during their last months in London. The cultivated circles that the students had gathered round them by this time shared with the young Muslims their growing interest in poetry and painting. This was, after all, one of the most dynamic eras in English arts and letters. Even so, there was a reciprocal interest among their friends in the cultural life of Iran. With their comfortably civilized upbringings, the class of Englishmen who traveled to Iran during the Regency were as fully attuned to the powers of art as the educated Iranians were in London. A large proportion of the period's travelers to Iran (almost all of whom were friends of the students) were accomplished amateur artists in their own right. Sir William Ouseley's and William Price's published accounts of the 1812 embassy to Iran (that Mirza Salih had accompanied) were illustrated with their own deft engravings. But the greater focus of William Ouseley's interest was in literature, and for his part Sir Gore Ouseley became one of Europe's earliest connoisseurs of Persian poetry, compiling in his spare time a voluminous compendium of Persian poets. He was by no means the first to turn to the pleasures of Persian verse, since England's interest in the sweet songs of Shiraz had developed a generation earlier through Sir William Jones's attempts at "Englishing" Persian poetry. Jones's translations—particularly of the languorous lyrics of Hafiz—appeared in many popular publications, such as the *Gentleman's Magazine* and *Town and Country*. As the classicism of the eighteenth century began to give way to the exoticism of the Romantics, "Oriental Jones" had offered the new movement an elective Eastern affinity:

> Speak not of fate:—ah! change the theme,
> And talk of odours, talk of wine,
> Talk of the flowers that round us bloom:
> 'Tis all a cloud, 'tis all a dream.

By 1819, England was at the height of the orientalist fashion that Jones first cultivated and Byron brought to fruition. In 1812, he had become an overnight sensation through the first canto of his *Childe*

Harold's Pilgrimage. In 1813 and 1814 Byron had then published the verse novellas of his four *Oriental Tales* after traveling through the western territories of the Ottoman Empire. Though Byron claimed firsthand experience of piratical *giaours* and almond-eyed odalisques from the seraglio, we do know from the correspondence of the students' friend, Sir John Malcolm, that Byron at least received a copy of Malcolm's *History of Persia*, for which the poet wrote him a letter of thanks. Even if Byron's oriental language learning remained superficial, there were other Englishmen writing not only poetry about Persians but poetry *in* Persian. These included Colonel John Baillie (1772–1838), a relative of Mirza Salih's associate James Baillie Fraser. Like Sir Gore Ouseley, Fraser spent many years at the court of Sa'adat 'Ali Khan in Lucknow and learned there the improvised art of versified Persian repartee.

Mirza Salih does not seem to have had much interest in poetry, and his diary is virtually devoid of the snatches of verse that characterize most Persian travel accounts of the period. On the rare occasion when he did cite poetry, he preferred the humanely sardonic verses of his fellow son of Shiraz, the medieval Sa'di. But if his high-minded diary is reticent on the frivolous pleasures of poetry, we know enough about the other students' interests to prove that they were fully aware of the literary fashion for "the Orient." In a short memoir of Mirza Ja'far written by one of his English friends, he was said to be "a man of cultivated mind, and was able to enter into the spirit of our best poets, whose works he had perused." Moreover, in an interview he gave to a newspaper Mirza Ja'far declared that he was "pleased with the poems of Lord Byron, and with the *Lalla Rookh* of Mr. Moor." While we can only guess whether it was Byron's *Oriental Tales* that he had in mind, in the case of *Lalla Rookh* we have unquestionable evidence of his liking for orientalist verse. Having just been published in 1817, *Lalla Rookh* was written by the Irish poet Thomas Moore (1779–1852). It contained the versified adventures of its titular heroine, Lalla Rookh, a daughter of the Mughal Emperor Awrangzeb, following her as she traveled from India to Iran. If modern literary critics have often decried such works as the artistic detritus of empire, Mirza Ja'far clearly read them differently. However exoticized the poem's depiction of his country, its storyline was not altogether different from the narrative poems on which the students would themselves have been raised in Iran. With its familiar title—*lala rukh* was a Persian nickname meaning "rosy-cheeked"—the young Mirza Ja'far perhaps found solace far from home in Mr. Moore's romantic tale. For though it was written in a foreign language, from its very opening lines *Lalla Rookh* celebrated his Iranian homeland:

> In that delightful Province of the Sun,
> The first of Persian lands he shines upon.
> Where all the loveliest children of his beam,
> Flowerets and fruits, blush over every stream

So it was that long before Iranians were reading *Lolita* in Tehran, they were reading *Lalla Rookh* in London.

The artistic traffic between Mirza Salih's Iran and Jane Austen's England came not only in terms of literature. It also came in terms of the visual arts. At this time, the grand portrait in oil and canvas was just becoming popular in Iran. Its Qajar monarchs and courtiers were having themselves painted in their finest robes, jewels, and medals, creating a style that for all its adaptations of European techniques remains one of the most unmistakably original in art history. In his palace at Tabriz, the students' patron 'Abbas Mirza even had a private gallery of paintings of his European heroes that he liked to show off to his diplomatic guests. In a reciprocal gesture, when the Iranians visited the house of Sir Gore Ouseley, they were shown his collection of Persian canvas and miniature paintings. When Ambassador Abu'l-Hasan visited, he remarked on the fine portrait of Asaf al-Dawla, the ruler of Lucknow, which Sir Gore had respectfully hung beside paintings of European noblemen.

This shared interest in the arts saw several paintings commissioned from the Iranians' circle in London. Of these, the most lavishly Romantic were the several portraits made of Abu'l-Hasan. One was painted by the famous society artist Sir Thomas Lawrence (1769–1830) and commissioned by Sir Gore Ouseley. Abu'l-Hasan recounted his many sittings for Sir Thomas in his diary. Another portrait of the ambassador, one of two painted by Sir William Beechey (1753–1839) and seen in the Introduction to this book, shows him in more relaxed guise, reclining in an azure-lined scarlet cloak. It depicted Abu'l-Hasan—then

Fig. 28. Persia Britannica: Mirza Jaʿfar's Literary Beloved *Lalla Rookh*.
Source: *Lalla Rookh*, by Thomas More (London, 1816).

aged thirty-five and in the prime of his manhood—as a kind of Byronic hero, a living embodiment of the poet's black-bearded *Corsair*. It was an image that Abu'l-Hasan was not averse to cultivating through his daily exercises in Regent's Park that, widely observed, involved hurling javelins for his unfortunate retainers to catch in full flight. Judging by the fact that Abu'l-Hasan sat for no fewer than eight portraits during his two visits to England in 1809 and 1819, he clearly enjoyed the attention. Though Mirza Salih was little interested in poetry, he did take an interest in painting and paid several visits to the Royal Academy in Somerset House on the Strand. There he described seeing artists sitting at work every day with life models frozen motionlessly before them. Such was the popularity of the *surat*, or portrait, as an art form, he noted, that every year all of London's artists exhibited paintings at the Royal Academy that masses of visitors would travel to see every day during the Academy's Summer Exhibition. Ambling through the galleries that summer of 1819 and passing comment, we might think of Mirza Salih as England's first Muslim art critic.

The students' entry into these artistic circles was a sign of their increasing social stature during their final months in England. Indeed, they were almost becoming celebrities. For their interest in the English arts found a fitting echo when portraits of two of the students were displayed at the Royal Academy. Several years earlier, Sir Thomas Beechey's portrait of Abu'l-Hasan had been shown there, but now it was the students' time in the spotlight. At the Royal Academy's 1819 Summer Exhibition, London's most prestigious annual art show, there hung on display a *Portrait of Mearza Riza, a Persian* and another of *Meerza Saulih, a Persian.* Since the Royal Academy did not purchase or otherwise acquire the paintings displayed at the Summer Exhibitions but either sold them to private collectors or returned them to the artist, it is unclear what happened to the two portraits or even what they looked like. What a loss! We do, though, know something about the man who painted them, Samuel John Stump (1778–1863). An American who had moved to England to study fine art, by 1815 Stump had successfully established himself in the fashionable circles of Brighton and London. Since around this time Mr. Stump lived on Leicester Square, where the students had first lodged with Mr. D'Arcy, it may have been there that he first encountered them. After all, Ambassador Abu'l-Hasan's second portrait painter, Sir William Beechey, similarly lived just one street west of Abu'l-Hasan's lodgings. However it was that Mr. Stump first met the students, by 1819 when he painted them he clearly regarded them as celebrities: the other portraits he painted that year were all of leading thespians like Edmund Keane.

It was appropriate company to be keeping in paint, for we have already seen Mirza Salih's taste for the theater. It is only natural that he enjoyed the company of such jolly bohemians as the artist Sam Stump and the theater manager Sam Beazley, for despite Dr. Gregory's scientific connections he was hardly an ideal noctural comrade. Already forty-three years old when he came into contact with the students, Gregory was too old to compete with the theater-loving Sam Beazley when it came to evenings of entertainment. Another good-time companion was Dr. Dennis, a young physician closer to the students' age who Mirza Salih described as the son of a well-known surgeon and who may also have been a friend of the medical student, Hajji Baba. Mirza Salih wrote of Dr. Dennis fondly as someone with whom he always had fun.

Yet it was not all friendship, and by the summer of 1819, the students' relationship with their first English friend, Mr. D'Arcy, had sunk to an all-time low. They had even begun to suspect him of trying to deliberately thwart the completion of their studies. Mirza Salih wrote in his diary that Mr. D'Arcy lied to him that Sir Gore Ouseley did not want to see any more of the students or even hear their names spoken when in fact Sir Gore remained their firmest friend. Sensitive to social infelicities as he was, Mirza Salih took particular offense at Mr. D'Arcy's habit of referring to the students as *atfal*, or "kids." It was not only his criticisms that were voiced that summer. For in a letter written to Mr. Planta at the Foreign Office, in July 1819 Mirza Ja'far also plainly condemned Mr. D'Arcy, who, he stated, far from helping the students had only used his influence "to annoy and vex us." If the students' last summer in London was therefore not without its annoyances, they still enjoyed evenings of gaiety with such friends as Dr. Dennis, Sam Beazley, and Robert Abraham, the companion of Mirza Salih's Devonshire trip whom the students often met in London. Remembering how Mr. Abraham's family had cried when he had left them in Plymouth at the end of his tour through Devonshire, Mirza Salih now reflected on how sincere and dear friendships could be made among peoples of such different countries. Summing up his thoughts in a short Persian phrase, he wrote *ikhtilaf-i mazhab chi?*—"What does the difference of religion matter?"

Though he was formally recording English rituals of friendship to guide Iranians who would follow him to England, Mirza Salih took much pleasure in the tea parties, dinners, theater trips, and garden walks he described that summer. Like many others in Jane Austen's England, he held these simple pleasures to be of value and was not afraid to state as much. For the right kinds of entertainment and pleasure were part of the making of a man, part of what, as a citizen of the world, he had come to regard as a rounded education for both Christians and Muslims. These were after all civilized pastimes that he was describing. He made no mention of the drinking and whoring that were the other "gentlemanly" pursuits of the day. Whether Sam Beazley also introduced him to these more furtive pleasures we do not know. But we have seen the large shipment of wine and champagne that he imported for himself and, as we will now see, the places he was spending his evenings were rife with the prostitutes to whom Regency Englishmen turned with alarming regularity. This was the case especially with Covent Garden, where by night poor girls sold themselves to theatergoing "gentlemen." So associated was the area with prostitution that in Regency London venereal disease was nicknamed "Covent Garden gout."

Though we cannot be sure whether the students also befriended the "Druly Lane vestals" who leased their bodies by night around theaterland, we can re-create the settings in which Mirza Salih described his friends socializing and draw our own quiet conclusions. For his diary was always only a partial testimony, a document that placed both his English and Iranian friends in a flattering if not always revealing light. Lest his fellow countrymen charge the Christian English with the immoral vices of infidels, he portrayed their friendships and pleasures as taking place in the symbolic epitome of civilized order: the garden. And it was in Regency London's greatest pleasure park that Mirza Salih gave fullest vent to his xenophilia, his love and admiration for the peoples of *Inglistan*. That pleasure park was Vauxhall Gardens.

Park Life

Now that summer had arrived, the students took advantage of the famous parks that were first taking shape in Regency London. Park life there was both familiar and different to the Iranians. Like the tea drinking that Mirza Salih celebrated as a shared social ritual between England and Iran, the cultivation of gardens was another custom that Iranians held in common with the English. Continuing his ethnography of amity, Mirza Salih penned a series of depictions of London's gardens and parks that were intended to strike a chord of recognition with Iranian readers by reflecting their own love of gardens. "In London, there are four 'parks,'" he explained, "That is to say, public gardens." He continued in more detail:

> One is Hyde Park; another is St James' Park; another is Green Park; and another is Regent's Park. In each of them, the people of London come there at one o'clock in the afternoon to spend time strolling around and conversing. Men and women, who might be family or friends, lock hands as they stroll. Those who have their own carriages go there in their carriages; other people ride horses. They stay there, ambling around, till it gets dark. But it is the custom there that no-one at all speaks loudly. If a blind person went there, he would imagine that none of them could speak or that speaking had been banned there!

As spaces for the public expression of good manners, for Mirza Salih gardens were vivid proof of English civility and public spiritedness, all the more so because every social class seemed to have access to these places. His remark about driving in open carriages was an implicit comparison with the enclosed palanquins of Iran. Indeed, everyone he encountered in London's parks seemed to be on public display, which encouraged them to be well-dressed and well-mannered.

He added to this impression at various other points in the diary. He especially admired south London's Vauxhall Gardens and the tearooms and firework displays visitors enjoyed there. Then there were the *baghchas*, or "little gardens," surrounded by iron railings and set in residential squares—classic Georgian design features—to which entry was only allowed to those deemed appropriate and lent a key. On his earlier travels in the West Country with Mirza Ja'far, he had praised Sydney Gardens in Bath, completed in 1795 to the designs of Charles Harcourt Masters. Jane Austen once wrote to her sister that "It would be very pleasant to be near Sydney Gardens; we might go into the labyrinth every day." Her horticultural enthusiasms were persuasive, since between 1801 and 1804 the adjacent 4 Sydney Place became the Austen family home. During their journey, Mirza Salih and Mirza Ja'far had also taken a stroll around Cheltenham's Thomson Garden, which Mirza Salih correctly recorded as being named in honor of the Scottish poet James Thomson (1700–1748; now best remembered as the composer of *Rule Britannia!*). He described visitors coming to drink its special well water as a cure for their ailments. Back in London, he noted that even the insane were taken on daily walks through the pleasant gardens that adjoined what he called the "madhouse," namely the infamous Bedlam Asylum. As he interpreted matters, when made available to all classes of citizen, such parks and gardens were the architectural key to public civility. They offered a concrete—or, rather, a grassy—explanation for the manners and social rituals that so impressed him. And as he well recognized, it was a context that could be re-created in Iran and elsewhere if city governors could be persuaded to create public spaces.

Given that we know Mirza Salih was associated with at least two architects—the theatrical architect Samuel Beazley and the home and garden architect Robert Abraham—there is good reason to suppose that he learned of the philosophical ideals behind England's gardens through discussions with his friends. The students' years in England after all coincided with the heyday of both formal garden design and the commissioning of public parks. In the years when Mirza Salih knew Robert Abraham, he was working as the business partner of John Nash, the greatest architect of the Regency who during the students' last summer in London was designing the jewel of its public gardens, Regent's Park. The young Muslims were well aware of these horticultural transformations around them, and Mirza Salih recorded in his diary discussing the prince regent's plans for the area around Regent's Street.

His diary discussion of London's other parks shows that he and his friends visited most of them, including Vauxhall Gardens, the city's grandest pleasure park. Although Vauxhall Gardens dated back to the seventeenth century, in terms of their popularity Mirza Salih and his companions were visiting during their halcyon days. Vauxhall Gardens were quite distinct from the more serene public gardens of Bath and the more private gardens of residential London squares; in today's terminology, they would be better described as an amusement park. Since the introduction of admission charges in 1785, the amusements on offer at Vauxhall had become ever more spectacular, ranging from musical entertainments and historical reenactments to open-air banquets, hot-air balloon flights, and the massive firework displays described by Mirza Salih. Clearly, the students were making the most of their final few months.

An advertisement from the *Morning Post* newspaper describes one such spectacle that Mirza Salih and his friends may have attended:

> VAUXHALL—Under the patronage of His Royal Highness the Prince Regent—Madame Sucran's astonishing performance on the TIGHT ROPE . . . Will be repeated every Gala Night until further notice . . . Tomorrow evening will be a splendid Gala and brilliant display of Fireworks . . . Doors open at seven and the concert begins at eight.

The students would have been happy to learn that the "price is lowered to 3s 6d," for the entrance fees were deliberately priced to be open to all comers. The only people forbidden entry were servants in uniform: they broke the garden's illusion of being a place of equality as nature intended. Yet there was more than fireworks and music on offer. With its notorious "dark walks," deliberately created by the designer Jonathan Tyers as retreats for many a beau and belle, Vauxhall Gardens were London's largest open secret: a meeting place for adulterers and lovers. So boisterous were these lovers in dark groves that Vauxhall's owners received public complaints about "loose women and their male companions, whose yells have been described as issuing from the dark walks in sounds as terrific as 'the imagined horror of Cavalcanti's bloodhounds.'" Perhaps this was what Mirza Salih was alluding to in his reference to lone female visitors, though he glossed over the troupes of prostitutes for which the gardens were infamous.

By their last months in England, our six young men were surely aware of this nocturnal dimension to London park life. Ambassador Abu'l-Hasan certainly noticed the vast numbers of prostitutes on London streets and wrote of them in his diary. But Mirza Salih was deliberately more tactful in painting his more pleasing picture of park life, cultivating an image of public propriety that would reassure his readers in Iran of the morality of their Christian allies. What is striking is the vivid contrast between his positive portrayal of English civility and the gross image of Western depravity penned by such later Muslim travelers as the Islamist Sayyid Qutb who went to America as a student in the 1950s. Both xenophilia and xenophobia have their political purposes.

And so too did parks have their political, or at least diplomatic, purposes. For in May 1819, newspapers all across England reported that Ambassador Abu'l-Hasan "accompanied by Sir G. Ouseley and his secretary, mounted upon three white Persian horses and took a ride through Hyde Park." Though the decadent prince regent was associated with the louche entertainments of Vauxhall Gardens, it was Hyde Park that he chose as the more dignified space for the ambassador's reception. There the Muslim dignitary could be publically shown to his greatest advantage, as he "rode a beautiful grey horse, with a Persian bridle and saddle, and was dressed in his national costume in rich crimson satin and had a highly finished dirk with a large diamond in the centre of the hilt." With the students' firmest friend Sir Gore Ouseley playing host, the park had become a place for performing the friendship between England and Iran.

As public spaces for pleasure or diplomacy, Mirza Salih understood gardens to lie at the heart of English civility. Not every Iranian visitor was so high-minded, though, as James Fraser learned a decade later when he guided the two Iranian princes through Regent's Park. Archly, Fraser noted that the princes "made some shrewd remarks on several of the full-length statues, particularly on some antique ones of females in the nude state." Juvenile as they now seem, such "shrewd remarks" were an honest response to the parks' association with sex that Mirza Salih downplayed. For his depiction of London's parks was as places for more dignified friendships than rolling in clover with courtesans.

Whether because he was prude or shrewd, throughout his diary Mirza Salih cast a veil over the subject of romantic friendships with females, a silence that is tantalizing to say the least. Weakening the case for his prudity, a newspaper reporter wrote that Mirza Salih "has much humour, and is social and easy, particularly with the ladies." So we must question the reticence of his diary and see if, when confronted with other evidence, Mirza Salih will finally break his vow of discretion over the matter of women—and love.

Women and Love

Despite his enthusiastic discussion of London's gardens, except for describing Covent Garden's opera house and theaters Mirza Salih brushed over with little detail the evenings he and his companions spent in that most notorious of all English "gardens." For as we have seen earlier, while by day it served as the city's main fruit and vegetable mart, by night Covent Garden became its most famous haunt of prostitutes. It was the bordellos' proximity to the respectable theaters and opera houses, as well as the aristocratic houses along the Strand and on Leicester Square where the students originally lodged with Mr. D'Arcy, that made Covent Garden so successful a resort for the sex trade. We can be sure that the students knew about this side to London life: Muhammad ʿAli's lodgings on King Street looked out onto the central piazza of Covent Garden; it was the location of the theaters Mirza Salih described in detail and a two-minute walk from the Lyceum Theatre of his best friend, Sam Beazley. Ambassador Abu'l-Hasan also described visiting Covent Garden in the company of Sir Gore Ouseley. Since Abu'l-Hasan wrote openly (if disapprovingly) about the city's sex workers, it is unclear why Mirza Salih never mentioned Regency London's vast population of prostitutes. It came partly perhaps from his desire to portray the English positively. As an unmarried youth, or *bacha*, he may also have been considered too young to write about such things. Moreover, his patron ʿAbbas Mirza may have taken umbrage had he learned of his protégé's costly expertise in English strumpets.

Whatever the reasons for Mirza Salih's reticence, almost the only young women who featured in his diary were the talkative country girls between whom he was squeezed on his coach journey through Devonshire and the young female Methodists with whom he and Mirza Jaʿfar spent a happy evening in Gloucester. Abu'l-Hasan felt no such compunctions and wrote freely on the topic of women, whether prostitutes or otherwise. With as good an eye for detail as Mirza Salih, the ambassador described London's prostitutes with precision, estimating their number to stand at thirty thousand. Even so, the context of his discussions was often moralizing: one of his diary entries has him shaving his servant's head in punishment for a night spent in a London brothel. Humiliating as the punishment was, it doesn't seem to have been an effective deterrent. For less than three weeks later, Abu'l-Hasan was infuriated to learn that another of his servants, Muhammad 'Ali Beg, cuddled up with a prostitute after a pub crawl through four different taverns. Noting how many of these prostitutes were finely dressed and kept their own carriages, servants, and households, elsewhere Abu'l-Hasan recounted how wealthy Englishmen took the prettier prostitutes on as salaried mistresses. He also recorded the price range for different classes of prostitute and the fact that there was a house of correction called Magdalen House where former prostitutes were sent to mend their ways.

The place Abu'l-Hasan was discussing was one of the many charitable "Magdalene hospitals" that existed in London and other cities. Despite his usual reticence, Mirza Salih did describe a Magdalene Hospital and a prostitutes' reform house. Yet all this was acknowledgement in the abstract. And even if Abu'l-Hasan pointed to the existence of prostitutes, he did so in an indirect way that reflected badly on neither himself nor his English friends. As for Mirza Salih, the Magdalene Hospital's existence was a sign of the charity and so, paradoxically, of the morality of the English. Hypocritical as their discretion may have been, both Muslim and Christian elites shared a gentlemen's code.

When it came to the more respectable women of England, Abu'l-Hasan's diary again contained more observations than Mirza Salih's. Nor was the ambassador above recording the masculine banter he shared with that illustrious philanderer, the prince regent. With its worldly anecdotes, observations, and occasional dash of ribaldry, Abu'l-Hasan's diary was often (though not always) complimentary about the women of England. And as we saw in an earlier chapter, London hostesses in return "looked [at him] with their hearts in their eyes," though he was displeased when one of them dared to stroke his beard in public. Yet if Englishwomen showed such interest in these high-class Muslim visitors, then the question still remains of how much interest they took in Englishwomen apart from Abu'l-Hasan's mysterious "Miss Pul" (probably Emily Wellesley-Pole, niece of the foreign secretary). We find more evidence when we turn to the Indian Muslim traveler Abu Talib Khan, who came to London a decade before the students. Abu Talib claimed in his diary that he was the perpetual target of female affections which, in the case of Miss Julia Burrell at least, he reciprocated by penning odes to her in Persian. Judging by the scale of his efforts, his affection seems to have been sincere. For he wrote separate poems in celebration of her beautiful appearance (*husn-i a'za*); her lips (*lab*); her moles (*khal*); her neck and breasts (*gardan u sina*); her bearing and manner (*qad u raftar*); her hat (*kulah*); her veil (*niqab*); her dress (*jama*); her jewels (*zivarha*); her tiara (*tara*); her bracelet (*dastband*); her artlessness (*subuki*); her morals (*akhlaq*); and her many other admiring lovers (*'ushaq*). We might manage a digestible sample of these rich eulogies:

> *Safa'i-yi gardan-ish hangam-i nushin*
> *Namayad mai chu az jam-i bullurin*

> So limpid her skin that when she sips wine
> Its color is seen through her throat crystalline.

Yet more inventively, Abu Talib declaimed:

> *Chu 'umr-i khizr gawn-ish dar darazi*
> *Ba-'aql-i falisufan dar babazi.*

> Her "gown" is as long as the life of Methuselah:
> For philosophers' wits, it's a real bamboozler.

The final poem in his Miss Burrell cycle was a *munazara*, or "internal debate," in which his heart and mind fought for control over his actions. In this Persian lover's complaint written in London at the height of the Romantic movement, the bearded Abu Talib wrestled similarly grandiose emotions as Shelley and Byron:

> *Junun guyad ke didar-ish garan nist*
> *Taqavvud-i din u hasti-yi kharad chist?*

> Insanity says I can handle the sight of her:
> As for creed and for caution, they tell me, "Why bother?'

These were by no means the only Persian poems written in praise of an Englishwoman in the years either side of the students' time in London. The sweet talk of another Indian Muslim also survives, namely Muhammad Isma'il Khan, an emissary of the Nawwab of Awadh who

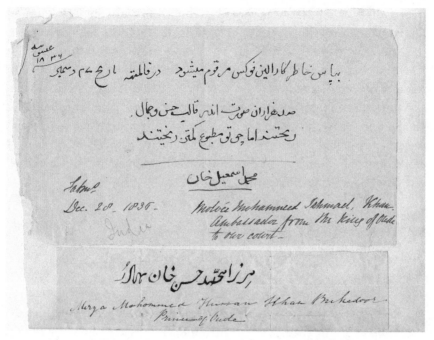

Fig. 29. Persian Flirtations: Muhammad Isma'il's Poem from Caroline Fox's Autograph Album.   Source: Collection of the author.

quickly won the reputation of a charmer. No sooner had he disembarked at Falmouth than he met the young society diarist, Miss Caroline Fox. The most vivacious of the bluestockings, Miss Fox entertained the most interesting men of the time, including such celebrated poets as Coleridge and Wordsworth. In a period usually seen as the Romantic era of a narrowly English literature, Muhammad Isma'il was another of the poets who visited her.

In her diary, Miss Fox described her meeting with Muhammad Isma'il and his wife, Mariam Begum:

> On showing him the Begum's writing in my book, he was much pleased at her having inserted his name as an introduction to her own. "Ha! She no me forget, I very glad to see that." He added some writing of his own in Persian, the sense of which was, "When I was young I used to hunt tigers and lions, but my intercourse with the ladies of England has driven all that out of my head."

Her diary is not the only record of their flirtation. She also kept an autograph album filled with messages from the most famous men of the era— this was the "book" she mentioned in the quotation. Though it was broken up a century ago, a single-leaf page that was torn from the album somehow survived as a scrap of paper unearthed in a London antique shop during the research for this book. On it, Muhammad Isma'il had signed his autograph and, following custom, left a personal message. In a few lines of Persian that have till now never been read since he wrote them, beneath his name Muhammad Isma'il inscribed a couplet of his own composition:

> *Sad hazaran surat andar qalib husn u jamal rikhtand*
> *Amma chun tu matbu'a kamtar rikhtand*

A hundred thousand fine faces were cast from the dye:
But like yours they printed few.

Whether this is the verse Miss Fox described in her diary is unclear: since she couldn't read Persian, she could easily have misunderstood its meaning or had someone make a garbled translation. In any case, the verse that Muhammad Isma'il dedicated to Miss Fox is the vestige of a forgotten history of flirtation between Persian-speaking Muslims and Jane Austen's misses.

For all its playfulness, Muhammad Isma'il's verse echoed the industrializing age in which the students were participants. For in drawing its guiding metaphor from Persian's new vocabulary of printing— *matbu'a, qalib*—it lends insight into the kinds of verse that, had he been so inclined, Mirza Salih might have composed as he spent those last summer months learning to print in Richard Watts's workshop.

Although the brief encounter between Miss Fox and Muhammad Isma'il was far from a full-blown love affair, with their much longer sojourn in London the students had time for more serious affections. Newspaper reports and diaries of those who met them portray the *mirzas* taking great pleasure in the way women were attracted to them. We have just seen Mirza Salih described as "social and easy, particularly with ladies." And after seeing him and Mirza Ja'far at a dinner party, the society hostess Hester Piozzi declared that they "flirt with the girls famously," pointedly adding that after meeting them, "ladies leave cards." Such was their inveterate flirting over the dinner table that Mrs. Piozzi admonished them with another impromptu poem:

> The glowing dames of Persia's royal court
> Have faces flushed with more exalted charms . . .
> Arriv'd 'mong these, the prince will soon forget
> Our pale unripen'd beauties of the North.

Former verbal sparring partner of Dr. Johnson as she was, Mrs. Piozzi had a mind well-stocked with clever put-downs. In fact, she was quoting lines from Joseph Addison's *Cato; A Tragedy*, a play from 1712, albeit wittily inserting "Persia" into Addison's line "The glowing dames of Zama's royal court." It was probably not the first or last verse that an Englishwoman recited to the dashing *mirzas*; other verses seem to have been more romantic. For even Mirza Salih, usually so reticent about such matters in his diary, was forced to admit that Englishwomen found him fascinating. Like his friends, he was invited to the houses of more than one society hostess and knew the genteel cover that rendered such flirtatious visitations respectable. Describing such occasions, when men called on women around four in the afternoon and were served cheese and wine, he noted coyly, "and they call this 'tiffin.'"

Only once in his diary had Mirza Salih come close to confessing anything approaching an actual love affair, albeit a chastely Austenesque kind of courtship. It had been during his tour of Devonshire with his architect friend Mr. Abraham and, more importantly, his sister, Sarah. He already knew Miss Abraham from London and enjoyed sitting next to her during their long journeys through the wild and remote country of Devonshire. Laced with the laconic humor that often sneaked into his diary entries, the romantic episode took place during the festivities for King George's birthday in Plymouth. Since it was a special occasion, Mirza Salih donned his finest Persian outfit and, dressing as dandily as he could, took Miss Abraham's hand as they walked into town. What neither of them had reckoned with was the effect that the sight of so exotic a foreigner holding hands with a young English lady would have on the provincial good people of Plymouth. And so there was an uproar as they walked into the celebrating crowds, and the couple (if such we can call them) were forced to retreat to the Abrahams' home. There Mirza Salih changed back into his English clothes and out they walked again, hand-in-hand; devoid of his fancy dress, he wrote, no one batted an eyelid. Aptly enough, it was also on vacation in Devonshire—that rustic county so far from the protocols of the capital—that Jane Austen once fell in love with a charming young clergyman (he died shortly afterward). As for Mirza Salih, he allowed the episode into his diary as a way of telling something else—the attitudes to foreigners of the provincial English, the prejudice the students surely sometimes faced—but the suggestion of something more is writ through the anecdote, hinting at an infatuation or an affair. But Mirza Salih was too careful, too downright diplomatic, to divulge anything more.

One love affair that we know a little more about concerned Mirza Ja'far, who by the summer of 1819 was completing his engineering studies at the Royal Military Academy. Despite the moral zeal we have seen Dr. Gregory distilling into his geometry lessons, Mirza Ja'far found himself helplessly attracted to an Englishwoman. Her name, alas, has not been recorded (again, the gentleman's code). What we know of the affair survives only in the mannered prose of a letter that Mirza Ja'far wrote to the anonymous "Madam" on June 14, 1819, weeks before the students' final departure. In the long letter, Mirza Ja'far voiced his "deep regret" at "leaving this happy land" and his determination to rein in his feelings and "not repine at this unavoidable separation." Echoing in reverse the autograph album in which the Indian Muhammad Isma'il wrote his message to Caroline Fox, Mirza Ja'far mentioned that he too had an album in which various "ladies . . . have so kindly offered me such proofs of their elegant acquirements and increased the value of it so greatly." So he had taken to keeping one of the fashionable albums in which lovers, friends, and acquaintances inscribed private messages. Yet Mirza Ja'far's discretion did not prevent him from turning poetical, and in his letter to the unnamed lady he dedicated to her these lines of prose poetry:

> May no clouds arise to obscure your happiness! May wisdom and virtue more and more illumine your path, as long as the shadows of night shall be dispelled by the appearance of the morn, and the dust of with-

eredness shall be washed by gentle showers from the rosy cheeks of tulips!

We know nothing more about this romance, nor about Mirza Jaʿfar's relationships with the other women who wrote "proofs of their elegant acquirements" in his autograph book. Even so, the letter is a tantalizing hint of the friendships and even romances that, more than the pursuit of algebra, filled the students' last summer in London.

Yet Mirza Jaʿfar's was far from the students' only liaison that season. For according to Mirza Salih's diary, during their last months in London their fellow student, Muhammad ʿAli, fell in love with an English girl and then dramatically married her! Since Mirza Salih said the marriage took place "in the English manner" and in a church, we may assume that, like many a sacrifice of faith in favor of love, it involved as a precondition Muhammad ʿAli's conversion to Christianity. At last, it seems, the evangelicals had found a convert among the six Muslim students. But such as it was, Muhammad ʿAli's acceptance of Christ was prompted by love for his bride and not by polemics from the likes of Dr. Macbride. Perhaps Muhammad ʿAli had learned to see Christianity and Islam as two muddied versions of a universal higher truth, to see the two faiths through the Deist lenses of the radical artisans he met through his apprenticeship to Alex Galloway that year. Whatever the details of the matter, it is clear that their radical notions of friendship had rubbed off on him: none of the other students dared do anything so bold. And true to the proletarian universalism of his radical workmates, Muhammad ʿAli's bride, Mary Dudley, was not a society hostess but a market girl. She was the sister of his metalworking landlord at King Street, Covent Garden.

Whether by nature or nurture, Mirza Salih was more cautious than the former blacksmith and recorded how he and the other four students tried to dissuade Muhammad ʿAli from marrying the English girl. As we have seen, by this time Mirza Salih was envisaging a future for himself as a diplomat, as a replacement perhaps for Ambassador Abuʾl-Hasan, whose return to London had now heralded the end of his education. So it is unlikely that he would ever have compromised his appearance of diplomatic neutrality by a hasty marriage. But despite being warned about the repercussions by his companions, Muhammad

'Ali had gone ahead with the marriage nonetheless. Here, as the adventures of England's first Muslim students reached their end, was the beginning of a love story.

While Mirza Salih only committed to his diary the most indirect testament to his romantic dealings with Englishwomen, Muhammad 'Ali was unafraid to pledge an oath of his love in public. He even signed a marriage register to prove it. The handwritten registry book entry for his marriage to Mary Dudley at St. James's Church, Westminster, survives to this day. Their names are entered beneath those for a wedding earlier the same day between the more likely English partnership of Charles Jewett and Mary Taylor. It was May 27, 1819. That the marriage took place against the wishes of the other students and without the knowledge of Mr. D'Arcy is clear from the marriage certificate. For it lists as the two witnesses a Mr. W. A. Portal and a Miss Mary Birkinshaw, presumably friends of the bride (perhaps also the groom) from their working-class circle. Setting aside the concerns that surrounded the wedding, let us imagine it as a happy occasion. Surrounded by the graceful proportions of a church designed by Sir Christopher Wren, they walked down the aisle after the bride entered with her friend Mary Birkinshaw (for her father was dead). Then there they stood at the altar at St. James's, the foreign former blacksmith and the metal worker's sister, facing the delicately wrought-iron railings and gorgeous woodwork of the master craftsman Grinling Gibbons. It is an apt and happy picture.

Yet more mundane matters soon surrounded the newlyweds. Given the fact that the marriage took place at the end of May, just two months before the students' impending departure, it caused alarm among their English friends no less than the other students. While the relationship between Muhammad and Mary had clearly been going on for some time, its public announcement caught everyone by surprise. Not least surprised was Mr. D'Arcy, to whom Muhammad 'Ali sent only an *ex post facto* note telling him what was already done. The note also bore a bold request.

> Dear Sir,
>
> My having married an Englishwoman, I shall deem it as a great favour if you will so far interest yourself for me as to procure permission

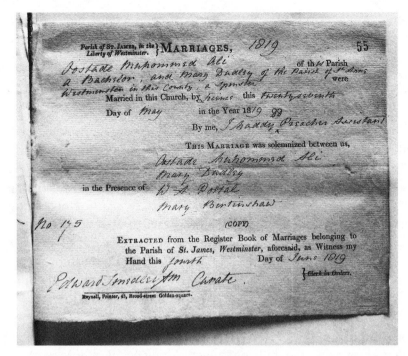

Fig. 30. The *Ustad*'s Sweetheart: Marriage Certificate of Muhammad ʿAli and Mary Dudley. Source: Courtesy The National Archives. F.O. 60/15 (55)

from the Foreign Office for my wife to accompany me out to Persia, and to have the passage in the Cabin of the Ship arranged for her on the same plan as it is done for myself. I must again return you my thanks for the trouble I have given and subscribe myself yours Gratefully,

Muhommed Ali.

In this sole remaining record of the Muslim artisan's own words, we detect a different personality from the socially elevated *mirzas* who made up the rest of the student party. Born of his much humbler background, the tone of Muhammad ʿAli's supplication to Mr. D'Arcy was strikingly different from how the latter was addressed in Mirza Salih's diary and the ruder letters written by the other students. Unlike his compatriots, who by the summer of 1819 had made friends with influential Englishmen in the military, diplomacy, and politics, Muhammad ʿAli had spent the previous years learning from artisans and living in the household of his new brother-in-law, the "ornament man" Thomas Dudley. Unlike the other students, he had no friends in high places to call on. And so, out of love, he had to beg a "great favour" of Mr. D'Arcy.

It was in fact two favors that were needed by Muhammad 'Ali and Mrs. Mary Ali, as she now proudly called herself. First, the newlyweds required permission for Mary to leave the country; second, they needed funds for the feminine decency of a private cabin passage all the way to Iran. In response, Mr. D'Arcy passed the message up the chain and wrote to Mr. Planta, his contact at the Foreign Office; in June 1819, Mary Ali's family took the more desperate measure of writing directly to the foreign minister, Lord Castlereagh. It must have taken considerable courage for a family of artisans to write a collective letter to one of the most powerful aristocrats in England. Fortunately, it would not be for another two months that Shelley would write ominously of Castlereagh that "seven blood-hounds followed him. . . . He tossed them human hearts to chew."

Describing the Peterloo Massacre that took place later that summer, Shelley was writing about the plight of working people whose requests were brutally put down by the "smooth . . . yet grim" Castlereagh. But in his letter to Castlereagh, Thomas Dudley was not demanding rights for an entire class, merely a favor for a few of its members. He was writing on behalf of his sister Mary and her relatives, who all put their signatures to the letter. Unlike the bold old Etonian Percy Shelley, Tom Dudley declared himself "reluctantly compelled to obtrude myself on your Lordship's notice." With its dropped Cockney aitches, its menial obeisance, its proletarian piety that echoed the Book of Common Prayer, Tom Dudley's letter deserves quoting:

> Painful as it is to the whole family to reflect on the step she as taken, which may probably be the cause of separating us for ever, yet as she is of mature age and the marriage has been solemnized according to the rites and ceremonies of the Church of England, and she is willing to becometh a wife, to share with her husband in his future prospects, whether good or ill: Her family feel themselves bound to acquiesce to her wishes on the principle laid down in Holy Writ that they whom God hath joined, let no man put asunder . . .

I beg leave in the name of his wife and her surviving relatives to solicit the honour of Your Lordship's permission for her to accompany him and that your Lordship should so far condescend as to give such directions as would secure to her suitable accommodation in the same ship with her husband; as I am sorry to say she as not the means of procuring it on her own account, even should she receive your Lordship's sanction to accompany him.

When all was said and done, it was a begging letter. What else could a family of iron workers do? But even at a distance of two centuries, it is moving in its dignity. Undersigned at the end of the letter, "in testimony of our concurrence in this application," were the names "Mary Ali, late Dudley; Thos Dudley, her brother; Isaac Dudley, her brother; Sarah Willingdale, her only sister." We can only imagine the circumstances in which it was written, on the kitchen table at 36 King Street, Covent Garden, surrounded by the hammering and sawing of the smiths and carpenters who worked in the surrounding houses. There was surely great anxiety in the air; perhaps a draft or two was drawn up in preparation of the final version; maybe Mary interrupted her brother now and then to correct a form of address or rephrase a request. Since no record of Mary's own words survives, it is perhaps not too fanciful to think that we can hear her voice behind her brother's written words, directing a plea to a lord of the realm that, as a craftsman's orphaned sister, she was not allowed to write for herself? Perhaps in any case she didn't know how to write: the Sunday Schools that Mirza Ja'far had urged his Unitarian friends to found in Bristol had not yet reached many of London's working women.

Whoever's words the letter ultimately contained, it was dispatched on June 20th to Lord Castlereagh. There is no record of any reply.

Departures

With the exception of the medical student Mirza Ja'far, who stayed behind to complete his course with Dr. Babington, the students left London on July 23, 1819. Mirza Salih recorded the scene for us in his diary. "In truth, as I said farewell to each of my friends, everyone expressed their heartfelt sorrow at being separated from me when I departed. From the bottom of my heart, I too prayed for them and wished them well. And I will always do so in future." For all of the students, taking leave of their friends was heart-rending. In return, there were many prayers said for their safety, the prayers of Christian friends that as foreign Muslims they were happy to accept.

During their last days in London, many of their friends came to bid them farewell, even venturing down to the unnamed inn beside the Thames at East India Dock from where the students set sail for Gravesend. There was Mr. Dennis, the surgeon's son with whom Mirza Salih had spent many an entertaining evening. There was his printing master Mr. Watts, who had brought his family along too. There was Mr. Garrett, his erstwhile teacher of French, Latin, and the natural sciences, along with his son Lieutenant Edward. There were his two recent Indian friends, Muhyi al-Din and Mir Afzal 'Ali. There were surely also friends of the other students there that day whom Mirza Salih did not think to mention. And there was Mr. D'Arcy, who despite all the harsh words and disappointments of the previous years had brought along his wife and daughters to say goodbye. Departing together with Mirza Salih were Mirza Riza, Hajji Baba, the other Mirza Ja'far, and Muhammad 'Ali. And, yes, there was Muhammad 'Ali's English wife, now Mrs. Mary Ali, for whom permission had been granted and funds somehow found to sail away with her husband. Despite all the opposition, the young couple were aboard ship when the students set sail for Gravesend, Constantinople and from there to Mary's new home in Iran. Mirza Salih was far from the only member of his party who harbored a love of strangers.

Nor was Muhammad 'Ali's bride the only English prize that the students were carrying home. On his return to London a few months earlier, Ambassador Abu'l-Hasan had authorized the students to spend up to five hundred pounds on the equipment they would need to practice their new skills in Iran; the Foreign Office had again overseen the expenditure. Keen to take credit for the arrangement, Mr. D'Arcy had written a letter to the foreign secretary declaring that he had "furnished them with a selection of such books, instruments and implements of trade as appeared to me most necessary to enable them to pursue their different studies and mechanical labours hereafter with advantage." Along with the medical equipment that we earlier saw Hajji Baba and Mirza Riza ordering, there was also Mirza Salih's apparatus of modernity. It comprised a telescope (provided by the astronomer Sir John Herschel) and a printing press with Arabic type (purchased on his behalf by his printing master, Mr. Watts). Mirza Salih remarked that this was a "small printing press," likely an iron handpress of the kind invented twenty years earlier by Lord Stanhope, since when hundreds had been made. If so, it was a good choice, for at the time these cheap and portable machines were for the first time bringing printing to many other countries around the world. When Mirza Salih left Iran four years earlier, no Persian book had ever been printed there: he had high hopes of becoming Iran's Gutenberg.

With such prospects, he and his companions had reason to be pleased with themselves. They had mastered arts and sciences known to none of their countrymen. As Mirza Salih reckoned it, the length of their studies came to a total of three years, nine months, and twenty days. It was about the same length of time as an undergraduate degree today. With their financial concerns, their search for supportive teachers, and their festive nights in an unfamiliar city, their adventures form a recognizable student experience even two centuries later. Like many a student after them, in those busy few years they had transformed and reinvented themselves. Back when it all began in September 1815, apart from what Mirza Salih had learned from his earlier contacts with the giant soldier Henry Lindsay-Bethune and the diplomat Ouseley brothers, the students had arrived in Great Yarmouth with only as much English as they had learned aboard ship from Mr. D'Arcy. By the time they sailed from Gravesend in July 1819, as testified in the surviving letters from their final year, they had an enviable command of the elegant idioms of the age. Apart from Muhammad ʿAli, they had also learned Latin and French. And not only had they mastered England's language and customs, they had also learned its new sciences. This was especially true of the lowly Muhammad ʿAli, who had seen steam engines being manufactured before his own eyes.

Having studied the history of English political and scientific institutions, as Mirza Salih sat in his berth on the brig *Starling,* he could reassure himself that he had discovered the mechanisms behind England's prosperity. For in his diary, he concluded that the answer lay in its being a *vilayat-i azadi*, a "country of freedom." And before boarding ship, he had mastered what was perhaps the most liberating skill of the age. After all, no less a revolutionary than his fellow Freemason Benjamin Franklin had learned printing as a foreign apprentice in Covent Garden. Though Mirza Salih had written of Franklin's London visits in his diary, he didn't know that the great libertarian was also apprenticed to a Mr. Watts, albeit a John rather than a Richard.

Having reached London as a boatload of bewildered youths, Mirza Salih and his companions were returning home transformed: between them they were scholars and engineers, scientists and Freemasons, doctors and a would-be diplomatist. Then as now, none of this came for free. When the students sailed away that midsummer night, for the education of his protégées the crown prince 'Abbas Mirza was left owing the British government a total of £4,252, 12 shillings, and 2 pence—today around £325,000, or $520,000.

But the value of an education can never be boiled down to pounds and pence. Their education had been a journey through knowledge and faith into friendship. From the lifelong pledge of Muhammad 'Ali's wedding vows to Mirza Salih's evenings of camaraderie around Covent Garden, their friendships had taken many forms. Encompassing Unitarians and evangelicals, Freemasons and radicals, diplomats and tradesmen, the students' friends comprised a varied circle. Although in their movements through the neoclassical hallways of Regency London, Bath, and Cambridge we have often made comparisons with the refined society of Jane Austen, the comparison is ultimately a limited one. For the students explored a far more diverse England than the one encompassed in Miss Austen's novels. And so if Mirza Salih's diary is infinitely less famous than *Pride and Prejudice*, then it is no less important a record of the age, revealing a more complex society, evangelical and imperial, behind the decorous civility of Pemberley. Yet for all that the story told by Mirza Salih was one of a struggle for education, it was not a tale of confrontation with Christians or of resistance to empire. It was a story of his affinity and admiration for a foreign people and his tenacious (and at times thwarted) attempts to share in their intellectual, religious and social lives. And as a counterpoint to *Pride and Prejudice*, it is not Mr. D'Arcy but Mirza Salih who is its hero. In the stories of Jane Austen, the purpose of a hero is to reveal the development of humane and reasoned virtue. In the case of our hero, that virtue was xenophilia, the love of strangers.

It was not only Mirza Salih who was grateful to his English friends. Aboard the *Starling* at Gravesend on the verge of their final departure, Hajji Baba dashed off a brief letter to Mr. Planta at the Foreign Office to thank "the English Government for the very liberal manner in which my education has been conducted." Like the other students, he had come to see personal friendships as the root of the friendship of nations. In that last communication with the English, he voiced his hope that "the government and the people of this highly favoured land enjoy that degree of prosperity and eminence with which it is at present blessed." Then, just as it seemed that all's well that ends well, as though in a Shakespearean comedy there lurked from the background a scowling malcontent, a Mr. D'Arcy to the bard's Malvolio. Having seen the students aboard the *Starling*, he wrote in relief to Lord Castlereagh to officially resign his responsibilities. "I will be honoured with a general discharge," he wrote; for his years with the students had "been a most arduous duty, attended with unusual anxiety and rendered extremely irksome from the restless and intractable disposition of some of these foreigners." With this bitter Parthian shot, Mr. D'Arcy crept off into obscurity.

As for the students, it was the end of a most unusual education. The last words must go to Mirza Salih: "It was four o'clock in the afternoon. In the harbour at Gravesend, the sails of our ship filled with wind and we departed, sailing straight down the middle of the Thames." They were going home.

Afterlives

When the students reached Tabriz toward the end of 1819 after a long journey via the Ottoman Empire, the Middle East was just beginning its long and fraught path to modern development. In asking what the students achieved after they returned to Iran, it would be naïve to expect that six young men could transform an entire society. The purpose of following their educations has not been to claim that they turned the world on its head. Instead, it has been to show that these young Muslims were part of the social, cultural, and intellectual life of Jane Austen's England—to show that Muslims shared the sophisticated dinners, the scientific discoveries, and the reasoned discussions that are too often seen as the narrow preserve of Europeans' past. Even so, the students did have an impact on their own society. In significant ways, they influenced diplomacy, education, medicine, science, engineering, industry, cartography, and warfare. They also helped spread a spectrum of cultural influences from cutlery to uniforms. Perhaps most significantly of all, Mirza Salih was instrumental in bringing printing to Iran, in promoting that most crucial of all technologies for public knowledge and debate.

We have seen how in his last six months in London Mirza Salih acquired mechanical skills that were unique among his countrymen and how, in the weeks before he sailed home, he arranged with Mr. Watts to export a small printing press. As far as Mirza Salih was aware, he was about to become Iran's first Muslim printer, a Persian Gutenberg. But by the time he reached Tabriz, during his absence ʿAbbas Mirza had managed to import a press from Russia. Operating under the supervision of another secretarial *mirza*, Zayn al-ʿAbidin, it had been brought from Saint Petersburg, which Zayn al-ʿAbidin had visited through briefly improved relations with Russia. It was from this press that Iran's first Persian book was printed in 1817; it was two years before Mirza Salih came home. Nonetheless, the press from Richard Watts that Mirza Salih carried back to Tabriz did print at least one book. Its choice is a telling one. When seeking solace in London, Mirza Salih had often turned to the verses of Saʿdi, the wise old Sufi of Shiraz, and when he came home it was his *Gulistan* (or "Rose Garden") that he printed. His choice also hints at the reciprocity we have seen so often in his education, for the *Gulistan* was the standard book with which Iranians and Englishmen alike learned to read Persian. Perhaps he even sent a copy to his friends, the Ouseley brothers. In physical terms, Mirza Salih's *Gulistan* was a small book, its verses squeezed onto petite pages that resulted from the shortage of suitable paper and the narrow platen of the portable press he had carried from London. But it was at least printed with delicate Persian type. Today only one copy is known to survive, having made its way via Saint Petersburg and Paris to the Bavarian State Library in Munich.

In a reflection of the intellectual exchanges we have seen the students involved with, another of the earliest books to be printed in Iran was the *Risala-yi Taʿlim dar ʿAmal-i Abila Zadan* ("Treatise on Smallpox Vaccination"). Though not written by any of the students, it emerged from the same connections that had carried them to London, for it was written by ʿAbbas Mirza's personal physician, the former East India Company employee, John Cormick (d. 1833). The small steps that were made by these first printed books were enough to gain Tabriz the nickname of Basma-Khana, "The House of Printing." From ʿAbbas Mirza's capital there spread to the rest of Iran what Thomas Carlyle later called one of "the three great elements of modern civilization."

Though Zayn al-ʿAbidin had beaten Mirza Salih to be Iran's first printer, just three years after departing for home from Gravesend, Mirza Salih achieved his larger ambition of becoming a diplomat. In 1822, he was sent back to London as special emissary on an important mission. It must have been a gratifying few months, as the former student who just five years earlier had been forced by a lack of funds to retreat from the capital to Croydon now took up residence at 25 Great Coram Street, Russell Square. It was one of the grand new mansions recently developed by Lord Francis Russell, the 5th Duke of Bedford. His brief for this mission was to buy weapons to protect Iran from Russia, which was threatening to invade again, and to broach the delicate matter of replacing Captain Henry Willock, the obstreperous *chargé d'affaires* in Tehran. Given the fact that Captain Willock accompanied him from Iran on an assignment secretly intended to undermine him, Mirza Salih must have called on his mastery of English civility to disguise his true purpose. In the event, he argued successfully for Captain Willock's replacement. For his other task of defending Iran, he tried to enlist the help of his old friend, Sir John Malcolm, but it was to no avail. Britain was now better friends with Russia.

Various documents survive from this mission, including letters in which Mirza Salih described his chief goal as "the friendship of the two countries." But the most interesting document is a letter he was entrusted to deliver from prince ʿAbbas Mirza to the prime minister, Lord Liverpool. The Persian original is preserved in the Bodleian Library at Oxford. It was written on heavy and durable cloth paper, made with traditional craft techniques rather than the mechanized papermaking Mirza Salih that had inspected near Oxford five years earlier. Its key theme—and indeed term—was that of the "friendship," the *dusti*, between ʿAbbas Mirza and Lord Liverpool and "the maintenance of the friendship existing between the two powers." If his entry into international politics required him to smile as he stabbed Captain Willock in the back, Mirza Salih remained an advocate of friendship. He was also a bearer of gifts that served as artistic symbols of amity, presenting the newly crowned George IV with a twin portrait mirror. It was like the one presented earlier by Ambassador Abu'l-Hasan, except this one hinged a portrait of ʿAbbas Mirza (not Fath ʿAli Shah) beside a mirror in which King George could see his own image with that of his distant friend, peeping over his shoulder from Tabriz. Amid the attempted gun-running triggered by the threat of a belligerent Russia, there was something sincere about this search for friendly shelter. And in a gesture of openness toward the artistic innovations the students witnessed in England, ʿAbbas Mirza had his portrait carved in alabaster rather than painted in traditional style. Sculpted in the neoclassical style of Canova, he appears like a more hirsute cousin of Jane Austen's Regency gentlemen. And there was also another gift. Though it had little intrinsic worth, it would prove to be of great historical value. It was a manuscript copy of Mirza Salih's diary that he presented to

Captain Willock's brother, George. Later bequeathed to the India Office Library, it would become the sole surviving record of his years in England. It was the diary on which this book has drawn.

But the most extraordinary element of Mirza Salih's mission was a message he carried from 'Abbas Mirza in which the prince tried to persuade people from England to come and settle in Iran. Published in several newspapers, in his letter 'Abbas Mirza promised that if English families moved to Iran he would "immediately assign to them portions of land, with residences attached, and every requisite for their comfort and subsistence." Moreover, such English settlers would "be exempt from all taxes or contributions of any kind; their property and persons be held sacred, under the immediate protection of the Prince himself . . . as is the custom of Persia, be at full liberty to enjoy their own religions opinions and feelings, and to follow, without control or interruption, their own mode of worship." It was an astonishing if perhaps fanciful offer of friendship to the English people who had aided his student protégés.

Statesmanship aside, the London mission of 1822–23 marked Mirza Salih's triumphant return to the city in which he had struggled to pay tuition and rent. After studying printing with Richard Watts, he must have been delighted to learn that the Persian language guide he had written years earlier for the Ouseley brothers had been published in a fine edition (it was later reissued several times). Lodged in one of London's finest new districts and holding official meetings with the highest officials of the foreign office, Mirza Salih had fulfilled the ambition of his student years. Since his mission was at least a partial success—a new *chargé d'affaires* was appointed to replace Captain Willock in Tehran— he wished to commemorate his triumph. Recalling his earlier visits to the art galleries of the Royal Academy, he decided to commission a sculpture of his own while he was still in London. The artist he selected was Robert William Sievier (1794–1865), a respected society sculptor for whom he sat in 1823 to have his likeness carved in marble. Sievier had studied at the Royal Academy Schools and by 1823 had a studio on Bloomsbury's Southampton Row, close to Mirza Salih's mansion on Great Coram Street. The same year that he carved his bust of Mirza Salih, Sievier also began work on a statue of a more famous pioneer of the new learning, the discoverer of smallpox vaccination, Edward Jenner. The statue still stands today in the cathedral at Gloucester that Mirza Salih himself had earlier visited. The personality revealed by Sievier's bust of the Iranian is already different from that of the younger, more uncertain youth of the diary. Now Mirza Salih was the chief emissary of the shah, a commanding figure in fine uniform, a dashing and dare we say Austenesque Muslim. It was what he had dreamed of during those drizzly early days in Camden Town.

Yet Mirza Salih never forgot his friends in England. From Bloomsbury in 1823, he wrote to his old Cambridge host, Professor Lee, who was then translating the Arabic and Persian polemics between the Cambridge missionary Henry Martyn and the Muslim clerics of Shiraz. Lee was troubled that he had no idea who wrote what he called the *Controversial Tracts* that James Morier had carried from Istanbul among Martyn's possessions after the latter's death in 1812. Hearing that Mirza Salih had returned to London, Lee wrote in Persian to his former house guest to request advice on the identity of Martyn's disputants. Ever keen to show off his talents, in the introduction to the *Controversial Tracts* Lee reprinted his own Persian letter, in which he referred to himself in the self-deprecating Persian idiom as Mirza Salih's *banda-yi kamtarin*, his "humblest of servants." The professor's former translator had certainly risen up in the world! Mirza Salih wrote him a helpful reply and later, on his second return home, corresponded with him on various matters and even sent him manuscripts. It seems reasonable to suppose that, in return, the professor dispatched English books to Mirza Salih. So it was that long after his student years ended, the knowledge, faith, and friendship of his English years stayed intertwined.

The London mission of 1822–23 would not be Mirza Salih's only diplomatic endeavor. During the following decade, he featured in many of Iran's most important international negotiations. As one later historian has described him, "he seems to have been a specialist in delicate missions . . . a master of tact." In 1827, with Russia again threatening to invade, he was dispatched to the frontier fortress at Abbasabad to negotiate an alternative to war. His frank report on the negotiations shows him drawing on the diplomatic skills he acquired in England, trying to manipulate the rituals of friendship by repeatedly dining and taking tea with General Ivan Paskievich, the MacArthur of imperial Russia. In spite of his skills, no solution could be reached. Within three months, the Russians invaded Iran and seized control of ʿAbbas Mirza's capital at Tabriz. Through the Treaty of Torkmanchai in 1828, Iran surrendered all of its Caucasian provinces that Russia still dominates today. No amount of diplomacy could constrain the Russians in their most expansionist phase.

Mirza Salih never lost the other interests he discovered in London. In 1829, he learned of a new printing technology called lithography, or *chap-i sangi*. As committed as ever to the printer's métier, he accompanied the embassy of Prince Khusraw Mirza to Saint Petersburg to oversee the acquisition of Iran's first lithographic presses. Having moved up in the world since his oil-spattered afternoons with Mr. Watts, he ordered his own understudy Mirza Asadullah to learn how to use the new press. It was a great step forward for learning. With lithography, Iran was not only able to print its cursive Persian script more easily. It could also for the first time print the maps and scientific diagrams that the other students had learned to draw in London. It was with the lithographic press that Mirza Salih imported from Saint Petersburg that in 1832 the Quran was printed in Iran for the first time. While this may seem out of character for the Freemasonic *mirza*, we should remember that his fellow cosmopolitan Freemason Sir Gore Ouseley similarly oversaw scripture printing as the vice president of the Bible Society. In an age when religion was seen as a natural part of life, Sir Gore and perhaps Mirza Salih like him believed that providing access to scripture promoted reasoned interpretation over illiterate superstition.

We also have another reason to be thankful for Mirza Salih's continued commitment to printing. For it was through his interest in lithography during that journey to Russia that he sat for the only surviving portrait of him: an engraving by the Russian artist Karl Karlovich Gampeln (1794–1880) that was then printed as a lithograph in Saint Petersburg. As he appeared in that portrait of 1829, Mirza Salih had the stern countenance of the statesman. In the title beneath his portrait he was described in Persian script as the *munshi-yi khas*, or "chief secretary," of prince ʿAbbas Mirza. In practice, this made him the closest advisor of the heir to Iran's throne. Using his knowledge of European society and history, he advised the prince on international policy and used the French he had learned in London to draft the

Fig. 31. From Student to Statesman: Lithographic Portrait
of Mirza Salih. Source: *Majmū'a-i Safarnāmahhā-yi Mīrzā Sālih
Shīrāzī*, ed. Ghulām Husayn Mīrzā Sālih (Tehran: Nashr-i Tārīkh-i Īrān,
1364/1985).

prince's diplomatic mail. In later years, he established links with the
Royal Asiatic Society of Great Britain: his old friends, including Sir
Gore Ouseley, were among its founding members. Apparently through
Mirza Salih, the Society's library acquired copies of two of the earliest
Persian books issued through the printing industry he had helped es-
tablish in Tabriz.

True to what he had learned in London, Mirza Salih would leave his
most lasting mark on Iranian history as a bringer of news. For in January 1837, almost twenty years after he had read the newspapers printed
around Mr. Watts's workshop on Fleet Street, he founded Iran's first-
ever newspaper. Called simply *Kaghaz-i Akhbar*, or "Newspaper," it
lasted for only one issue. As determined as he was in his youth, five
months later he founded another newspaper called *Akhbar-i Vaqa'a*,
or "Current News." It became Iran's first regular newspaper. Remembering his learned friends in London and their help so many years

earlier, he sent a sample copy of *Akhbar-i Vaqaʻa* to the Royal Asiatic Society. It consisted of just a few dense pages printed with the lithographic press he had brought back from Saint Petersburg. In 1839, "to show not only what matters are thought likely to engage the attention of the public in Persia, but also to give a specimen of the language and orthography in use among ordinarily educated persons," the *Journal of the Royal Asiatic Society* reprinted the April/May 1837 issue of *Akhbar-i Vaqaʻa* in both its original Persian and English translation. Among the snippets of foreign and domestic political news, Mirza Salih had included in his newspaper an account of a party at the British Embassy in Tehran in honor of King William IV's birthday. For Mirza Salih, it must have brought back memories of when he first learned the English custom of celebrating the King's birthday during his tour of Devonshire: it was the night when he and Miss Abraham joined the merry throngs of Plymouth for the birthday of George III. Given his English connections, and his residence by this time in Tehran, it seems likely that Mirza Salih was present that night at the embassy, for his report noted that "a numerous assemblage of the nobles, and chiefs, and principal servants of this [Iranian] state, were also invited." Since it was likely penned by Mirza Salih himself, the report of the party in the embassy gardens deserves quoting as a counterpart to his earlier account of London park life:

> The palace of the English embassy was splendidly illuminated. The garden of the palace is filled with beautifully-variegated roses and tulips, and enchanting trees. Thousands of crystal lamps, besides gold and silver candelabras, were suspended in the porticos, saloons, galleries, and walls, making the night vie with the day. The portrait of His Majesty the Shahanshah, painted on canvas, was placed in the highest position in the palace, encompassed by innumerable lights; while that of His Majesty the King of England, painted on another piece of canvass, was placed opposite, being also surrounded by lamps. There was so brilliant an exhibition of fireworks, that the spectators were dazzled, and the sun, had it been day, would have been obscured.

Here in this earliest of Iranian newspapers was a slice of English history celebrated in the Persian idioms of *gul u lala, fanus u qandil,* of roses and tulips, lamps and candelabras. In Tehran, Mirza Salih had found a little part of England that he could occasionally and fondly visit.

In the long run, his trust in the English was misplaced, and in his later career his reputation for being too close to the *Inglis* seems to have become a liability. The death of Prince ʿAbbas Mirza in 1833 dealt Mirza Salih another strong blow, for he was closely linked with his reforms. Although he managed to establish his second newspaper a few years later, it survived only five years, and in the illiberal following decade he gradually slipped from view. But he was still remembered in London. For among a list of corresponding members of the Royal Asiatic Society in 1841, his name appeared as "Mirza Salih, Editor of the Teheran Gazette." Along with him on the list were several of his old friends and teachers: Sir Gore and Sir William Ouseley, Professor John Shakespear, Professor Samuel Lee, and Mr.—by now Lieutenant-Colonel—Joseph D'Arcy. It is not clear when Mirza Salih died; perhaps in 1845. But through his central role in introducing the printing press and the newspaper to Iran, he had transformed his society. He had transferred to Iran the media of public opinion and education that he considered so crucial to England's development into a *vilayat-i azadi*, a "land of freedom."

Mirza Salih was not alone in bringing the "new sciences" to the Middle East. His London companions were also major conduits, and adapters, of English learning to Iran. While we know less about what happened to the other students, there is evidence enough to sketch something of their careers. Shortly after their return home in 1819, the medical student Hajji Baba became the assistant to Prince ʿAbbas Mirza's personal physician, the Irish doctor John Cormick, whose book on smallpox vaccination we have seen being printed shortly afterward. A decade later, when ʿAbbas Mirza's brother, Muhammad Shah, became king in 1834, Hajji Baba was raised to the position of *hakim-bashi*, or "physician-in-chief," to the king. Despite holding this position of high influence for the rest of his career, he was always annoyed by the fact that his former acquaintance James Morier used his name in his satirical novel, *The Adventures of Hajji Baba of Ispahan*. Clearly, not all of their friends could be trusted.

We do not know what happened to the other medical student, Mirza Jaʿfar, but he probably pursued a similar, if perhaps less distinguished, career to Hajji Baba. Turning to the other Mirza Ja'far—the frequent companion of Mirza Salih during their London days —after he returned home he worked first as a teacher of engineering and mathematics in Tabriz. But Mirza Ja'far's unique skills were clear to all around him and he soon rose up to become the country's *muhandis-bashi* or "engineer-in-chief." Through him, many other Iranians learned the engineering and cartographic techniques he had mastered at the Royal Military Academy. Over the following years, his knowledge of European ways saw him selected to negotiate trade treaties with Belgium and Spain. Then, in 1834, he was appointed ambassador to the Ottoman Empire in Istanbul; at the time, it was the highest ranking post in Iranian diplomacy. He served as ambassador in Istanbul for a decade. Drawing on the surveying skills he had learned in Woolwich, he was next appointed by his government to the international boundary commission set up to determine the Iranian-Ottoman border. It was a task of national importance in which he played a leading and expert role and on which he also wrote a memoir. Though Mirza Ja'far never had a mountain named after him like his fellow alumnus of the Royal Military Academy, Sir George Everest, he received many Persian titles that were at least the equal of an English knighthood.

Never forgetting what he had learned as a young man thirty years earlier, in 1847 Mirza Ja'far published a Persian manual on mathematics entitled *Khulasat al-Hisab* ("A Summary of Mathematics"). In it, he abridged the various books he had studied in London; he may have drawn in particular on the mathematical manual written by his tutor at the Royal Military Academy, Dr. Olinthus Gregory. Using his varied skills as both surveyor and diplomat, Mirza Ja'far also wrote a Persian book on world geography and another comparing Iran's style of government with those of Europe. After the coronation of Nasir al-Din Shah in 1848, Mirza Ja'far put his knowledge into practice by helping persuade the new ruler to set up the Majlis-i Shura-yi Dawlati, the "State Consultative Assembly." Through it, Iran made its first ever steps toward democratic government. Finally, at the end of a glorious career, in 1861 Mirza Ja'far returned to London. This time he was ambassador. He spent one more year of his life there, in quite different circumstances to those he knew as a young man in Croydon. He died in Tehran in 1879.

Mirza Ja'far's world history book was not the only such work to be written by the former students. For Mirza Riza, his old companion at the Royal Military Academy, used his knowledge of the English language to translate into Persian histories of Peter the Great and Napoleon. Since Prince 'Abbas Mirza greatly admired these modernizers, his influence may have been behind Mirza Riza's choice to translate these books. Like Mirza Ja'far again, Mirza Riza also drew on his training at the Royal Military Academy to rise up to the position of *muhandis-bashi*, in his case as engineer-in-chief to the Iranian army. Like Mirza Salih, Mirza Riza remembered his English friends with fondness and played host to any English people who passed through Iran. In 1831, he even hosted the missionary Joseph Wolff. As interest gradually spread in the new learning that the students brought back with them, Mirza Riza was appointed to design Iran's first polytechnic, the Dar al-Funun, which finally opened in 1851. As Iran's first institution dedicated to the teaching of modern science, the Dar al-Funun transmitted more widely the new sciences that Mirza Riza and his companions had studied in London. It was later transformed into Tehran University, still today Iran's most prestigious seat of secular learning.

And as for the former blacksmith Muhammad 'Ali, he too made contributions to his country's development. Drawing on the understanding of steam power gained through his apprenticeship to Alex Galloway, he imported from England one of Iran's first ever steam engines. It was used to operate a lathe in a workshop that perhaps resembled that of James Wilkinson & Sons where he had learned to make rifles. A newspaper report from 1826 gives a tantalizing glimpse into the life of Muhammad 'Ali—and his English bride—in Iran:

> At Tabreez, also, resides an Englishwoman, a native of London, the daughter of an eminent gun-maker, who is married to a Persian of the name of Mahomet Ally, who was sent to England some years since by the Prince Abbas Mirza, to learn some of the English mechanic arts, and who since his return to Persia has been intrusted with the superintendance of the arsenal of the Prince, who has also in his employ a Scotsman, formerly a private in the Royal artillery, who accompanied Sir Gore Ouseley in his embassy to Persia, and who superintends the construction of the carriages for the artillery, and the casting of brass ordnance.

So Muhammad ʿAli had risen to become superintendent of the royal arsenal. And back in Tabriz, he still worked alongside at least one British artisan just as he had in London. Whether the mysterious Scottish ordnance caster was as radical a companion as Alex Galloway, we cannot know, nor do we know whether he brought a wife who kept company with Mrs. ʿAli, née Dudley. It was later reported that Mary had to live according to Iranian ways, but was allowed to receive European guests in far Tabriz and always insisted on the use of knives and forks in her household. They were at least comfortably off, far more so than they had been back in Covent Garden. In 1835, Muhammad ʿAli was placed in charge of the royal foundry in Tehran. There in the capital, Mary ʿAli may have found English company through the embassy, as Mirza Salih did. Whether she needed such friends or not, as she had sworn at St. James's Church, Westminster, in the spring of 1819, her marriage to Muhammad ʿAli lasted till death did them part.

All in all, then, the impact the students had on their homeland was considerable. That the story of these six young Muslims has never been told is perhaps because it is a quiet tale of cooperation: there was no great conflict or bloodshed, no acts of aggression or repression that fit European or Middle Eastern stereotypes of each other. Yet those Muslims stood amid the scientific and industrial revolution taking place around Jane Austen's sedate Pemberley, every one of them keen to spread the new sciences back home. That they were patriots is beyond question: more interesting is that they were partisans of reason, science, and reform. Though their homeland was repeatedly invaded by Russia, they felt no impulse to blame the entirety of Christendom, or "the West," as we would call it today. Instead, they made many Christian friends and cultivated that rare virtue that is the love of strangers.

Ultimately, it was not only Iran that they helped transform. Through their presence in England—through the humanizing effect of meeting people from so many walks of life—they contributed to the transformation of England itself. For in the course of the nineteenth century, England in general and London in particular would be slowly transformed by the presence of foreign and non-Christian peoples. London was more than an imperial capital; it was, as Mirza Salih himself declared, a liberal capital. And this was not only the achievement of the

English themselves; it was the achievement of the foreign visitors and residents who in making friendships with the English made liberalism a practice no less than a philosophy. Mirza Salih and his companions stood at the start of a long process of the sharing of knowledge, faith, and friendship that transformed London into the global city it is now. Their story forms a genesis for today's London of kebab shops and mosques, an origin story not a whit less civilized than *Sense and Sensibility*.

For during their years in London, our six Muslims learned a good deal about sense and sensibility, about reason and compassion, about science and sympathy, and about the tolerance that is the fair child of their union. That they learned these things, cherished them, and exported them, is the most important lesson they can teach us two hundred years later. For there are no such things as "Western" values, "European" values, or even "English" values. There are only values, which people from different places can choose to adopt and carry wherever they will. Whether and to what extent such values do spread afar is a larger question. But the students have shown us that they can, they have, and they do. Mirza Salih and his companions did not see reason, science, or liberty as uniquely English values, still less as being in conflict with their Muslim faith. This is the final lesson they have passed down to us: such values have no innate homelands; they belong nowhere more than elsewhere; they travel wherever people will take them.

A Note on Sources and Method

$\mathcal{W}$hile I am aware of arguments that make a case for interpreting Persian travelogues primarily as literary texts, I have chosen instead to conceive of Mirza Salih's *safarnama* as a reliable eyewitness source. While much might be said elsewhere of the stylistic and literary features of this "diary," I have found that its most useful purposes are as a historical document that sheds wide revealing light onto the living arena of social and intellectual interactions in which these first Muslim students abroad participated. As a microhistory devoted to the contours and contexts of the students' London, this book has not widened its horizontal vision to compare them with other Iranian travelers of the period. Since many effective overviews of Iranian and other Middle Eastern travelers now exist, I have opted instead for a more detailed excavation of the evidence surrounding their particular, four-year journey. I have in any case discussed and drawn on the evidence of the university evangelicals, Mirza Salih's work with them and his access to print technology in another book, *Terrains of Exchange*. With the different aims of that book, Mirza Salih is compared with a wider range of historical actors and situated into a more vertical picture of transformation, and indeed antagonism, over time.

While this book is not explicitly structured around historical debates, I hope academic readers can taste the mustard of analysis and argument that is blended into the narrative. In many respects, writing it has been an exercise in prosopography, of reconstructing as carefully as possible the social circles in which Mirza Salih and his companions moved and using the evidence of this reconstructed circle to in turn identify the people named in the Arabic script of his diary. For the largest challenge in researching *The Love of Strangers*—and the most significant contribution to knowledge it may claim—is in identifying for the first time the majority of the people with whom Mirza

Salih and his fellow students were associated in London. This has been no easy task, since the various Persian editions of his diary contain variant Arabic-script spellings of the English names of the students' associates, variations that emerge from both the palaeographic ambiguities of Mirza Salih's original diary manuscript and the unfamiliarity of its Iranian editors with English surnames. (I have not listed in the notes the various page references to the different Persian editions of the diary, since this appears superfluous to most readers' requirements. Instead, except where there was a particular reason to demonstrate comparisons between the different editions or the manuscript, I have restricted the references to the diary to the latest and most complete edition, that of Ghulam Husayn Mirza Salih from 1985.)

In reading the English names in the Arabic script of the diary, my method has been to compare the various printed editions with the original surviving manuscript (British Library, Add. 24034) and to work from the most likely readings that emerge from the prosopographical evidence of the circle that gathered around Mirza Salih's best known associates, such as Dr. Olinthus Gregory and the Ouseley brothers. While the latter, along with other well-known historical figures, are identified in notes to the Iranian editions of the diary, most of the people with whom they interacted are not. It is here, in identifying the wider cast of characters in their story, that my method, at once prosopographical and palaeographical, has been brought to bear. Wherever possible, I have corroborated my identifications through cross-references to the persons in question via either Foreign Office correspondence or the journals and letters of the persons themselves.

While future research by other scholars may disprove one or two of my identifications, I am confident that the majority will stand scrutiny. While Mirza Salih's diary has long been known to specialists, the result of the research here for the first time provides Mirza Salih and his companions with a social and intellectual context in England and, in so doing, demonstrates the full range of ideas and technologies to which these pioneering middlemen were exposed. In places, I may appear to have made the historical transgressions of planting words in Mirza Salih's mouth or emotions in his mind. Here I can offer two explanations. First, I have tried to draw on his own written testimony even though my attempts to avoid such frequent usages as "he wrote" and "he described" means that this may not always be apparent. Second, after nine years of reading and reflecting on his diary, I have drawn on the elusive but essential historical asset that is empathy. For heuristic and narrative purposes, on a few occasions I have also found it necessary to slightly amend the sequence of certain events (such as the journeys to Bristol and Bath) or to narrativize a few of the diary's descriptive sections (such as the park visits).

I hope this has all paid off. For if Mirza Salih previously walked through a social vacuum in England, then he and his companions can now take their place amid the full *tamasha* (to adopt one of his favorite terms) of the orientalists, evangelicals, and tradesmen of the early nineteenth century. He can also be seen among his friends, across centuries and nations. I hope in some measure to have made a case for the students' importance as intellectual mediators and cultural explorers. And I aspire to have made a case for the virtues of what Mirza Salih has so often been condemned for by his countrymen: xenophilia. For in his time as in ours, it is more a virtue than a vice and one that is today more important than ever. Perhaps Mirza Salih has something to teach us all.

Acknowledgments

In the nine years of researching and writing of this book, I have been helped by many people and institutions whom I would now like to acknowledge. I thank the Bibliographical Society for awarding me the Katharine F. Pantzer Fellowship for 2009–10 to work in various libraries in London, Oxford, and Munich. Among the many librarians and archivists who aided me elsewhere, I offer my sincere gratitude to Dr. Toby Barnard, Archivist, Hertford College, Oxford; Martin Cherry, Librarian, and Diane Clements, Director, Library and Museum of Free-masonry, Freemasons' Hall, London; Jacqueline Cox, Archivist, Cambridge University Archives; Linda Haynes, Archivist, Oxfordshire County Records Office; Dr. David Hirsch, Librarian for Middle Eastern, Islamic, South Asian and Jewish Studies, UCLA; Reverend Jonathan Holmes, Keeper of the Records, Queens' College, Cambridge; Dr. Anthony Morton, Archivist, Sandhurst Collection (including the archives of the Royal Military Academy, Woolwich), the Royal Military Academy, Sandhurst; Dr. Peter Nockles, Director, Methodist Archives and Research Centre, Manchester University; Toby Parker, Archivist, The Haileybury Archives, Haileybury College; Andrew Potter, Research Assistant, the Royal Academy Library, London; Dr. Winfried Riesterer, Librarian for Turkish and Persian Rare Books, Bayerische Staatsbibliothek, Munich; Nigel Roche, Librarian of the St. Bride Printing Library, London; Dr. Graham Shaw, Dr. Muhammad Isa Waley, and Dr. Ursula Sims-Williams, Asia, Pacific & Africa Collections, the British Library, London; Dr. Jonathan Smith, Archivist, Trinity College, Cambridge; William G. Wood, Archivist, the Whitgift School, Croydon; the staff of the National Archives (former Public Record Office), Kew, London; the staff of the library and archive of the British and Foreign Bible Society, Cambridge University Library; the staff of Croydon Local Studies Library and Archives; the staff of the Center for Oxfordshire Studies,

Oxford Public Library; the staff of the Bodleian Library and the Oriental Institute Library, Oxford University; and the Master and Fellows of Trinity College, Cambridge, for permission to print their portrait of Professor Samuel Lee.

Several of the chapters draw in places on sections from my earlier articles, albeit in heavily revised and expanded form. I therefore gratefully acknowledge the following publishers and organizations for permission to reprint (parts of) the following articles: Cambridge University Press for "Among the Dissenters: Reciprocal Ethnography in Nineteenth-Century Inglistan," *Journal of Global History* 4, 2 (2009); the American Printing History Association for "The Development of Arabic-Script Printing in Georgian Britain," *Printing History* n.s., 5 (2009); Edinburgh University Press for "Kebabs and Port Wine: The Culinary Cosmopolitanism of Anglo-Persian Dining, 1800–1835," in Derryl Maclean and Sikeena Karmali (eds.), *Cosmopolitanisms in Muslim Contexts* (Edinburgh, 2012); Taylor & Francis for "The *Madrasas* of Oxford: Iranian Interactions with the English Universities in the Early Nineteenth Century," *Iranian Studies* 44, 6 (2011); and the British Institute of Persian Studies for "Paper Modernity? Notes on an Iranian Industrial Tour, 1818," *Iran: Journal of Persian Studies* 46 (2008). My translation of Mirza Salih's description of the Oxford degree ceremony previously appeared in my article "The *Madrasas* of Oxford, 1818," *Oxford Magazine* 253 (2006).

Among the academic colleagues who have made useful suggestions or commented on various iterations of the research presented in this book, I gratefully thank Firuza Melville, Abbas Amanat, Mehrdad Amanat, Maziar Behrooz, Ali Boozari, C. Edmund Bosworth, Willem Floor, Edmund Herzig, Homa Katouzian, Nikki Keddie, Arash Khazeni, Ulrich Marzolph, Anne Mellor, Ali Mousavi, Daniel Newman, Geoffrey Roper, A. Reza Sheikholeslami, Sanjay Subrahmanyam, Naghmeh Sohrabi, Mohamad Tavakoli-Targhi, and Farzin Vejdani. I am especially grateful to Michael H. Fisher, Ali Gheissari, David Motadel, and the two anonymous readers for Princeton University Press for their comments and suggestions on the manuscript as a whole.

In a book I have researched by walking history, there have also been many companions on the road. A special shout out to Bradley Jones for joining me on marches through London in search of the students' former residences (and drinking dens); Nigel Eltringham for taking me to the remnants of the East India Seminary at Addiscombe; Arash Khazeni for roving conversations on the wide Persianate world; Hendrik Müller for playing host at Oxford high tables and helping me with Philoxenus's Latin; Norbert Schurer for generously sharing his knowledge about the Austen family's Indian connections; Roy Shadbolt for assistance with the history of James Wilkinson the gun- and swordsmith; Jenn Whiskerd for initiating me into the dissenting history of the Stroud Valley mill towns and for taking the photograph of Belvedere Mill; Teri-Lee Wagstaff of Langley Priory, Derbyshire, for local memories of the former squire John Shakespear; and the doorman I cajoled into escorting me round the house of William Hazlitt in Soho. I am also grateful to the staff of the Coalbrookdale Museum of Iron for helping with my many questions about cast iron; to David Baddeley and John Boucher of the Society for the Protection of Ancient Buildings (Mills) for teaching me about mill technology on a private tour of Staffordshire's Worston Mill (built in 1805); and to Ann Reeve, whose family has farmed outside Oxford since the time of Mirza Salih, for helping me find the lost papermaking village of Hampton Gay. Back in the United States, my acquisitions editor at Princeton, Brigitta van Rheinberg, has been a paragon of the three editorial virtues of efficiency, energy, and enthusiasm. Quinn Fusting, Sara Lerner, and Jennifer Harris helped enormously with various practical dimensions of the editing process, while Dimitri Karetnikov and David Cox used their cartographical skills to attend to my every request in drawing the maps.

In writing this book, I have often had in mind my own travels through Iran in my twenties, learning Persian, wandering lonely and sometimes lost, meeting Sufis, nomads, and day laborers—making friends. During those years, there were many kind Iranians who fed me, helped me, told me jokes, and taught me a great deal about not just their country but about being human, about *insaniyat*. I owe them all a great deal. And across the centuries I also shared with Mirza Salih the same patron of our studies in Sir Gore Ouseley, whose family endowed the Ouseley Memorial Scholarship that funded my doctoral studies in London, setting up the latter-day reciprocity that saw me learning Persian as Mirza Salih learned English. So in writing this book, I hope to have repaid a double debt, both to the Ouseleys and to the many Iranians who befriended me: without them, my own student days would have been literally and figuratively far poorer. And finally, for sharing our home for so long with her *ambagh*, Mirza Salih, thanks to my beloved wife, Nushin, whom I first met as an Afghan student in London.

Notes

Introducing Mr. D'Arcy's Persians

Page

1 "Iranian students": On the subsequent history of other Iranians studying abroad, see Mohammad Hossein Azizi and Farzaneh Azizi, "Government-Sponsored Iranian Medical Students Abroad (1811–1935)," *Iranian Studies* 43, 3 (2010); Homa Nategh, "Les Persans à Lyon (1884–1907)," in Christophe Balaÿ, Claire Kappler, and Živa Vesel (eds.), *Pand-u Sukhan* (Paris-Tehran: Institut Français de Recherche en Iran, 1995); and Ghulām ʿAlī Sarmad, *Iʿzām-i Muhassil bih Khārij az Kishvar dar Dawra-yi Qajāriya* (Tehran: Chāp va Nashr-i Bunyād, 1372/1993). Note that throughout the following chapters, I have written of "England" rather than "Britain" because it was only England, rather than Scotland or Wales, that the students visited and because England (or *Ingland/Inglistan*) was their name for the country. For better or worse, I have stuck to this term for the sake of consistency, though wherever appropriate I have labeled various persons as specifically Scottish, Irish, or Welsh.

2 "Rifaʿa al-Tahtawi": While Muslims of various kinds, including some scholars, had visited Western Europe over the previous few centuries, I have been unable to find evidence of any of them formally studying there before the Iranian students, bar one possible exception. This was a certain ʿUthman Nur al-Din sent from Egypt in 1809 to study military engineering, shipbuilding, and printing in Pisa, Livorno, and then for less than two years in Paris, before returning to Egypt in 1817, thus overlapping with the Iranian students in London. However, aside from fragmentary evidence in Russian and French archives, Nur al-Din left no record of his time in Europe comparable to that of his Iranian contemporaries. See René Cattaui, *Le règne de Mohamed Aly d'après les archives russes en Égypte* (Cairo: Imprimerie de l'Institut français d'archéologie orientale du Caire, 1931), vol. 1, pp. 387–89; and James Heyworth-Dunne, *An Introduction to the History of Education in Modern Egypt* (London: Luzac and Company, 1939), p. 105. While some Ottoman Christians had undertaken theological studies in Rome, these form a separate category, as do elite Ottoman Greek "phanariots," who studied, for example, in (what was in any case Ottoman-ruled) Bucharest. On the latter, see Christine M. Philliou, *Biography of an Empire: Governing Ottomans in an Age of Revolution* (Berkeley: University of California Press, 2011), pp. 38–40. Even when it did draw on European science for its *nizam-i cedid*, the Ottoman Empire preferred to import European professors rather than export its own students (thanks to Christine Philliou for this insight). The breakaway province of Egypt under Muhammad ʿAli Pasha (r. 1805–48) became the exception to this Ottoman general rule. Hence, on Egyptian scholars (particularly Arab Christians) in early nineteenth-century France, see Ian Coller, *Arab*

France: Islam and the Making of Modern Europe, 1798–1831 (Berkeley: University of California Press, 2011); and on the Egyptian students' in Paris in the late 1820s, see Daniel Newman (trans. and ed.), *An Imam in Paris: Al-Tahtawi's Visit to France (1826–1831)* (London: Saqi Books, 2004). On the earliest Indian formal students in Britain, dating only from the 1840s, see Rozina Visram, *Ayahs, Lascars and Princes: Indians in Britain 1700–1947* (London: Pluto Press, 1986), pp. 178–79. On subsequent Iranian students, see the previous note.

2 "the diary": Based on the manuscript of the diary (British Library, Add. 24034), three editions of Mirza Salih's diary have been published: *Safarnāma-yi Mīrzā Sālih Shīrāzī*, ed. Ismāʿīl Rāʾīn (Tehran: Rūzan, 1347/1968); *Guzārish-i Safar-i Mīrzā Sālih Shīrāzī (Kāzarūnī)*, ed. Humāyūn Shahīdī (Tehran: Rāh-i Naw, 1362/1983); and *Majmūʿa-yi Safarnāmahā-yi Mīrzā Sālih Shīrāzī*, ed. Ghulām Husayn Mīrzā Sālih (Tehran: Nashr-i Tārīkh-i Īrān, 1364/1985). While I have compared all three editions in checking names and other details, except in problematic cases I have cited the editon of Ghulām Husayn Mīrzā Sālih (as Shīrāzī [1364/1985]) for the sake of bibliographical simplicity. For a critical assessment of Rāʾīn's edition, see Sayyid Muhammad ʿAlī Shahristānī, "Safarnāmahā-yi Mīrzā Sālih Shīrāzī," *Ganjīna-yi Asnād* 33–34 (1378). Thanks to Ali Gheissari for providing access to the latter. I have also consulted the British Library manuscript (Add. 24,034) for significant variances with the printed editions.

2 "Recounting their escapades": A short informative account of the students' fortunes in England (albeit without using Mirza Salih's diary) appears in Denis Wright, *The Persians amongst the English: Episodes in Anglo-Persian History* (London: I. B. Tauris, 1985), chapter 7. Short treatments of Mirza Salih and the other students also appear in Husayn Mahbūbī Ardakānī, "Duvvumīn Kārvān-i Maʿrifat," *Yaghmā* 18 (1965); and idem, *Tārīkh-i Muʾassasāt-i Tamaddunī-yi Jadīd dar Īrān*, 3 vols. (Tehran: Anjūman-i Dānishjūyān-i Dānishgāh-i Tihrān, 1975), vol. 1, pp. 176–79, 222–24. On the genre to which Mirza Salih's diary belonged, see William L. Hanaway, "Persian Travel Narratives: Notes toward the Definition of a Nineteenth-Century Genre," in Elton Daniel (ed.), *Society and Culture in Qajar Iran: Studies in Honor of Hafez Farmayan* (Costa Mesa, CA: Mazda Press, 2002).

2 "Edward Said": Edward W. Said, *Culture and Imperialism* (London: Chatto & Windus, 1993).

2 "Mirza Salih": For brief but helpful contextualization of Mirza Salih's writings, see Kamran Rastegar, *Literary Modernity between the Middle East and Europe: Textual Transactions in Nineteenth Century Arabic, English and Persian Literatures* (London: Routledge, 2007), pp. 80–82; Mohamad Tavakoli-Targhi, *Refashioning Iran: Orientalism, Europology, and Nationalist Historiography* (Basingstoke: Palgrave, 2001), pp. 32–33, 43–45, 75–76; and Farzin Vahdat, *God and Juggernaut: Iran's Intellectual Encounter with Modernity* (Syracuse, NY: Syracuse University Press, 2002), pp. 27–28.

3 "Joseph D'Arcy": On D'Arcy's career, see Alan H. Barrett, "A Memoir of Lieutenant-Colonel Joseph D'Arcy, R.A. 1780–1848," *Iran* 43 (2005); and Kambiz Eslami, "D'Arcy, Joseph," in *Encyclopaedia Iranica*.

3 "writing to the Foreign Office in London": UK National Archives, FO 248/32 (173): Joseph D'Arcy to James Morier (May 18, 1815).

3 "their names": Ibid. On the students' title, *mirza*, see John R. Perry, "Ethno-Linguistic Markers of the Turco-Mongol Military and Persian Bureaucratic Castes in Pre-

modern Iran and India," in Irene Schneider (ed.), *Militär und Staatlichkeit* (Halle-Wittenberg, 2003), pp. 112–13.

4 "two young Iranians": Mujtaba Minuvī, "Avvalīn Kārvān-i Maʿrifat," *Yaghmā* 18 (1965).

4 "students to London until 1818, with a larger group reaching Paris in 1826": Coller (2011), chapter 8; Heyworth-Dunne (1939), pp. 105–6; and Newman (2004).

5 "Regency gentlemen": Throughout this book, the term "Regency" is used as a general reference to the culture of the period from 1811 to 1820 when, due to the "madness" of George III, his son ruled by proxy as a "Prince Regent."

5 "new diplomatic ties": On Iranian motivations and strategies, see Manoutchehr M. Eskandari-Qajar, "Between Scylla and Charybdis: Policy-Making under Conditions of Constraint in Early Qajar Persia," in Roxane Farmanfarmaian (ed.), *War and Peace in Qajar Persia: Implications Past and Present* (London: Routledge, 2008); and Colin Meredith, "The Qajar Response to Russia's Military Challenge, 1804–28" (PhD dissertation, Princeton University, 1973).

6 "the embassy": Barrett (2005). On the early history of Anglo-Iranian diplomatic relations, see Edward Ingram, *Britain's Persian Connection, 1798–1828: Prelude to the Great Game in Asia* (Oxford: Clarendon Press, 1992); and Dennis Wright, *The English amongst the Persians* (London: I. B. Tauris, 1985).

6 "distrust among some Iranians": On changing Iranian attitudes, see Abbas Amanat, "Through the Persian Eye: Anglophilia and Anglophobia in Modern Iranian History," in Abbas Amanat and Farzin Vejdani (eds.), *Iran Facing Others: Identity Boundaries in a Historical Perspective* (New York: Palgrave, 2012).

6 "threat posed by Europeans": On Iranian relations with the French and Russians in this period, see Iradj Amini, *Napoleon and Persia: Franco Persian Relations under the First Empire* (Washington, DC: Mage, 1999); Muriel Atkin, *Russia and Iran, 1780–1828* (Minneapolis: University of Minnesota Press, 1980); Laurence Kelly, *Diplomacy and Murder in Tehran: Alexander Griboyedov and Imperial Russia's Mission to the Shah of Persia* (London: I. B. Tauris, 2002); and Irène Natchkebia, "Envoys of Napoleon: General Gardane's Mission to Persia, 1807–1809," *Qajar Studies* 7 (2007). For primary documents, see ʿAbbās Mīrzā Iʿtizād al-Dawla, *Tārīkh-i Ravābit-i Īrān va Nāpuliyūn: bih Inzimām-i Siyāsat-i Rūs va Ingilīs dar Īrān* (Tehran: Intishārāt-i Zarrīn, 1363/1984).

6 "diplomatic relations with Britain": Abbas Amanat, "'Russian Intrusion into the Guarded Domain': Reflections of a Qajar Statesman on European Expansion," *Journal of the American Oriental Society* 113, 1 (1993). For further context, see Hamid Algar, *Religion and State in Iran, 1785–1906: The Role of the Ulama in the Qajar Period* (Berkeley: University of California Press, 1969), pp. 73–101.

6 "Treaty of 1812": On the background to the treaty, see Edward Ingram, "An Aspiring Buffer State: Anglo-Persian Relations in the Third Coalition, 1804–1807," *Historical Journal* 16, 3 (1973).

6 "diplomatic exchanges": Examples of the Persian diplomatic correspondence exchanged between Sir John Malcolm and the court of Fath ʿAli Shah are published in Charles Stewart (ed.), *Original Persian Letters and Other Documents with Fac-Similes* (London: Kingsbury, Parbury, Allen & Co., 1825), pp. 174–203.

6 "ʿAbbas Mirza": ʿAbbas Mirza is still poorly served by biographers: see Emineh Pakravan, *Abbas Mirza* (Paris: Buchet-Chastel, 1973); and Mustafā Musavī Tabarī,

'Abbās Mīrzā Qājār: Sharh-i Hāl va Siyāsat va Khidāmat-i Ū (Tehran: Ibn Sīnā, 1974).

6 "Russian expansion": On the conflicts and their consequences, see Firoozeh Kashani-Sabet, *Frontier Fictions: Shaping the Iranian Nation, 1804–1946* (Princeton, NJ: Princeton University Press, 1999); and Firouzeh Mostashari, *On the Religious Frontier: Tsarist Russia and Islam in the Caucasus* (London: I. B. Tauris, 2006).

7 "European ideas": Some of these influences can be discerned in the letters 'Abbas Mirza exchanged with the later British envoy, Sir John Kinneir MacDonald (1782–1830). See Kamran Ekbal (ed. and trans.), *Der Briefwechsel Abbas Mirzas mit dem britischen Gesandten MacDonald Kinneir im Zeichen des zweiten russisch-persischen Krieges (1825–1828): e. Beitr. zur Geschichte der pers.-engl. Beziehungen in d. frühen Kadscharenzeit* (Freiburg im Breisgau: Schwarz, 1977).

7 "Napoleon Bonaparte": On the 1808 Iranian diplomatic mission to Napoleon's Paris, see Iradj Amini, "Askar Khan Afshar: Fath Ali Shah's Ambassador in Paris," *Qajar Studies* 7 (2007).

8 "Moritz von Kotzebue": Moritz von Kotzebue, *Narrative of a Journey into Persia in the Suite of the Imperial Russian Embassy in the Year 1817* (London: Longman, Hurst, Rees, Orme, and Brown, 1819), p. 164. See also p. 184 for a further description.

8 "Mr. D'Arcy": Barrett (2005), p. 243.

8 "article in *The Times*": Untitled article, *The Times* (April 12, 1819).

8 " 'Abbas Mirza": Sir Henry Willock, "Biographical Sketch of His Late Royal Highness Abbas Mirza, Prince Royal of Persia, Hon. MRAS, etc, etc," *Journal of the Royal Asiatic Society* 1, 2 (1834), p. 322.

9 "Abu'l-Hasan Khan": Hasan Mursilvand (ed.), *Hayratnāma: Safarnāma-yi Mīrzā Abū al-Hasan Khān Īlchī bih Landan* (Tehran: Mu'assasa-yi Khidamāt-i Farhangī-yi Rasā, 1364/1986), selectively translated by Margaret Morris Cloake as Mirza Abul Hassan Khan, *A Persian at the Court of King George 1809–10: The Journal of Mirza Abul Hassan Khan* (London: Barrie & Jenkins, 1988). Note that Mursilvand's Persian edition and Cloake's English translation are made from two separate (and differing) manuscripts. To aid specialist and nonspecialist readers, in the subsequent notes I have given references to both the Persian edition and translation. Where conflicts arise, I have relied on the Persian version. However, for a critique of the Persian edition, see Abbas Amanat, "The Study of History in Post-Revolutionary Iran: Nostalgia, Illusion, or Historical Awareness?," *Iranian Studies* 22, 4 (1989).

9 "blazing a trail": In *The Times* alone, articles (often frivolous) on Ambassador Abu'l-Hasan appeared on December 21, 1809; December 30, 1809; January 12, 1810; January 18, 1810; February 23, 1810; March 24, 1810; March 29, 1810; April 27, 1819; May 1, 1819; May 24, 1819; June 1, 1819; and June 10, 1819.

9 "his own Persian diary": For a critical reading of Abu'l-Hasan's diary, see Naghmeh Sohrabi, *Taken for Wonder: Nineteenth Century Travel Accounts from Iran to Europe* (New York: Oxford University Press, 2012), chapter 1.

9 "precocious daughter": Abul Hassan Khan (1988), p. 111; Mursilvand (1364/1986), pp. 173–74.

9 "library": Abul Hassan Khan (1988), p. 86; Mursilvand (1364/1986), p. 153.

9 "painter Aqa 'Ali Naqash": William Price, *Journal of the British Embassy to Persia: Embellished with Numerous Views Taken in India and Persia; Also, a Dissertation upon the Antiquities of Persepolis* (London: Kingsbury, Parbury & Allen, 1825), p. 36.

10 "quaff wine and brandy": Philoxenus Secundus, *Persian Recreations, or Oriental stories, with Notes, to which is Prefixed some Account of Two Ambassadors from Iran to James the First and George the Third* (London: S. Rousseau, 1812), p. 34.

10 "expensive asparagus": Abul Hassan Khan (1988), p. 235; Mursilvand (1364/1986), p. 305. I have relied here on the slightly different version recounted in the Persian text.

10 " 'ladies flirting' ": Abul Hassan Khan (1988), p. 236; Mursilvand (1364/1986), p. 306. I have modified the quotation from Cloake's translation through reference to the Persian text.

10 " 'Pretty beautiful ladies' ": From Abu'l-Hasan's letter to the *Morning Post*, May 29, 1810 (reprinted in Wright [1985], appendix 4).

12 "the latifa": Philoxenus Secundus (1812), pp. i–ii.

12 " 'handsome dark man' ": Ibid., p. 23.

12 "epithet in Latin": Ibid., p. 21.

12 "from Virgil's Aeneid": *Aeneid*, Book VIII, lines 265–67. I am grateful to Dr. Hendrik Müller for guidance on the original source of these verses.

13 "be 'gallant' ": Philoxenus Secundus (1812), pp. 37–39.

13 "Stephen Weston": The identification of Philoxenus is given in William Cushing, *Initials and Pseudonyms: A Dictionary of Literary Disguises* (New York: T. Y. Crowell & Co., 1885), p. 233.

13 "Abu'l-Hasan": Sohrabi (2012), chapter 1.

13 "Henry Lindsay-Bethune": Bethune is mentioned by Mirza Salih in his diary: see Mīrzā Sālih Shīrāzī, *Majmūʿa-i Safarnāmahā-yi Mīrzā Sālih Shīrāzī*, ed. Ghulām Husayn Mīrzā Sālih (Tehran: Nashr-i Tārīkh-i Īrān, 1364/1985) [henceforth Shīrāzī (1364/1985)], p. 44. See also Farīd Qāsimī, *Avvalīnhā-yi Matbuʿāt-i Īrān* (Tehran: Nashr-i Ābī, 2004), p. 15.

14 "warrior hero, Rustam": Sir Percy Molesworth Sykes, *A History of Persia*, 2 vols. (London: Macmillan & Co., 1921), vol. 2, p. 308.

14 " 'pure dialect of Shiraz' ": William Price and Mirza Muhammad Saulih Shirazi, *A Grammar of the Three Principal Oriental Languages, Hindoostanee, Persian and Arabic to Which Is Added, a Set of Persian Dialogues by Mirza Muhammad Saulih of Shiraz* (London: Kingsbury, Parbury & Allen, 1823), p. vi.

15 "language guide": Mirza Salih Shirazi, *Suʾal va Javab*, Bodleian Library, Oxford, Ouseley Collection, ms 390.

15 "Journal of Mīrzā Mohammed Sāleh": Bodleian Library, Ouseley ms 159; colophon dated 1812. For Ouseley's own description, Sir William Ouseley, *Catalogue of Several Hundred Manuscript Works in Various Oriental Languages, Collected by Sir William Ouseley* (London: A. J. Valpy, 1831), appendix, no. 687.

15 "traveled with the embassy": ʿAbbās Amānat, "Hamrāh-i Mīrzā Sālih az Isfahān bih Tihrān," *Āyanda* 9 (1983), pp. 36–49, 86.

15 "Sir Gore wrote": "Diary of the Right Hon. Sir Gore Ouseley, Bt, KCH, FRS," Bodleian Library, Manuscripts Department, ms b250. Page 1 lists the names of the Britons accompanying the embassy, along with nine unnamed "Persian servants."

16 " 'Age of Discovery' ": William H. Goetzmann, *New Lands, New Men: America and the Second Great Age of Discovery* (New York: Viking, 1986), pp. 1–5.

17 "Jane Austen's brother": On the Burmese escapades of Charles Austen, see John H.

Hubback and Edith C. Hubback, Jane *Austen's Sailor Brothers* (London: J. Lane, 1906), pp. 278–82.

18 "fog of misunderstanding": Ali M. Ansari, " 'Persia' in the Western Imagination," in Vanessa Martin (ed.), *Anglo-Iranian Relations since 1800* (London: Routledge, 2005).

20 "story of xenophilia": Although *xenophilia* is not attested in classical Greek, and purists may favor the classically attested *philoxenia* ("love of strangers," "hospitality"), I have preferred the former since it is the more obvious antonym of the familiar term *xenophobia*.

Chapter One. In Search of a Teacher

Page

23 "study the *'ulum-i farang*": Shīrāzī (1364/1985), p. 141.

24 "matched curiosity": Mohamad Tavakoli-Targhi, *Refashioning Iran: Orientalism, Occidentalism, and Historiography* (New York: Palgrave, 2001).

24 "recorded the date": Shīrāzī (1364/1985), p. 150.

24 "steamship *Margery*": Frank L. Dix, *Royal River Highway: A History of the Passenger Boats and Services on the Thames* (Newton Abbot: David & Charles, 1985), pp. 50–60.

25 "D'Arcy's family": Barrett (2005), p. 244.

25 "harp and guitar": Shīrāzī (1364/1985), p. 153.

25 "Mansfield Park": The harp-playing of Mary Crawford features in chapter 7 of *Mansfield Park*.

26 "sailor brothers": John H. Hubback and Edith C. Hubback, *Jane Austen's Sailor Brothers* (London: J. Lane, 1906), chapters 4–12.

26 "Austen visited Rochester": See Austen's letter no. 9 (October 24, 1798), in R. W. Chapman (ed.), *Jane Austen's Letters to Her Sister Cassandra and Others*, 2 vols. (Oxford: Clarendon Press, 1932), vol. 1, p. 20.

26 " 'great priests' ": Shīrāzī (1364/1985), p. 154.

26 "Mirza Salih described": Ibid., p. 153.

27 "Mirza Salih described": Ibid., p. 155.

27 "noted simply": Ibid., p. 154.

27 "bathhouses": *The Original Picture of London*, 24th ed. (London: Longman, Rees, Orme, Brown & Green, 1826), p. 370.

28 "Even Jane Austen": Paula Byrne, *The Real Jane Austen: A Life in Small Things* (New York: HarperCollins, 2013), p. 306.

29 " 'at your service' ": Shīrāzī (1364/1985), p. 156.

29 "breakdown of the funds": UK National Archives, FO 60/11 (68): "D'Arcy to Edward Cooke" (February 7, 1816).

29 "sum of £1,200": For the sum's modern equivalent (in 2013), I have relied on the Bank of England's Historical Inflation Calculator: www.bankofengland.co.uk/education/Pages/resources/inflationtools/calculator/index1.aspx (accessed January 2015).

30 "D'Arcy was writing": UK National Archives, FO 60/11 (73): "D'Arcy to Edward Cooke" (March 11, 1816).

30 "avoidance of responsibilities": Shīrāzī (1364/1985), pp. 157–61, 167–69.

30 " 'their extravagances' ": UK National Archives, FO 60/11 (73): "D'Arcy to Edward Cooke" (March 11, 1816).

31 "27 Leicester Square": Given what we will see later of Mirza Salih's regular excursions to the theater, there is a pleasing symmetry in the fact that when his former lodgings on Leicester Square were demolished in 1854, it was to make way for the Alhambra Theatre. In 1936, that theater in turn gave way for England's most famous cinema, The Odeon on Leicester Square.

32 "bathhouse": Original Picture of London(1826), p. 370.

32 "Huntly's Coffee House": Original Picture of London (1826), p. 368; and UK National Archives, FO 60/11 (102): "Statement of Accounts" (June 10, 1816).

32 "London house": I have again relied here on the Bank of England's Inflation Calculator.

34 "Francis Balfour": On Balfour's printing activities, see C. A. Storey, "The Beginnings of Persian Printing in India," in J. D. Cursetji Pavry (ed.), *Oriental Studies in Honour of Cursetji Erachji Pavry* (London: Oxford University Press, 1933), p. 457.

34 "Francis Belfour": *Oxford University Calendar for 1821* (Oxford: University Press, 1821), p. 277; and UK National Archives, FO 60/11 (102): "Statement of Accounts" (June 10, 1816).

35 "Muhammad Kazim": The quotation regarding the funeral is found in UK National Archives, FO 60/8 (1), "Lord Castlereagh to Gore Ouseley" (April 5, 1813).

35 "*Adventures of Hajji Baba*": For critical investigations of the links between the Abu'l-Hasan and Morier's *Hajji Baba*, see Henry B. McKenzie Johnston, "*Hajji Baba* and Mirza Abul Hasan Khan—A Conundrum," Iran 33 (1995); Kamran Rastegar, "The Unintended Gift: The Adventures of Hajji Baba Ispahani as a Transactional Text between English and Persian Literatures," *Middle Eastern Literatures* 10, 3 (2008); and Naghmeh Sohrabi, "Looking behind Hajji Baba of Ispahan: The Case of Mirza Abul Hasan Khan Ilchi Shirazi," in Amy Singer, Christoph Neumann, and Selcuk Aksin Somel (eds.), *Untold Histories of the Middle East: Recovering Voices from the 19th and 20th Centuries* (London: Routledge, 2010).

35 "'a conversation'": Shīrāzī (1364/1985), p. 156.

36 "farmland into housing": Edward Walford, "Camden Town and Kentish Town," in idem, *Old and New London*, 6 vols. (London: Cassell & Co., 1878), vol. 5, pp. 309–12.

36 "The address": The Camden Town address is found in UK National Archives, FO 60/11 (70): "Letter from Hajee Baba" (February 11, 1816).

36 "visited Sir John": Shīrāzī (1364/1985), p. 162.

37 "blessed with a daughter": The birth was announced in "Births, Deaths, Marriages and Obituaries," in the *Morning Post* (November 1, 1815).

37 "extensive tour": John William Kaye, *The Life and Correspondence of Major-General Sir John Malcolm, GCB*, 2 vols. (London: Smith, Elder, and Co., 1856), vol. 2, chapter 3.

38 "'in town'": On Jane Austen's visits to London's theaters, see Byrne (2013), pp. 141–46.

38 "Theatre Royal": On Beazley's additions to the Theatre Royal, see David Watkin, *Regency: A Guide and Gazetteer, The Buildings of Britain*, vol. 4 (London: Barrie & Jenkins, 1982), p. 161.

38 "distinguished ancient schools": Shīrāzī (1364/1985), pp. 273–75.

39 "reform schools": Ibid., pp. 287–88.

39 "charity schools": Ibid., p. 206.

39 "still say no": Ibid., p. 163.

40 "advertising their services": Michael H. Fisher, Counterflows *to Colonialism: Indian Travellers and Settlers in Britain, 1600–1858* (Delhi: Permanent Black, 2004), p. 105.

41 "Indian teachers": Michael H. Fisher, "Persian Professor in Britain: Mirza Muhammad Ibrahim at the East India Company's College, 1826–44," *Comparative Studies of South Asia, Africa and the Middle East* 21, 1–2 (2001).

42 "Mir Hasan 'Ali": Ibid., pp. 26–27.

43 "'disgusted with the style'": William Price and Mirza Mohammed Saulih, *A Grammar of the Three Principal Oriental Languages, Hindoostanee, Persian and Arabic to Which Is Added, a Set of Persian Dialogues by Mirza Mohammed Saulih of Shiraz* (London: Kingsbury, Parbury & Allen, 1823), pp. vi–vii.

43 "Mirza Ibrahim": Fisher (2001), p. 28.

43 "collective letter": UK National Archives, FO 60/11 (77), "Persian Students to D'Arcy" (March 18, 1816).

44 "second letter": UK National Archives, FO 60/11 (78), "Persian Students to D'Arcy" (March 20, 1816).

45 "wrote to Edward Cooke": UK National Archives, FO 60/11 (73), "D'Arcy to Cooke" (March 11, 1816).

45 "scrupulous accounts": For example, UK National Archives, FO 60/11 (89), "Annual Stipend for the Five Persians, 1816" (undated, 1816); and UK National Archives, FO 60/11 (102), "Statement of Accounts" (June 10, 1816).

45 "check the expense": UK National Archives, FO 60/11 (99), "William Ouseley to Edward Cooke" (June 26, 1816).

45 "'cannot be in want'": UK National Archives, FO 60/11 (73), "D'Arcy to Cooke" (March 11, 1816).

45 "expenses": UK National Archives, FO 60/11 (102), "Statement of Accounts" (June 10, 1816).

46 "cold mathematics": The comparisons are based on my own calculations from other expenses in the accounts statements cited earlier.

47 "students' activities": UK National Archives, FO 60/12 (285), "Brief Statement of the Circumstances Attending the Persian Officers" (December 8, 1817).

47 "John Shakespear": Shīrāzī (1364/1985), p. 167. Details on the teachers at Addiscombe can be found in Anonymous, *Haileybury College and Addiscombe Military Seminary: A Return of the Number of Writers and Cadets Educated* (London: Published for the House of Commons, 1822); and Henry Meredith Vibart and Frederick Sleigh Roberts, *Addiscombe: Its Heroes and Men of Note* (Westminster, UK: Archibald Constable and Co., 1894).

47 "Mir Hasan 'Ali": Vibart and Roberts (1894), p. 39.

47 "the young John Shakespear": Ibid., p. 40.

47 "oil painting": I am grateful to Teri-Lee Wagstaff of Langley Priory, Derbyshire, for showing me the portrait of John Shakespear kept at his former country seat.

48 "endowment": Julia Thomas, *Shakespeare's Shrine: The Bard's Birthplace and the Invention of Stratford-upon-Avon* (Philadelphia: University of Pennsylvania Press, 2012), p. 62.

49 "enduring dictionaries": John Shakespear, *Dictionary, Hindustani and English* (London: Printed for the author, by Cox and Baylis, and sold by Black, Parbury, and Allen, 1817).

49 "his definition of the adjectival form": Ibid., *s.v.*, "Mirzāʾī."

49 "Shakespear was paid": UK National Archives, FO 60/11 (102), "Statement of Accounts" (June 10, 1816).

50 "golden age": For Croydon's history, I have relied on John Corbet Anderson, *A Short Chronicle Concerning the Parish of Croydon in the County of Surrey* (London: Reeves & Turner, 1882); Robert Bannerman, *Forgotten Croydon* (Croydon: Croydon Times Ltd, 1933); John W. Brown, *Walford's History of Croydon Towns and Suburbs* (London: Local History Reprints, 1993); and William Page, *Recollections of Croydon in the 1820's* (London: Local History Publications, 1998).

50 "stagecoach system": Shīrāzī (1364/1985), pp. 177–78, 277, and on hackney carriages, pp. 293–94.

52 "landlady in Croydon": UK National Archives, FO 60/11 (102), "Statement of Accounts" (June 10, 1816).

52 " 'stately Gothic structure' ": Dr. Garrow (1818), cited in Brown, *Walford's History* (1993), no pagination.

52 "Samuel Pepys Cockerell": Howard Colvin, *A Biographical Dictionary of British Architects, 1600–1840* (New Haven, CT: Yale University Press, 1995), *s.v.* "Cockerell, Samuel Pepys."

53 "Daniells' drawings": Here I have relied on Mildred Archer, *Indian Architecture and the British* (London: Royal Institute of British Architects, 1968), pp. 11–25.

53 "eating habits": Shīrāzī (1364/1985), pp. 309–10, 311–13.

53 "colloquial terms": Stephen Hart, *Cant: A Gentleman's Guide to the Language of Rogues in Georgian London* (Sydney: Improbable Fictions, 2014), p. 31.

54 " the theater ": Shīrāzī (1364/1985), pp. 290–91, 310–11.

54 " 'fine black men' ": Page (1998), p. 17.

55 " 'foreign beret' ": Shīrāzī (1364/1985), p. 170.

55 " 'far from reason' ": Ibid., pp. 169–70.

55 "boot-maker": On these and other shops in Croydon around 1820, see Page (1998), pp. 22–23.

56 " 'Baldwin' or 'Bordwine' ": Shīrāzī (1364/1985), pp. 167–68.

56 "Joseph Bordwine": Vibart and Roberts (1894), p. 39.

56 "at the East India College": Ibid.

56 " 'two gold coins' ": Shīrāzī (1364/1985), p. 168.

56 "John Bisset": Shīrāzī (1364/1985), pp. 169–70. "John Bisset," Papers of Freddie Percy (SM/17/1), Whitgift School Archives, Croydon. I am grateful to William G. Wood, Archivist of the Whitgift School, for providing access to this material.

57 " 'Academy for Gentlemen' ": F.H.G. Percy, *Whitgift School: A History* (Croydon: Whitgift Foundation, 1991), p. 103.

57 "Jane Austen's father": Byrne (2013), p. 20.

57 "supplement to his salary": I draw here on the information in the file "John Bisset," Papers of Freddie Percy (SM/17/1), Whitgift School Archives.

57 " 'a stout, jolly fellow' ": Quoted in Anderson (1882), p. 200.

57 " 'admiring company' ": Quoted in Ronald R. B. Bannerman, *Forgotten Croydon* (Croydon: Croydon Times Press, 1933), p. 45.

59 "fled to Paris": UK National Archives, FO 60/11 (109), "D'Arcy to Thomas Bidwell" (July 23, 1816).

59 "his own money": UK National Archives, FO 60/11 (97), "D'Arcy to Cooke" (July 12, 1816).

60 " 'we know not what to do' ": UK National Archives, FO 60/11 (156), "Persian Gentlemen to Lord Castlereagh" (undated [December 1816?]).

60 " 'I met Murder' ": Percy Shelley, *The Mask of Anarchy (Written on the occasion of the massacre carried out by the British Government at Peterloo, Manchester 1819)*, lines 5–8, 11–12.

61 " 'considerable difficulties' ": UK National Archives, FO 60/11 (13), "Lord Castlereagh to D'Arcy" (November 30, 1816).

61 " 'advance the further sum' ": Ibid.

61 "assign £300": UK National Archives, FO 60/12 (238), "Cooke to D'Arcy" (April 23, 1816); and FO 60/12 (267), "Cooke to Hamilton" (July 14, 1816). Note that the assigned funds took some time after these dates to actually appear.

62 " 'fabricating guns, sabres, etc' ": UK National Archives, FO 60/11, "The Meerzas to Lord Castlereagh" (October [?] 10, 1816).

62 "Muhammad ʿAli": UK National Archives, FO 60/12 (285), "Brief Statement of the Circumstances Attending the Persian Officers" (December 8, 1817).

62 "James Wilkinson": Wilkinson and Son are named in UK National Archives, FO 60/12 (260, 262), "Morier to Lord Castlereagh" (July 22, 1817). On the business address and other details, see Critchett and Woods, *The Post Office Directory for 1819, Including a New Guide to Stage Coaches, Waggons, Carts, Vessels etc, for 1819* (London: T. Maiden, 1819), p. 371.

63 "castellated style": David Watkin, *Regency: A Guide and Gazetteer, The Buildings of Britain*, vol. 4 (London: Barrie & Jenkins, 1982), p. 79.

63 "Mirza Jaʿfar and Mirza Riza": UK National Archives, FO 60/11 (64), "Colonel Mudge to Lord Castlereagh" (undated).

63 " 'Dr. Gregory' ": Ibid.

63 "wrote many works": Olinthus Gregory, *Lessons Astronomical and Philosophical for the Amusement and Instruction of British Youth*, 5th ed. (London: J. Conder, 1815); and idem, *Mathematics for Practical Men* (London, 1825). Gregory dedicated the latter book to the great engineer, Thomas Telford.

64 "*Treatise of Mechanics*": Olinthus Gregory LLD, *A Treatise of Mechanics: Theoretical, Practical and Descriptive*, 3rd ed. in 2 vols. (London: P. C. & J. Rivington et al., 1815).

65 "surveying skills to Iran": On these mapmaking preoccupations, see Firoozeh Kashani-Sabet, *Frontier Fictions: Shaping the Iranian Nation, 1804–1946* (Princeton, NJ: Princeton University Press, 1999).

65 "Sir William Congreve": James Earle, *Commodore Squib: The Life, Times and Secretive Wars of England's First Rocket Man, Sir William Congreve, 1772–1828* (Newcastle, UK: Cambridge Scholars, 2010); and Simon Werrett, "William Congreve's Rational Rockets," *Notes & Records of the Royal Society* 63 (2009).

65 "*Fath al-Mujahidin*": The Persian manuscript (the original of which remains in the British Library) has been printed as Mir Zayn al-ʿAbidin Shushtari, *Fath-ul-Mujahideen: A Treatise on the Rules and Regulations of Tipu Sultan's Army and His Principles of Strategy*, edited by Mahmud Husain (Karachi, Pakistan: Urdu Academy Sind, 1950). On the circumstances of the manuscript's find, see Earle (2010), chapter 5.

66 "assigned to a London surgeon": UK National Archives, FO 60/12 (285), "Brief Statement of the Circumstances Attending the Persian Officers" (December 8, 1817).

66 "George Babington": Babington's qualifications and career are outlined in the *London Medical Gazette* (1834) and in an obituary in *Gentleman's Magazine* 200 (1856).

66 "St. George's": Terry Gould and David Uttley, *A Short History of St. George's Hospital and the Origins of its Ward Names* (London: Athlone Press, 1997), chapter 1.

67 "famous physicians": Ibid., pp. 73–76, 116–20.

67 "John Shaw": UK National Archives, FO 60/13 (211), "Extract from a Letter from John Shaw" (December 1, 1818).

67 "Royal College of Surgeons": Shīrāzī (1364/1985), pp. 284–85.

68 "'an elementary course'": UK National Archives, FO 60/8 (98), "Plan of Education for the Persian Youth" (undated [1813]).

69 "Mirza Sadiq": Hormoz Ebrahimnejad, "La Médecine Française, un choix stratégique de l'Iran Qajar," in N. Pourjavady and Živa Vesel (eds.), *Sciences, techniques et instruments dans le monde Iranien, X–XIX siècle* (Tehran: Presses Universitaires d'Iran, 2004), pp. 287–91; and Denis Wright, *The Persians among the English: Episodes in Anglo-Persian History* (London: I. B. Tauris, 1985), pp. 141–42.

70 "John Garrett": UK National Archives, FO 60/12 (285), "Brief Statement of the Circumstances Attending the Persian Officers" (December 8, 1817); and Shīrāzī (1364/1985), p. 170.

70 "as a lodger": Shīrāzī (1364/1985), pp. 170–71.

70 "imported shawls": On Jane Austen and shawls, I have drawn on Byrne (2013), pp. 29–30.

71 "closest confidants": Shīrāzī (1364/1985), p. 318. On Percy and the CBC, see Michael Port, *Six Hundred New Churches: The Church Building Commission, 1818–1856* (London: Church Historical Society, 1961).

71 "no more classes": Shīrāzī (1364/1985), p. 176.

72 "Robert Abraham": Ibid., pp. 177–92, 350.

72 "buildings of Regent Street": The discussion of Regent Street, directly after his travels with Mr. Abraham, appears in Shīrāzī (1364/1985), p. 193. For a list of Mr. Abraham's major commissions, see Howard Colvin, *A Biographical Dictionary of British Architects* (New Haven, CT: Yale University Press, 1995), pp. 47–48.

72 "Catholic nobleman": Shīrāzī (1364/1985), p. 191.

72 "Iran whose roads": On Iranian attempts to found an efficient postal travel system in the wake of Ambassador Abu'l-Hasan's return from England, see Willem Floor, "The *Chapar-Khāna* System in Qajar Iran," *Iran* 39 (2001), pp. 257–91.

72 "England's roads": Ibid., pp. 177–78, 277, 293–94, 308.

73 "'much of his conversation either'": Ibid., p. 178.

74 "Salisbury's civic assets": Ibid., pp. 178–79.

74 "female relatives": Ibid., pp. 182–85.

74 "the Catholics": Ibid., pp. 190–91.

74 "D'Arcy twice swore": Ibid., p. 192.

74 "Roman conquest": Ibid., p. 194.

75 "common law": Ibid., p. 199.

75 "foundation of Cambridge": Ibid., pp. 199–200.

75 "Austen even owned": Byrne (2013), p. 60.

338 • Notes to Chapter Two

75 "Magna Carta and the Civil War": Shīrāzī (1364/1985), pp. 216–18, 233–35.

76 "champion of liberty": Ibid., pp. 233–34.

76 "North America's history": Ibid., pp. 243–49.

76 "Benjamin Franklin": Ibid., p. 247.

76 "British in India": Ibid., pp. 253–59.

76 "centers of learning": Ibid., pp. 262–306.

77 *Pantologia*: J. M. Good, O. Gregory, and N. Bosworth, assisted by other gentlemen of eminence, *Pantologia: A New (Cabinet) Cyclopædia* (London: G. Kearsley et al., 1813).

77 "writing his *Letters*": Olinthus Gregory, *Letters to a Friend, on the Evidences, Doctrines, and Duties of the Christian Religion*, 9th ed. (London: H. G. Bohn, 1851 [1815]).

78 "'absurdity of Deism'": Ibid., p. 65.

78 "'incomprehensible elements'": Ibid., p. 46; on the uselessness of equations for solving the divine mysteries, see pp. 58–61.

78 "evidence of miracles": Ibid., pp. 129–56.

79 "'at their pleasure'": Olinthus Gregory, *The Works of Robert Hall, MA* (London: Holdsworth & Ball, 1832), p. 298. The sermon (pp. 275–316) was originally preached in London in 1814.

79 "Royal Society and the British Museum": Shīrāzī (1364/1985), pp. 284–90.

80 "Joseph Banks": Ibid., p. 284. While Mirza Salih may have learned of the Royal Society from Dr. Gregory, there also remains the possibility that he learned of Sir Joseph's public audiences through Sir Gore Ouseley, who around this time exchanged letters with Sir Joseph. See "Letter from Sir Joseph Banks to Sir Gore Ouseley" (July 6, 1819), British Library, Add. MSS 35230.63.

80 "lectures were freely given": Shīrāzī (1364/1985), p. 284.

80 "fifty thousand visitors": Ibid., pp. 289–90.

81 "Elgin Marbles": William St. Clair, *Lord Elgin and the Marbles*, rev. ed. (Oxford: Oxford University Press, 1998), chapter 22.

81 "connection and comparison": Shīrāzī (1364/1985), pp. 193–260.

81 "'travels of Captain Cook'": Ibid., p. 290.

82 "preliminary visit": Ibid., p. 319.

82 "journey to Oxford": Ibid., pp. 318-20.

Chapter Two. The *Madrasas* of Oxford

Page

83 "Oxford graduates": M. G. Brock, "The Oxford of Peel and Gladstone, 1800–1833," in M. G. Brock and M. C. Curthoys (eds.), *The History of the University of Oxford*, vol. 7, part 2, *Nineteenth-Century Oxford* (Oxford: Oxford University Press, 2000), p. 9.

83 "clergymen": Byrne (2013), p. 204. For more detail, see Irene Collins, *Jane Austen and the Clergy* (London: Hambledon Press, 2003), chapter 1.

84 "'Master of Arts'": J. G. Lockhart, *Reginald Dalton: A Study of English University Life* (London: Frederick Warne & Co., n.d.[1823]), p. 60.

84 "Oxford undergraduates": For statistics on the social class of Oxford undergraduates in 1810, see L. Stone, "The Size and Composition of the Oxford Student Body, 1580–1909," in Lawrence Stone (ed.), *The University in Society*, 2 vols. (Princeton, NJ: Princeton University Press, 1975), vol. 1, table 2, p. 93.

85 "fancies of men": Josiah Bateman, *Daniel Wilson*, 2 vols. (London: John Murray, 1860), vol. 1, p. 113, cited in Brock (2000), pp. 34–35.

85 "evangelical movement": In writing of "evangelicals," I recognize the social and theological differences between the different movements discussed in subsequent chapters. By certain technical standards, the Anglican and establishment Bible Society and Church Missionary Society were not "Evangelical" (uppercase) in the narrow sense of being direct heirs to Whitefield and the Wesleys. However, for the general reader, the distinction is less pressing, leading me to use the term "evangelical" (lowercase) for the various "conversionist" movements discussed in this book. Here I draw on the broader definition of David W. Bebbington, *Evangelicalism in Modern Britain: A History from the 1730s to the 1980s* (London: Routledge, 1993).

86 "admonished freshmen": John Campbell, *Hints for Oxford* (Oxford: Munday and Slatter, 1823), pp. 17, 38.

86 "'no zeal of enquiry'": Ibid., pp. 63–64.

88 "'branches of my heart'": Mirza Itesa Modeen, *Shigurf Namah i Velaët, Or, Excellent Intelligence Concerning Europe: Being the Travels of Mirza Itesa Modeen in Great Britain and France*, trans. by James Edward Alexander (London: Parbury, Allen & Co., 1827), p. 63. On Iʿtisam al-Din's journey, see also Michael H. Fisher, *Counterflows to Colonialism: Indian Travellers and Settlers in Britain, 1600–1858* (Delhi: Permanent Black, 2004), pp. 86–90.

88 "college libraries": Mirza Itesa Modeen (1827), pp. 66–67.

88 "Thomas Hunt": Ibid., pp. 64, 70.

88 "unacknowledged help": Ibid., pp. 64–66. For further context and case for the Indian teachers' role, see Mohamad Tavakoli-Targhi, "Orientalism's Genesis Amnesia," *Comparative Studies of South Asia, Africa and the Middle East* 16, 1 (1996).

88 "Asiatic Society of Bengal": On the early history of the Asiatic Society of Bengal, and Jones's role within it, see Om Prakash Kejariwal, *The Asiatic Society of Bengal and the Discovery of India's Past, 1784–1838* (Calcutta: Oxford University Press, 1988).

88 "Indian scholar": Mīrzā Abū Tālib Khān, *Masīr-i Tālibī yā Safarnāma-yi Mīrzā Abū Tālib Khān*, ed. Husayn Khadīv-Jam (Tehran: Sāzmān-i Intishārāt va Āmūzish-i Inqilāb-i Islāmī, 1363/1985), translated as Mirza Abu Taleb Khan, *The Travels of Mirza Abu Taleb Khan in Asia, Africa, and Europe*, 2 vols. (London: Longman, Hurst, Rees, Orme & Brown, 1814). For an overview of Abu Talib's career in Britain, see Fisher (2004), pp. 104–9.

89 "traveled to Oxford": "A Chip off the Old Block," [William Bayzand], "Coaching in and out of Oxford from 1820 to 1840 [Ms. Bod. Add. A. 262]," in *Collectanea*, fourth series (Oxford: Clarendon Press, 1905).

89 "'public in general'": Ibid., p. 273.

89 "'mob-cap'": Ibid.

89 "students' story": My translation of the degree ceremony section of the diary is based on Shīrāzī (1364/1985), pp. 321–24.

89 "'Dr Macbride'": The printed edition of Mirza Salih's *safarnama* by Ghulām Muhammad Mīrzā Sālih has the unlikely name of *Mistar Bakrīd* for this figure. By consulting the original manuscript (British Library, Add. 24,034, f. 157v), I have deduced that this must be the editor's palaeographic misreading of "Macbride"

(*Makbrīd*) in the original manuscript via a flattening of the *mim* and a misreading of the location of the dot of *ba.*

90 "'Mr Dunmill'": While it is unclear who this Mr. Dunmill was, he was certainly not the warden of New College in 1818, for the actual warden at the time of his visit was Samuel Gauntlett.

90 "'Mr Pitt'": I have been able to trace two possible contenders in 1818 for the Mr. Pitt in question—namely, Joseph Pitt, a BA of Christ Church College, and Charles Pitt, a Commoner of the same college. See *Oxford University Calendar* (1819), pp. 224–25.

91 "'*bashliq*'": In the clothing of the Caucasus, where Mirza Salih had previously traveled, a *bashliq* is a kind of hood worn attached to an accompanying black cloak, or *burqa.*

91 "'proctors'": On the occasion of Mirza Salih's visit, the two university proctors were B. P. Symons of Wadham College and William Russell of Magdalen College. See *Oxford University Calendar* (1819), p. 42.

92 "'tomfoolery and excess'": For Mirza Salih's account of the pomp and circumstance surrounding the royal burial of Queen Charlotte at Windsor, see Shīrāzī (1364/1985), pp. 340–43.

93 "Austen's brother Charles": Charles Austen's Malaya diaries are summarized and quoted extensively in Hubback and Hubback (1906), chapter 14.

94 "honorary degree": John William Kaye, *The Life and Correspondence of Major-General Sir John Malcolm, GCB*, 2 vols. (London: Smith, Elder, and Co., 1856), vol. 2, p. 141.

95 "Frodsham Hodson": Kaye (1856), vol. 2, p. 141; and *Oxford University Calendar* (1819), p. 11.

95 "grand duke Michael": "University Intelligence," *Oxford University and City Herald* (October 17, 1818). Mirza Salih recorded the English date of the degree ceremony as Thursday, October 13, 1818, but since no such date existed I have assumed that he must have referred to the ceremony described on Friday, October 16, 1818.

95 "Maximillian of Austria": "University Intelligence," *Oxford University and City Herald* (October 17, 1818). Oxford's Star Inn, at which coaches from London arrived, has long since disappeared, though its location was just to the west of the current Cornmarket Street in the center of the city.

95 "degrees were conferred": "University Intelligence," *Oxford University and City Herald* (October 31, 1818). A complete list of everyone examined and given degrees throughout the whole Michaelmas term 1818 is found in the *Oxford University Calendar* (1819), pp. 127–28, with details for the entire academic year of 1818–19 following on pp. 135–44.

96 "'degree'": "Martaba," *s.v., Encyclopaedia of Islam*, 2nd ed.

97 "bestowing gowns": Gail Minault, "The Emperor's Old Clothes: Robing and Sovereignty in Late Mughal and Early British India," in Stewart Gordon (ed.), *Robes of Honour: Khilʿat in Pre-Colonial and Colonial India* (Delhi: Oxford University Press, 2002).

97 "'beau-ideal of a Warden'": Quoted in Robert Sangster Rait and Hastings Rashdall, *New College* (London: F. E. Robinson, 1901), p. 212.

97 "dining at New College": Shīrāzī (1364/1985), pp. 321, 349–50. Mirza Salih named

his host at New College as "Mister Dunmill," though as note earlier the actual warden at the time of his visit was Samuel Gauntlett.

97 "Spanish visitor": Javier Marias, *All Souls* (New York: New Directions Publishing, 2000), particularly pp. 39–49.

97 "'(obsequious) comment'": Ibid., p. 40.

97 "Samuel Gauntlett": Shīrāzī (1364/1985), p. 321. Also Deirdre Le Faye (ed.), *Jane Austen's Letters*, 4th ed. (Oxford: Oxford University Press, 2011), p. 526.

98 "'mince Pies'": James Woodforde, *The Diary of a Country Parson, 1758–1802* (Oxford: Oxford University Press, 1949), pp. 86–87.

98 "'small Beer'": Ibid., p. 98.

100 "linguistic commodity": On the slow expansion of language studies in Oxford and other universities during this period, see Yusef Azad, "The Limits of University: The Study of Language in Some British Universities and Academies, 1750–1800," *History of Universities* 7 (1988); P. J. Marshall, "Oriental Studies," in L. S. Sutherland and L. G. Mitchell (eds.), *The History of the University of Oxford*, vol. 5, *The Eighteenth Century* (Oxford: Oxford University Press, 1986); and Rebecca Posner, "Modern Languages and Linguistics," in Brock and Curthoys (2000).

101 "chair in Arabic": M. Feingold, "Patrons and Professors: The Origins and Motives for the Endowment of University Chairs—in Particular the Laudian Professorship of Arabic," in G. A. Russell (ed.), *The "Arabick" Interest of the Natural Philosophers in Seventeenth-Century England* (Leiden: Brill, 1994); and Lucy Sutherland, "The Origin and Early History of the Lord Almoner's Professorship in Arabic at Oxford," in idem, *Politics and Finance in the Eighteenth Century* (London: Hambledon Press, 1984).

101 "'degrade the Hebrew'": Benjamin Holloway, *The Primævity and Preeminence of the Sacred Hebrew, above all other languages, vindicated from the repeated attempts of the Reverend Dr. Hunt to level it with the Arabic, and other oriental dialects; in a letter to a friend* (Oxford: Printed at the Theatre for S. Parker, and E. Withers, London, 1754), p. 3.

101 "study of Persian": Anonymous [Warren Hastings], *A Proposal for Establishing a Professorship of the Persian Language in the University of Oxford* (Oxford: s.n., 1768), pp. 6–7 (my italics).

102 "'that Language'": Ibid., pp. 10–11.

102 "'native of Persia'": Ibid., pp. 13–15.

102 "sum of £5,000": Byrne (2013), p. 36.

102 "Hastings and Austen families": Byrne (2013), pp. 31–39; and Hubback and Hubback (1906), pp. 260–62.

104 "John Hill": J. S. Reynolds, "Hill, John," in D. M. Lewis (ed.), *The Blackwell Dictionary of Evangelical Biography, 1730–1860*, 2 vols. (Oxford: Blackwell, 1995).

104 "vice principal": *The Oxford University Calendar, 1818* (Oxford: University Press, 1818), p. 262.

104 "home for tea": On Hill's address, see Henry Robinson, "St Alban Hall, Oxford," in Lilian M. Quiller Couch (ed.), *Reminiscences of Oxford by Oxford Men* (Oxford: Clarendon Press, 1892), p. 348.

104 "Oxford's first branch": J. S. Reynolds, "Hill, John."

105 "son of John Macbride": Short accounts of both men are found in the *Oxford Dic-*

tionary of National Biography (Oxford: Oxford University Press, 2004) [henceforth *ODNB*]. I have also consulted the small collection of materials related to Macbride in the Hertford College archive. I am grateful to Dr. Tony Barnard, the college archivist, for providing access to Macbride's papers.

105 "list of subscribers": See the list of subscribers in Sir William Ouseley (ed.), *The Oriental Collections for April, May, June 1797* (London: Oriental Press, 1797), which includes "John Macbride, Esq., Exeter College, Oxford."

105 "Oxford's two endowed positions": On the earlier endowment of Oxford's professorship and readership of Arabic, see Feingold (1994). The Laudian professor at the time of the students' visit was another theologian, Thomas Winstanley, DD, who was also principal of Alban Hall. See *Oxford University Calendar* (1819), p. 53.

105 "he was traveling": Untitled article, *Oxford University and City Herald* (October 31, 1818).

106 "other appointments": *Oxford University Calendar* (1819), pp. 12, 13, 14, 58.

106 "Francis Belfour": Mr. Belfour's membership of the college during Macbride's tenure as principal is stated in *Oxford University Calendar for 1821* (Oxford: University Press, 1821), p. 277.

106 "Magdalen Hall": On the history of Magdalen Hall, see Sidney Graves Hamilton, *Hertford College* (London: F. E. Robinson & Co., 1903).

106 "Oxford Arabism": On Pococke's career, see P. M. Holt, "Edward Pococke (1604–91), the First Laudian Professor of Arabic at Oxford," *Oxoniensia* 56 (1991). On the development of Arabic studies in early modern England more generally, see G. J. Toomer, *Eastern Wisdom and Learning* (Oxford: Oxford University Press, 1996).

106 "member of Magdalen":"Lord, Henry," *s.v.*, in *ODNB*.

107 "letter in his hand": Copy of letter from Dr. John David Macbride, then principal of Magdalen Hall, Oxford, to the undergraduates containing "advice to candidates for ordination" (dated October 16, 1815), Bristol Record Office, Hale Bequest, ref. 14182/HB/C/9.

107 "his leadership": On Macbride's various early offices, see *Oxford University Calendar* (1819). On Magdalen Hall under Macbride, see Hamilton (1903), chapters 6 and 7, and Reynolds (1975), p. 86.

107 "lecture to the undergraduates": John David Macbride, *Lectures Explanatory of the Diatessaron, or the Life of our Lord and Saviour Jesus Christ, Collected from the Four Evangelists* (Oxford: Bartlett and Hinton, 1824), p. iv. Numerous later editions were published.

107 "*Mohammedan Religion*": Reverend John David Macbride, *The Mohammedan Religion Explained: With an Introductory Sketch of Its Progress, and Suggestions for Its Confutation* (London: Seeley, Jackson and Halliday, 1857).

108 "Christian approach to empire": Ibid., pp. i–iii.

108 " 'false religions, fall' ": Ibid., p. ii.

108 " 'disinclination for it' ": Letter to Cassandra Austen (January 24, 1809), no. 45 (66), in Jane Austen, *Selected Letters*, ed. Deirdre Le Faye with Vivien Jones (Oxford: Oxford University Press, 2004), p. 115.

108 "anti-Muslim slander": Macbride (1857), pp. 180–224.

108 "Church Missionary Society": Pileus Quadratus, *Observations on the Defence of the*

Church Missionary Society against the Objections of the Archdeacon of Bath (Oxford: J. Parker, 1818).

109 "major libraries": Shīrāzī (1364/1985), p. 284.

109 "devouring histories": Ibid., p. 346.

109 "reading histories": When, after leaving England, Mirza Salih toured Russia with Ambassador Abu'l-Hasan, he added to the account of his Russian journey an overview of Russia's past that he based on a book he had read during his stay in England, so passing onto Iran a distinctly Anglocentric vision of Russian history. On the visits to Russia of Mirza Salih and other Qajar Iranian travelers and their writings on that country, see Maryam Ekhtyar, "An Encounter with the Russian Czar: The Image of Peter the Great in Early Qajar Historical Writings," *Iranian Studies* 29, 1–2 (1996), especially p. 66.

110 "Persian manuscripts": Abul Hassan Khan (1988), p. 86; Mursilvand (1364/1986), p. 153.

110 " 'little pleasure' ": James Baillie Fraser, *Narrative of the residence of the Persian princes in London, in 1835 and 1836, With an Account of their Journey from Persia, and Subsequent Adventures*, 2 vols., 2nd ed. (London: Richard Bentley, 1838), vol. 1, p. 187.

110 "interest in books": More generally, see Denis Wright, "British Travelers in Qajar Persia and Their Books," in Elton Daniel (ed.), *Society and Culture in Qajar Iran: Studies in Honor of Hafez Farmayan* (Costa Mesa, CA: Mazda, 2002).

110 "purchase the manuscripts": For the contents of Sir Gore's collection, see Anonymous, *Books and Manuscripts from the Library of Sir Gore Ouseley, Orientalist and Diplomat* (Edinburgh: Grant & Shaw Ltd, 1989).

111 "Persian scripts": William Ouseley, *Persian Miscellanies, An Essay to Facilitate the Reading of Persian Manuscripts* (London: printed for Richard White, 1795).

111 "two unique manuscripts": Sir William Ouseley, *Catalogue of Several Hundred Manuscript Works in Various Oriental Languages, Collected by Sir William Ouseley* (London: A. J. Valpy, 1831).

111 "Bodleian's collection": On the earlier development of the Bodleian's oriental collections, see Colin Wakefield, "Arabic Manuscripts in the Bodleian Library: The Seventeenth Century Collections," in Russell (1994).

111 "received a donation": William Dunn Macray, *Annals of the Bodleian Library, Oxford, A.D. 1598–A.D. 1867*, 2nd ed. (Oxford: Oxford University Press, 1890), year entry for 1818.

112 "the manuscripts": Bodleian Library, MS Pers e 93, MS Pers d 116.

113 "other manuscripts": Bodleian Library, MS Pers c 18, MS Pers d 119, MS Pers d 118, MS Pers d 117.

114 "Hajji Baba's possessions": ʿAbbās Iqbāl, "Kitāb-i Ḥājjī Bābā va Dāstān-i Nukhustīn Muhsilīn-i Īrānī dar Farang," *Yādgār* 1, 5 (1944), pp. 33–34.

114 "Cuvier rose to fame": For the best overview of Cuvier's career, see Dorinda Outram, *Georges Cuvier: Vocation, Science, and Authority in Post-Revolutionary France* (Manchester, UK: Manchester University Press, 1984).

114–115 "gift to Hajji Baba in 1815": Georges Cuvier, *Essay on the Theory of the Earth*, trans. Robert Kerr, "with mineralogical notes and an account of Cuvier's geological discoveries by Professor Jameson" (Edinburgh: William Blackwood; London: John

Murray, 1813). The professor of natural history at Edinburgh University from 1803 until his death half a century later, Robert Jameson (1774–1854) was a strong supporter of Cuvier's theories and was later to distance himself from Buckland's scripturalist geology. See "Jameson, Robert," *s.v., ODNB.*

115 "'Sacred History'": Reverend William Buckland, BD FRS MGS, *Vindiciæ Geologicæ; or The Connexion of Geology with Religion Explained, in an Inaugural Lecture delivered before University of Oxford, May 15, 1819, on the Endowment of a Readership in Geology by His Royal Highness the Prince Regent* (Oxford: printed at the University Press for the author, 1820), p. 23.

115 "'natural history'": Ibid., p. 18.

115 "geology—and geologists": Nor, according to Buckland, was the new geological science even a threat to the Oxford curriculum in which Paley's *Natural Theology* played so central a part. Buckland elaborated these assurances for the rest of his career, particularly in his two-volume *Geology and Mineralogy, Considered with Reference to Natural Theology,* in which he used his vast collection of fossils to present scientific evidence for the theological proof by design of God's existence by way of the "design" of fossilized vertebrate animals, vegetables, and mollusks. See Reverend William Buckland, *Geology and Mineralogy, Considered with Reference to Natural Theology,* 2 vols. (London: William Pickering, 1836).

115 "intellectual discretion": For overviews of Buckland's career, I have relied on "Buckland, William," *s.v., ODNB*; and Mrs. [Elizabeth Oke] Gordon, *The Life and Correspondence of William Buckland, D.D., F.R.S., sometime Dean of Westminster, Twice President of the Geological Society, and First President of the British Association* (London: John Murray, 1894). Unfortunately, the latter text contains no reference to Buckland's meeting with Hajji Baba. Certain oriental interests may be surmised from the existence of Ouseley's *Asiatic Researches* in Buckland's library. See J. C. Stevens (auctioneer), *A Catalogue of the Valuable Scientific Library of the Late Very Rev. Dr. Buckland, Dean of Westminster . . . Which will be Sold by Auction, by Mr. J.C. Stevens, at his Great Room, 38, King Street, Covent Garden, on Monday, the 26th Day of January 1857* ([London]: Alfred Robins, n.d. [1857]), item no. 206. Although Buckland never traveled to Asia himself, he later wrote a commentary on fossils brought back from John Crawfurd's 1826–27 military expedition to Burma, in which he referred to studies on Indian geology by the oriental scholars Colebrooke and Fraser. See John Crawfurd, *Journal of an Embassy from the Governor-General of India to the Court of Ava . . . 1827, with an Appendix by Prof. Buckland and Mr. Clift* (London: Henry Colburn, 1829), appendix xiii, pp. 78–88.

116 "advertisements": Shīrāzī (1364/1985), p. 278.

117 "oriental rugs": *Oxford University and City Herald,* October 10, 1818.

118 "'place like paradise'": Shīrāzī (1364/1985), p. 324.

118 "its heyday": Anonymous, *The Oxford Botanic Garden* (Oxford: Basil Blackwell, 1957), pp. 5–7.

118 "George Williams": Charles Daubeny, *Oxford Botanic Garden; or, A Popular Guide to the Botanic Garden of Oxford,* 2nd ed. (Oxford: n.p. , 1853), pp. 9–10. Daubeny was Williams's more energetic professorial successor, who was responsible for changing the garden's official name to the Botanic (rather than Physic) Garden and for rebuilding its greenhouses and importing a greatly increased number of trees from India, America, and China.

118 "seven thousand species": Anonymous (1957), p. 7.

118 "Charles Dubois": Daubeny (1853), p. 58. In total, Dubois's *Herbarium* contained approximately 13,000 specimens. It was supplanted by the later *East Indian Herbarium* presented by Dr. Wallich.

119 "Abraham's sister": On the meeting with Abraham's sister, see Shīrāzī (1364/1985), pp. 184–85.

119 "Mr. Garrett": Ibid., pp. 170–71.

119 "Sir Joseph": Shīrāzī (1364/1985), p. 284; and UK National Archives, FO 60/13 (175 & 177), "Sir Joseph Banks to Lord Castlereagh" (April 8, 1818).

119 "garden squares": Shīrāzī (1364/1985), p. 285.

119 "oriental trees": On the planting dates of the trees, see Anonymous (1957), pp. 12–13, 18–19. The species mentioned are the *morus alba*, *sophora japonica*, and *picea smithiana*, respectively.

120 "death in Isfahan": On Aucher-Eloy, see Daubeny (1853), pp. 6, 19.

120 "*chahar-bagh*": On gardens in Persian poetry, see Dominic Brookshaw, "Palaces, Pavillions and Pleasure-Gardens: The Context and Setting of the Medieval Majlis," *Middle Eastern Literatures* 6, 2 (2003); and Julie Scott Meisami, "Allegorical Gardens in the Persian Poetic Tradition: Nezami, Rumi, Hafez," *International Journal of Middle East Studies* 17, 2 (1985).

120 " 'for Pleasure made' ": *Vertnumaus, an Epistle to Mr. Jacob Bobart* (1713), reprinted in Anonymous (1957), p. 2. Jacob Bobart was the garden's first keeper and in 1648 was responsible for publishing the first catalogue of its plants.

120 "horticultural plunder": Adrian P. Thomas, "The Establishment of Calcutta Botanic Garden: Plant Transfer, Science and the East India Company, 1786–1806," *Journal of the Royal Asiatic Society* 16, 2 (2006).

120 " 'vegetables and melons' ": John Gurney, "Legations and Gardens and Their Subalterns," *Iran* 40 (2002), p. 204.

121 "medical writings": However, on early modern Indo-Islamic pharmacological writings, see A. A. Husain, *Scent in the Islamic Garden: A Study of Deccani Urdu Literary Sources* (Karachi: Oxford University Press, 2000).

122 "tours he made": For the factory visits and description of industries, see Shīrāzī (1364/1985), pp. 178, 308, 330–31, and 333–35..

122 "paper mills": For the list of village paper mills, see Harry Carter, *Wolvercote Mill: A Study in Paper-making at Oxford* (Oxford: Printed for the Society at the University Press, 1957), appendix IV.

123 "Charles Venables": Shīrāzī (1364/1985), p. 324. On the village, see "Hampton Gay," in *The History of the County of Oxford* (Oxford: Oxford University Press, 1959), vol. 6, pp. 56–71; and Ianto Wain, "Hampton Gay, Deserted Medieval Village," *South Midlands Archaeology* 30 (2000).

124 "water wheel": On the preparation of paper for printing during the early nineteenth century, see Richard-Gabriel Rummonds, *Nineteenth-Century Printing Practices and the Iron Handpress, with Selected Readings*, 2 vols. (London: British Library, 2004), vol.1, pp. 447–82.

124 "source of employment": Hampton Gay parish registers (transcribed and typed by Brigadier F.R.L. Goadby, 1975), copies lodged with the Diocean archivist, Bodleian Library, and the churchwarden, Hampton Gay.

124 "medieval mill": Frances Wakeman, *Notes towards an Account of Paper Mills in*

Oxfordshire (Kidlington, UK: Plough Press, 1991), n.p. On English paper mills more generally, which were always relatively few given the competition of the cheaper imported paper produced in the mills of northern France, see Alfred H. Shorter, *Paper Mills in England* (London: Society for the Protection of Ancient Buildings, 1966). On the industrialization during this period of the paper mills in the splendidly named Lancashire twin villages of Nob End and Little Lever, see Denis Lyddon and Peter Marshall, *Paper in Bolton: A Papermaker's Tale* (Altrincham, UK: Trinity Paper Mills Ltd, 1975), pp. 75–102.

124 "other paper mills": For the list of village paper mills in 1816, see Harry Carter (1957), appendix IV. On Oxfordshire's paper mills, see also A. H. Shorter (1957), pp. 225–27.

124 "steam engine": Carter (1957), p. 6.

125 "Charles Venables": Documents on Venables's later papermaking ventures are preserved in the Centre for Buckinghamshire Studies, Aylesbury, Taplow Paper Mills files, D-GR/17/1.

125 "'and whipped'": *Some Selected Reports from The Windsor and Eton Express 20th October 1827.* http://freepages.genealogy.rootsweb.ancestry.com/~dutillieul/ZWind sorEtonExpress/20thOctober1827B.html (accessed June 2009).

125 "married his wife": Hampton Gay parish registers, "Marriages."

125 "aforementioned George": He died in 1906 and was buried back in Hampton Gay, the village of his birth.

125 "Fourdrinier machine": Wakeman (1991), n.p. A list of the machinery of the mill as it survived some thirty years after Mirza Salih's visit is found in *Auction Catalogue of the Estate and Paper Mill, 13th July 1849* (copy held at the Bodleian Library, Oxford).

126 "twenty Fourdrinier machines": On the impact of the machine in Britain, see Richard L. Hills, *Papermaking in Britain 1488–1988: A Short History* (London: Athlone Press, 1988), while on the technical aspects of the machine's workings, see R. H. Clapperton, *The Paper-Making Machine: Its Invention, Evolution and Development* (Oxford: Pergamum Press, 1967); and G. H. Nuttall, *The Theory and Operation of the Fourdrinier Paper Machine* (London: Phillips, 1967).

126 "Amin al-Zarb": Shireen Mahdavi, *For God, Mammon and Country: A Nineteenth Century Persian Merchant* (Boulder, CO: Westview Press, 1999), pp. 48–51. For an Anglocentric perspective on the diffusion of nineteenth-century British technology to the Middle East and elsewhere, see R. A. Buchanan, "The Diaspora of British Engineering," *Technology and Culture* 27, 3 (1986), especially pp. 513–18.

126 "artisans in Iran": On this traditional process, see L.-J. Olmer, "Rapport sur une mission scientifique en Perse," *Nouvelles archives des missions scientifiques et litteraires* 16 (1908), pp. 104–6 (cited in Floor, "Paper and Paper-Making").

127 "Swann brothers": Wakeman (1991), n.p. John and James Swann were in fact the earliest licensees of the Fourdrinier patent.

127 "750,000 Bibles": Carter (1957), p. 35.

127 "Oxford's Bibles": D. N. Griffiths, "Prayer-Book Translations in the Nineteenth Century," *The Library*, 6th series, 6, 1 (1984).

128 "'Greek College'": E. D. Tappe, "The Greek College at Oxford, 1699–1705," *Oxoniensia* 19 (1954).

Chapter Three. Among the Dissenters

Page

133 "'Isis' coach": On the coach route, see "A Chip off the Old Block" [William Bayzand], "Coaching in and out of Oxford from 1820 to 1840 [Ms. Bod. Add. A. 262]," in *Collectanea*, fourth series (Oxford: Clarendon Press, 1905), p. 272. Unfortunately, the Plough Hotel was demolished to build a shopping center in the early 1980s. An etching of the building—a classic Regency coaching inn—as it appeared in the early 1820s can be found in Samuel Young Griffith, *New Historical Description of Cheltenham and Its Vicinity* (London: Longman, Rees, Orme, Brown & Green, 1826).

133 "night in an inn": Mīrzā Sālih Shīrāzī, *Majmūʿa-yi Safarnāmahā-yi Mīrzā Sālih Shīrāzī*, ed. Ghulām Husayn Mīrzā Sālih (Tehran: Nashr-i Tārīkh-i Īrān, 1364/1985), p. 328.

134 "final illness": Byrne (2013), p. 120.

134 "James Morier": For the fullest account of Morier's career, see Henry McKenzie Johnston, *Ottoman and Persian Odysseys: James Morier, Creator of Hajji Baba* (London: I. B. Tauris, 1998).

134 "accompanied Ambassador Abu'l-Hasan": Ibid., p. 128.

134 "Hajji Baba": On the debate over the "real" Hajji Baba's identity, see Abbas Amanat, "Hajji Baba of Ispahan," *Encyclopaedia Iranica*; and Henry McKenzie Johnston, "Hajji Baba and Mirza Abul Hasan Khan: A Conundrum," *Iran* 33 (1995).

134 "their tour": For the sake of exposition, I have slightly modified the sequence of their itinerary. Mirza Salih and Mirza Jaʿfar actually visited Bath after Bristol and again, as noted in the following, later in "the season."

135 "'so fine a city'": Shīrāzī (1364/1985), p. 337.

135 "'view of Bath'": See Jane Austen's letter no. 35 (May 5, 1801) to Cassandra Austen in Chapman (1932), vol. 1, p. 123.

135 "city's shallowness": Keiko Parker "'What Part of Bath Do You Think They Will Settle In?' Jane Austen's Use of Bath in *Persuasion*," *Persuasions: The Jane Austen Journal* 23 (2001).

135 "Grand Pump Room": Shīrāzī (1364/1985), p. 329.

135 "famous Royal Crescent": Ibid., p. 336.

136 "newspaper report recounts": "The Persian Princes," *The Times* (December 7, 1818), p. 3. Mirza Salih also made a second visit to Bath in November 1818, and it is may be this later visit that is described in the report. However, I have placed the account here for the sake of continuity. For this later visit, see Shīrāzī (1364/1985), pp. 337–39.

136 "Sir George": "Gibbes, Sir George Smith," *s.v.*, *ODNB*. He did not receive his knighthood until 1820.

136 "seeing them strolling": The anecdote appears as a footnote by Fellowes in revised versions of his original edition of the letters of his friend, Hester Piozzi. See Hester L. S. Thrale Piozzi, *Autobiography, Letters and Literary Remains of Mrs. Piozzi (Thrale)*, 2 vols. (London: Longman, Green, Longman & Roberts, 1861), vol. 2, p. 415.

136 "'any old pelisse'": Jane Austen, *The Annotated Persuasion*, ed. David M. Shapard (New York: Random House, 2012), p. 124, with an image of a pelisse on p. 121.

137 "'European manners'": Piozzi (1861), vol. 2, p. 415.

137 "'distinguished personages'": *Gloucester Herald* (November 21, 1818; reprinted in *Morning Chronicle*, November 24, 1818).

138 "pottery and cloth manufactory": Shīrāzī (1364/1985), pp. 183–84.

138 "'iron road'": Ibid., p. 329.

139 "early witnesses": Strictly speaking, by the late nineteenth century a short railroad was carrying small numbers of passengers between Tehran and the suburban shrine of ʿAbd al-ʿAzim. However, it was not until the 1930s that Iran truly developed a rail system.

139 "cloth mills": On the road and Nailsworth mills, see Albion Urdank, *Religion and Society in a Cotswold Vale: Nailsworth, Gloucestershire, 1780–1865* (Berkeley: University of California Press, 1990), pp. 43, 170–207.

139 "mechanized": Julia de Lacey Mann, *The Cloth Industry in the West of England from 1640 to 1880* (Oxford: Clarendon Press, 1971), pp. 134–35; and Betty Mills, *A Portrait of Nailsworth* (Nailsworth, UK: B. A. Hathaway, n.d.), pp. 13–14.

139 "steam-powered wheels": Shīrāzī (1364/1985), pp. 330–31, 334–35.

139 "spent five hours": Ibid., p. 330.

139 "Ditherington flax mill": David Watkin, *Regency: A Guide and Gazetteer, The Buildings of Britain*, vol. 4 (London: Barrie & Jenkins, 1982), p. 112.

140 "industrial strikes": Mann (1971), pp. 152, 156–57.

140 "Indo-Persian travelers": Mirza Itesa Modeen, *Shigurf Namah i Velaët, Or, Excellent Intelligence Concerning Europe* (London: Parbury, Allen & Co., 1827); see pp. 95–120 for the generalizing account of English religion. Abu Talib showed even less interest in English religiosity: see Mirza Abu Taleb Khan, *The Travels of Mirza Abu Taleb Khan in Asia, Africa, and Europe*, 2 vols. (London: Longman, Hurst, Rees, Orme & Brown, 1814). For an overview of these prior travelers' descriptions of religious life in England, see Gulfishan Khan, *Indian Muslim Perceptions of the West during the Eighteenth Century* (Karachi: Oxford University Press, 1998), chapter 4.

140 "quickly bored": McKenzie Johnston (1998), p. 128.

141 "Dissent had long flourished": Urdank (1990)

141 "Protestant refugees": Shīrāzī (1364/1985), pp. 262–69.

141 "Catholics": Ibid., pp. 190–91.

141 "Catholics and Protestants": Ibid., p. 269.

141 "statues intact": Ibid.

141 "'Methodists'": Ibid., p. 329.

141 "Miss Bleechley": I have been unable to trace any record of this woman (or persons with similar names) in the Methodist Archives and Research Centre at Manchester University. I am, however, grateful to Dr. Peter Nockles for assistance.

142 "gossiping and laughing": Shīrāzī (1364/1985), p. 329.

142 "'its pious use'": *Gloucester Herald*, November 21, 1818.

143 "Bishop Ryder": Grayson Carter, *Anglican Evangelicals: Protestant Secessions from the Via Media, c. 1800–1850* (Oxford: Oxford University Press, 2001), p. 143.

143 "short and mean": Shīrāzī (1364/1985), pp. 329–30. For Mirza Salih's description of Gloucester itself, see pp. 330–31.

143 "private cells": Ibid.

143 "new prisons": On the new prison buildings of the period, see Watkin (1982), pp. 87–88.

143 "these factories": *Gloucester Herald*, November 21, 1818; Shīrāzī (1364/1985), pp. 330–31. On Gloucester's mills in this period, see Mann (1971), especially pp. 244, 301–5 on the Davis family.

144 "Levant Company": Mann (1971), p. 41; Shīrāzī (1364/1985), p. 167.

144 "Anglican polemicist": The exchanges were reprinted with a commentary in Theophilus Browne MA, *Religious Liberty and the Rights of Conscience and Private Judgement Grossly Violated* (Gloucester, UK: T. Critchley, 1819).

144 "stirred further controversy": For the Gloucestershire debate on secession, and the role of Mirza Salih's acquaintances Ryder and Hannah More in it, see Carter (2001), pp. 105–51.

144 "bottle and crystal factories": Shīrāzī (1364/1985), p. 331.

145 "Barley Wood": Ibid.

145 "John Loudon McAdam": On the Bristol turnpike trust, see Anthony Ridley, "Other Means of Communication," in Brian Bracegirdle (ed.), *The Archaeology of the Industrial Revolution* (London: Heinemann, 1973), pp. 71–72.

145 "interesting Englishwoman": For other Muslim accounts of British women in this period, see Michael H. Fisher, "Representing 'His' Women: Mirza Abu Talib Khan's 1801 'Vindication of the Liberties of Asiatic Women,'" *Indian Economic and Social History Review* 37, 2 (2000); and Mohammad Tavakoli-Targhi, "Eroticizing Europe," in Daniel (2002).

145 "Mendip Schools": Arthur Roberts, *The Mendip Annals, or a Narrative of the Charitable Labours of Hannah and Martha More* (London: James Nesbet, 1859).

145 "no fewer than 114": Patricia Demers, *The World of Hannah More* (Lexington: University Press of Kentucky, 1996), p. 109. On other female religious leaders in this period, see Deborah M. Valenze, *Prophetic Sons and Daughters: Female Preaching and Popular Religion in Industrial England* (Princeton, NJ: Princeton University Press, 1985).

146 "'I dislike it.'": Letter to Cassandra Austen (January 24, 1809), no. 45 (66), in Jane Austen, *Selected Letters*, ed. Deirdre Le Faye with Vivien Jones (Oxford: Oxford University Press, 2004), p. 115.

146 "Christian education": Jeremy and Margaret Collingwood, *Hannah More* (Oxford: Lion Publishing, 1990), p. 99.

147 "quiet cottage door": On the poets and other famous visitors to Hannah More, see Collingwood (1990), p. 137.

147 "'odiferous herbs'": Shīrāzī (1364/1985), p. 331.

147 "'large library'": Ibid., p. 332.

147 "she wrote her name": Ibid., p. 332.

148 *"Practical Piety"*: Ibid.

148 "'decided assent'": William Roberts, *Memoirs of the Life of Hannah More*, 2 vols. (London: R. B. Seeley & W. Burnside, 1836), pp. 246–47.

148 "no Persian translation": However, printed translations of English technical works did follow in the wake of the students' return to Iran. See Iraj Afshar, "Book Translations as a Cultural Activity in Iran, 1806–1896," *Iran* 41 (2003).

149 "ten editions": Rev. James Skinner, *Hannah More: Christian Philanthropist; A Centenary Biography* (London: Thynne & Co. Ltd, 1934), p. 96.

149 "social activism": Hannah More, *Practical Piety*, 2 vols., 3rd ed. (London: T. Cadell

and W. Davies, 1811); see in particular chapter 2, "Christianity: A Practical Principle."

149 "'direct the creed'": Ibid., vol.1, pp. 28–29.

150 "'Christian principles'": Ibid., vol.1, p. 40.

150 "'this-worldly' religiosity": Francis Robinson, "Other-Worldly and This-Worldly Islam and the Islamic Revival," *Journal of the Royal Asiatic Society* 14, 1 (2004).

150 "medical missions": On medical missions, see Shireen Mahdavi, "Shahs, Doctors, Diplomats and Missionaries in 19th Century Iran," *British Journal of Middle Eastern Studies* 32, 2 (2005).

151 "'practical moral duties'": "The Persian Princes," *The Times* (December 7, 1818), p. 3.

151 "'of ethics'": Ibid.

151 "William Paley": On Paley's career, see the extensive entry "Paley, William," in *ODNB*.

151 "same time as orientalists": Tavakoli-Targhi (2001), chapter 3.

152 "divine watchmaker": William Paley, *Natural Theology* (Oxford: Oxford University Press, 2006); the famous watchmaker analogy is on pp. 7–10.

152 "emerged from the Enlightenment": Here I have in mind the post-Eurocentric approach to the Enlightenment outlined in Sebastian Conrad, "Enlightenment in Global History: A Historiographical Critique," *American Historical Review* 117, 4 (2012).

152 "scriptural authority": Olinthus Gregory, *Letters to a Friend, on the Evidences, Doctrines, and Duties of the Christian Religion*, 9th ed. (London: H. G. Bohn, 1851 [1815]).

154 "'God's providence'": Quoted in Johnston (1998), chapter 16.

154 "spent five days": Shīrāzī (1364/1985), pp. 332–35.

154–55 "slave trade": On Bristol and slavery, see Madge Dresser, *Slavery Obscured: The Social History of the Slave Trade in an English Provincial* Port (London: Continuum, 2001); see especially pp. 195–200 on Mirza Salih's period.

155 "'trade and manufactures'": *Mathews's Bristol Guide; being a Complete Ancient and Modern History of the City of Bristol, the Hotwells and Clifton; Including a Description of the Interesting Curiosities of their Vicinity; Fifth Edition, Revised and Carefully Corrected to the Present Time* (Bristol: Printed and sold by Joseph Mathews, and sold by the booksellers, 1819), p. 87. For an argument on the early emergence of industrial modernity in the rural West Country, see David Rollison, *The Local Origins of Modern Society: Gloucestershire 1500–1800* (London: Routledge, 1992).

155 "Mr. Harford": Shīrāzī (1364/1985), p. 333. On the interior design of other houses Mirza Salih visited, see pp. 313–15. This Mr. Harford cannot have been the diplomat and former envoy extraordinary to Iran, Sir Harford Jones Brydges (1764–1847), since his family connections and residence were in Radnorshire in Wales and not Bristol.

155 "Harford family": On the family, see Alice Harford (ed.), *Annals of the Harford Family* (London: Westminster Press, 1909). On the Harfords' earlier slave trading associations and the ties between "gentility and slavery" in Bristol, see Dresser (2001), pp. 96–128, especially 99–100, 132.

155 "social transformation": "Harford Family," *s.v.*, *ODNB*.

155 "Harford's own manufactory": *Mathews's Bristol Guide* (1819), p. 89.

155 "'even India'": Shīrāzī (1364/1985), p. 331.

156 "supplier of soaps": *Mathews's Bristol Guide* (1819), pp. 90, 91.

156 "spectacle of glass-blowing": *Mathews's Bristol Guide* (1819), pp. 91–92; Shīrāzī (1364/1985), pp. 333–34. On glass as a cultural spectacle, see Isobel Armstrong, *Victorian Glassworlds: Glass Culture and the Imagination, 1830–1880* (Oxford: Oxford University Press, 2008).

156 " 'Persian princes' ": This article was reprinted in *The Times* (December 7, 1818), p. 3.

156 " 'true charity' ": Ibid.

156 "medical fees of Louisa": On More's years of covering Louisa's expenses, see Collingwood (1990), pp. 65–66. On evangelicals, Dissenters, and emancipation in Bristol, see Dresser (2001), pp. 130–42.

156 "Infirmary": *Mathews's Bristol Guide* (1819), p. 161.

157 " 'own maintenance' ": Ibid., p. 162.

157 "basket maker": Shīrāzī (1364/1985), p. 334.

157 "coarse baskets": *Mathews's Bristol Guide* (1819), p. 162. On the many other charitable foundations in Bristol at this time, including dispensaries, alms houses, and girls' orphanages, see ibid., pp. 155–65.

157 "Dissenters": Jonathan Barry and Kenneth Morgan (eds.), *Reformation and Revival in Eighteenth-Century Bristol* (Bristol, UK: Bristol Record Society, 1994).

157 "no need for sails": Shīrāzī (1364/1985), pp. 334–35.

158 "Horton's bold idea": "*Vulcan*," s.v., in I.C.B. Dear and Peter Kemp (eds.), *The Oxford Companion to Ships and the Sea*, 2nd ed. (Oxford: Oxford University Press, 2005); and John Grantham, *Iron Ship-Building* (London: J. Weale, 1858), p. 7.

158 "Aaron Manby": W. H. Chaloner and W. O. Henderson, "Aaron Manby, Builder of the First Iron Steamship," *Transactions of the Newcomen Society* 29 (1953–55); and "*Aaron Manby*," s.v., in Dear and Kemp (2005).

159 "Unitarian and Quaker families": Shīrāzī (1364/1985), pp. 333–34, mentioning meetings and factory visits with the (former?) Quaker industrialist Mr. Harford and the Unitarian Reverends John Rowe and Lant Carpenter.

160 "Unitarian *kalisa*": Shīrāzī (1364/1985), pp. 332–33.

160 "Unitarian minister": "Rowe, John," s.v., *ODNB*.

160 "Lewin's Mead Chapel": On the chapel in the eighteenth and nineteenth centuries, see O. M. Griffiths, "Side Lights on the History of Presbyterian-Unitarianism from the Records of Lewin's Mead Chapel, Bristol," *Transactions of the Unitarian Historical Society* 6, 2 (1936).

160 "Unitarian Relief Act": Ibid., p. 117.

160 " 'principal public buildings' ": *Mathews's Bristol Guide* (1819), p. 146.

161 " 'frenzy and barbarism' ": John Rowe, *A Letter from an Old Unitarian to a Young Calvinist* (Bristol, UK: John Evans & Co., 1816), p. 22.

161 " 'guide to happiness' ": Ibid., p. 23. In the year of Mirza Salih's Bristol fieldwork, this critique of Islam as "superstition" rather than "true religion" also featured in "On the General Prevalence of Superstition," *The Monthly Repository of Theology and General Literature*, vol. 13 (1818), pp. 313–14.

161 "John Rowe": John Rowe, *Scripture and Reason the Only Test of Christian Truth, a Sermon* (London: n.p., 1817). Details on Rowe's career are also found in the records of the Lewin's Mead Unitarian Congregation, Bristol Record Office, Bristol and in his obituary, which appeared in the first edition of the Unitarian magazine, *Christian Reformer, or, Unitarian Magazine and Review* 1 (1834).

161 "Lant Carpenter": Shīrāzī (1364/1985), p. 334. In the edition of Mirza Salih's diary prepared by Humāyūn Shahīdī (ed.), *Guzārish-i Safar-i Mīrzā Sālih Shīrāzī (Kāzarūnī)* (Tehran: Rāh-i Naw, 1362/1983, pp. 350–51), the name Carpenter (*karpintar*) is variously mistranscribed from the manuscript as *karinstar* and *karpinaz.*

162 "Champion's Brass Works": Griffiths (1936), p. 120.

162 "new critical spirit": See Lant Carpenter's early work, *Discourses on the Genuineness, Integrity, and Public Version of the New Testament* (Exeter, UK: P. Hedgeland, 1809), in which he concluded his vindication of the Gospels' genuineness with a long quotation from Paley (pp. 18–19).

163 "to be worshipped": Lant Carpenter, *Proof from Scripture that God, even the Father, Is the Only True God, and the Only Proper Object of Religious Worship* (Exeter, UK: R. Cullum, 1812), pp. 1–2, which cites John xvii: 3 as the basis of its evidence and continues its anti-Trinitarian theme throughout the following pages. On the faithfulness of the Unitarians to "original" apostolic Christianity, see Lant Carpenter, *The Primitive Christian Faith: A Discourse delivered in the Evening Service at the opening of the Chapel in York Street, St James's Square, London, December the 19th, 1824* (London: Rowland Hunter, 1825).

164 "Carpenter may have presented": Shīrāzī (1364/1985), p. 334.

164 " 'backward here' ": Russell Lant Carpenter (ed.), *Memoirs of the Life of the Rev. Lant Carpenter, LLD, with Selections from his Correspondence* (Bristol, UK: Philip and Evans, 1842), p. 243.

165 " 'acquired permanency' ": Ibid., p. 244.

166 " 'corruption of the Gospel' ": Ibid.

166 "Joseph Hunter": On Hunter's career, see Peter B. Godfrey, "Joseph Hunter, 1783–1861," *Transactions of the Unitarian Historical Society* 18, 2 (1984).

166 " 'rational views' ": Godfrey (1984), p. 20; and Joseph Hunter, *A Tribute to the Memory of the Rev. John Simpson, contained in a Sermon delivered at the Unitarian Chapel in Bath, on Sunday August 29th, 1813* (Bath, UK: Richard Cruttwell, n.d. [1813]), pp. 9, 34. On Carpenter's moderate liberalism, his condemning of the Peterloo Massacre of 1819, and his support of parliamentary reform, see "Carpenter, Lant," *s.v.*, *ODNB.*

167 "emotive sermons": Alex Kolaczkowski, "Jerom Murch and Unitarianism in Bath, 1833–45," *Transactions of the Unitarian Historical Society* 21, 1 (1995), p. 19. On the dilemmas of high-brow preaching style of Hunter's Unitarian contemporaries, see David L. Wykes, " 'A Good Discourse, Well Explained in 35 Minutes': Unitarians and Preaching in the Early Nineteenth Century," *Transactions of the Unitarian Historical Society* 21, 3 (1997). One local consequence of this was the huge rise in popular support for evangelicalism in Bath. See P. T. Philips, "The Religious Side of Victorian Bath, 1830–1870," *Social History* 6 (1973).

167 " 'free inquiry' ": W. J. Fox, *A Sermon on Free Inquiry in Matters of Religion* (London: R. Hunter and D. Eaton, 1815), p. 23.

167 " 'most liberal' ": Ibid., pp. 21–22.

167 "praised Bath's contribution": Reverend Joseph Hunter, *The Connection of Bath with the Literature and Science of England* (Bath, UK: R. E. Peach, 1853), especially pp. 45–50. On Mirza Salih's meeting with Herschel, see Shīrāzī (1364/1985), pp. 340–44.

168 "rejection of the Trinity": Joseph Hunter, *The Deist, the Christian, the Unitarian: A*

Sermon delivered at the Chapel in Trim-Street, Bath, on Sunday November 28th, 1819 (Bath, UK: Richard Cruttwell, 1819), pp. 21–22.

168 "Bath sermon of 1819": Hunter (1819), p. 15. On the slightly later fortunes of the Trim-Street chapel, see Kolaczkowski (1995), especially pp. 18–21.

168 "'priest,' or *kashish*": Shīrāzī (1364/1985), p. 336.

170 "lodge in Calcutta": Walter Kelly Firminger, *The Early History of Freemasonry in Bengal and the Punjab* (Calcutta: Thacker, Spink and Co., 1906), pp. 5–6.

170 "1758 and 1793": Ibid., pp. 6–7.

170 "eight lodges": Ibid., p. 198.

170 "by no means unknown": Hamid Algar, "An Introduction to the History of Free-masonry in Iran," *Middle Eastern Studies* 6 (1970); and idem, "Freemasonry ii: In the Qājār Period," *s.v., Encyclopaedia Iranica.*

171 "'frequently urged'": Abu Taleb Khan, *The Travels of Mirza Abu Taleb Khan in Asia, Africa, and Europe during the Years 1799, 1800, 1801, 1802, and 1803,* 2 vols. (Broxbown: R. Watts, 1810), vol. 1, p. 193.

171 "'alter his faith'": Ibid.

171 "first Iranian Freemason": Algar (1970), p. 266; and Iradj Amini, "Askar Khan Af-shar, Fath Ali Shah's Ambassador in Paris," *Qajar Studies* 7 (2007), pp. 58–59.

171 "Freemason in England": Mirza Abul Hassan Khan, *A Persian at the Court of King George, 1809–10* (London: Barrie & Jenkins, 1988), pp. 17, 265; and Harry Carr, "The Foundation of the Grand Lodge of Iran," *Ars Quatuor Coronatorum: Transactions of the Research Lodge* 81 (1968).

171 "'mysteries from him'": Abul Hassan Khan (1988), p. 38; and Mursilvand (1364/1986), p. 130.

171 "rationalists and cosmopolitans": Margaret C. Jacob, *The Radical Enlightenment: Pantheists, Freemasons and Republicans* (London: George Allen & Unwin, 1981), es-pecially pp. 215–55 on "pantheistic religion."

172 "Yusuf Aqa Effendi": Personal communication, Diane Clements, director, Library and Museum of Freemasonry, Freemasons' Hall, London (September 19, 2007). Their initiation is also mentioned in Abu Taleb Khan (1810), vol. 1, p. 194. On that embassy, see Mehmet Alaaddin Yalçinkaya, "Mahmud Raif Efendi as the Chief Sec-retary of Yusug [*sic*] Agah Efendi, the First Permanent Ottoman Turkish Ambas-sador to London (1793–1797)," *Ankara Üniversitesi Osmanlı Tarihi Araştırma ve Uygulama Dergisi* 5 (1994).

172 "'magic house'": Zahīr al-Dīn Munshī, *Ifshā'ī-yi Asrār-i Frīmishan* (Lucknow, India: Nawal Kishawr, 1299/1882). For a general history of Freemasonry in India, see G. S. Gupta (ed.), *Freemasonic Movement in India* (Delhi: Indian Masonic Publi-cations, n.d. [1981]).

172 "Sufi brotherhoods": Matthijs van den Bos, *Mystic Regimes: Sufism and the State in Iran, from the Late Qajar Era to the Islamic Republic* (Leiden: Brill, 2002), pp. 123–24; and Thierry Zarcone, *Mystiques, philosophes, et francs-maçons en Islam: Riza Tevfik, penseur Ottoman (1868–1949), du soufisme à la confrérie* (Istanbul: Institut français d'études anatoliennes d'Istanbul, 1993).

172 "'House of Forgetting'": On the origins of the Persian term *faramush-khana* in eighteenth-century Calcutta, see Algar (1970), pp. 279–80.

172 "master among the Freemasons": Shīrāzī (1364/1985), p. 318. The Mr. Percy in question may have been the foreign office official, mentioned elsewhere, with

whom the students were in frequent contact. However, such is the nature of Freemasonry that I have been unable to confirm this identification.

173 "long-term ambitions": Ibid., p. 186.

173 *"faramush-khana"*: Ibid.

173 "Mirza Ja'far": Algar (1970), p. 278.

173 "'marks of decapitation'": Cuthbert Bede, *The Adventures of Mr. Verdant Green, an Oxford Freshman* (London: James Blackwood & Co., n.d.), p. 86.

174 "'as Brothers'": Abu Taleb Khan (1810), vol. 1, p. 192.

174 "Mr. Harris": Shīrāzī (1364/1985), p. 341.

174 "account of this meeting": Ibid., p. 344.

175 "oil painting": Personal communication, Diane Clements, director, Library and Museum of Freemasonry, Freemasons' Hall, London (September 19, 2007).

175 "preparatory drawing": Ibid. The drawing is now kept in the collections of the Library and Museum of Freemasonry at Freemasons' Hall. I am grateful to Diane Clements for providing me with a copy.

175 "Freemason lodge in Iran": It was another erstwhile Iranian resident in London (and Paris), Mirza Malkum Khan (1834–1908), who in 1858 brought Freemasonry institutionally home with him to Iran and opened the first lodge there. However, the liberal and republican ideas associated with this lodge meant that it was short lived. See Algar (1970), p. 276. On subsequent developments, see A.K.S. Lambton, "Secret Societies and the Persian Revolution of 1905–6," in A.K.S. Lambton, *Qajar Persia: Eleven Studies* (London: I. B. Tauris, 1987); and Jacob M. Landau, "Muslim Opposition to Freemasonry," *Die Welt des Islams*, New Series, 36, 2 (1996).

Chapter Four. Evangelical Engagements

Page

180 "Samuel Lee": Alice M. Lee, *A Scholar of a Past Generation: A Brief Memoir of Samuel Lee, by His Daughter* (London: Seely and Co. Limited, 1896).

180 "'not a pretty sight!'": Shīrāzī (1364/1985), pp. 349–52.

181 "noted his relief": Ibid., p. 352.

181 "'learned the languages'": Ibid., p. 350.

181 "according to Mirza Salih": Ibid., p. 351.

181 "recorded in a letter": Lee's letter to Scott is printed in Alice M. Lee (1896), pp. 2–8.

183 "Buchanan arranged": In a letter dated January 13, 1814, Buchanan stated: "I consulted the college to-day concerning the proposed admission of Mr. Lee, the Shrewsbury linguist. It was agreed to admit him at Queen's." Printed in Reverend Hugh Pearson, MA, *Memoirs of the Life and Writings of the Rev. Claudius Buchanan, DD*, 2 vols., 3rd ed. (London: T. Cadell & W. Davies, 1819), vol. 2, p. 344. On the circumstances of Buchanan's own supported admission to Queen's and his ambitiously industrious activities there, see ibid., pp. 43–132.

184 "Regius professor": Alice M. Lee (1896), p. 24.

185 "evangelical agenda": J. S. Reynolds, *The Evangelicals at Oxford, 1735–1871: A Record of an Unchronicled Movement*, 2nd ed. (Abingdon, UK: Marcham Manor Press, 1975).

185 "John Bisset": "John Bisset," Papers of Freddie Percy (SM/17/1), Whitgift School Archives, Croydon.

185 "large cash prize": Pearson (1819), vol. 2, p. 174.

186 "'translating the Scriptures'": John Willis Clark, *Endowments of the University of Cambridge* (Cambridge: Cambridge University Press, 1904), p. 382.

186 "first Persian translations of the Gospel": Maulvi Abdul Wali, *The Life and Work of Jawad Sabat, an Arab Traveller, Writer and Apologist* (Calcutta: Thacker, Spink & Co., 1925); and Edward Rehatsek, *Catalogue Raisonné of the Arabic, Hindostani, Persian, and Turkish Mss. in the Mulla Firuz Library* (Bombay: Managing Committee of the Mulla Firuz Library, 1873), pp. 185–86.

186 "almost unintelligible": John Sargent, *Memoir of the Rev. Henry Martyn, B.D.: Late Fellow of St. John's College, Cambridge, and Chaplain to the Honourable East India Company*, 2ⁿᵈ ed. (London: J. Hatchard and Son, 1819), p. 281.

186 "Martyn's efforts": *The Christian Observer, Conducted by Members of the Established Church for the Year 1819*, vol. 18 (1820), p. 372.

186 "made a mockery": The incident was reported in James Morier, *A Second Journey through Persia, Armenia, and Asia Minor, to Constantinople, between the year 1810 and 1816* (London: Longman, 1818), p. 225.

187 "letters of introduction": The circumstances are described in Ouseley's own account: Archive of the British and Foreign Bible Society, Cambridge University Library [henceforth BFBS], BSA/D1/1/(14–), Ouseley to Turgeneff (14 March 1815), p. 2. References to Martyn and Ja'far 'Ali's day-to-day collaborations can be found in S. Wilberforce (ed.), *Journal and Letters of the Rev. Henry Martyn, B.D.* (New York: M. W. Dodd, 1851), pp. 452–58.

187 "Persian New Testament": Sargent (1819), pp. 364–80, 372–74.

187 "featured in the newspapers": For example, Reverend Daniel Wilson MA, "A Defence of the Church Missionary Society, against the Objections of the Rev. Josiah Thomas, Archdeacon of Bath," *Oxford University and City Herald*, January 17, 1818. The debate continued in previous and successive issues of the *Herald*.

187 "Austen stated": Letter to Cassandra Austen (January 24, 1809), no. 45 (66), in Jane Austen, *Selected Letters*, ed. Deirdre Le Faye with Vivien Jones (Oxford: Oxford University Press, 2004), p. 115.

187 "Samuel Blackall": Austen's short-lived "romance" with Blackall is the subject of Andrew Norman, *Jane Austen: An Unrequited Love* (Stroud, UK: History Press, 2009), chapter 11.

188 "Cambridge Chronicle": From there, the report was picked up by *The Times* and reprinted on September 29, 1818.

189 "'and their rank'": *The Times* (September 29, 1818), p. 3.

190 "Queens' College": Shīrāzī (1364/1985), pp. 350–52.

190 "zealous coterie": On the history of the Cambridge evangelicals, see Marcus L. Loane, *Cambridge and the Evangelical Succession* (London: Lutterworth Press, 1952); and J. C. Pollock, *A Cambridge Movement* (London: John Murray, 1953), which mainly however deal with the post-Regency period.

190 "Venn family": Reverend Jonathan Holmes, private communication.

191 "Milner and Simeon": "Simeon, Charles" and "Milner, Isaac," *s.v.*, *ODNB*. For a survey of the activities of the BFBS, see Stephen Batalden, Kathleen Cann, and John Dean (eds.), *Sowing the Word: The Cultural Impact of the British and Foreign Bible Society, 1804–2004* (Sheffield, UK: Sheffield Phoenix Press, 2004).

191 "Milner's support": Milner's testimonial is printed in Pearson (1819), vol.1, pp. 131–32.

191 " 'fell asleep' ": Shīrāzī (1364/1985), p. 353.

192 "Joseph Jee": I am most grateful to Reverend Jonathan Holmes, keeper of the records, Queens' College, Cambridge, for identifying Jee and Mandel and providing biographical information on them.

192 "William Mandell": Private communication, Reverend Jonathan Holmes, Queens' College, Cambridge.

192 " 'sincere Christians' ": William Mandell, *The Blessedness of Dying in the Lord, a Sermon, Preached on Occasion of the Death of King George the Third* (Cambridge, 1820).

192 "Austen's cousin": I have relied for this section on Edward Cooper on Byrne (2013), pp. 201–2; and Gaye King, "Jane Austen's Staffordshire Cousin: Edward Cooper and His Circle," *Persuasions: The Jane Austen Journal* 15 (1993).

193 " 'quite uproarious' ": H. Gunning, *Reminiscences of the University, Town, and County of Cambridge, from the Year 1780* (1854), cited in "Milner, Isaac," *s.v., ODNB.*

193 "Regency varsities' subculture": Sheldon Rothblatt, "The Student Subculture and the Examination System in Early Nineteenth Century Oxbridge," in Lawrence Stone (ed.), *The University in Society,* 2 vols. (Princeton, NJ: Princeton University Press, 1975), vol. 1, pp. 254–55, 270–72.

193 " 'liquid state' ": Anonymous, *Oxford Night Caps: A Collection of Receipts for Making Various Beverages Used in the University* (Oxford: Slatter & Rose, n.d. [1827]), p. 5.

194 "vegetables and herbs": Shīrāzī (1364/1985), p. 351.

194 "Mr. Lambert": I am grateful to Jonathan Smith, archivist of Trinity College, Cambridge, for identifying James Lambert and providing information on his career.

195 "sent to Parliament": Shīrāzī (1364/1985), p. 352.

195 "evangelical tract": Alice M. Lee (1896), p. 13. The fullest account of Lee's early Cambridge years is found in his obituary in the Church Missionary Society's *Intelligencer* (March 1853).

195 "curate at Chesterton": Alice M. Lee (1896), p. 16.

195 "Missionary Society": Private communication, Reverend Jonathan Holmes, Queens' College, Cambridge.

196 "Lee's critics": For a sample, see Anonymous, *Remarks on Professor Lee's Vindication of His Edition of Jones's Persian Grammar, Published in the July and August Numbers of The Asiatic Journal, 1824* (Glasgow: James Brash & Co., 1825).

196 "panegyric puff piece": "Account of the Rev. Mr. Lee," *Oxford University and City Herald,* September 26, 1818. It seems the article was written as part of the campaign to elect Lee to the professorship at Cambridge.

197 " 'grammar of that language' ": Alice M. Lee (1896), pp. 19–20.

198 "MA by Royal Decree": I am grateful to Reverend Jonathan Holmes, Queens' College, Cambridge, for explaining the circumstances of Lee's election to the chair.

198 "letter of recommendation": Cambridge University Archives, CUR 39.7.12 (1), pp. 8–9. The letter, addressed to the vice chancellor, was composed in Persian and here translated in literal form; the handwritten Persian document appears to have been lost. The letter was dated Rabiʿ al-Sani 1234 (February 1819), being the same month

in which the other testimonials were written. A somewhat amended extract from the letter is printed in Alice M. Lee (1896), p. 20.

199 "in translating scripture": On the employment of foreign travelers to London in Bible translation, Leslie Howsam, *Cheap Bibles: Nineteenth-Century Publishing and the British and Foreign Bible Society* (Cambridge: Cambridge University Press, 1991), pp. 21–22.

199 "testimonial letter": "To the Honourable and Reverend the Vice Chancellor, Heads of Houses, and Members of the Senate, of the University of Cambridge," Cambridge University Archives, CUR 39.7.12 (1), p. 8.

199 "'a learned Persian'": Alice M. Lee (1896), p. 18. On Lee's early involvement in biblical translation into Islamic languages, see also Samuel Lee, *Remarks on Dr. Henderson's Appeal to the Bible Society, on the Subject of the Turkish Version of the New Testament Printed at Paris in 1819* (Cambridge: J. Smith, 1824).

200 "'with Mirza Khaleel'": "Account of the Rev. Mr. Lee," *Oxford University and City Herald*, September 26, 1818, back page.

200 "guest at his vicarage": The slight discrepancy in dates (the 1818 of Alice Lee versus the 1819 of Mirza Salih) might also be explained either by the existence of the earlier visit suggested previously or by the fact that Lee's daughter was writing his memoirs in the middle of the 1890s.

200 "Mirza Khalil": A brief account of Mirza Khalil's career at the college is found in Andrew Hambling, *The East India Company at Haileybury, 1806–1857* ([n.p.], 2005), p. 38.

200 "grammatical correctness": Cambridge University Archives, CUR 39.7.12 (1), p. 8.

200 "'opinions of intelligent and learned Persians'": Sir William Jones (ed. Samuel Lee), *A Grammar of the Persian Language, with Considerable Additions and Improvements by S. Lee*, 9th ed. (London: W. Nicol, 1828), p. xix.

200 "the visits to Cambridge": Shīrāzī (1364/1985), pp. 349–50.

203 "request further funds": UK National Archives, FO 60/13 (178), "D'Arcy to Planta" (May 18, 1818).

203 "'under my charge'": UK National Archives, FO 60/13 (180), "D'Arcy to Planta" (May 30, 1818).

203 "'finish their education'": UK National Archives, FO 60/13 (173), "Sir Gore Ouseley to Planta" (February 18, 1818).

204 "taught to print books": Shīrāzī (1364/1985), pp. 344–46, 353.

204 "differences of rank": UK National Archives, FO 60/11 (68), "D'Arcy to Edward Cooke" (February 7, 1816). This document also refers to Muhammad 'Ali by his title "Ustad" in differentiation to the other students' titles of "Mirza."

204 "Muhammad 'Ali": UK National Archives, FO 60/12 (260, 262), "Morier to Lord Castlereagh"; and FO 60/12 (285), "Brief Statement of the Circumstances Attending the Persian Officers" (December 8, 1817). I have taken the addresses from Critchett and Woods, *The Post Office Directory for 1819, Including a New Guide to Stage Coaches, Waggons, Carts, Vessels etc, for 1819* (London: T. Maiden, 1819), pp. 130 and 371.

205 "'scientific enquiries'": UK National Archives, FO 60/15 (86), "Olinthus Gregory to Planta [?]" (July 10, 1819); and FO 60/15 (90), "Jaafar Hewsainey to Planta" (July 14, 1819).

206 "'Mr. Butterworth'": UK National Archives, FO 60/15 (90), "Jaafar Hewsainey to Planta" (July 14, 1819).

206 "Butterworth pledged £50": J.B.B. Clarke, *An Account of the Infancy, Religious and Literary Life of Adam Clarke, LLD* (New York: B. Waugh & T. Mason, 1833), vol. 3, p. 7.

206 "publishing industry": Howsam (1991).

206 "Bible Society": Stephen Batalden, Kathleen Cann, and John Dean (eds.), *Sowing the Word: The Cultural Impact of the British and Foreign Bible Society, 1804–2004* (Sheffield, UK: Sheffield Phoenix Press, 2004).

207 "'true charity'": "The Persian Princes," *The Times* (December 7, 1818), p. 3.

207 "scholar of Persian and Hindustani": Ram Babu Saksena, *European and Indo-European Poets of Urdu and Persian* (Lucknow, India: Newul Kishore Press, 1941), pp. 42–43.

208 "'expense of printing'": Charles John Shore Teignmouth, *Memoir of the Life and Correspondence of John, Lord Teignmouth*, 2 vols. (London: Hatchard, 1843), vol. 1, p. 104.

208 "'their own country'": Quoted in William Roberts, *Memoirs of the Life of Hannah More*, 2 vols. (London: R. B. Seeley & W. Burnside, 1836), pp. 246–47.

209 "Scottish and German missions": Nile Green, "The Trans-Colonial Opportunities of Bible Translation: Iranian Language-Workers between the Russian and British Empires," in Michael Dodson and Brian Hatcher (eds.), *Trans-Colonial Modernities in South Asia* (London: Routledge, 2012).

209 "John Shakespear": Shīrāzī (1364/1985), pp. 167–68.

209 "'Hindostanee and Persian printing'": "Account of the Rev. Mr. Lee," *Oxford University and City Herald* (September 26, 1818), back page.

209 "Arabic presses": Geoffrey Roper, "Arabic Printing and Publishing in England before 1820," *Bulletin (British Society for Middle Eastern Studies)* 12, 1 (1985); and *Typographia Arabica* (1971), pp. 20–21.

209 "university press": Stanley Morison, *John Fell, the University Press and the "Fell" Types: The Punches and Matrices Designed for Printing in the Greek, Latin, English, and Oriental Languages Bequeathed in 1686 to the University of Oxford by John Fell, D.D., Delegate of the Press, Dean of Christ Church, Vice-Chancellor of the University and Bishop of Oxford* (Oxford: Clarendon Press, 1967).

210 "'fount [sic] of Persian types'": Sir William Ouseley (ed.), *The Oriental Collections*, vol. 3, no. 2 (April–June 1799), p. 195.

210 "Vincent Figgins": *A Specimen of New Persian Types, in Imitation of the Talik Character, Cast by Vincent Figgins, for Wilson and Co. of the Oriental Press* (London: Printed at The Oriental Press, by Wilson and Co., 1800). Further examples of the craftsmanship of Figgins (d. 1861) can be found in Bertholde Wolpe (ed.), *Vincent Figgins: Type Specimens, 1801 and 1815, Reproduced in Facsimile* (London: Printing Historical Society, 1967).

210 "William Bulmer": Peter Isaac, *William Bulmer: The Fine Printer in Context, 1757–1830* (London: Bain & Williams, 1993), especially pp. 61–66. A checklist of the oriental works printed by Bulmer is found in the appendix. On Martin's and Bulmer's common dealings, see "Memoir of William Bulmer, Esq.," *Gentleman's Magazine* 100, part 2 (October 1830), pp. 305–10.

211 "5,000 copies": On the New Testament, see *The Fifteenth Report of the British and*

Foreign Bible Society (London: BFBS, 1819), p. xciv. On the two Bibles, see *The Seventeenth Report of the British and Foreign Bible Society* (London: BFBS, 1821), p. l000v. Note that at the same time the Bible Society was also printing Malay Bibles in Roman script.

211 "Persian and Turkish New Testaments": *The Thirteenth Report of the British and Foreign Bible Society* (London: BFBS, 1817), p. 338; and *The Fifteenth Report* (1819), p. xciv.

211 "massive 10,000": *The Seventeenth Report* (1821), p. l000iv.

211 "Richard Watts": The various printed editions of Mirza Salih's diary present a range of orthographical problems, none of which has proved more perplexing than the name of his printing master. For example, Ghulām Husayn's edition has *mistar dāns* (دانس), while other editions give the name as *wāns* (وانس) or *wāls* (والس). See Shīrāzī (1364/1985), pp. 353, 355 (*dāns*); *Guzārish-i Safar-i Mīrzā Sālih Shīrāzī (Kāzarūnī)*, ed. Humyūn Shahīdī (Tehran: Rāh-i Naw, 1362/1983), p. 369 (*wāns*); *Safarnāma-yi Mīrzā Sālih Shīrāzī*, ed. Ismāʿīl Rāʾīn (Tehran: Rūzan, 1347/1968), p. 375 (*dāns*). To add further to the confusion, a secondary source, Husayn Mīrzāʾī Golpāʾīgānī, *Tārīkh-i Chāp va chāpkhāna dar Īrān* (Tehran: Intishārāt Gulshan-i Rāz, 1378/1999), pp. 10–11, quotes two versions of the name: *vāls* and *vāns*. Consultation of the original manuscript diary suggests that the various editors have misread the placement of the unclear and adjoined dots of the Arabic letter *ta* as either a *lam* (thus "wals") or *nun* (thus "wans") and the *waw* as a *dal* (thus "dans"). I have finally come to the conclusion that the name "Watts" is the only viable English name that fits with the orthography of the original manuscript; Mirza Salih's description of his printing master's specialities; and the name of a master printer who was actually active in London in 1818. On Watts, see Talbot Baines Reed, *A History of the Old English Letter Foundries* (London: Eliot Stock, 1887), pp. 362–63.

212 "Welsh Bible": David E. Jenkins, *The Life of the Rev. Thomas Charles, B.A., of Bala*, 3 vols. (Denbigh, UK: Llewelyn Jenkins, 1908), vol. 3, p. 68.

212 "attention of Professor Lee": Alice M. Lee (1896).

212 "different type sets": W. M. Watts, *Oriental and Other Types in 67 Languages or Dialects, Principally Prepared by R. Watts and Now in Use in W. M. Watts's Office* (London: W. M. Watts, 1851).

212 "translated into Hindustani": D. N. Griffiths, "Prayer-Book Translations in the Nineteenth Century," *The Library*, 6th series, 6, 1 (1984), pp. 3, 15.

212 "several hundred printers": Philip A. H. Brown, *London Publishers and Printers: A Tentative List, c. 1800–1870* (London: British Museum, 1961); and William B. Todd, *A Directory of Printers and Others in Allied Trades, London and Vicinity 1800–1840* (London: Printing Historical Society, 1972).

212 "chief oriental printer":William Canton, *A History of the British and Foreign Bible Society*, 5 vols. (London: John Murray, 1904–10), vol. 1, p. 64.

213 "Hindustani New Testament": *The New Testament of Our Lord and Saviour Jesus Christ; Translated into the Hindoostanee Language from the Original Greek by H. Martyn; and Afterwards Carefully Revised with the Assistance of Mirza Fitrit and Other Learned Natives* (London: Printed by Richard Watts for the British and Foreign Bible Society, 1819).

213 "project's supervisor": On Lee's involvement, see T. H. Darlow and H. F. Moule, *Historical Catalogue of the Printed Editions of Holy Scripture in the Library of the*

British and Foreign Bible Society (London: Bible House, 1903–11), vol. 2, part 1, p. 744.

213 "Book of Psalms": Darlow and Moule (1903–11), vol. 2, part 1, pp. 69–70.

214 "Arabic version of the New Testament": *Kitāb al-ʿAhd al-Jadīd, yaʿnī, Injīl al-Muqaddas, li-Rabbinā Yasūʿ al-Masīh* [New Testament] (Landan [London]: Richārd Wāts, 1821). Also Darlow and Moule (1903-11), vol. 2, part 1, p. 69.

214 " the date 1821": Darlow & Moule (1903–11), vol. 2, part 2, p. 1204.

214 " Sir Gore Ouseley ": Canton (1904–10), vol. 1, p. 64.

214 "Oriental Type-Foundry": The building that contained Watts's own workshop was demolished in the 1870s to make way for the Royal Courts of Justice, whose Victorian Gothic turrets now hover over Temple Bar.

215 "new iron handpresses": For superlative detail, see Richard-Gabriel Rummonds, *Nineteenth-Century Printing Practices and the Iron Handpress*, 2 vols. (London: British Library, 2004). On the operating of imported hand presses later in Iran, see Golpāʾīgānī (1378/1999), pp. 12–13.

215 "diplomatic correspondence": UK National Archives, FO 60/13 (199), "Meerza Riza to Hamilton" (December 7, 1818).

215 "knowledge of Arabic and Hindustani": On the Iranians' knowledge of several Asian languages, see UK National Archives, FO 60/15 (132), "Salame to Planta" (April 28, 1819).

215 "Sullivan Law Hyder": Michael H. Fisher, *Counterflows to Colonialism: Indian Travellers and Settlers in Britain, 1600–1857* (Delhi: Permanent Black, 2004), pp. 121–23.

216 "'processes of hegemony'": Edward W. Said, *Culture and Imperialism* (London: Chatto & Windus, 1993), p. 131 and chapter 3.

217 "worked for the missionaries": Shīrāzī (1364/1985), p. 345.

217 "*Sense and Sensibility*": While Roworth was the printer, the better-known publisher was T. Egerton.

217 "8 Salisbury Court": I have taken the address from a letter written by Mirza Jaʿfar: UK National Archives, FO 60/15 (90), "Jaaʿfar Hewsainey to Planta" (July 14, 1819).

217 "Samuel Richardson": On the literary associations of Salisbury Court, see T. C. Duncan Eaves and Ben D. Kimpel, "Samuel Richardson's London Houses," *Studies in Bibliography* 15 (1962).

218 "nearby inn": Shīrāzī (1364/1985), p. 345.

218 "workers' cant": For the period's dialectical "cant," I have relied here on Hart (2014), pp. 3, 5, 10–11.

218 "Friedrich König": Colin Clair, *A History of Printing in Britain* (London: Cassell, 1965), pp. 210–18.

218 "program of studies": UK National Archives, FO 60/8 (98), "Plan of Education for the Persian Youth" (undated [1813]).

220 "Survey of India": On the survey, I have relied on Rama Deb Roy, "The Great Trigonometrical Survey of India in Historical Perspective," *Indian Journal of History of Science* 21, 1 (1986). For Everest's biography, I have referred "Everest, Sir George," *q.v., ODNB.*

220 "manufacture of iron": In this section, I have relied on Richard Hayman, *Ironmaking: The History and Archaeology of the Iron Industry* (Stroud, UK: History Press,

2005); and Jacqueline Fearn, *Cast Iron* (Princes Risborough, UK: Shire Publications, 1990).

221 "John Nash": On Nash's use of cast iron, see Fearn (1990), pp. 19–20.

221 " 'Iron King' ": On John Wilkinson, see Hayman (2005), pp. 40–41, 55, 86, 96–97.

221 "James Wilkinson": Robert Wilkinson-Latham, *Mr. Wilkinson, Pall Mall, London: The History of the Wilkinson Sword in Two Volumes, 1772–1972* (Hampshire, UK: RL Publishing, 2000), vol. 1, chapter 2. I am grateful to Roy Shadbolt for further advice on Messrs. Nock and Wilkinson.

221 " 'busy at work there' ": Shīrāzī (1364/1985), p. 334.

222 "Alexander Galloway": Critchett and Woods, *The Post Office Directory for 1819, including a New Guide to Stage Coaches, Waggons, Carts, Vessels etc, for 1819* (London: T. Maiden, 1819), p. 130. More generally, I have relied in this section on "Galloway, Alexander," *q.v., ODNB.*

223 "writing to magazines": One such letter from Galloway is reproduced in full in Cadwallader D. Colden, *The Life of Robert Fulton; Comprising Some Account of the Invention, Progress and Establishment of Steam-Boats* (New York: Kirk & Mercein, 1817), pp. 328–30.

223 "Matthew Boulton's company": Jennifer Tann and John Aitken, "The Diffusion of the Stationary Steam Engine from Britain to India 1790–1830," *Indian Economic and Social History Review* 29, 2 (1992).

223 "Austen's sailor brother": On Francis Austen in Alexandria, see Hubback and Hubback (1906), pp. 94–103.

Chapter Five. Diplomatic Friendships

Page

227 "daily routine": Shīrāzī (1364/1985), p. 345. I have rendered Mirza Salih's traditional Persian timekeeping into standard Western format.

227 "brought bad news": Shīrāzī (1364/1985), pp. 318–19.

228 " 'vessel for Constantinople' ": UK National Archives, FO 60/13 (187), "Foreign Office to D'Arcy" (November 23, 1818).

228 "passage to Constantinople": UK National Archives, FO 60/13 (189), "D'Arcy to Hamilton" (November 24, 1818).

228 " 'Constantinople & Persia' ": UK National Archives, FO 60/13 (193), "Sir Gore Ouseley to Hamilton" (November 29, 1818).

228 "persuade Captain Powell": UK National Archives, FO 60/15 (34), "Powell to Hamilton" (May 10, 1819).

229 "remain in London": A translation of Abu'l-Hasan's letter is included in UK National Archives, FO 60/13 (199), "Meerza Riza to Hamilton" (December 7, 1818).

229 "angrily litigious letter": Ibid.

231 " 'this country and ours' ": UK National Archives, FO 60/12 (232), "Persian Students to Lord Castlereagh" (May 8, 1817).

231 " 'for their maintenance' ": UK National Archives, FO 60/11 (13), "Lord Castlereagh to D'Arcy" (November 30, 1816).

232 " 'politics of friendship' ": Leela Gandhi, *Affective Communities: Anticolonial Thought, Fin-de-Siècle Radicalism, and the Politics of Friendship* (Durham, NC: Duke University Press, 2006).

233 "public reception": Abul Hassan Khan (1988), p. 35; and Mursilvand (1364/1986), p. 128.

234 "public reception gifts for the shah": On diplomatic gifts exchanged between the rulers of Iran and Russia in this period, see Edward Kasinec and Robert Davies, "Graphic Documentation of Gift Exchanges between the Russian Court and Its Islamic Counterparts, Seventeenth to the Nineteenth Century," in Linda Komaroff (ed.), *Gifts of the Sultan: The Arts of Giving at the Islamic Courts* (Los Angeles: Los Angeles County Museum of Art, 2011).

234 "'enamelled looking-glass'": *The Times* (May 24, 1819), p. 3.

234 "mirror or *aʾina*": On the extension of mirror metaphors into the realm of mystical love, see Riza Feiz, "Le symbole du miroir dans la gnose musulmane," in M. Hossein Beikbaghban (ed.), *Images et representations en terre d'Islam* (Tehran: Presses Universitaires d'Iran, 1997); and Akhtar Qamber, "The Mirror Symbol in the Teaching and Writing of Some Sufi Masters," *Islamic Culture* 62, 4 (1988).

235 "'ʿAbbas Mirza's sentiments'": *The Times* (December 21, 1822), p. 2.

235 "made only of glass": Mirza Abul Hassan Khan (1988), pp. 288–89; Mursilvand (1364/1986), pp. 351–52.

237 "his own father": Shīrāzī (1364/1985), p. 163.

237 "rituals of dinner": I have borrowed this phrase and my understanding of the social functions of dining from Margaret Visser, *The Rituals of Dinner: The Origins, Evolution, Eccentricities, and Meaning of Table Manners* (New York: HarperCollins, 1992).

237 "*halal* meat": Mirza Itesa Modeen [*sic*], *Shigurf Namah i Velaët, Or, Excellent Intelligence Concerning Europe* (London: Parbury, Allen & Co., 1827), pp. 214–17.

237 "ritually slaughtering sheep": Abu'l-Hasan, though, does seem to have had his meat specially slaughtered, since he traveled with a substantial entourage of servants and stayed in more spacious accommodations.

238 "Englishman's daily cycle": Shīrāzī (1364/1985), pp. 309–10. Cf. the observations of Indo-Muslim travelers summarized in Gulfishan Khan, *Indian Muslim Perceptions of the West during the Eighteenth Century* (Karachi: Oxford University Press 1998), pp. 189–94.

238 "'father reads Cowper'": See Jane Austen's letter no. 14 (December 18, 1798) to Cassandra in Chapman (1932), vol. 1, p. 39.

238 "Atlantic fishing": Shīrāzī (1364/1985), p. 308.

239 "'fish they call *kad* [cod]'": Ibid., p. 308.

239 "pheasant, or goose": Ibid., p. 309.

239 "times at which they ate": Ibid., pp. 311–13.

239 "described breakfast": Ibid., p. 311.

240 "'grace and propriety'": Hester L. S. Thrale Piozzi, *Autobiography, Letters and Literary Remains of Mrs. Piozzi (Thrale)*, 2 vols. (London: Longman, Green, Longman & Roberts, 1861), vol. 2, p. 415.

240 "plates and cutlery": Shīrāzī (1364/1985), p. 312.

240 "sat opposite her": Ibid., pp. 312–13.

241 "fruit and almonds": Ibid., p. 313.

241 "embassy to Saint Petersburg": Muhammad Gulbun (ed.), *Safarnāma-yi Khusraw Mīrzā bih Pītirizbūrgh va Tārīkh-i Zindigānī-yi ʿAbbās Mīrzā Nāʾib al-Salṭāna bih Qalam-i Hājjī Mīrzā Masʿūd* (Tehran: Mustawfī, 1349/1970), pp. 362–65.

241 "imperial Russian capital": Gulbun (1349/1970), p. 362.

241 "hunting practices": Shīrāzī (1364/1985), p. 309. Cf. Sir John Malcolm, *Sketches of Persia from the Journals of a Traveller in the East*, 2 vols. (London: J. Murray, 1828), vol. 1, pp. 52–59.

242 "hurling javelins": Ismāʿīl Rāʾīn, *Mīrzā Abū al-Hasan Khān Īlchī* (Tehran: Jāvīdān, 1357/1978), p. 35; and Philoxenus Secundus, *Persian Recreations, or Oriental Stories, with Notes, to which is Prefixed Some Account of Two Ambassadors from Iran to James the First and George the Third* (London: S. Rousseau, 1812), pp. 23–24.

242 "*ashpaz-khana*": Shīrāzī (1364/1985), p. 293.

242 "novelty of the restaurant": Rebecca L. Spang, *The Invention of the Restaurant: Paris and Modern Gastronomic Culture* (Cambridge, MA: Harvard University Press, 2000).

242 "coffeehouses served curries": I have based this curry section on David Burnett and Helen Saberi, *The Road to Vindaloo: Curry Cooks and Curry Books* (Totnes: Prospect Books), pp. 25–26, 40, 161.

243 "hotels Mirza Salih saw": Shīrāzī (1364/1985), p. 293.

243 "English cutlery set": Rāʾīn (1357/1978), p. 59. Technically, this was on his earlier visit to London.

243 "800,000 sheep": Shīrāzī (1364/1985), p. 265.

243 "milk of sheep": Ibid., p. 265.

244 "improved hotels": On the construction of new-style inns and hotels during these years, see David Watkin, *Regency: A Guide and Gazetteer, The Buildings of Britain*, vol. 4 (London: Barrie & Jenkins, 1982), pp. 105–6.

244 "Star Inn": On the Star Inn, see Shīrāzī (1364/1985), p. 320.

244 "young women": Shīrāzī (1364/1985), p. 293. For a rather less decorous picture of pleasure-seekers and women sex workers in this period, see Jane Rendell, *The Pursuit of Pleasure: Gender, Space & Architecture in Regency London* (New Brunswick: Rutgers University Press, 2002).

245 "'Syllabub, Tea, Coffee'": See Jane Austen's letter no. 73 (May 31, 1811) to Cassandra in Chapman (1932), vol. 1, p. 285.

245 "wines [*sharab*] exquisite": Mirza Abu Taleb Khan, *The Travels of Mirza Abu Taleb Khan in Asia, Africa, and Europe*, 2 vols. (London: Longman, Hurst, Rees, Orme & Brown, 1814), vol. 1, pp. 197–98, with Persian terms taken from Mīrzā Abū Tālib Khān, *Masīr-i Tālibī yā Safarnāma-yi Mīrzā Abū Tālib Khān*, ed. Husayn Khadīv-Jam (Tehran: Sāzmān-i Intishārāt va Āmūzish-i Inqilāb-i Islāmī, 1363/1985), p. 106.

245 "'Asiatic notions of hospitality'": James Baillie Fraser, *Narrative of the Residence of the Persian Princes in London, in 1835 and 1836, with an Account of Their Journey from Persia, and Subsequent Adventures*, 2 vols. (London: Richard Bentley, 1838), vol. 1, p. 62.

245 "'British ladies'": Philoxenus Secundus (1812), pp. 21–22.

245 "attendance": Many of the newspaper reports have been reprinted in Mirza Abul Hassan Khan (1988).

246 "loanword, '*parti*'": See for example Mursilvand (1364/1986), pp. 304 and 306.

246 "fancy dress": On the shift toward more negative Iranian assessments of English social customs after the failed embassy of 1838, see Tavakoli-Targhi (2001), chapter 4.

246 "Romans and hoary seadogs": Mirza Abul Hassan Khan (1988), p. 239; and Mursil-vand (1364/1986), pp. 310–11.

246 "'ta'am va sharab va kabab'": Mursilvand (1364/1986), p. 310.

246 "'helpless and bewildered'": Ibid., p. 311.

246 "'together with spices'": The newspaper is cited in Mirza Abul Hassan Khan (1988), p. 61.

247 "12 Bruton Street": I have taken Sir Gore's address from the 1818 voting register: see "Parish of St George," in *A List of the Poll for the City and Liberty of Westminster, June 18–July 4, 1818* (London: n.p., 1818), p. 78.

247 "'Asiatic table delicacy'": Advertisement section, *Morning Post* (December 14, 1816).

247 "'first time in my life'": Sarah Austin (trans.), *A Regency Visitor: The English Tour of Prince Pückler-Muskau Described in His Letters, 1826–1828* (London: Collins, 1957), p. 279.

249 "'Mivart's'": Managed by James Edward Mivart (1781–1856), the establishment in question was the early Claridge's hotel, which was "known in the 1820s as a fashionable discreet address for senior *corps diplomatique* personnel." See Elaine Denby, *Grand Hotels: Reality and Illusion* (London: Reaktion Books, 2004), p. 154.

249 "'sort of thing it is!'": Fraser (1838), vol. 1, pp. 280–81.

250 "'at their table'": Ibid., vol. 1, pp. 281–82.

250 "'Malcolm's plum'": Malcolm (1828), vol. 1, pp. 37–38.

250 "Irish ate potatoes": Shīrāzī (1364/1985), p. 309.

250 "Arabic literary tradition": On earlier Arabic panegyrics to the pleasures of the table, see G.J.H. van Gelder, *God's Banquet: Food in Classical Arabic Literature* (New York: Columbia University Press, 2000).

250 "sensuality of Islam": For corresponding Iranian perceptions of English licentiousness in the nineteenth century, see Henry A. Stern, *Dawnings of Light in the East* (London: Charles H. Purday, 1854), pp. 192–93.

251 "powers of talismans": Philoxenus Secundus (1812), p. 39.

251 "brother's penis": Mirza Abul Hassan Khan (1988), pp. 151–52; and Mursilvand (1364/1986), p. 211.

251 "'ingratiating manners'": "The Persian Princes," from an unnamed "Bristol newspaper," reprinted in *Caledonian Mercury*, December 14, 1818.

251 "dining with the Freemasons": Shīrāzī (1364/1985), p. 176.

252 "coffin of the queen": Ibid., pp. 340–43.

252 "'the finest artist'": William Wharry, *A Funeral Sermon [on Job 23] Written on the Death of Queen Charlotte of Great Britain* (Horncastle, UK: Bontoft, 1818), p. 29.

252 "the funeral service": Shīrāzī (1364/1985), pp. 342–43.

253 "'solemn concluding ceremony'": Walley C. Oulton, *Authentic and Impartial Memoirs of her Late Majesty: Charlotte Queen of Great Britain and Ireland Containing a Faithfull Retrospect of her Early Days, her Marriage, Coronation, Correspondence, Illness, Death, Funeral Obsequies* (London: T. Kinnersley, 1819), p. 467.

253 "'Meerza Jaaffa and Meerza Saalih'": "Lying in State of the Queen," *Liverpool Mercury* (December 11, 1818).

253 "8 Salisbury Court": I have taken the address from a letter written by Mirza Ja'far: UK National Archives, FO 60/15 (90), "Ja'far Hewsainey to Planta" (July 14, 1819).

253 "36 King Street": I have taken the address from a letter concerning Muhammad

'Ali written by Thomas Dudley: UK National Archives, FO 60/15 (64), "Dudley to Lord Castlereagh" (June 20, 1819).

253 "Charles Fowler": David Watkin, *Regency: A Guide and Gazetteer, The Buildings of Britain*, vol. 4 (London: Barrie & Jenkins, 1982), p. 100.

254 "corn dealers, and victuallers": "Parish of St Ann," in *A List of the Poll for the City and Liberty of Westminster, June 18–July 4, 1818* (London: n.p., 1818), p. 211.

254 "'water bewitched'": Thomas Dudley's occupation and address are listed in ibid. For "water bewitched," see Hart (2014), p. 12.

255 "'country squire'": Piozzi (1861), vol. 2, p. 415.

255 "'number of ingredients'": Anonymous (n.d.), p. 11.

255 "Englishwomen drank little": Shīrāzī (1364/1985), p. 312.

255 "wine drinking in Iran": Rudi Matthee, *The Pursuit of Pleasure: Drugs and Stimulants in Iranian History, 1500–1900* (Princeton, NJ: Princeton University Press, 2005), chapter 7.

255 "'Orange Wine'": See Jane Austen's letter no. 54 (June 30, 1808) to Cassandra in Chapman (1932), vol. 1, p. 209.

256 "Freemasons' Tavern": Located on Great Queen Street, the Freemasons' Tavern was a distinct entity from the present-day Freemasons' Arms on Longacre, which is a later, Victorian building. The Tavern was later renamed the Connaught Rooms and survives today as a hotel of the same name.

256 "'course of my life'": Abu Taleb Khan, *The Travels of Mirza Abu Taleb Khan in Asia, Africa, and Europe during the Years 1799, 1800, 1801, 1802, and 1803*, 2 vols. (Broxbown: R. Watts, 1810), vol. 1, p. 193.

256 "'for my own use'": National Archives (Kew), FO 60/23, letter nos. 22 (dated April 3, 1823) and 24 (undated). The letters were actually written a few years later during his second visit to England, as discussed in the section "Afterlives." However, the letters strongly suggest that Mirza Salih picked up his taste for wine during his earlier student years in London.

256 "'great occasions'": Philoxenus Secundus (1812), p. 34.

257 "'inconvenience from it'": Moritz von Kotzebue, *Narrative of a Journey into Persia in the Suite of the Imperial Russian Embassy in the Year 1817* (London: Longman, Hurst, Rees, Orme & Brown, 1819), p. 123.

257 "'liqueurs, in immense quantities'": Von Kotzebue (1819), p. 122.

257 "'Has it *kayf*?'": Fraser (1838), vol. 1, p. 193.

257 "religious contradictions": For a survey of earlier contradictions in Muslim attitudes toward alcohol, see Daniel S. Feins, "Wine and Islam: The Dichotomy between Theory and Practice in Early Islamic history" (unpublished PhD thesis, University of Edinburgh, 1997).

258 "'not be included in the law'": Stern (1854), p. 148.

258 "'days of enjoyment!'": Fraser (1838), vol. 1, p. 290.

258 "spaces of sociability": On cultures of coffee consumption, see Brian Cowan, *The Social Life of Coffee: The Emergence of the British Coffeehouse* (New Haven, CT: Yale University Press, 2005); and Ralph Hattox, *Coffee and Coffee-Houses: The Origins of a Social Beverage in the Medieval Near East* (Seattle: University of Washington Press, 1985). On increasing tea consumption in Iran during this period, see Matthee (2005), chapter 9.

258–60 "Iranian tea imports": Abdollah Mostofi, *The Administrative and Social History of the Qajar Period: The Story of My Life*, 3 vols. (Costa Mesa, CA: Mazda Publishers, 1997), vol. 3, p. 783.

260 "planting tea in India": John Keay, *India Discovered: The Recovery of a Lost Civilization* (London: HarperCollins, 2010), p. 209.

260 "Twinings's doorway": The teahouse's portico had been constructed by Richard Twining in 1787.

263 "Thomas Belcher": Karen Downing, "The Gentleman Boxer: Boxing, Manners, and Masculinity in Eighteenth-Century England," *Men and Masculinities* 12, 3 (2010).

264 "Alexander Galloway": Here I have relied mainly on the entry on "Galloway, Alexander," *s.v., ODNB*.

265 "Tom Galloway": Antoine B. Zahlan, "The Impact of Technology Change on the Nineteenth-Century Arab World," in Charles E. Butterworth and I. William Zartma (eds.), *Between the State and Islam* (Cambridge: Cambridge University Press, 2001), p. 47.

265 "Galloway Bey": For details of Galloway Bey's life, I have relied on the obituary in the *Morning Chronicle* (August 18, 1836).

Chapter Six. The Love of Strangers

Page

267 "Persian word *ulfat*": Shīrāzī (1364/1985), pp. 150, 192.

267 "remain in London": A translation of Abu'l-Hasan's letter is included in UK National Archives, FO 60/13 (199), "Meerza Riza to Hamilton" (December 7, 1818).

268 "flee his house": Shīrāzī (1364/1985), pp. 156, 166.

269 " 'I were your father' ": Shīrāzī (1364/1985), p. 163.

269 "recalled for duty": John William Kaye, *The Life and Correspondence of Major-General Sir John Malcolm, GCB*, 2 vols. (London: Smith, Elder, and Co., 1856), vol. 2, pp. 133–34.

269 "Indians residing in London": Michael H. Fisher, *Counterflows to Colonialism: Indian Travellers and Settlers in Britain, 1600–1858* (Delhi: Permanent Black, 2004), chapters 3–6.

270 " 'obsolete words' ": William Price and Mirza Mohammed Saulih, *A Grammar of the Three Principal Oriental Languages, Hindoostanee, Persian and Arabic to which is Added, a Set of Persian Dialogues by Mirza Mohammed Saulih of Shiraz* (London: Kingsbury, Parbury & Allen, 1823), p. vii.

270 "Muhyi al-Din": Shīrāzī (1364/1985), p. 346. On the Indian emissary's visit, see Fisher (2004), pp. 193–96.

270 "with Sam Beazley": Shīrāzī (1364/1985), p. 162.

270–71 "ten major theaters": Ibid., pp. 290–91.

272 "his prior routine": Ibid., p. 346.

272 "Royal Society and the British Museum": Ibid., pp. 284, 288–90.

272 "Olinthus Gregory": Ibid., pp. 319–20, 331–32.

272 " 'every one of us' ": UK National Archives, FO 60/15 (90), "Jaafar Hewsainey to Planta" (July 14, 1819).

272 "Joseph Butterworth": Echoing again the strangely enabling role played by missionaries in the students' education, a month after the students' departure later in

the summer of 1819 Mr. Butterworth became the general treasurer of the Wesleyan Methodist Missionary Society.

273 "famous astronomer": Shīrāzī (1364/1985), pp. 340–44.

273 "forty feet long": Ibid., pp. 340–41.

274 " 'with the treaty' ": Price (1825), p. 63.

275 "traditional map of the heavens": On the impact of European astronomy in late Qajar Iran, see Kamran Arjomand, "The Emergence of Scientific Modernity in Iran: Controversies Surrounding Astrology and Modern Astronomy in the Mid-Nineteenth Century," *Iranian Studies* 30, 1–2 (1997).

275 "no one in their home country": I make this claim in full recognition of Indo-Persian scholars' awareness of European scientific developments , as demonstrated by in Kapil Raj, *Relocating Modern Science: Circulation and the Construction of Knowledge in South Asia and Europe, 1650–1900* (New York: Palgrave Macmillan, 2007).

275 "collection of seeds": UK National Archives, FO 60/13 (175 & 177), "Joseph Banks to Foreign Office" (April 8 and April 23, 1818).

275 " 'purchased of Mr Galloway' ": UK National Archives, FO 60/15 (104), "D'Arcy to Planta" (August 12, 1819).

275 " 'machinist and engineer' ": Critchett and Woods, *The Post Office Directory for 1819, including a New Guide to Stage Coaches, Waggons, Carts, Vessels etc, for 1819* (London: T. Maiden, 1819), p. 130.

276 " 'gold Persian characters' ": UK National Archives, FO 60/12 (262), "James Morier to Lord Castlereagh" (July 22, 1817).

276 "bill of £367": UK National Archives, FO 60/13 (191), "Statement of the Allowance Account to the Five Persians" (November 24, 1818). For the sum's modern equivalent (in 2013), I have again relied on the Bank of England's Historical Inflation Calculator.

276 " 'drawings and coloured casts' ": UK National Archives, FO 60/13 (191), "John Shaw to Mirza Jafer Tabeeb" (December 1, 1818).

276 "best medical supplies": UK National Archives, FO 60/13 (213), "Memorandum Concerning Mirza Jiaffer [*sic*]" (undated [December 1818]).

276 "sum of £500": UK National Archives, FO 60/15 (41), "Planta to D'Arcy" (May 22, 1819).

277 "compendium of Persian poets": Sir Gore Ouseley, *Biographical Notices of Persian Poets, with Critical and Explanatory Remarks, to which is Prefixed a Memoir of Gore Ouseley by James Reynolds* (London: Oriental Translation Fund of Great Britain and Ireland, 1846).

277 " 'Englishing' Persian poetry": I have borrowed Jones's own term of "Englishing" via Ahmad Karimi-Hakkak, "Beyond Translation: Interactions between Persian and English Poetry," in Nikki R. Keddie and Rudi Matthee (eds.), *Iran and the Surrounding World: Interactions in Culture and Cultural Politics* (Seattle: University of Washington Press, 2002), p. 39.

277 "Jones's translations": Karimi-Hakkak (2002), p. 59. For a fuller study of Jones's literary output, see Garland H. Cannon, *Oriental Jones: A Biography of Sir William Jones, 1746–1794* (Bombay: Asia Publishing House, 1964).

277 " ''tis all a dream' ": From "A Persian Song of Hafiz," in William Jones, *The Works*

of Sir William Jones, 6 vols. (London: G. G. and J. Robinson and R. H. Evans, 1799), vol. 4, p. 450.

277 "Lord Byron": The extent to which Byron drew on the more academic writings of the orientalists remains unclear, and literary critics have argued endlessly about of the scale of Byron's background research. The contemporary Iranian Byron scholar Seyed Mohammad Marandi regards claims that Byron took the trouble to study Persian or Arabic as merely part of "the myth of Byron's extensive and profound knowledge of the East." See Seyed Mohammad Marandi, "The Concubine of Abydos," *Byron Journal* 33, 2 (2005), p. 106. For a fuller survey of the debate, see Seyed Mohammad Marandi, "The Oriental World of Lord Byron and the Orientalism of Literary Scholars," *Critique: Critical Middle Eastern Studies* 15, 3 (2006); and Naji B. Oueijan, *A Compendium of Eastern Elements in Byron's Oriental Tales* (New York: Peter Lang, 1999).

278 "letter of thanks": John William Kaye, *The Life and Correspondence of Major-General Sir John Malcolm, GCB*, 2 vols. (London: Smith, Elder, and Co., 1856), vol. 2, p. 93.

278 "court of Saʿadat ʿAli": Ram Babu Saksena, *European and Indo-European Poets of Urdu and Persian* (Lucknow, India: Newul Kishore Press, 1941), p. 42. On the family's genealogy, see Joseph G. Baillie Bulloch, *A History and Genealogy of the Family of Baillie of Dunain, Dochfour and Lamington* (Green Bay, WI: Gazette Print, n.d.).

278 "snatches of verse": Samples of these remembered verses are found in Muzaffar Alam and Sanjay Subrahmanyam, *Indo-Persian Travels in the Age of Discoveries, 1400–1800* (New York: Cambridge University Press, 2007).

278 " 'he had perused' ": Russell Lant Carpenter (ed.), *Memoirs of the Life of the Rev. Lant Carpenter, LLD, with Selections from his Correspondence* (Bristol, UK: Philip and Evans, 1842), p. 244.

278 "Mirza Jaʿfar declared that he was 'pleased' ": "The Persian Princes," *The Times* (December 7, 1818), p. 3.

279 "grand portrait in oil": For an overview of developments, see S. J. Falk, *Qajar Paintings: Persian Oil Paintings of the 18th & 19th Centuries* (London: Faber and Faber, 1972); and Basil W. Robinson, "Persian Royal Portraiture and the Qajars," in Edmund Bosworth and Carole Hillenbrand (eds.), *Qajar Iran: Political, Social, and Cultural Change, 1800–1925* (Edinburgh: Edinburgh University Press, 1983).

279 " 'Abbas Mirza had a private gallery": Moritz von Kotzebue, *Narrative of a Journey into Persia in the Suite of the Imperial Russian Embassy in the Year 1817* (London: Longman, Hurst, Rees, Orme& Brown, 1819), pp. 164, 184. On Iranian military painting in this period, see Layla S. Diba, "Making History: A Monumental Battle Painting of the Perso-Russian Wars," *Artibus Asiae* 66, 2 (2006).

279 "Asaf al-Dawla": Mirza Abul Hassan Khan (1988), p. 86, and Mursilvand (1364/1986), p. 153.

279 "Thomas Lawrence": For a short but erudite study of the painting, see Charles W. Millard, "A Diplomatic Portrait: Lawrence's 'The Persian Ambassador,' " *Apollo* (February 1967).

279 "recounted his many sittings": Mursilvand (1364/1986), pp. 320–23, 333, 340.

279 "Sir William Beechey": The Beechey portrait illustrated in the Introduction is on display at Compton Verney, Warwickshire, having been bought at Christie's in June

2006 for £181,600. Beechey's other portrait of Abu'l-Hasan hangs in the Asian and African Studies Reading Room at the British Library.

280 "hurling javelins": Philoxenus Secundus (1812, pp. 23–24) recalled one occasion when Abu'l-Hasan's javelin flew straight through his attendant's cheek, whom he then "called a lazy awkward dog, that he did not know how to get out of the way."

281 "eight portraits": Millard (1967), p. 119.

281 "Summer Exhibition": Shīrāzī (1364/1985), p. 284.

281 *Portrait of Mearza Riza, a Persian*: Algernon Graves, *The Royal Academy of Arts: A Complete Dictionary of Contributors and their Work from its Foundation in 1769 to 1904*, 8 vols. (London: H. Graves and Co., 1905–6), vol. 7, p. 299, items #866 (1819) and #808 (1819).

281 "Samuel John Stump": My thanks to Andrew Potter, Research Assistant at the Royal Academy Library, for help in identifying Samuel John Stump.

281 "Abu'l-Hasan's lodgings": Mirza Abul Hassan Khan (1988), p. 121, footnote 1.

281 "Edmund Keane": Stump's 1819 stipple engraving of Edmund Keane now belongs to the National Portrait Gallery, London (NPG D19334).

282 "wrote of Dr. Dennis": Shīrāzī (1364/1985), p. 353.

282 "remained their firmest friend": Ibid., p. 192.

282 "*atfal,* or 'kids'": Ibid.

282 "'to annoy and vex us'": UK National Archives, FO 60/15 (90), "Jaafar Hewsainey to Mr. Planta" (July 14, 1819).

282 "*ikhtilaf-i mazhab chi?*": Shīrāzī (1364/1985), p. 192.

283 "'Covent Garden gout'": Hart (2013), p. 158.

284 "love of gardens": On the physical forms of the Iranian and Indo-Persian garden, see Sylvia Crowe and Sheila Haywood, *The Gardens of Mughal India: A History and a Guide* (London: Thames and Hudson, 1972); and J. Lehrmann, *Earthly Paradise: Garden and Courtyard in Islam* (Berkeley: University of California Press, 1980).

284 "'speaking had been banned there!'": Shīrāzī (1364/1985), p. 280.

284 "Vauxhall Gardens": Ibid., pp. 292–93. For Abu'l-Hasan's description of Vauxhall Gardens, see Mirza Abul Hassan Khan (1988), pp. 261–62; and Mursilvand (1364/1986), p. 352.

284 "*baghchas,* or 'little gardens,'": Shīrāzī (1364/1985), p. 285.

284 "'labyrinth every day'": See Jane Austen's letter no. 32 to Cassandra Austen (January 21, 1801) in Chapman (1932), vol. 1, p. 115.

285 "Thomson Garden": Shīrāzī (1364/1985), pp. 328, 336.

285 "the 'madhouse'": Ibid., p. 277.

285 "Regent's Street": Ibid., p. 193.

285 "Vauxhall Gardens": David E. Coke and Alan Borg, *Vauxhall Gardens: A History* (New Haven, CT: Yale University Press, 2011).

286 "firework displays": Shīrāzī (1364/1985), p. 292. On the fireworks and balloon rides, see also Coke and Borg (2011), pp. 265–67.

286 "advertisement from the *Morning Post*": Advertisements section, *Morning Post* (June 6, 1816), p. 1. The "Madame Sucran" in question was presumably the French tightrope artist Madame Saqui (1786–1866), who in 1816 had just arrived in London for her first performances at Vauxhall Gardens. See Coke and Borg (2011), pp. 276–77.

286 "'Cavalcanti's bloodhounds'": Quoted in Coke and Borg (2011), p. 194.

286 "vast numbers of prostitutes": Mirza Abul Hassan Khan (1988), p. 252; and Mursil-vand (1364/1986), p. 318.

287 "Islamist Sayyid Qutb": Sayyid Qutb, "The America I Have Seen," in Kamal Abdel Malik and Mouna El Kahla (eds.), *America in an Arab Mirror* (New York: Palgrave Macmillan, 2011).

287 "'ride through Hyde Park'": *Lancaster Gazette and General Advertiser* (May 8, 1819).

287 "'nude state'": Fraser (1838), vol. 1, p. 117.

287 "'with the ladies'": "The Persian Princes," *The Times* (December 7, 1818), p. 3.

288 "haunt of prostitutes": Jane Rendell, *The Pursuit of Pleasure: Gender, Space & Architecture in Regency London* (New Brunswick, NJ: Rutgers University Press, 2002), p. 109.

288 "theaters Mirza Salih described": Shīrāzī (1364/1985), p. 161 on Beazley, and pp. 290–91 on the Opera House and the other theaters of London.

288 "company of Sir Gore Ouseley": Mursilvand (1364/1986), p. 158.

288 "evening in Gloucester": Shīrāzī (1364/1985), pp. 185, 329.

288 "topic of women": On accounts of European women in Persian travel accounts from this period, see Michael H. Fisher, "Representing 'His' Women: Mirza Abu Talib Khan's 1801 'Vindication of the Liberties of Asiatic Women,'" *Indian Economic and Social History Review* 37, 2 (2000); and Mohamad Tavakoli-Targhi, "Imagining Western Women: Occidentalism and Euro-Eroticism," *Radical America* 24, 3 (1993).

288 "described London's prostitutes": Mirza Abul Hassan Khan (1988), p. 252; and Mursilvand (1364/1986), pp. 317–18.

289 "night spent in a London brothel": Mirza Abul Hassan Khan (1988), p. 252; and Mursilvand (1364/1986), pp. 317–18.

289 "Muhammad 'Ali Beg": Mirza Abul Hassan Khan (1988), p. 270; and Mursilvand (1364/1986), p. 337.

289 "Magdalen House": Mirza Abul Hassan Khan (1988), p. 252; and Mursilvand (1364/1986), pp. 317–18. For details, see Martha J. Koehler, "Redemptive Spaces: Magdalen House and Prostitution in the Novels and Letters of Richardson," *Eighteenth-Century Fiction* 22, 2 (2010).

289 "prostitutes' reform house": Shīrāzī (1364/1985), pp. 288–89.

289 "masculine banter": Mirza Abul Hassan Khan (1988), pp. 151–52; and Mursilvand (1364/1986), p. 211. Note that elsewhere the Iranian edition has been bowdlerized: the editor notes that he has cut several licentious sentences from the ambassador's conversation with the prince regent. See footnote 1 in Mursilvand (1364/1986), p. 191.

289 "stroke his beard": Philoxenus Secundus (1812), pp. 22, 30.

289 "Abu'l-Hasan's mysterious 'Miss Pul'": Miss Pole appears in Mursilvand (1364/1986), p. 219. On her identification, see Cloake's note in Mirza Abul Hassan Khan (1988), pp. 100–101, where Cloake also suggests the less likely identification of Emily's married elder sister, Priscilla. A chalk drawing of Emily and her sisters by Sir Thomas Lawrence is reproduced in Mirza Abul Hassan Khan (1988), plate 43 (opposite p. 256).

290 "Julia Burrell": Mirza Abu Taleb Khan (1810), vol. 1, p. 187. On Abu Talib's complex attitude toward European women, see Fisher (2000).

290 "poems in celebration": The verses were privately printed in Persian with an ac-

companying English translation by Abu Talib's friend, George Swinton. See Abu Taleb Khan/George Swinton, *Masnavī-yi Nazm-i Mirzā Abū Tālib Khān with an English Translation by George Swinton, Esq.* (London: privately printed, 18–).

290 "ʿ*az jam-i bullurin*' ": Ibid., p. 10; the translation is mine.

290 "ʿ*falisufan dar babazi*' ": Ibid., p. 16; again, the translation is mine.

290 "ʿ*hasti-yi kharad chist?*' ": Ibid., p. 26. Alack! Once again, my translation.

290 "Muhammad Ismaʿil Khan": On Muhammad Ismaʿil Khan's mission, see Fisher (2004), pp. 264–75.

291 "ʿout of my head' ": Caroline Fox, *Memories of Old Friends, being Extracts from the Journals and Letters of Caroline Fox, of Penjerrick, Cornwall, from 1835 to 1871*, ed. H. N. Pym (Philadelphia: J. B. Lippincott & Co., 1882), pp. 14–15.

292 "ʿ*matbuʿa kamtar rikhtand*' ": The original manuscript from Caroline Fox's autograph book is now in my own collection.

292 "ʿparticularly with ladies' ": "The Persian Princes," *The Times* (December 7, 1818), p. 3.

293 "ʿladies leave cards' ": Hester L. S. Thrale Piozzi, *Autobiography, Letters and Literary Remains of Mrs. Piozzi (Thrale)*, 2 vols. (London: Longman, Green, Longman & Roberts, 1861), vol. 2, p. 415.

293 "ʿcall this "tiffin"' ": Shīrāzī (1364/1985), p. 312.

293 "King George's birthday": Ibid., p. 189.

294 "charming young clergyman": Byrne (2013), pp. 179–80.

294 "letter that Mirza Jaʿfar wrote": The letter was then printed in *The Times* on June 24, 1819. The entire letter is also quoted in Wright (1985), pp. 79–80.

294 "fashionable albums": On the fashion for such autograph albums, see Margaret A. E. Nickson, *Early Autograph Albums in the British Museum* (London: Trustees of the British Museum, 1970).

295 "ʿcheeks of tulips!' ": "Letter to a Lady," *The Times* (June 24, 1819).

295 "dramatically married her!": Shīrāzī (1364/1985), p. 349.

295 "Mary Dudley": Wright (1985), p. 77.

296 "registry book entry": The handwritten registry book entry for Muhammad ʿAli's marriage is found on page 18 (no. 175) of *Marriages Solemnized in the Parish of St. James, Westminster, in the County of Middlesex, in the Year 1819*.

296 "the marriage certificate": The marriage certificate is filed in UK National Archives, FO 60/15 (55).

296 "caused alarm": Shīrāzī (1364/1985), p. 349.

297 "ʿGratefully, Muhommed Ali' ": UK National Archives, FO 60/15 (53), "Muhommed Ali to D'Arcy" (June 7, 1819).

298 "writing directly to the foreign minister": UK National Archives, FO 60/15 (51), "D'Arcy to Mr. Planta" (June 10, 1819).

298 "ʿyour Lordship's notice' ": UK National Archives, FO 60/15 (64), "Thomas Dudley to Lord Castlereagh" (June 20, 1819).

299 "ʿto accompany him' ": Ibid.

300 "ʿdo so in future' ": Shīrāzī (1364/1985), p. 353.

300 "prayers of Christian friends": Ibid., p. 353.

300 "set sail for Gravesend": Ibid., p. 354.

300 "young couple were aboard": Ibid., p. 355. On other early British female travelers

in Iran (mostly diplomatic wives), see Denis Wright, "Memsahibs in Persia," *Asian Affairs* 14, 1 (1983).

300–301 "'hereafter with advantage'": UK National Archives, FO 60/15 (102), "D'Arcy to Lord Castlereagh" (August 12, 1819).

301 "'small printing press'": Shīrāzī (1364/1985), p. 353. For fuller discussion of the evidence for identifying the press, see Nile Green, "Persian Print and the Stanhope Revolution: Industrialization, Evangelicalism and the Birth of Printing in Early Qajar Iran," *Comparative Studies of South Asia, Africa and the Middle East* 30, 3 (2010).

301 "length of their studies": Shīrāzī (1364/1985), p. 357.

302 "'country of freedom'": Ibid., p. 193.

302 "a John rather than a Richard": I have been unable to ascertain whether, a generation or two apart, Franklin's John Watts (d. 1763) was related to Mirza Salih's Richard Watts, born around 1765. However, given that Richard had an elder brother called John and hailed from a London family, there is every possibility.

302 "total of £4,252": The sum is given in Mr. D'Arcy's final report to the Foreign Office in UK National Archives, FO 60/15 (102), "D'Arcy to Lord Castlereagh" (August 12, 1819). Again, for the modern equivalent (in 2013), I have relied on the Bank of England's Historical Inflation Calculator.

303 "'education has been conducted'": UK National Archives, FO 60/15 (96), "Hajee Baba to Mr. Planta" (July 23, 1819).

303 "'some of these foreigners'": UK National Archives, FO 60/15 (102), "D'Arcy to Lord Castlereagh" (August 12, 1819).

303 "'middle of the Thames'": Shīrāzī (1364/1985), p. 358.

Afterlives

Page

305 "Persian Gutenberg": For fuller discussion, see Nile Green, "Journeymen, Middlemen: Travel, Trans-Culture and Technology in the Origins of Muslim Printing," *International Journal of Middle East Studies* 41, 2 (2009).

305 "first Persian book": Nile Green, "Persian Print and the Stanhope Revolution: Industrialization, Evangelicalism and the Birth of Printing in Early Qajar Iran," *Comparative Studies of South Asia, Africa and the Middle East* 30, 3 (2010); and Ulrich Marzolph, "Zur frühen Druckgeschichte in Iran (1817–ca. 1900): 1: Gedruckte Handschrift / Early Printing History in Iran (1817–ca. 1900): 1: Printed Manuscript," in Eva Hanebutt-Benz, Dagmar Glass, and Geoffrey Roper (eds.), *Sprachen des Nahen Ostens und die Druckrevolution: Eine interkulturelle Begegnung* (Westhofen: WVA-Verlag Skulima, 2002).

306 "his *Gulistan*": Qāsimī (2004), p. 191.

306 "Bavarian State Library": I am grateful to Dr. Winfried Riesterer of the Bayerische Staatsbibliothek, Munich, for allowing me to inspect the immensely rare *Gulistan* printed by Mirza Salih.

306 "'Treatise on Smallpox'": Willem M. Floor, "Cāp" in *Enclopaedia Iranica*; and Kamran Ekbal and Lutz Richter-Bernburg, "Cormick, John,"http://www.iranica.com/newsite/articles/v6f3/v6f3a017.html in ibid.

306 "Basma-Khana": A near contemporary account of the arrival of printing in Tabriz

is found in ʿAbd al-Razzāq Dunbulī, *Maʾāsir-i Sultāniya: Tārīkh-i Janghā-yi Avval-i Īrān va Rūs*, ed. Ghulām Husayn Zargarīnizhād (Tehran: Rūznāma-yi Īrān, 1383/2004), pp. 218–19. For the term *Basma-Khana*, see Edward G. Browne, *The Press and Poetry of Modern Persia, Partly Based on the Manuscript Work of Mīrzá Muḥammad ʿAlí Khán 'Tarbiyat' of Tabríz* (Cambridge: Cambridge University Press, 1914), p. 8.

306 "becoming a diplomat": Dunbulī (1383/2004), pp. 523–24.

306 "25 Great Coram Street": The address is given in several of Mirza Salih's letters from 1823 filed in the UK National Archives, FO 60/23.

307 "Willock's replacement": Wright (1985), pp. 83–84.

307 " 'friendship of the two countries' ": Letter from Mirza Salih in Paris (January 30, 1823) in the UK National Archives, FO 60/23.

307 " 'between the two powers' ": "Letter from Abbas Mirza to Lord Liverpool, with English translation," Bodleian Library, Ms. Pers. c. 7.

307 "Mirza Salih's diary": The circumstances of the manuscript's presentation to George Willock are given on its opening folio. See British Library, Add. 24,034, f. 1r. The manuscript subsequently formed the basis of the several editions of the diary printed in Tehran since the late 1960s.

308 " 'for their comfort and subsistence' ": ʿAbbas Mirza's letter was reprinted in the *Edinburgh Annual Register*, vol. 16 (1824), pp. 263–64. A follow-up announcement from Mirza Salih was also printed in the *Morning Chronicle* on July 16, 1823.

308 "Persian language guide": William Price and Mirza Muhammad Saulih Shirazi, *A Grammar of the Three Principal Oriental Languages, Hindoostanee, Persian and Arabic to Which Is Added, a Set of Persian Dialogues by Mirza Muhammad Saulih of Shiraz* (London: Kingsbury, Parbury & Allen, 1823).

308 "Robert William Sievier": A photograph of the sculpture, along with the date and artist's name, is found in Ismāʿil Raʾīn's edition of the diary. See Mīrzā Sālih Shīrāzī, *Safarnāma*, ed. Ismāʿīl Raʾīn (Tehran: Rawzan, 1347/1969), unpaginated frontispiece. However, for Sievier's identification as *Robert William* (not, pace Raʾīn, E. V. Sevier), I have relied on the editorial discussion in Shīrāzī (1364/1985), p. 35.

309 "Persian polemics": Reverend Samuel Lee, *Controversial Tracts on Christianity and Mohammedanism, by H. Martyn and Some of the Most Eminent Writers of Persia, Translated and Explained; to which is Appended an Additional Tract* (London: W. Nicol, 1828). For a full elucidation of the debate, see Abbas Amanat, "Mujtahids and Missionaries: Shiʿi Responses to Christian Polemics in the Early Qajar Period," in Robert Gleave (ed.), *Religion and Society in Qajar Iran* (London: Routledge, 2004).

309 " 'humblest of servants' ": Lee (1828), p. cxviii.

309 "corresponded with Lee": The letters are filed in Archive of the British and Foreign Bible Society, Cambridge University Library, BSA/D1/1/185–186.

309 " 'master of tact' ": L. P. Elwell-Sutton, "Parleying with the Russians in 1827," *Journal of the Royal Central Asian Society* 49, 2 (1962), p. 183. The negotiations are also described in Laurence Kelly, *Diplomacy and Murder in Tehran: Alexander Griboyedov and Imperial Russia's Mission to the Shah of Persia* (London: I. B. Tauris, 2002), chapter 18.

309 "tea with General Ivan Paskievich": Elwell-Sutton (1962), p. 184.

310 "first lithographic presses": Shahlā Bābāzādah, *Tārīkh-i Chāp dar Īrān* (Tehran: Tahūrī, 1378/1999), p. 21; and Farīd Qāsimī, *Sarguzasht-i Matbūʿāt-i Īrān: Rūzgār-i*

Muhammad Shāh va Nāsir al-Dīn Shāh, 2 vols. (Tehran: Vizārat-i Farhang va Irshād-i Islāmī, 1380/2001), vol. 1, pp. 191–94. More generally, see Nile Green, "Stones from Bavaria: Iranian Lithography in its Global Contexts," *Iranian Studies* 43, 3 (2010).

310 "only surviving portrait of him": On the portrait and its companion pieces, see Edward Kasinec and Robert Davies, "Graphic Documentation of Gift Exchanges between the Russian Court and Its Islamic Counterparts, Seventeenth to the Nineteenth Century," in Linda Komaroff (ed.), *Gifts of the Sultan: The Arts of Giving at the Islamic Courts* (Los Angeles: Los Angeles County Museum of Art, 2011), p. 199.

311 "earliest Persian books": The books in question were Mulla Mahdi of Naragh's *Muhriq al-Qulub* ("Purifier of the Hearts") and Mulla Ibrahim's *Husayniya* ("On Husayn"). Their donation to the Society is described in a footnote to Sir Henry Willock, "Biographical Sketch of His Late Royal Highness Abbas Mirza, Prince Royal of Persia, Hon. M.R.A.S.," *Journal of the Royal Asiatic Society* 1, 2 (1834), p. 323. It is possible that the books were acquired for the Society through the offices of Captain Willock, the erstwhile *chargé d'affaires* in Tehran, though Mirza Salih's association with the Society suggests that he may have either sent them himself or had them sent via Willock.

311 "first regular newspaper": See the editorial introduction in Shīrāzī (1364/1985), pp. 20–26. Also Browne (1914), p. 11; and Floor, "Cāp," in *EIr*.

312 "May 1837 issue of *Akhbar-i Vaqaʿa*": "Persian Newspaper and Translation," *Journal of the Royal Asiatic Society* 5, 10 (1839), p. 355.

312 "party at the British Embassy": "Persian Newspaper" (1839), pp. 359–60 (Persian), pp. 367–68 (English).

312 "throngs of Plymouth": Shīrāzī (1364/1985), p. 189.

312 "'princely and noble entertainment'": "Persian Newspaper" (1839), p. 359 (Persian), p. 367 (English).

313 "little part of England": On the history of the gardens and buildings of the British Embassy in Tehran, see John Gurney, "Legations and Gardens and Their Subalterns," *Iran* 40 (2002).

313 "'Editor of the Teheran Gazette'": "List of the Members of the Royal Asiatic Society of Great Britain and Ireland, corrected to the 30th of June, MDCCCXLI," *Proceedings of the 18th Anniversary Meeting of the Society Held on 8th of May, 1841* (1841), p. 18.

313 "the other students": Short accounts of the students' later careers are found in Mihdī Bāmdād, *Sharh-i Hāl-i Rijāl-i Īrān dar Qarn-i 12 va 13 va 14 Hijrī*, 6 vols. (Tehran: Zavvār, 1363/1984), vol. 1, pp. 241–44, and vol. 2, pp. 175–79.

313 "Hajji Baba": H. Mahbūbī Ardakānī, "Afšār, Hājjī Bābā," in *EIr*.

314 "'engineer-in-chief'": For Mirza Jaʿfar's later career, I have relied on the Persian editorial introduction to Mīrzā Sayyid Jaʿfar Khān Muhandis-Bāshī Mushīr al-Dawla, *Risāla-yi Tahqīqāt-i Sarhadiya*, ed. Muhammad Mushīrī (Tehran: Intishārāt-i Bunyād-i Farhang-i Īrān, 1348/1969), pp. 8–15.

314 "wrote a memoir": The edited text of Mirza Jaʿfar's boundary report has been reprinted in ibid., pp. 33–193.

314 "*Khulasat al-Hisab*": Details of this and related books are found in Akram Masʿūdī (ed.), *Fihrist-i Kitābhā-yi Chāp-i Sangī-yi Īrān Mawjūd dar Kitābkhāna-yi Dānishgāh-yi Tihrān* (Tehran, 1379s/2001), pp. 136–39; and Sadīqa Sultānīfar (ed.),

Fihrist-i Kutub-i Darsī-yi Chāp-i Sangī Mawjūd dar Kitābkhāna-yi Millī-yi Jumhūrī-yi Islāmī-yi Īrān (Tehran, 1376s/1998), pp. 93–94.

314 "book on world geography": Mushīrī, "*Muqadima*," in Mushīr al-Dawla (1348/1969), p. 14.

315 "Peter the Great and Napoleon": Iraj Afshar, "Book Translations as a Cultural Activity in Iran, 1806–1896," *Iran* 41 (2003), p. 279.

315 "Joseph Wolff": Reverend Joseph Wolff, *Researches and Missionary Labours among the Jews, Mohammedans, and Other Sects* (London: James Nisbett, 1835), p. 39.

315 "'casting of brass ordnance'": Untitled article, *St James's Chronicle and General Post* (November 4, 1826), p. 4.

316 "forks in her household": Denis Wright, *The Persians amongst the English: Episodes in Anglo-Persian History* (London: I. B. Tauris, 1985), p. 82.

A Note on Sources and Method

Page
319 "*Terrains of Exchange*": Nile Green, *Terrains of Exchange: Religious Economies of Global Islam* (New York: Oxford University Press, 2015).

Index